HENRY VIII
MAN AND MONARCH

HR
VIII
AN
XXXV

HENRY VIII
MAN AND MONARCH

Exhibition guest curated by David Starkey

British Library curator: Andrea Clarke

Catalogue edited by Susan Doran

'Henry VIII: Man and Monarch' at The British Library
was made possible thanks to the kind generosity of

The British Library would also like to thank Vermeer Associates and
Melvin R. Seiden for their generous support of this catalogue

First published in 2009 by
The British Library
96 Euston Road
London NW1 2DB

On the occasion of the exhibition at The British Library:

'Henry VIII: Man and Monarch'
23 April – 6 September 2009

British Library Cataloguing-in-Publication Data
A catalogue record is available from The British Library

ISBN 978 0 7123 5025 9 (HB)
ISBN 978 0 7123 5026 6 (PB)

Designed and typeset by Andrew Shoolbred
Colour reproductions by Dot Gradations
Printed in Italy by Printer Trento S.r.l.

CONTENTS

LENDERS TO THE EXHIBITION

The British Library would like to thank the following institutions and collections for their generous loans to the exhibition

Archivo General de Simancas, Simancas
The Berger Collection at Denver Art Museum, Denver
Bibliothèque de Méjanes, Aix-en-Provence
Bodleian Library, Oxford
British Museum, London
Cambridge University Library
Canterbury Cathedral
Clare College, Cambridge
Collection of Mark Pigott OBE
College of Arms, London
Corpus Christi, Parker Library, Cambridge
Duke of Bedford
Duke of Buccleuch
Duke of Northumberland
Fitzwilliam Museum, Cambridge
Glastonbury Abbey
Kunsthistorisches Museum, Vienna
Lambeth Palace, London
Lambeth Palace Library, London
Marquess of Salisbury
Mary Rose Trust, Portsmouth
Merton College, Oxford
National Archives, Kew
National Maritime Museum, London
National Portrait Gallery, London
Private Lenders
Queens' College, Cambridge
Ripon Cathedral
Royal Armouries, London
Royal Collection, London
Royal Library, Windsor
Society of Antiquaries, London
St John's College, Cambridge
Trinity College, Cambridge
Ushaw College, Durham
Victoria and Albert Museum, London
Vatican Library, Rome
Westminster Abbey Library, London
Worshipful Company of Barber Surgeons, London

CONTRIBUTORS TO THE CATALOGUE

AA Adrian Ailes, The National Archives
PB Peter Barber, The British Library
NB Nicolas Bell, The British Library
GB George Bernard, University of Southampton
JC James Carley, York University, Toronto
DC David Carlson, University of Ottawa
AC Andrea Clarke, The British Library
GC Gloria Clifton, National Maritime Museum
TC Tarnya Cooper, National Portrait Gallery
SD Susan Doran, Jesus College, University of Oxford
ED Eamon Duffy, Magdalene College, University of Cambridge
SG Steven Gunn, Merton College, University of Oxford
JG John Guy, Clare College, University of Cambridge
JH Julian Harrison, The British Library
RH Ralph Houlbrooke, University of Reading
AH Ann Hutchinson, Glendon College, York University, Toronto
EI Eric Ives, University of Birmingham
DM Diarmaid MacCulloch, St Cross College, University of Oxford
RM Rory McEntergart, American College, Dublin
SMcK Scot McKendrick, The British Library
PM Peter Marshall, University of Warwick
SR Susan Reed, The British Library
RR Richard Rex, Queens' College, University of Cambridge
JR Judith Richards, La Trobe University, Melbourne
GR Glenn Richardson, St Mary's University College, Strawberry Hill
TR Thom Richardson, Royal Armouries
AR Alec Ryrie, University of Durham
DS David Starkey, Fitzwilliam College, Cambridge
TS Tatiana String, University of Bristol
DW Daniel Williman, State University of New York, Binghamton

ACKNOWLEDGEMENTS

The curators and the editor would like to thank the following for their assistance in the preparation of the exhibition and the catalogue:

Archivo General de Simancas, Valladolid: Isabel Aguirre Landa, Agustín Carreras Zalama, Eduardo J. Marchena Ruiz, José Luis Rodríguez de Diego

His Grace the Duke of Bedford and Chris Gravett

Bibliothèque de Méjanes, Aix-en-Provence: Philippe Ferrand, Isabelle Lang

The Bodleian Library, Oxford: Bruce Barker-Benfield, Chris Fletcher, Maddy Slaven

The British Library: Peter Barber, Nicolas Bell, Claire Breay, Gareth Burfoot, Greg Buzwell, Robert Davies, Adrian Edwards, Laura Fielder, Moira Goff, Chris Grohman, Julian Harrison, Arnold Hunt, Kristian Jensen, Chris Lee, Scot McKendrick, Kumiko Matsuoko, Sally Nicholls, Laura Nuvoloni, Barbara O'Connor, Tony Parker, Lara Speicher, Alan Sterenberg, David Way

The British Museum, London: Silke Ackermann, Robert Owen, Janice Reading, Dora Thornton

His Grace the Duke of Buccleuch: and Gareth Fitzpatrick, Sandra Howat

Cambridge University Library: Brian Jenkins

Canterbury Cathedral: Cressida Williams

James Carley: York University, Toronto

Clare College, Cambridge: Anne Hughes

The College of Arms, London: Robert Yorke

Corpus Christi College, Cambridge: Gill Cannell, Christopher de Hamel

Denver Art Museum, Colorado: Bridget O'Toole, Kathleen Stuart

The Fitzwilliam Museum, Cambridge: David Scrase, Thyrza Smith

Glastonbury Abbey: Janet Bell

Historic Royal Palaces:Brett Dolman, Kent Rawlinson

Kunsthistorisches Museum, Vienna: Ruperta Pichler, Karl Schütz, Elisabeth Wolfik

Lambeth Palace, London: The Most Rev. and the Rt Hon. the Archbishop of Canterbury, Dr Rowan Williams, Andrew Nunn

Lambeth Palace Library, London: Richard Palmer

The Mary Rose Trust, Portsmouth: Andy Elkerton, Mark Jones, John Lippiett

Merton College, Oxford: Dame Jessica Rawson, Julia Walworth

The National Archives, Kew: Adrian Ailes, Nancy Bell, Paul Carlyle, Sean Cunningham, Nicola Harold

The National Maritime Museum, London: Gloria Clifton, Emily Hope Thomson

The National Portrait Gallery, London: Tarnya Cooper, David McNeff

His Grace the Duke of Northumberland and Clare Baxter

Mark Pigott OBE

Queens' College, Cambridge: Murray Milgate

Ripon Cathedral: Dean of Ripon, Very Revd. Keith Jones, Ian Horsford

Royal Armouries, London: Thom Richardson, Ciara Gallagher

Her Majesty the Queen and The Royal Collection & Royal Library: Sir Hugh Roberts, the Hon. Lady Jane Roberts, Elena Greer, Kate Heard, Theresa-Mary Morton, Jennifer Scott

The Most Hon. the Marquess of Salisbury: and Robin Harcourt-Williams

Society of Antiquaries of London: Julia Dudkiewicz, David Gaimster, Heather Rowland, Julia Steele

St John's College, Cambridge: Jonathan Harrison

Trinity College, Cambridge: Paul Simm

Trinity College Library: David McKitterick

Ushaw College, Durham: Peter Seed

The Vatican Library, Rome: Monsignor Cesare Pasini, Amalia D'Alascio, Christine Grafinger

The Victoria and Albert Museum, London: Clare Brown, Marian Campbell, Rebecca Wallace, Christopher Wilk

Westminster Abbey Library, London: Tony Trowles

The Worshipful Company of Barbers, London: Jeremy Bolton, Christopher Buckland-Wright, Peter Durrant, Adam Lewis, William Shand

INTRODUCTION

David Starkey

In 1519 or 1520, Henry VIII, who was then in his late twenties, wrote a short note to his minister, Cardinal Wolsey. It deals with the most delicate and secret affairs of state. Yet it is only a few lines long and the King himself felt the need to apologize for its shortness. 'Wryttyng to me', Henry explained, 'Is sumwhat tedius and paynfull' (cat. no. 84).

A glance at the letter shows why. The King's hand is bold and heavy, with square, rather awkward letter forms. There is nothing of the grace of the new italic script, as famously practised by his daughter Elizabeth (cat. no. 230), or of the crisp, regular 'secretary' hands of Sir Thomas More or Wolsey himself, who wrote the copper-plate of the day (cat. nos 155, 118). Instead, the writing is like the man: massive, overbearing, unmistakeable.

And this unmistakeable handwriting is everywhere in this exhibition. Held to mark the 500th anniversary of Henry VIII's accession to the throne, it features important and rarely displayed items from the British Library's unrivalled Henry VIII collections – including the King's personal letters, key official documents, maps and books from Henry's own Royal Library – alongside loans from other national and international museums and collections. Here are Henry's school-books (cat. nos 18, 19, 34) and his boyhood aid to devotion (cat. no. 35), as well as the book which won him the title of Defender of the Faith (cat. nos 95–6). And here is tapestry and armour and weapons and portraits – of Henry and his family and of his courtiers, friends and councillors, including masterpieces by Hans Holbein, Quentin Matsys and Lucas Horenbout.

But, among all these treasures, what will stick in the mind, I hope, is Henry's handwriting. For this is the *primum mobile* of his universe, that sets everything else in motion – for better and for worse. It confides in Wolsey, 'as hartely as hart can thynke'. It proffers that same heart – graphically – to his new love, Anne Boleyn, when he signs the letter in which the two pledge their troth, 'H. seeks AB no other R.' (cat. no. 106). It shifts, at a stroke, the foundations of the monarchy, when it re-writes the Coronation Oath that was the very contract between King and People, which Henry had sworn to and had then broken (cat. no. 153). It dares to alter the mysteries of the Catholic faith and presumes even to correct the text of the Ten Commandments which Henry, now Supreme Head on Earth of his own Church of England, felt that God had left dangerously vague (cat. no. 189). It deals life and death to the greatest in the land (cat. no. 266). And it seeks – and for once fails – to govern England from beyond the grave in his Will (cat. no. 269).

This was a rare defeat. For Henry sat more securely in the throne than any of his predecessors and wielded the sceptre more confidently too. Thanks largely to the anti-royalist zeal of the English Republican regime of the 1650s, none of these showy emblems of Henry's sovereignty survives, not even the Imperial Crown itself which stands first in the Inventory – the comprehensive list of his myriad possessions, from trinkets to treasures – that was drawn up after his death in January 1547 (cat. no. 271).

But the real seat of Henry's power *does* survive and is exhibited here: his writing-desk (cat. no. 107). Its drawers and compartments are empty now. Then they would have been bursting with papers and ink, pens and penknives, pencils and rulers – as well as the spectacles that his increasing addiction to reading and writing forced him to wear.

The writing-desk may also contain the clue that explains how the strapping, somewhat cack-handed athlete of 1519/20, who found 'wryttyng … sumwhat tedius and paynfull', turned into the most literate – and literary – monarch yet, who ruled England with the pen more than the sword (though he was not shy to use the latter either). For the desk is decorated with the emblems of Henry and his first wife, Katherine of Aragon. This means that it was made before 1527; it might even have been, as Andrea Clarke speculates, the very desk on which, in the first days of January 1527, Henry wrote his crucial love-letter to Anne Boleyn.

Thanks to the generosity of the Vatican Library, this letter too, which has been returned to England for the first time since it was written in the 16th century, is on display. It and its fellows were spirited to the Vatican, almost certainly, because they provided the best evidence for the Catholic view of Henry's Divorce: that he repudiated Katherine of Aragon, not because of conscientious scruples, but simply for love – or lust – for Anne.

This charge seems to me to be largely true. Which means in turn that Henry's love-letter is one of the crucial documents of English history, since it triggered its central event, the Henrician Reformation and everything that flowed from it. This is the centrepiece of the exhibition and of Henry's life. It is also the turning point, which transformed his attitude to reading and writing.

And it did so of necessity. When Henry wrote his love-letter to Anne, it is clear that both expected they would be married in the near future after a 'quickie' divorce obligingly provided by Wolsey, who was the Pope's legate or representative in England as well as Henry's minister. But Wolsey baulked and Rome blustered and delayed until finally Henry was driven to realize that he would get a divorce only in England and only from his own Church. To make that possible would require the legislation of the Reformation Parliament, culminating in the Act of Supremacy (cat. no. 150). But first Henry had to win the argument – or at least persuade himself that he had.

And that could only be done by royal reading and writing on an unprecedented scale. The Royal Library was transformed, as James Carley shows in his important essay (p. 273), from a showcase for lavishly illuminated luxury volumes into a hugely expanded workaday research library, in which the books were arranged alphabetically, catalogued numerically and combed for the evidence that would support Henry's case. Doing the combing and cross-referencing was a high-powered research team, which reported directly to Henry. And he, as his omnipresent marginalia and annotations prove, read, marked and inwardly digested their research report, the *Collectanea satis copiosa* ('the sufficiently full collections') (cat. no. 134) until he had made its arguments and evidence his own.

Here we not only display the *Collectanea*, with the books that both fed into it and resulted from it, we also use 'interactives' to recreate the process of its compilation and take the visitor into the very mind of Henry and his advisers. For books and words are not dull or dead things. On the contrary, it was the text of the *Collectanea* and Henry's resulting conviction that he was rightful head of his own national Church that brought about the huge political and physical changes of the 1530s: the break with Rome, the execution of Henry's closest and oldest friend, Thomas More, the Dissolution of the Monasteries, the crushing of Henry's once beloved daughter Mary – and the largest and most dangerous Tudor rebellion, Pilgrimage of Grace.

It was as though a ripple had spread from the Royal Library and Henry's writing-desk, and, gathering force as it went, turned into a tidal wave that swept into the furthest corners of England, uprooting, overturning and destroying anything that stood in its way. Here we display some of the debris: defaced sacred texts (cat. no. 203), the broken stones of demolished monasteries (cat. no. 171), the fragments of dismantled aristocratic tombs (cat. no. 168). What we cannot show, of course, are the human casualties: the broken and dismembered bodies, the destruction of ancient patterns of life and belief, the changing of the very fabric of a nation.

But it wasn't only a question of destruction. The cataclysm of the Reformation, unleashed by Henry's pen, threw up new structures – physical *and* intellectual – as well as demolishing old. New claims were made for English as a great language, with a grammar and literature able to stand comparison with any other (cat. no. 262). Brilliant propaganda was produced as potent words were combined with the new representational techniques of Renaissance art and disseminated by the new technologies of engraving and printing. And – highlighting yet again the connection between words and things, action and paper – England itself was reconceived as a single, mappable, strategic whole.

Once again, Henry himself was at the heart of the process. Instructions were sent out to local gentlemen and officials to map sections of the coast that were seen as vulnerable to invasion. The resulting maps, views and plans, often incorporating innovative techniques, were sent back to Westminster, where Henry pored over them in his map-room at Whitehall, with its extended drawers and shelves and massive, slate-topped drawing table (cat. nos 209–11, 213). Here too Henry oversaw the drawing up of plans of squat, heavily gunned castles and forts; decided where they should be placed at key points of the coastline and ordered their building at breakneck speed (cat. no. 212). And beyond the forts were his ships – rebuilt, rearmed and with the new dockyards, depots and administration that turned them into the embryo of a new Royal Navy (cat. no. 255).

The result is that the reign of Henry VIII was the most revolutionary period of change in English history since the Norman Conquest. It did not spring from nothing of course and we emphasize the strangeness of Henry's upbringing as a second son and the sophistication of his education. This made him the most Latinate king of England since at least the 12th century and the first since Alfred the Great to write a book. But the book, his broadside against Martin Luther known as the *Assertio septem sacramentorum*, was profoundly conservative, as was his policy in these early years of his reign. Abroad, it looked back firmly to the glory days of Henry V; at home, to the chivalric fantasies of Camelot.

In other words, if Henry had died, as many of his courtiers did, of the epidemic of 'sweating sickness' in 1528, he would have been forgotten. As he lived, and went on to divorce Katherine of Aragon, marry Anne Boleyn and break with Rome, he became one of England's most important kings: perhaps the greatest; certainly the most memorable. Claims for revolutionary change under Henry have of course been made before, but their author was supposed to have been the King's minister, Thomas Cromwell, and not the King. Here we use the unmistakeable evidence of Henry's handwriting to show, beyond doubt I think, that the real – if most unlikely – revolutionary was Henry himself.

THE YOUNG HENRY (1491–1509)

David Starkey

Henry, who was destined to be the most famous Tudor of them all, entered the world in comparative obscurity. Born on 28 June 1491, he was the third child and second son of Henry VII (1457–1509) and Elizabeth of York (1466–1503). Both his elder siblings were given splendid, carefully recorded births and baptisms, but Henry's – thanks to his comparative dynastic insignificance – was a more modest affair: at the time, his grandmother did not even bother to record his birth in her list of important Tudor family events. The only strictly contemporary evidence, indeed, is a bill for the supply of fine linens and other cloth used in his christening. But this is enough to establish that Henry received the full honours of a royal baptism.

Henry's upbringing and early education were equally coloured by his lack of dynastic status. His elder brother, Prince Arthur (1486–1502), was given a separate household from earliest infancy. Henry, instead, was brought up with his elder sister, Margaret (1489–1541). As other royal children were born, all but one of whom were girls, they too joined this junior royal nursery. For a Tudor boy, therefore, Henry's childhood was unusually feminized and he remained close to his mother, who, in a royal family of stridently assertive personalities, was gentle, affectionate and a peacemaker. He even seems to have learned to read and write at his mother's knee.

Henry's emergence from obscurity to the public stage was due to another throw of the dynastic dice. In 1493 a pretender, Perkin Warbeck (1477?–99), appeared. He passed himself off as Richard, Duke of York, the younger of the two Princes in the Tower, and received the enthusiastic endorsement of Margaret of York, the Dowager Duchess of Burgundy, who was the real Duke Richard's aunt. All this touched a sensitive nerve with Henry's father, who had been a scarcely more substantial figure when he had won the throne with foreign backing in 1485. To expose the falseness of Warbeck's claims, Henry VII decided to create his second son Henry Duke of York. The ceremony, in November 1494, was one of the most magnificent of the reign; Henry VII intervened

◀ Detail from cat. no. 15

repeatedly to make sure things went smoothly and Henry, though he was not yet four, impressed with his horsemanship and confident bearing.

Shortly afterwards, Henry began more formal instruction under his first schoolmaster, the priest-poet, John Skelton (*c.*1460–1529). Skelton boasts that he taught Henry, who had already learned to read and write from his mother, 'to spell'. He also wrote several pedagogical works for the boy, one of which, his *Speculum principis* (Mirror for a Prince) survives. Like its author, it is a strange mixture of the quirky and the commonplace. In 1499 Skelton and his young charge met the great Dutch scholar Erasmus (1469–1536), when Erasmus, then on his first visit to England, was introduced to Henry's household by William Blount, Lord Mountjoy (*c.*1478–1534), Henry's mentor and Erasmus' former pupil. The meeting was important for both sides: Henry's confident public demeanour made a great impression on Erasmus; Henry, for his part, would come to regard Erasmus as his model in Latinity.

Erasmus also paints an enchanting word-picture of the young Henry, his sisters and his short-lived brother Edmund as they assembled to greet their visitor. But this household, like Henry's own status, was about to undergo a revolution. In 1501 Henry's elder brother Arthur was married to Katherine of Aragon (1485–1536), youngest daughter of the 'Catholic Kings' of Spain, Ferdinand of Aragon, and Isabella of Castile. The wedding took place in St Paul's; Henry was Katherine's escort throughout the ceremonies and, indulged by his parents, he stole the show at the ensuing ball. Five months later, the fifteen-year-old Arthur, who had been sent to live with Katherine as man and wife in the Marches of Wales, was dead and Henry, once it became clear Katherine was not with child, became heir. Less than a year later, his mother was dead too, of complications following the birth of a child conceived in a desperate attempt to strengthen the weakened Tudor dynastic line.

Some years later, in a letter to Erasmus, Henry described his mother's death as 'hateful intelligence'. But, as etiquette dictated, he did not attend her funeral. His servants did, however, and the list of mourning given out provides a unique list of his household. Skelton, with his old-fashioned Latin, had been replaced by a professional schoolmaster, John Holt (d.1504), who was not only an expert in the new, Erasmian-style Latin but also the author of an innovative, illustrated textbook. There were also professionals to teach Henry music (both string and wind instruments), French and martial arts. He had five chaplains as well to oversee his religious instruction and practice, which, as his surviving bede or prayer roll shows, was a conventional late medieval piety in which magic and religion commingled. But still, at the age of twelve and as Prince of Wales, he was being brought up with his sisters.

Within a year, however, all had changed as his father decided to take him to court. Thomas More (1478–1535), who had formed one of the party when Henry first met Erasmus, had commemorated Queen Elizabeth's death with a *Lamentation* in which the Queen tells her husband that he must now be both father and mother to his children. Similarly, the Spanish ambassador was optimistic about the new arrangements, considering that Henry VII would be the best possible guide to introduce his son to his future role. It proved an optimistic view.

There were two problems. The first was a simple question of age. Henry's mother was thirty-seven when she died; his father was already forty-seven. He was prematurely aged, in poor health and politically disillusioned. At the beginning of his reign, he had tried hard to win over the Yorkist nobility to support the new regime. But they had been resistant. Pretender had followed pretender until finally Henry VII decided that fair means having been tried, only foul ones would work. The result was a regime of fiscal terrorism in which he aimed to bond and fine members of the elite into submission. It produced results – up to a point. But it also led to charges of tyranny. And many of the victims – like Lord Mountjoy – had close links to Prince Henry.

There was also a clash of style. Henry VII's personal courage was not in doubt: he had won his throne in personal combat and defended it twice at the head of his troops; he also tried hard (and spent good money) to maintain the chivalrous tone of his court. But he did not joust himself, while most of those who did were Yorkist by family connection and political affiliation.

Here Prince Henry quickly showed that he would take a very different line from his father. Already, by his mid-teens, it was clear that he had inherited the height and massive build of his Yorkist grandfather, Edward IV, which alone conferred a natural advantage in the tiltyard. He hero-worshiped the star jousters of the day and longed to emulate them. His head was stuffed with knightly lore and Arthurian myth (then of course devoutly believed to be real, at least by the English). And in 1506 he found a contemporary model with the enforced arrival in England of Philip the Fair, who had jousted with his own father just before his departure from the Netherlands.

Henry VII – strikingly – gave his son every encouragement: he provided horses, armour, weapons and instructors. He arranged contests and played the proud father as his son carried off the prizes. But he did set a strict limit on what Henry was allowed to do: he could take part in the training exercise known as 'running at the ring'. But jousting itself was considered too dangerous and was forbidden. Prince Henry chafed but acquiesced – as he did in most things to his father, including his on-off betrothal to his sister-in-law, Katherine of Aragon, who had remained in England in a curious and increasingly threadbare limbo between widow and wife.

There were diplomatic reasons why Henry VII kept postponing a new Spanish marriage. But there were strongly personal ones as well. It seems clear that Henry blamed himself for giving his eldest son Arthur the premature sexual experience to which contemporaries attributed the boy's early death. And he was not about to repeat the mistake with Henry. So instead of living with Katherine, he lived cheek by jowl with his father. His household followed the King's in all its wanderings; and, wherever they were, his apartments were next to his father's and interconnected with them.

What Henry thought of this, we do not know. Indeed – apart from his frustrated longing to joust – we know nothing directly of Henry's views at this time at all. Powerful figures in his father's court and council, including Edmund Dudley (*c*.1462–1510), gave him presents in the hope of ingratiating themselves with the rising sun. But Henry lost Dudley's ring and kept his opinion of the giver to himself.

Only when his father's iron grip on power – and Henry – was released would Dudley and everybody else find out what Henry's mind had been incubating.

Some at least of them would be surprised.

HENRY'S BIRTH

The future Henry VIII was the third child and second son of King Henry VII and Elizabeth of York, who had married in January 1486. The Prince was born on 28 June 1491 in the royal Palace of Greenwich, some five miles east of London, and baptized in the Church of the Friars Observant next to the Palace. At the baptism, the officiant was Richard Fox (1447/8–1528), then Bishop of Exeter and Lord Privy Seal (holder of the monarch's personal seal).

1 Henry as a Child

Unknown artist

Bibliothèque de Méjanes, Aix-en-Provence, MS 442 Res, MS 20

Inscribed: 'le Roy Henry Dangleterre'

This drawing shows a strapping two- or three-year-old infant. The child has a suggestion of Henry's long nose and rosebud mouth, though the chin is more distinctly cleft with a dimple than in the handful of unbearded portraits of the adult King; there is something of the mature Henry's pugnacious assertiveness as well. In short, this is what Henry *ought* to have looked like as a baby. Unfortunately, it is absolutely certain that the drawing – in its present form at least – cannot be authentic. The evidence is provided by the dress – in particular, the ostrich-plumed hat, which, as Sir Roy Strong has pointed out, clearly dates from the 1530s. Indeed, it is very similar to the costume worn by Henry's son, Prince Edward, in the Holbein painting and its associated drawing of 1539–40. But the face is too heavy to be another representation of Edward. (DS)

LITERATURE: Strong, *Tudor and Jacobean Portraits*; Starkey (ed.), *Henry VIII: A European Court in England*

2 The Birth of Prince Henry

Beaufort Book of Hours

British Library, Royal MS 2 A xviii, fol.30v

This Book of Hours, inherited from her mother's family by the matriarch of the House of Tudor, Henry's grandmother, Lady Margaret Beaufort, contains a calendar of Church festivals and saints' days which Lady Margaret turned into a chronicle of the important political and dynastic events in the foundation of Tudor power – including Henry's own birth. The calendar follows Roman usage and Henry's birth is entered under 'IV Kalendae Julii' 1491. But the entry also shows Henry's comparative dynastic insignificance at the time. For Henry's elder brother Arthur, Lady Margaret is scrupulously accurate, giving the exact time and place of birth: on 20 September 1486 'in the morning afore one of the clock after midnight was born Prince Arthur at Winchester'; likewise for his elder sister, Margaret, born 'at Westminster at night after the ninth hour a quarter' on 28 November 1489. In contrast, she merely notes the date of Henry's birth and, indeed, seems to enter the latter over a correction. After all, second sons did not rank very highly in the scheme of things! (DS)

LITERATURE: Starkey, *Henry: Virtuous Prince*

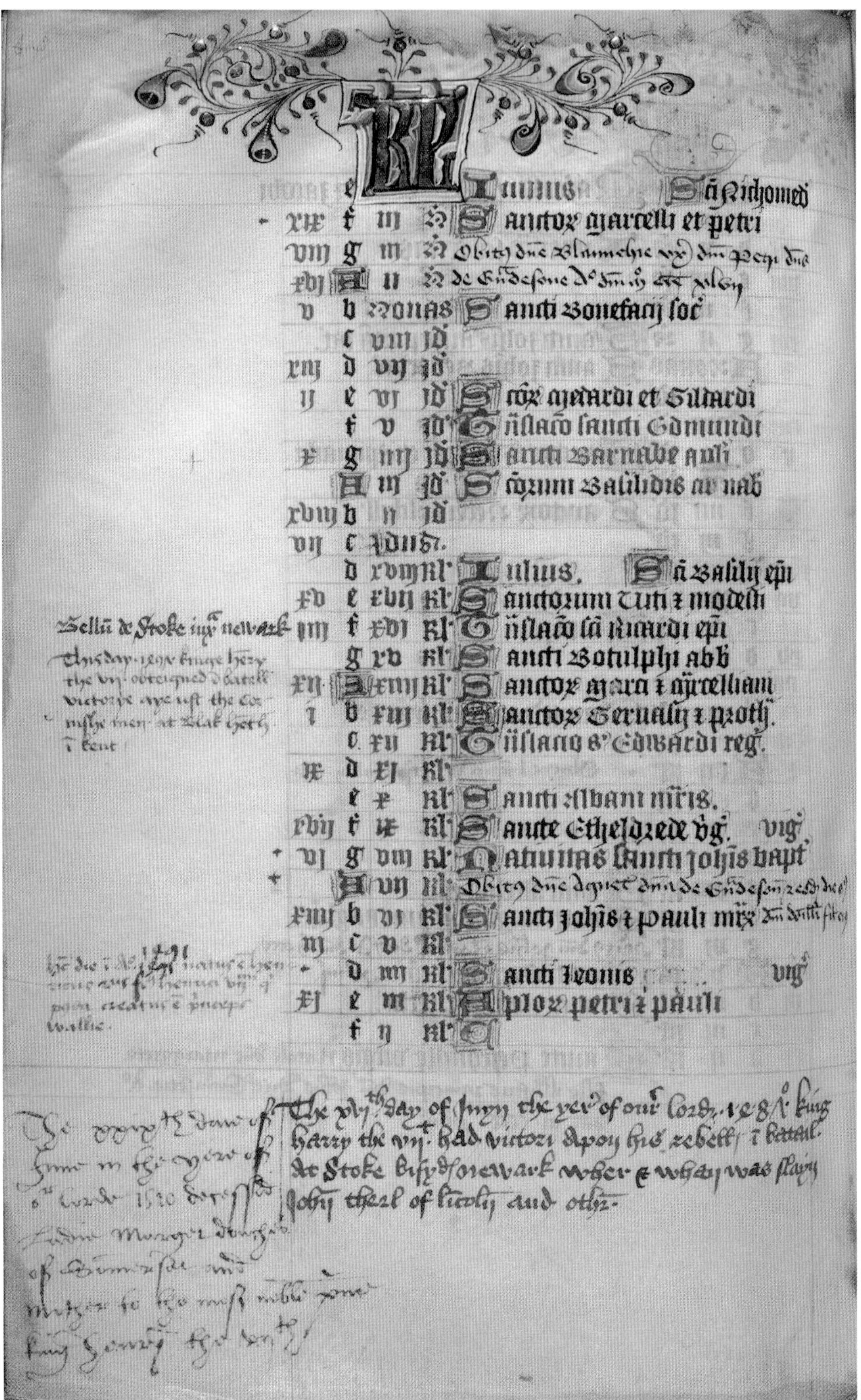

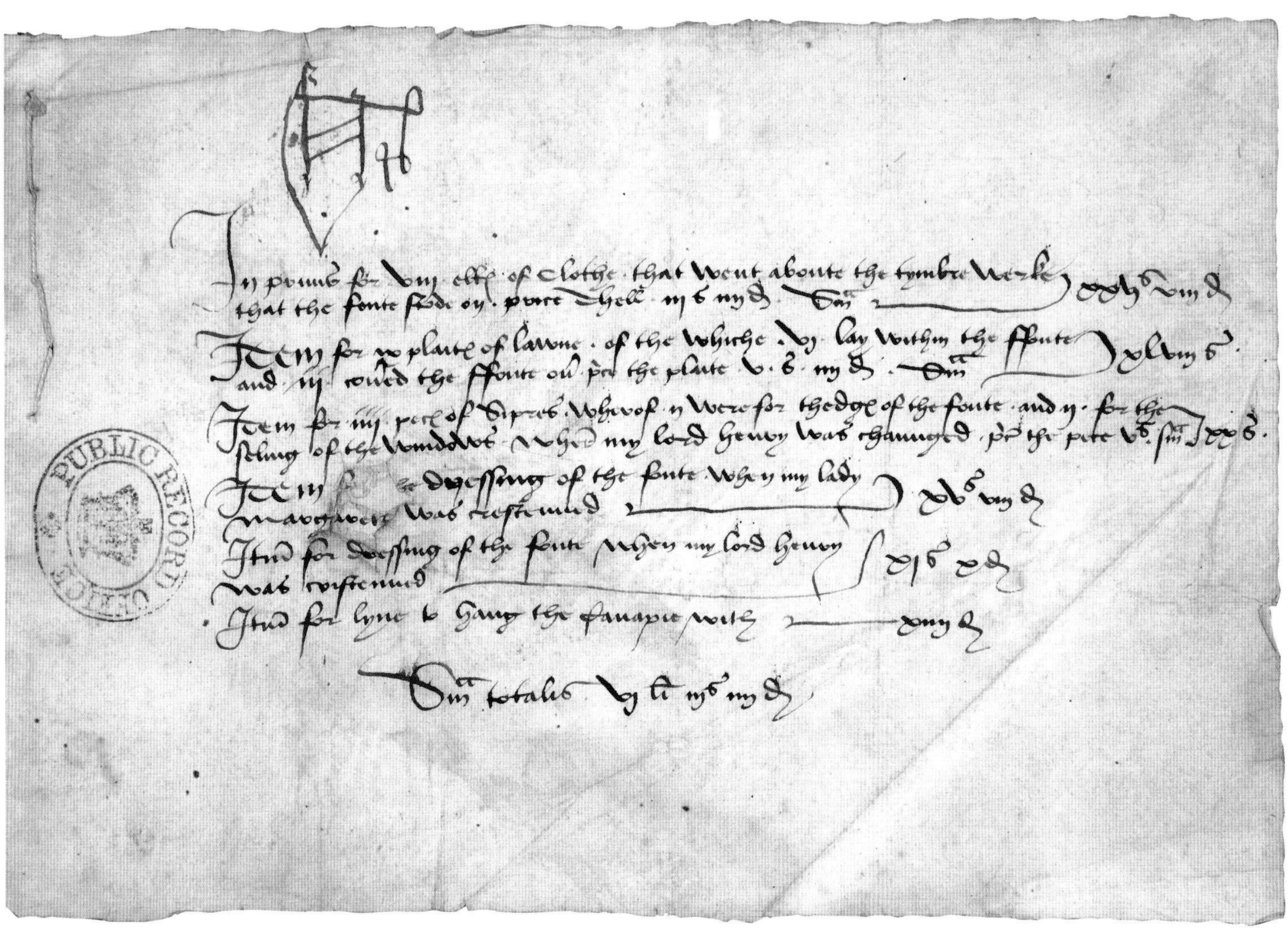

3 Henry's Baptism

Payment for the decoration of the font at the christening of Lord Henry, 1 September 1491

The National Archives, Kew, Richmond, Surrey, E404/81/1

This document is the only strictly contemporary record of Henry's christening. Brief though it is, it establishes that the elaborate ceremonies, laid down for a princely birth in the handbook of court protocol known as *The Ryalle Book*, were carried out to the letter. The document consists of two parts, both carrying the sign manual or initials, 'HR' (*Henricus Rex*) of Henry's father, Henry VII, which were made, at this stage of his reign, in the awkward rectangular strokes of an unpractised soldier's hand.

The first is a warrant or authorization to pay Benjamin Digby, Yeoman of the Queen's Wardrobe of the Beds, £6 3*s*. 4*d*. for his costs 'at the christening of our right dear son, the Lord Henry'; and the second (seen here) an attached bill which itemizes the actual expenses Digby incurred. They included: cloth to cover the tall wooden platform on which the font stood; 'line' or cords to suspend the cloth-of-gold canopy over the font and fine linen or 'lawn' to line and wrap the silver font to stop it abrading the delicate skin of the royal child. Finally, a sheer, almost translucent stuff, known as 'Cypress' from its original place of manufacture, was used to cover and draught-proof the windows near the 'traverse' or tent-like green-room, where Henry was undressed before being plunged bodily three times into the waters of the font. (DS)

LITERATURE: Starkey, *Henry: Virtuous Prince*

4 Panorama of London

Panorama of London by Anthonis van den Wyngaerde, *c.*1540
British Library, Maps 184.f.2(1)

The Panorama of London, dating from the last years of Henry VIII's reign, also shows the world of his childhood and youth. To the east, and sited in almost open country on a great meander of the Thames, is Greenwich Palace (shown here), where Henry was born and baptized. Then comes the Tower, where Henry took refuge with his mother from the Cornish rebel army in 1496, and where, in 1509, he was kept in purdah for the first weeks of his reign. In the centre is London Bridge, over which Katherine of Aragon, processed in 1501 on her way to her wedding with Henry's elder brother, Prince Arthur. Finally, to the west, is the great palace-monastery of Westminster, where Henry was created Duke of York in 1494, crowned with Queen Katherine on Midsummer's Day 1509 and celebrated the birth of his short-lived son, Prince Henry, in 1511. Finally, winding across the centre of the panorama, is the great artery of the city: the River Thames. All the major palaces had landing stages or 'bridges' on the Thames, and the gaily painted royal barges took the King, courtiers and councillors swiftly between them. (DS)

LITERATURE: Starkey, *Henry: Virtuous Prince*; Colvin and Foister (eds), *The Panorama of London circa 1544 by Anthonis van den Wyngaerde*

FAMILY BACKGROUND

On his father's side Henry VIII claimed descent from the Lancastrian dynasty; on his mother's side from the Yorkists. These two families had fought for the throne during the second half of the 15th century in the civil wars known, from the 18th century onwards, as the Wars of the Roses. Eventually the last Yorkist king, Richard III, was defeated in 1485 at the Battle of Bosworth by Henry Earl of Richmond, the last surviving male heir of the Lancastrian line, who took the throne as Henry VII. To end the dynastic wars Henry VII united the two families of Lancaster and York through his marriage to Elizabeth, the daughter of Edward IV and niece of Richard III.

5 Henry VI

Unknown artist, 16th century/probably 1530s
Society of Antiquaries of London, Scharf XVI
Inscribed, on the lower edge of the frame: 'HENRICVS VI'

The Lancastrian King Henry VI (1421–71) was Henry VIII's great-uncle. He was the son of the acclaimed warrior Henry V (1386/7–1422) and Catherine of Valois (1401–37), the daughter of Charles VI of France. On Henry V's death, Catherine took a young, handsome but undistinguished Welsh squire, Owen Tudor (*c*.1400–61), as her second husband, and their child (Henry VI's half-brother) was Edmund Tudor, the father of the future Henry VII.

Henry VI inherited the throne while an infant and grew up to be so incompetent a king that not only did England lose all its territories in France (apart from Calais) during his reign but also the realm descended into a long and disruptive civil war. Henry VI's violent death and reputation for piety, however, salvaged his reputation and allowed Henry VII to work for his canonization as a saint. From 1494 Henry VII ordered the compilation of a book of miracles allegedly worked by the King, and proposed to rebury his uncle's corpse in Westminster Abbey as Henry VI had originally wished. Nonetheless, Henry VI was an example of kingship to be avoided. (SD)

LITERATURE: Henry VI, *Oxford DNB*; Watts, *Henry VI and the Politics of Kingship*

6 Edward IV

Unknown artist, probably English, early 16th century
Society of Antiquaries of London, Scharf XVII
Inscribed: 'edward rex quart'

Henry VIII's maternal grandfather was Edward IV (1441–83), the son of Duke Richard of York (1411–60) and Cecily Neville (1415–95). Edward took the throne after deposing Henry VI in 1461, but lost it again in 1470 when he was driven into exile by resurgent Lancastrians allied to disaffected Yorkists. Backed by the French, Edward returned to England in March 1471 and won resounding victories over his opponents, the ex-Yorkists at the Battle of Barnet and the Lancastrians at Tewkesbury. With the defeat at Tewkesbury, the Lancastrian cause seemed entirely lost and Henry, Earl of Richmond (the future Henry VII), was forced to flee the country. After this, Edward ruled successfully for twelve years. However, on his death, his brother usurped the throne as Richard III, while his two underage sons were imprisoned and later murdered in the Tower of London. His eldest daughter, though, married Henry VII after the first Tudor king deposed Richard III.

Edward IV physically resembled his future grandson, Henry VIII. Both were tall, broad-shouldered and auburn-haired. They were also alike in character: Edward was a strong and ruthless ruler who managed men effectively and understood the politics of display. (SD)

LITERATURE: Edward IV, *Oxford DNB*; Starkey, *Henry: Virtuous Prince*

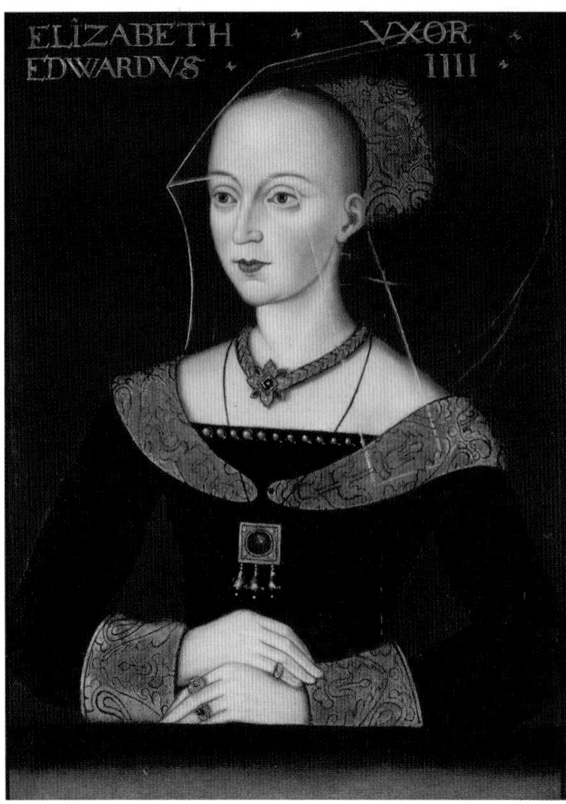

7 Elizabeth Woodville

Unknown artist, probably English School, 16th century

Queens' College, Cambridge

Elizabeth Woodville (*c*.1437–92), the wife of Edward IV, was Henry VIII's maternal grandmother. She was a beautiful, but unpopular, widow when the King secretly married her in April 1464, and together they had two sons and six daughters. In order to prevent Elizabeth's ambitious family ruling England during her son Edward V's minority, Duke Richard of Gloucester seized the throne and probably ordered the murder of Edward and his younger brother, Richard. Initially, Elizabeth became party to a conspiracy to depose the usurper, and so agreed to a marriage between her eldest daughter Elizabeth and the exiled Henry, Earl of Richmond (soon to be Henry VII). However, she quickly reached terms with Richard III when the conspiracy collapsed. Nonetheless, after Henry's accession, she was treated with respect as the new King's mother-in-law and became godmother to Prince Arthur in 1486. However, the following year, her lands were transferred to her daughter the Queen, while she retired to Bermondsey Abbey until her death. Queens' College, Cambridge, owns several portraits of Elizabeth, as she was the college's second foundress. (SD)

LITERATURE: Woodville, Elizabeth, *Oxford DNB*; Starkey, *Henry: Virtuous Prince*

8 Lady Margaret Beaufort, Countess of Richmond and Derby

Unknown artist, probably English School, late 16th century?

St John's College, Cambridge

Lady Margaret Beaufort (1443–1509) was a thirteen-year old widow when she gave birth to the future Henry VII, and it was through her line that her son had a claim to the English throne, though admittedly not a strong one. Her great-grandfather was John of Gaunt, Duke of Lancaster (1340–99), the third son of Edward III, but her great-grandmother was Gaunt's mistress, Katherine Swynford (1350?–1403), whose descendants, though legitimized, were excluded from the succession by Act of Parliament.

During Henry VII's reign Margaret enjoyed a dominant place at court, and, on his death, she supervised the arrangements for his funeral and her grandson's coronation. But, five days after the festive coronation, she died. In this portrait, she is shown at prayer before a devotional book, reflecting her reputation for piety. The arms in the picture display her ancestry: on the left light of the window are the royal arms used by the Tudors; on the right light is the portcullis badge of the Beauforts. This portrait is in St John's College, Cambridge, which was endowed after her death with money from her estates. (SD)

LITERATURE: Jones and Underwood, *The King's Mother*; Beaufort, Margaret, *Oxford DNB*

9 Henry VII

Unknown artist, probably English School, 16th century

Society of Antiquaries of London, Scharf XXIV

Henry VII (1457–1509) was crowned King on 30 October 1485, two months after his victory over Richard III at the Battle of Bosworth. Despite his marriage to Elizabeth of York, many Yorkists did not recognize him as king and plotted against him by supporting Perkin Warbeck – a pretender, who impersonated one of the murdered Princes in the Tower. So, although Henry's reign seemed blessed by the birth of first Arthur and then Henry, he could never feel his dynasty was secure. This insecurity grew more intense after the death of a third son, Edmund, in 1500 and Arthur in 1503. As a result, Henry VII closely watched his nobility and used financial bonds and recognisances to secure their good behaviour. On his death, Henry VII was strongly criticized for his rapaciousness and tyranny. Henry VIII, therefore, immediately distanced himself from his father's policies: he began his reign with a general pardon and the imprisonment (and later executions) of his father's most unpopular counsellors. Judging by this and other portraits, Henry VIII also did not look like his father, whose face was long and fine featured. (SD)

LITERATURE: Henry VII, *Oxford DNB*; Cunningham, *Henry VII*

10 Elizabeth of York

Unknown artist, British School, late 16th century

National Portrait Gallery, London, NPG 311

Inscribed: 'ELIZABETHA. VXOR/ HENRICI. VIII'

As the oldest child of Edward IV, Elizabeth of York had a far better claim to the throne of England than Henry VII. Perhaps it was for this reason that Henry chose to be crowned before taking Elizabeth as his Queen on 18 January 1486. The marriage was not intended to give his rule legitimacy but to unite the warring factions of York and Lancaster and bring about a lasting peace. Little is known of Elizabeth's personal character, but she was widely admired as a gracious and handsome princess. She was probably well educated, and may have taught her son Henry to read and write.

Elizabeth's portrait was in demand during the later part of the 16th century to fulfil orders for portraits sets of important monarchs. All the surviving examples are of a similar type and this portrait almost certainly derives from an Elizabethan set of monarchs. (SD and TC)

LITERATURE: Starkey, *Henry: Virtuous Prince*; Elizabeth of York, *Oxford DNB*; Strong, *Tudor and Jacobean Portraits*

PL.II
Three Children of K. HENRY VII and ELIZABETH his Queen.
I. Prince Arthur.
II. Pr. Henry. III. Ps. Margaret.
From the Royal Collection at Kensington Palace.
To his GRACE the most Noble THOMAS Duke of LEEDS, this is most humbly Inscribed by Geo. Vertue.

11 Prince Henry and his Older Siblings

George Vertue (1688–1756), after a picture of Christian II of Denmark's children by Jan Gossaert (dit Mabuse).

Copper engraving, 1748

Three Children of K. HENRY VII and ELIZABETH his Queen. I. Prince Henry. II. Prince Arthur. III. Ps. Margaret

British Library, 3.Tab.24.9

Initially, the marriage of Henry VII and Elizabeth seemed dynastically successful. Admittedly, three of their children died while still infants – including Elizabeth (1492–5), Edmund (1499–1500) and Katherine (1503) – but four others survived the dangerous years of infancy: Arthur, Margaret, Henry and Mary. However, by the time of the Queen's own death in 1503, only Margaret, Mary and Henry were still alive.

This engraving by George Vertue depicts (as he mistakenly believed) the three elder children – Arthur, Henry and Margaret – sitting at a table and playing with two apples and some cherries.

The picture is ornamented at the top with the portcullis (the Beaufort emblem) surmounted with roses. In reality, Henry had little to do with his older brother, who was educated at Ludlow in the Marches of Wales, while Henry remained with his sisters at Eltham Palace in Kent. (SD)

LITERATURE: Perry, *The Sisters of Henry VIII*; Starkey, *Henry: Virtuous Prince*

HENRY'S INFANCY

Since 1362, the usual title for the younger son of a ruling King of England had been Duke of Clarence. However, in 1474, at the age of eight months, Richard, the second son of Edward IV, was created Duke of York and a year later made a Knight of the Bath and Knight of the Garter. In 1494 Henry VII decided to follow this precedent for his second son, but in his case to make all the creations on one day in a more splendid court ceremony. In doing this, Henry VII was issuing a challenge to Perkin Warbeck, the Yorkist pretender then impersonating Richard of York, the younger of the Princes murdered in the Tower of London. No doubt Henry hoped to win over Yorkist sympathizers who might be tempted to join Warbeck at the Burgundian court in Malines.

12 A Mother's Boy

Warrant for payment of nursery servants

The National Archives, Kew, Richmond, Surrey, E404/81/3

The evidence for Henry's early upbringing is thin, consisting in the main of a series of warrants authorizing the payment of wages to his nursery staff. But these apparently unpromising sources can yield important biographical information. Above all, they show that Henry, unusually for a Tudor boy and unlike his brother Arthur, was brought up by women and in the same household as his sisters for the whole of his boyhood and beyond. The warrant exhibited here is dated 17 September 1493, when Henry was two years old. Listing Cecily Burbage, 'norice (nurse) to our right dearly well-beloved daughter the Lady Elizabeth', as well as the other women attending 'our right dearly well-beloved children, the Lord Henry [and] the Ladies Margaret and Elizabeth', the warrant establishes that Henry's younger sister Elizabeth, born in July 1492, had joined the nursery household which Henry was already sharing with his other sister Margaret, who was eighteen months his senior. Within two years, the warrants began to refer to this joint establishment as 'our nursery'. (DS)

LITERATURE: Starkey, *Henry: Virtuous Prince*

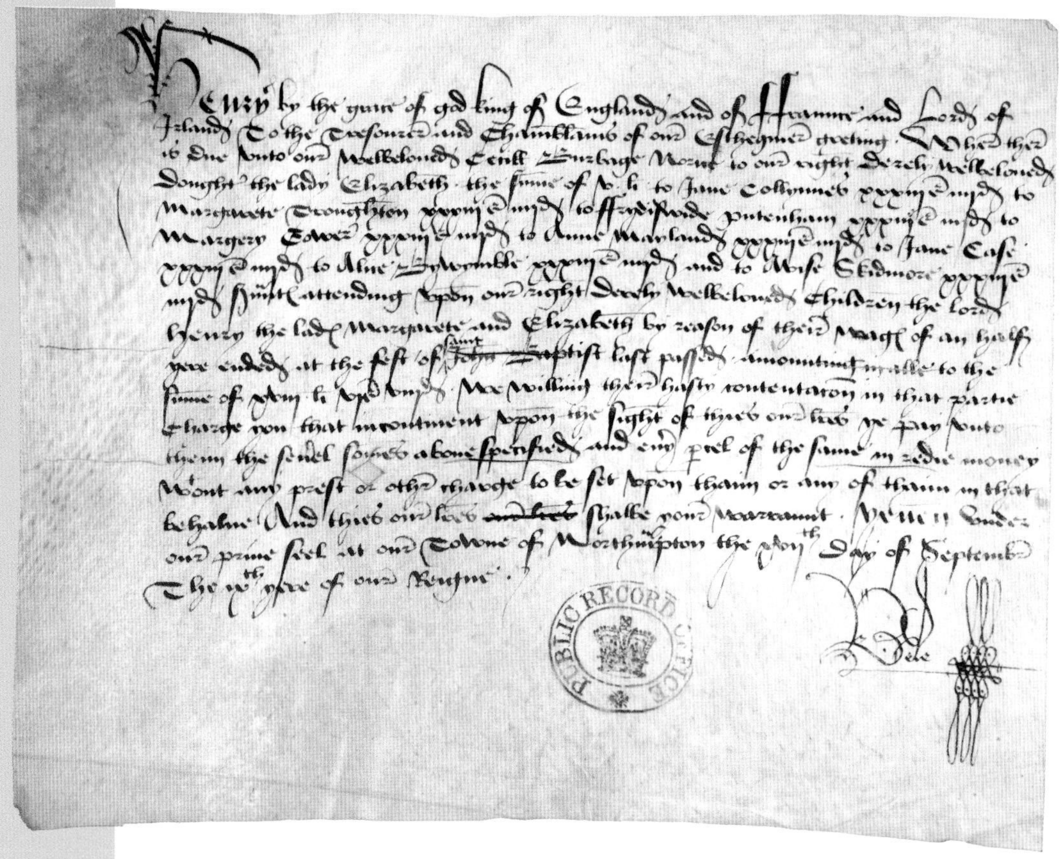

13 Perkin Warbeck:
a Serious Claimant for the Throne

Letter from Perkin Warbeck to Isabella, Queen of Spain, Dendermonde, 25 August 1493

British Library, Egerton MS 616, fol.3

This letter, addressed to Henry VII's principal ally, Queen Isabella of Castile, and signed 'Your cousin Richard Plantagenet, second son of the late King Edward, Duke of York etc: Richard', shows why Henry VII was obliged to take Perkin Warbeck seriously as a rival claimant. The letter provides a plausible account of 'Richard's' escape from Richard III's clutches and his subsequent adventures; boasts of the support he is already receiving from other European princes and seeks to use Isabella's mediation to win backing from her husband, Ferdinand of Aragon, as well.

The letter, dated *'octavo kallendas Septembris'* (25 August 1493), was written at 'Andermunda', one of the dower towns of Warbeck's principal backer, Margaret of York, Dowager Duchess of Burgundy. Margaret herself sent Isabella another letter, written at the same time and place, in a concerted attempt to win Spanish support. The attempt failed, and the Spanish remained consistently sceptical about Warbeck's claims. This letter is of major importance, as its discovery and publication in 1838 by the great librarian of the British Museum, Sir Frederick Madden, laid the foundation for all modern research on Warbeck. (DS)

LITERATURE: Arthurson, *The Perkin Warbeck Conspiracy, 1491–1499*

14 Henry's Creation as Duke of York: the Reasons

Warrant, issued at Woodstock near Oxford on 2 October 1494

The National Archives, Kew, Richmond, Surrey, E404/81/4

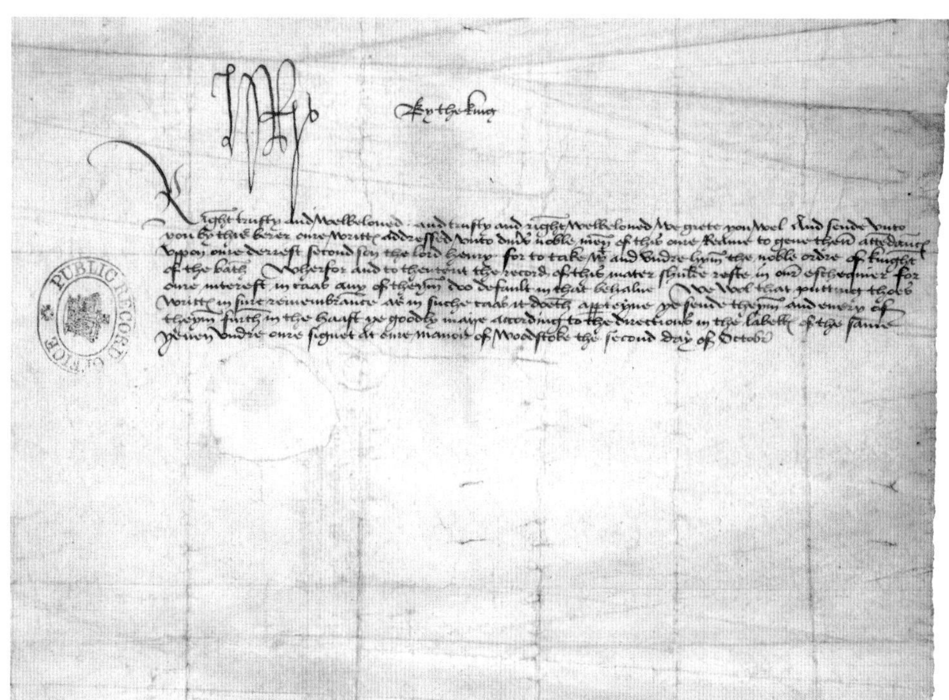

The decision to create the three-year-old Henry Duke of York in November 1494 was a direct riposte to the pretender, Perkin Warbeck, who had assumed the name, title and identity of 'Richard, Duke of York', the second son of Edward IV. This meant that the ceremony, Henry's first public event, had to be as ostentatious and well-publicized as his baptism had been comparatively modest. Which meant in turn that, right from the start, his father, King Henry VII, took the closest personal interest in its organization. In this warrant, issued at Woodstock near Oxford on 2 October 1494, the King uses the threat of Exchequer fines to make sure that a large and impressive list of gentlemen turned up to be dubbed Knights of the Bath with Henry as a preliminary to his creation as Duke. (DS)

LITERATURE: Starkey, *Henry: Virtuous Prince*

15 Henry Dubbed Knight of the Bath

Writhe's Garter book, the Ceremony of the Bath and the Earl of Salisbury roll, p.118

Collection of His Grace the Duke of Buccleuch

The well-established and elaborate ritual for dignifying important ceremonies with the dubbing of Knights of the Bath was graphically set out in a series of twenty-four coloured illustrations in this precedent book assembled for John Writhe, who was Garter King of Arms from 1478 to 1504. Writhe oversaw Henry's own dubbing in 1494 and no doubt made sure that the ceremonial blueprint was followed exactly. After nightfall, Henry and his fellow postulant knights were ceremonially undressed and bathed; then, each clad in a rough hermit's gown, they kept vigil in church, made confession and heard Mass before retiring to bed in the small hours. The following morning they mounted their horses, rode round the palace yard, entered the King's presence and were finally dubbed knight. The mounting and riding a horse, shown here, might be thought to be especially challenging to a three-year-old child, like Henry. But he was up to the challenge. He had already impressed observers by riding alone on a war-horse for his ceremonial entry into the City of London that had preceded his creation; now he displayed his equestrian skills once more. (DS)

LITERATURE: Starkey, *Henry: Virtuous Prince*

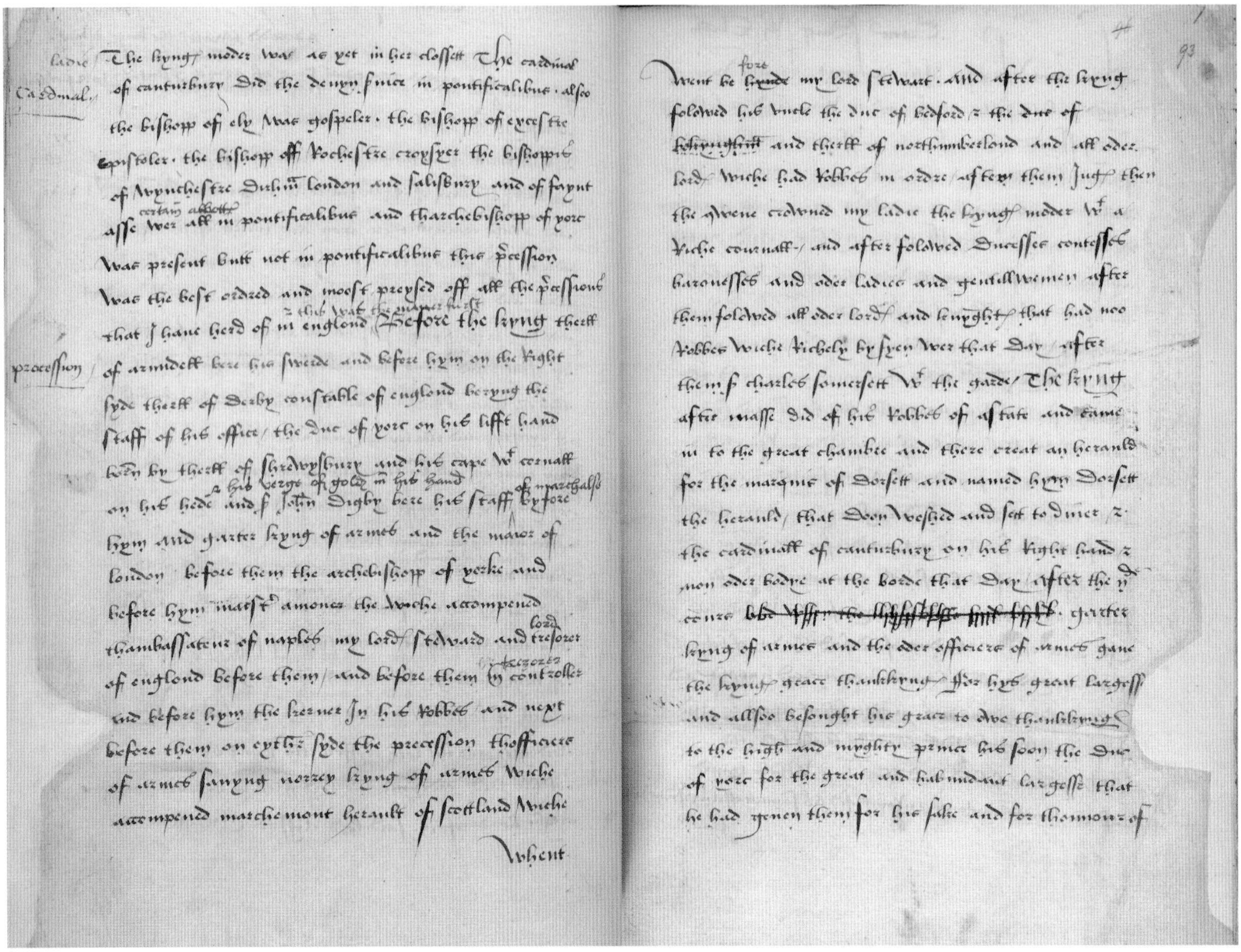

16 Henry's Creation as Duke of York: the Ceremony

British Library, Cotton MS Julius B xii, fols 92v–93

Unlike Henry's birth and baptism, his creation as Duke of York was deemed sufficiently important to be recorded. This account is one of the most elaborate ceremonial narratives of the reign; it also shows signs of having been read and corrected by Henry himself at some later date and with his typically pernickety attention to detail. This page describes the procession in which Henry, robed and coroneted, was carried round Westminster Hall after his father had created him Duke. The recording herald called it 'the best ordered and most praised of all the processions that I have heard of in England'. But Henry (or someone with a hand uncannily like his) found several inadequacies in the account. He altered titles to highlight the distinction between the Lord Treasurer of England, John, Lord Dynham, and the Treasurer of the Household, Sir Thomas Lovell, both of whom took part. He also noted that, as well as wearing his coronet and robe, he had carried 'his verge (rod) of gold in his hand'. Was Henry remembering all this? Or checking other, now vanished records? In any case it shows the importance he attached to his first appearance on the public stage. (DS)

LITERATURE: Starkey, *Henry: Virtuous Prince*

HENRY'S EARLY EDUCATION

Henry's informal education probably began when he was about five years old and his mother taught him to read and write. His first tutor, the poet John Skelton, was appointed in 1496 or 1497, and over the next five or so years Henry acquired a good grounding in Latin and was introduced to Classical writings. But, as Skelton's style of writing Latin was thought old-fashioned, he was dismissed on Prince Arthur's death in 1502, when greater attention was paid to the new heir's education. The task of tutoring the young prince then fell to better classicists, first John Holt and afterwards William Hone, both of whom were strongly influenced by the humanist scholar, Desiderius Erasmus. Throughout his education Henry was immersed in works of history and tales of chivalry, and the evidence points to Henry V and King Arthur emerging as potent role models for the future King.

17 Learning to Write at his Mother's Knee

Queen Elizabeth of York's Book of Hours

British Library, Additional MS. 50001, fol.22

Few examples of Queen Elizabeth of York's handwriting survive, of which this inscription in her Book of Hours is one: 'Elysabeth ye quene'. It consists of only three words and sixteen letters. But it is close enough in weight, letterforms and rhythm to the handwriting of Henry and his sisters to suggest very strongly that they learned to read and write at their mother's knee. (DS)

LITERATURE: Starkey, *Henry: Virtuous Prince*

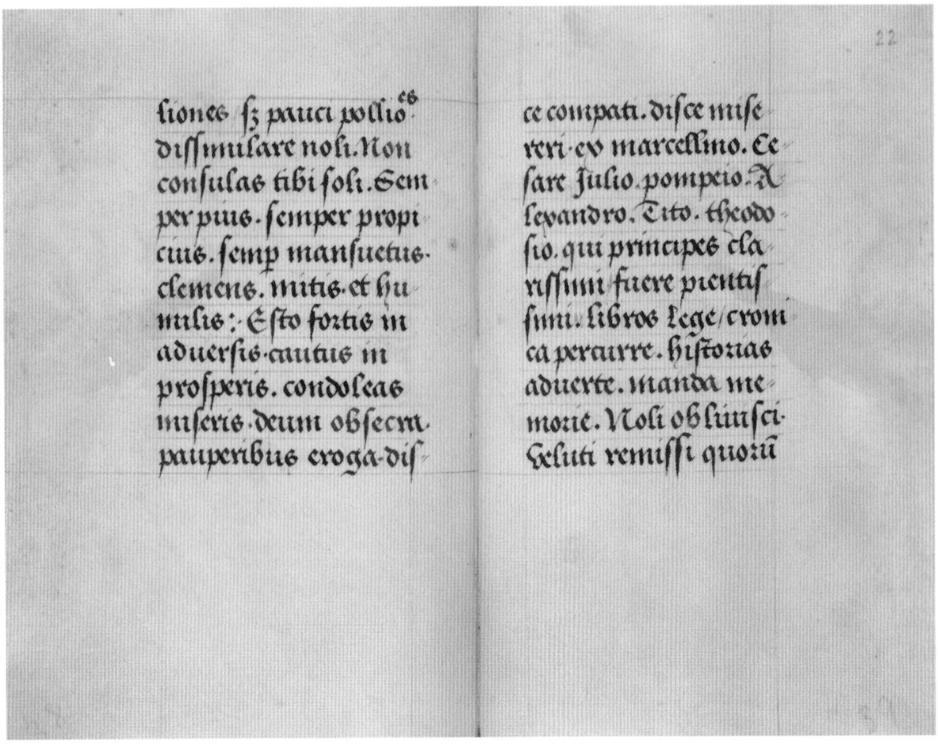
siones. s; pauca possio es
dissimulare noli. Non
consulas tibi soli. Sem
per pius. semper propi
cius. semp mansuetus.
clemens. mitis. et hu
milis :. Esto fortis in
adversis. cautus in
prosperis. condoleas
miseris. deum obsecra.
pauperibus eroga. dis
ce compati. disce mise
reri ex marcellino. Ce
sare Julio. pompeio. A
lexandro. Tito. theodo
sio. qui principes cla
rissimi fuere pientis
simi. libros lege. croni
ca perquire. historias
adverte. manda me
morie. Noli obliuisci.
Veluti remissi quorum

18 Henry's First Tutor, John Skelton

A moral treatise dedicated to Prince Henry, *Speculum principis*

John Skelton, Poet Laureate

British Library, Additional MS 26787, fols 21v–22

John Skelton wrote the treatise entitled *Speculum principis* (Mirror for a Prince) for Prince Henry that was originally dated 'at Eltham 28 August, in the year of Grace, 1501'. This manuscript copy, however, dates not from 1501, but from the moment of Henry's 1509 accession to the throne and forms part of Skelton's campaign to regain favour at court after his dismissal seven years earlier. Within the leather binding are several works by Skelton: the treatise, an epigram and a poem. In *Speculum principis* Skelton makes heavy reference to Classical history and literature in offering Henry advice about princely virtues. Many of Skelton's maxims were pretty banal: *Crapulam proscribe* (Leave drunkenness), *Virgines noli deflorare; viduas noli violare* (Do not deflower virgins; do not violate widows), but his emphasis on the importance of learning and the value of history reflected intellectual trends at the time and was a lesson absorbed by his young pupil. (SD and DC)

LITERATURE: Carlson, *The Latin Writings of John Skelton*

19 Lessons in History

Chronique de Rains

The Master and Fellows of Corpus Christi College, Cambridge, MS 432, fol.7

John Skelton used this 15th-century manuscript-chronicle of French affairs, now known as the *Récits d'un ménestrel de Reims,* for teaching Prince Henry history. The work provides a history of the Third Crusade, which recounts, among other things, the exploits of Richard I. Skelton presented the manuscript to the King in 1511, and attached to it a brief dedicatory Latin poem pointing out that the exploits of the English are usually belittled by French writers. In its margins, the manuscript has a series of the royal tutor's directions for reading – *Hic puer est natus* (This boy is born) next to an account of a royal birth; and shown here, *Nunc est ad sceptra vocatus* (Now he is called to the sceptre) next to a coronation; and so forth. Perhaps Henry acquired from his tutor something of his own well-attested propensity for defacing books in this way. Upon the accession, Skelton inscribed the book with a pair of new epigrams and presented it to his former charge. (DC and AC)

LITERATURE: Carlson, 'Royal Tutors in the Reign of Henry VII'; Scattergood (ed.), *John Skelton*

france filz au mauais mest uenuz ocirre. A
donc saillit li rois henris & prist .i. from & sa
alai es chambres quoies toz despatez & plaus
de lenemi. & sestranglai des taignes du froi.
Quant sa maignie uirent q li rois nestoit
mie entraus si le quisstrent p tout. & tant q
il le trouarent uilainnemant traitie. Car
il le trouarent estrangle. les taignes dou froi
entor son col. si en sont amerueilles esbahi.
Et lors le pristrent & le lauarent. & le mi
rent en son lit. & firent entendant au pue
ple que il estoit morz soudainnemant. mais
il nauient pas souant q tele auenture aueig
ne de tel home que on ne le saiche. Car ce
q maignie seuent nest mie souant celey.
Li cors du roy fu atornez & en seueliz
et fu portez a rouhant en normandie
et fu en foiz en la mere englyse.
Atant vos laissons aparler dou roy he
ri. si dirons dou roy richart son fil q
vint a terre & fu prouz & herdiz & cortois &
larges. & auenanz cheualiers. & uenoit tor
noier es marches de france et de pontous.
Et se demena vne grant piece ainsis q touz

20 Was Henry's Father, Henry VII, a Chivalric King?

Quentin Poulet, *L'Imaginacion de Vraye Noblesse*

British Library, Royal MS 19 C viii, fol.32v

It seems strange to doubt Henry VII's knightly qualities. He had won his throne in battle and defended it twice more against rebel armies. He frequently appeared in armour, with his helmet decorated by his wife. He led his troops into action against the French. He paid professional jousters to keep the tradition of the tournament going at his court; he had chivalric treatises in his library, like this lavishly illustrated presentation copy of *L'Imaginacion de Vraye Noblesse*; and he had himself represented as the supreme warrior-king when his new palace at Richmond was decorated. And yet the doubts persisted. Partly it was a matter of style, as he thought it beneath his dignity to take part in court tournaments himself. Partly it was a question of substance with his adoption, after 1501, of a policy of fiscal terrorism that resembled all too closely the unknightly vice of miserliness so that by his last years Henry VII resembled Poulet's unchivalrous knight, with his limbs literally dismembered with his broken reputation. In contrast, his son Henry went out of his way to present himself as a true knight who would bring order to the country that his father had put out of joint. (DS)

LITERATURE: Henry VII, *Oxford DNB*; Starkey, *Henry: Virtuous Prince*; Carley, *The Books of Henry VIII and his Wives*

21 An Arthurian Romance

Lancelot du Lac, c.1300

British Library, Royal MS 20 D iv, fol.1

Arthurian legends were well known at Henry VII's court and provided models of chivalric conduct for princes and gentlemen. This copy of the *Lancelot du Lac* was written and illuminated in France around 1300 but soon afterwards migrated to England, where it came into the possession of members of the Bohun family, whose arms have been inserted in the initials of the book. This miniature, which was added in England in the second half of the 14th century, encapsulates the tragedy of the Round Table. On the left, Arthur is engaged in conversation with his barons while Lancelot and Guenevere whisper together. In the scene to the right, the King and Queen preside over a state banquet. The book was one of a number of Arthurian romances in French that Henry VIII inherited and was possibly stored at Richmond Palace in 1535, when a French visitor, Palamède Gontier, included it on a list of books in the library. (JC)

LITERATURE: Sandler, *Gothic Manuscripts, 1285–1385*; Carley, *The Books of King Henry VIII and his Wives*

22 Henry V

Unknown artist, British School, probably mid- to late 16th century

National Portrait Gallery, London, NPG 545

Henry V (1386/7–1422) came to the throne in 1413 and ruled England for nearly ten years. In the early Tudor period he was celebrated as a great military leader, particularly for the English victory against the French at Agincourt in 1415. His military prowess provided the young Henry with an ideal of kingship, and helped inspire him to seek glory on the battlefield in France. Portraits of Henry V were popular during the 16th century and sometimes paired with Henry VIII. The only contemporary portraits of Henry V are found in extant illuminated manuscripts, in which he is shown either standing or seated receiving a book from the author. This portrait was probably produced for display among other kings and queens in an Elizabethan context. It shows the King in profile against an elaborate brocaded background which was fashionable for portraits of the Burgundian court in Henry V's lifetime, and the image may well have derived from a lost votive painting. (TC)

LITERATURE: Strong, *Tudor and Jacobean Portraits*; Scarisbrick, *Henry VIII*

23 Henry V: the Model Tudor King?

Beauchamp Pageant

British Library, Cotton MS Julius E iv, art. 6, fol.19v

Henry V features heavily in the 'Pageant' or illustrated history of Richard Beauchamp, Earl of Warwick (1389–1439), who had been one of the King's principal lieutenants in the French wars. This 'pageant' or scene shows the King and Earl in the English camp at the siege of Rouen. Henry V, helmeted and crowned (left), gives the kneeling Warwick charge of the city gate known as the Porte de Martainville; on the right, the Earl, standing in front of his tent, assumes his command. The 'Pageant' was made from about 1485 to 1490, but there is no reason to suppose that Henry VIII ever saw it.

By contrast, this same incident in the siege of Rouen also appears in the 'First English Life of Henry V', which *was* written for Henry VIII during his own French war of 1513–14. Its purpose was frankly didactic: that Henry 'maie in all thinges concerninge his person and the reigement of his people, conforme himselfe to [Henry V's] life and manners'. The 'First English Life' also drew heavily on the memories of one of the dominant figures of Henry's youth, Thomas Butler, 7th Earl of Ormond (*c.*1430–1515), who was Elizabeth of York's Lord Chamberlain and the stepfather of Henry's academic mentor, William Blount, Lord Mountjoy. As such, the 'First English Life' probably incorporates the actual tales of his great predecessor that Henry had first heard in his nursery. (DS)

LITERATURE: Starkey, 'King Henry and King Arthur'

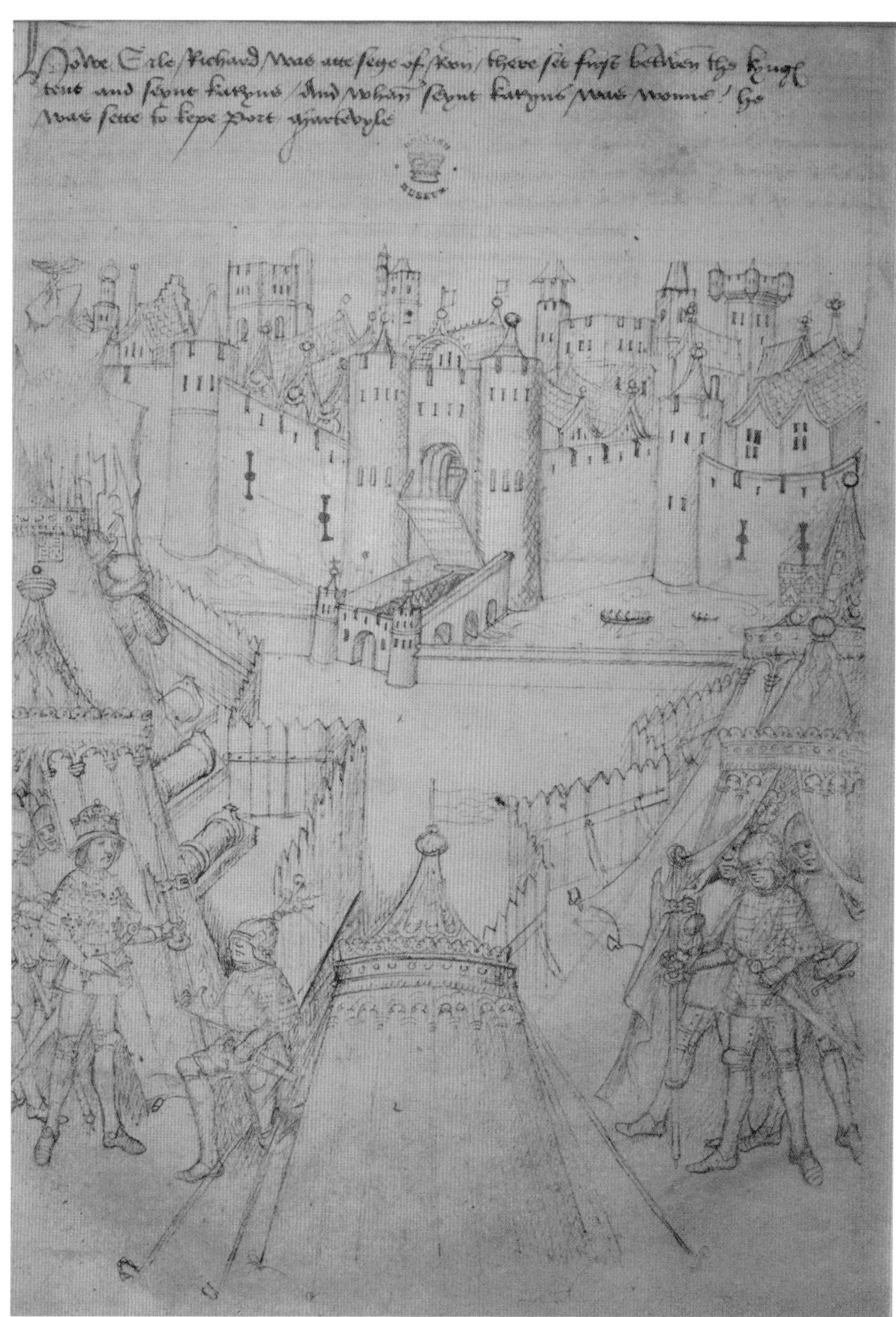

24 Desiderius Erasmus

Quentin Massys (1464/5–1530), 1517

RCIN 405759

This portrait is of the Dutch humanist scholar, Desiderius Erasmus, whose clear style of Latin was greatly admired within the intellectual circle around Prince Henry. Painted by Quentin Massys, the finest artist in Antwerp at that time, it was a gift for his old friend Thomas More, whom Erasmus had not seen since his third and last visit to England between 1511 and 1514. As is typical in his portraits, Erasmus is placed in a study with his books around him. Those on the shelf behind him have inscriptions relating to his recently published works: *Novum Testament[um]* (the New Testament) and *Hieronymus* (St Jerome); *Lovkianos* refers to Erasmus' and More's collaboration in translating Lucian's *Dialogues*; and *Hor*, originally *Mor*, both spells the first letters of his friend's name and refers to the 'Praise of Folly' (*Encomium Moriae*), a satirical essay written while Erasmus stayed with More in Bucklersbury in London in 1509. The words on the paper paraphrase Paul's Epistle to the Romans and the handwriting is a close imitation of Erasmus' own hand. (SD)

LITERATURE: Augustijn, *Erasmus*

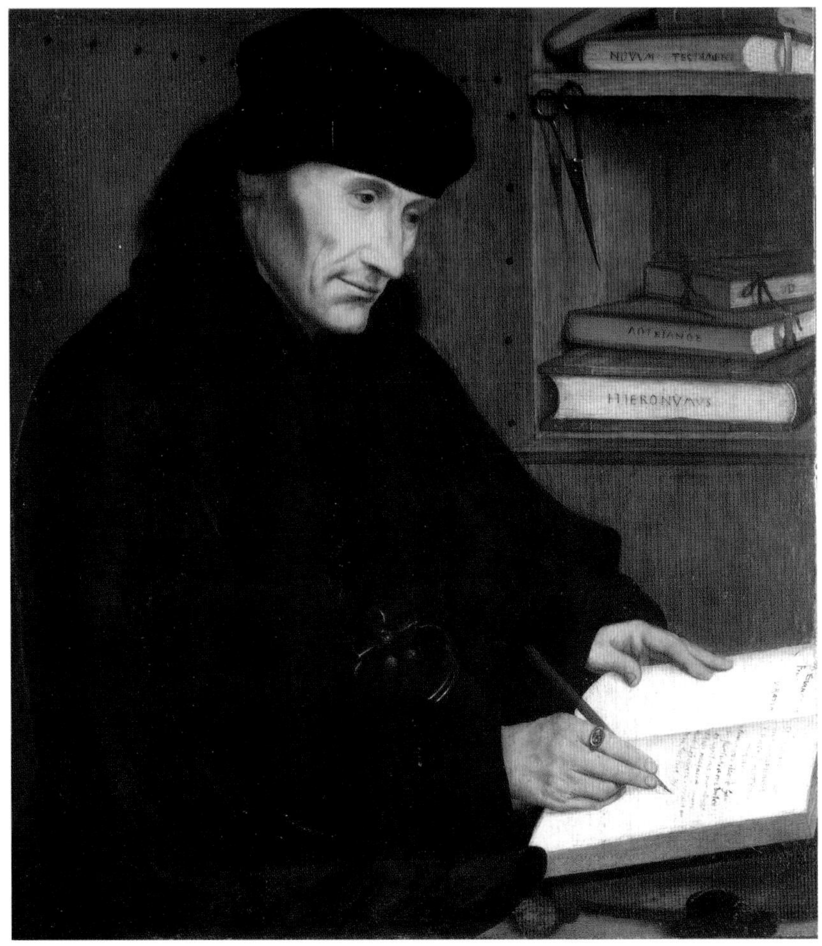

25 Erasmus' Offering to the Eight-year-old Henry

Erasmus' presentation letter to Henry VIII of 'Prosopopeia Britanniae', 1499

British Library, Egerton MS 1651, fol.1

This letter, addressed to 'the most illustrious prince, Duke Henry', marks the first contact between Henry and the most important scholar of the age, Desiderius Erasmus.

In 1499, Erasmus, then aged thirty and at the threshold of his European reputation, had been invited to England by his former pupil William Blount, Lord Mountjoy. Blount, who was acting as Henry's mentor, decided to introduce Erasmus to Henry; he also took along Erasmus' new friend, Thomas More. More began by presenting Henry with complimentary verses. But Erasmus, unfamiliar with English etiquette, had arrived empty-handed. Characteristically, Henry insisted on his pound of flesh and Erasmus, as he admitted later, laboured for three days 'partly out of shame and partly out of vexation' to produce the necessary poetical tribute. And this, almost certainly, is the actual copy Erasmus sent to Henry. Only ten leaves long, made up largely of reused materials, quickly and rather carelessly written, it is of no great merit. But Erasmus' prefatory letter, which justifies his gift on the grounds that only poets can confer eternal fame on kings, is more interesting. Is its theme a mere commonplace? Or does it mean that Erasmus already realized that the quest for fame would be what drove Henry? (DS)

LITERATURE: Starkey, *Henry: Virtuous Prince*

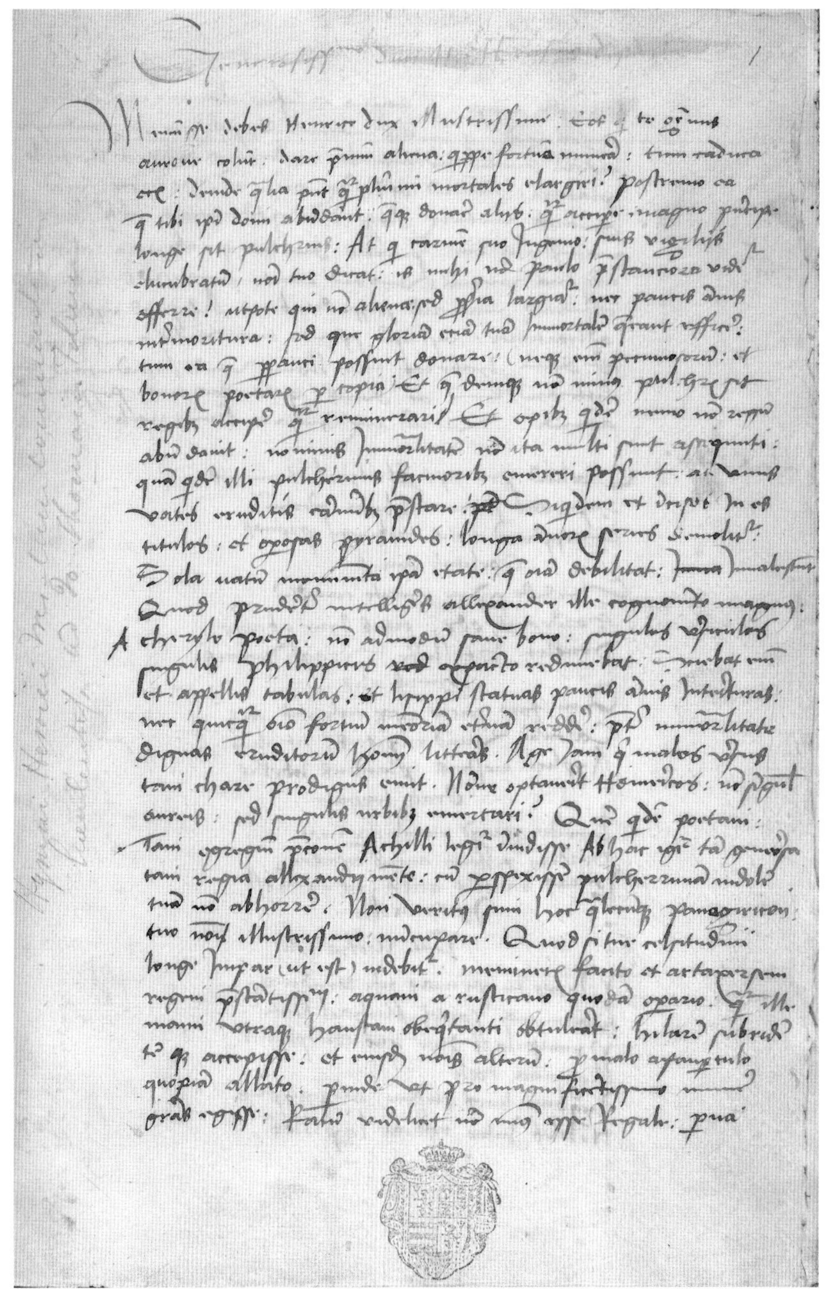

PRINCE ARTHUR'S MARRIAGE AND DEATH

After more than a year of negotiations, a marriage was agreed on 27 March 1489 between Henry VII's elder son Prince Arthur and Katalina (Katherine), the youngest daughter of Ferdinand of Aragon and Isabella of Castile, the joint monarchs of Spain. The marriage was delayed for a mixture of personal and political reasons, but eventually, on Sunday, 14 November 1501, their wedding took place in Old St Paul's Cathedral, London. A few days after Christmas the couple moved to Ludlow, where the fifteen-year-old Arthur was expected to gain experience in governing Wales. But did they consummate their marriage? One of his body servants later testified that Arthur had spent all night in his wife's bedchamber. Whatever the truth, Arthur was not to enjoy married life for long. On 2 April 1502, he died of the sweating sickness. Almost certainly Henry was not affected emotionally by the death of his elder brother, but it did change his life, as he was now heir to the throne. Barely a year later, though, Henry suffered a serious blow. His mother, Elizabeth of York, died unexpectedly shortly after giving birth to a daughter.

26 Prince Arthur

Collection of His Grace the Duke of Northumberland, cat. 04276

Born at St Swithun's Priory, Winchester, on 19 September 1486, the eldest son of Henry VII and Elizabeth of York was named after the mythical British King of Welsh descent, whom the Tudors claimed as an ancestor. In memory of Arthur, the baby prince was baptized in Winchester Cathedral, which some believed was the site of Camelot. When he was three years old, Arthur was dubbed a Knight of the Bath and invested as Prince of Wales and Earl of Chester, but, when six, he was packed off to Ludlow and had little further contact with his family.

Far more attention was paid to Arthur's education than that of his younger brother. He was first taught by John Rede (formerly headmaster of Winchester College) and then by the blind French poet, Bernard André. His death in 1502 was a cruel blow to his parents, but they tried to comfort each other for their loss. He was buried in Worcester Cathedral.

This is one of only two authenticated portraits of the Prince. In his hand is a gillyflower, or carnation, a symbol of purity or royalty. (SD)

LITERATURE: Arthur, Prince of Wales, *Oxford DNB*; Starkey, *Henry: Virtuous Prince*

27 The Parents of Katherine of Aragon

Spanish School, *c.*1470–1520

King Ferdinand II of Spain, King of Aragon (1452–1516) and Queen Isabella I of Spain, Queen of Castile (1451–1504)

The marriage in 1469 of Ferdinand, King of Aragon, to his cousin Isabella, Queen of Castile, was to unite their kingdoms and transform Spain into a major European power. The monarchs captured Granada from the Moors in 1492 and won the Kingdom of Naples from the French in 1503. Equally significant for the future of Spain, the monarchs offered patronage to Christopher Columbus, instituted the Spanish Inquisition and ordered the expulsion of the Jews. For their services to the Church, Pope Alexander VI awarded Ferdinand and Isabella the title of *Los Reyes Católicos* (The Catholic Kings). Given the prestige of the Spanish monarchs, it is little wonder that Henry VII was keen to marry his heir to their daughter, or that, after Arthur's death, he initially wanted Prince Henry to fill his brother's shoes and marry Arthur's widow. (SD)

LITERATURE: Edwards, *Ferdinand and Isabella*

28 The Betrothed Couple: Katherine and Arthur

Letter from Prince Arthur to Katherine of Aragon, endorsed 5 October 1499

British Library, Egerton MS 616, fol.14

Katherine and Arthur were formally betrothed in August 1497 at the ancient palace of Woodstock, Oxfordshire, with the Spanish ambassador, Pedro de Ayala, standing in for the bride. Katherine was due to travel to England in 1499, but her departure was delayed by disputes between Henry VII and Ferdinand over the payment of her dowry and by the insecurity of the Tudor dynasty, which made Isabella reluctant to let go of her youngest daughter. This is one of several love letters that Arthur sent to Katherine, his 'dearest spouse'. Writing in Latin, Arthur thanked her for her sweet letters and confessed an earnest desire to see her: 'let your coming to me be hastened, that instead of being absent we may be present with each other, and the love conceived between us and the wished-for joys may reap their proper fruit'. (AC)

LITERATURE: Mumby, *The Youth of Henry VIII*; Starkey, *Six Wives*

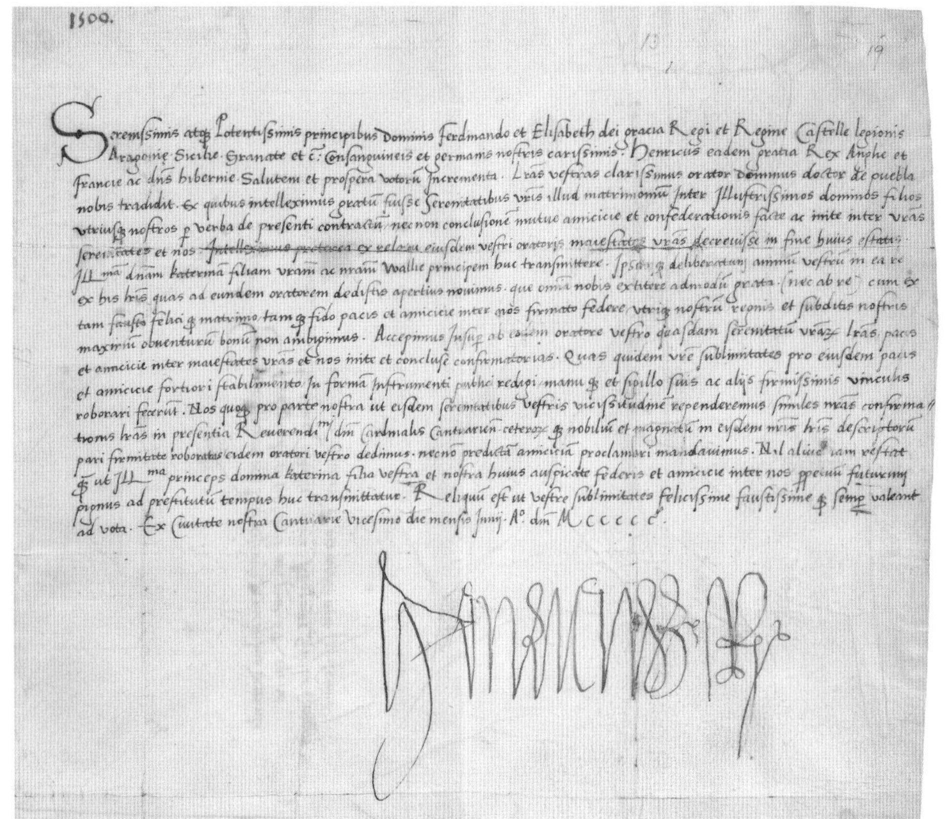

29 The Nuptials of Katherine and Arthur

Letter from Henry VII to Ferdinand and Isabella of Spain, Canterbury, 20 June 1500

British Library, Egerton MS 616, fol.19

In this letter to Ferdinand and Isabella, Henry VII informs them that he has received their letters expressing their pleasure at learning that the nuptials *per verba de praesenti* have been concluded between Arthur and Katherine. In return, Henry states how delighted he is to have learnt from De Puebla that they have resolved to send Katherine to England at the end of the summer. It was not until 21 June 1501, that Katherine finally bade farewell to her parents in Granada and travelled across Spain to La Coruña in Galicia, from where she departed for England on 27 September, and eventually landed at Plymouth on 2 October. It was the ten-year-old Prince Henry, who, on 14 November, proudly conducted Katherine's wedding procession from Baynard's Castle, the royal palace on the Thames, to Old St Paul's Cathedral, London, and escorted her to the altar to marry his older brother. (AC)

LITERATURE: Starkey, *Six Wives*; Weir, *The Six Wives of Henry VIII*

30 Henry's Mother: a False Prophet

Liber de optimo fato nobilissimi domini Henrici Eboraci ducis [afterwards Henry VIII] ac optimorum ipsius parentum . . . per Willielmum Parronum. Placentinum artium et medicine doctorem editus
(Book of the good fortune of Henry, Duke of York)

British Library, Royal MS 12 B vi, fols 1, 1v–2

This astrological treatise is the second work to be written for Henry. But it reflects his father's tastes rather than his own. Henry VII was addicted to relics, prophecies and prognostications, and it was to cater for this appetite that an Italian, known as William Parron, came to England and set up in practice as an astrologer. Each year, he produced a printed almanac, on Christmas Day, for general circulation, followed by a manuscript treatise as a New Year's gift to the King. The *Liber de optimo fato* is the New Year's gift for 1503, though it also exists in a version dedicated to Henry himself. The text offers Henry's parents condolences for the death of Arthur, for which it provides an astrological explanation. It declares that Prince Henry would enjoy a triumphant reign and father many sons. And it predicts that his mother would live until the age of eighty or ninety. Unfortunately for Parron, Queen Elizabeth died on her thirty-seventh birthday, only a month later, on 11 February 1503. The egregiousness of Parron's false prophecy is pilloried in More's *Lamentation*; it may also have left Henry with a lasting distaste for astrology. (DS)

LITERATURE: Starkey, *Henry: Virtuous Prince*

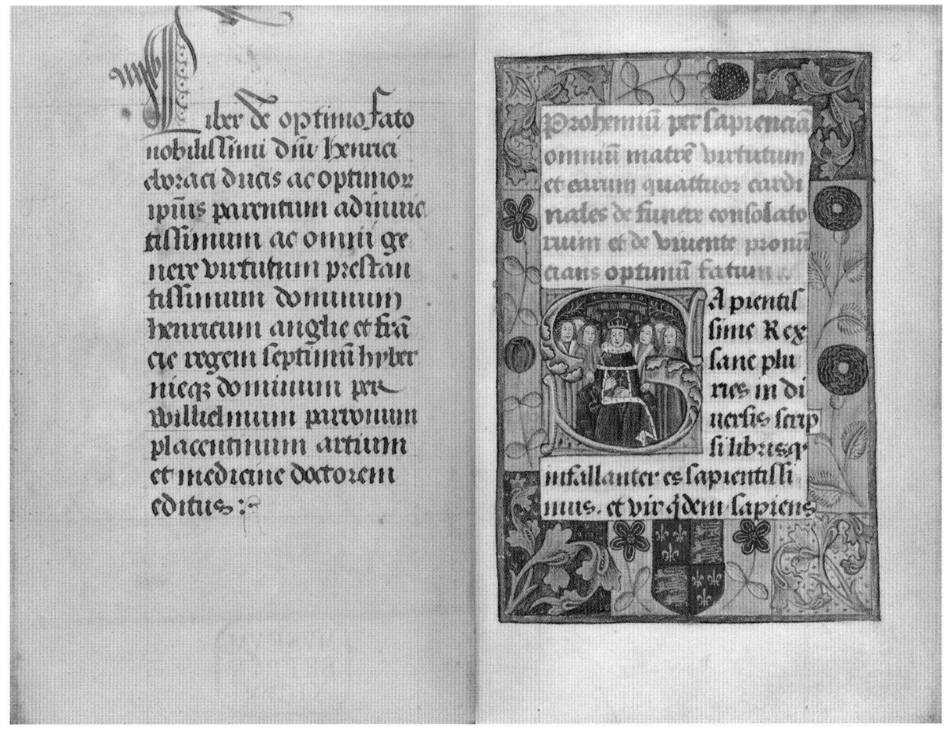

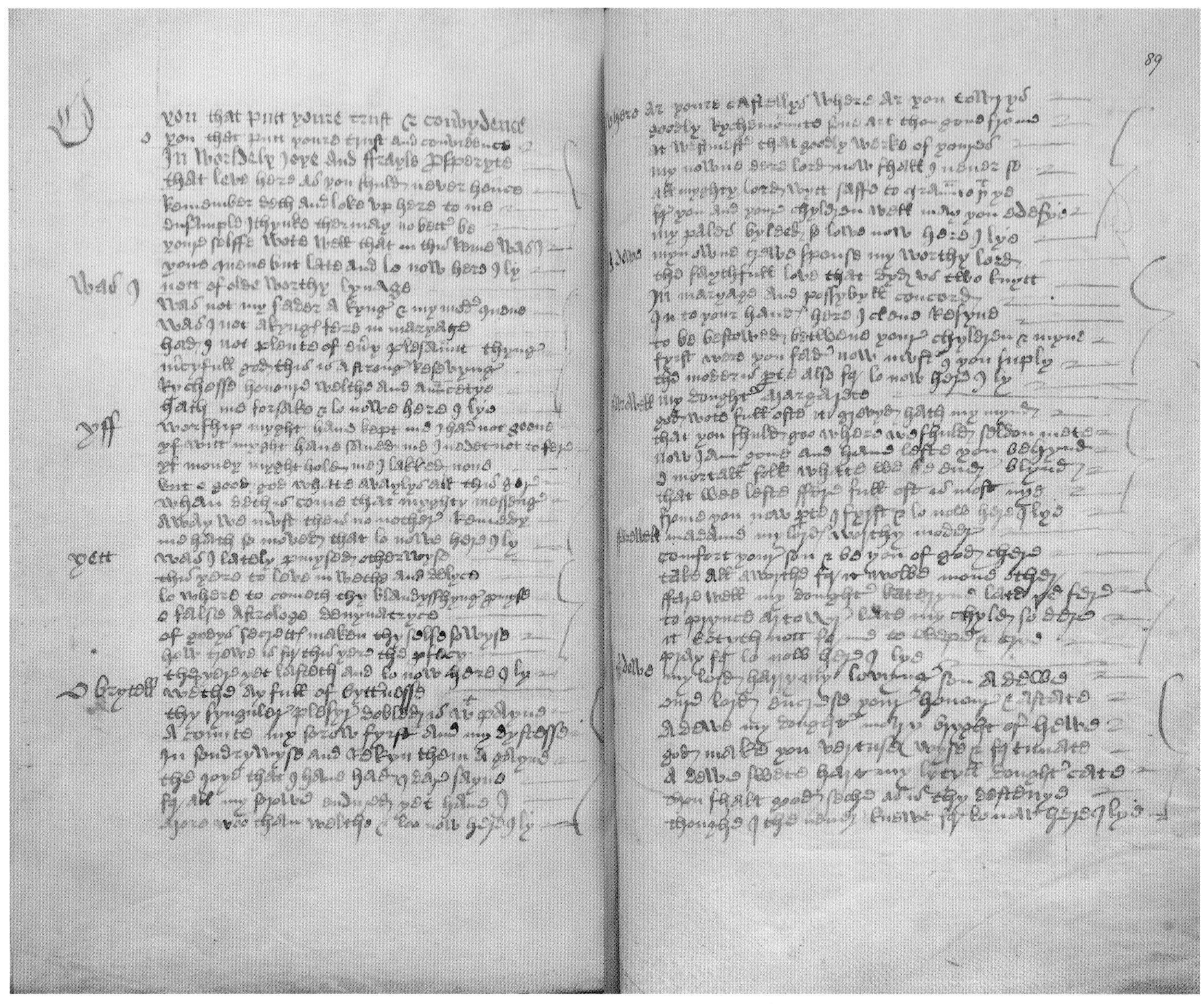

31 The Death of Queen Elizabeth of York

Thomas More's 'Rueful Lamentation' on the death of Queen Elizabeth, 1503

British Library, Sloane MS 1825, fols 88v–89

Queen Elizabeth of York, beautiful, pious, peace-loving and unimpeachably royal by descent, was by far the most popular member of Henry's family, and her tragically early death from complications following childbirth was the occasion for widespread grief: her husband was prostrate with grief; Henry mourned his mother 'bitterly'; Londoners wept openly at her funeral procession. There were also literary outpourings, of which this 'Rueful Lamentation' by Thomas More is the most impressive. It takes the conventional form of 'a dramatic soliloquy by the dead Queen, bidding farewell to all her earthly belongings'. Such poems were often wooden, but More personalizes the genre with unexpected flashes of sharp personal observation, such as Elizabeth's love of luxury (which she passed on to Henry). At the climax of the poem, Elizabeth says her farewells to her husband; she also begs him to bestow all his love on their children:

> Erst were you father, and now must you supply
> The mother's part also.

It is not a role that comes easily to most men, and Henry VII – as his surviving son would discover – was no exception. (DS)

LITERATURE: Starkey, *Henry: Virtuous Prince*

32 Elizabeth of York's Tomb

Cast by Domenico Brucciani (1815–80), after Pietro Torrigiano Torrigiani (1472–1528)

Electrotype of effigy in Westminster Abbey, 1512–18

National Portrait Gallery, London, NPG 291

Elizabeth of York's corpse lay in state for eleven days in the Tower of London. Then it was conveyed to Westminster Abbey for burial on 23 February 1503. Crowds came out to show their respect and watch the procession of several hundred mourners passing through the streets of London to the sounds of the tolling of church bells and the singing of friars. On top of the funeral bier was a wooden effigy of the Queen. A decade later, the Italian sculptor Pietro Torrigiano Torrigiani used the wooden effigy as a model for a gilt monument and tomb of Elizabeth that was erected in the new Henry VII chapel of Westminster Abbey. She lies alongside her husband and is shown, like him, with her hands clasped in prayer and in secular dress, without a crown or other royal insignia. The slim woman portrayed conforms to contemporary ideals of beauty, but differs from the Portuguese ambassador's description of Elizabeth as stout and large-breasted. (SD)

LITERATURE: Elizabeth of York, *Oxford DNB*; Doran, *The Tudor Chronicles*; Marks and Williamson, *Gothic*

HENRY, PRINCE OF WALES

On 23 February 1504, the twelve-year-old Henry was created Prince of Wales. However, unlike Arthur, he was not sent off to Ludlow but instead brought to court, where he was trained in the art of kingship by observing his father and learning from his tutors. Arrangements were also made for his marriage. His father's choice of bride was Katherine, Arthur's widow. However, the death of her mother, Queen Isabella, on 26 November 1504, made the marriage a less attractive prospect to Henry VII. Ferdinand of Aragon had no constitutional right to rule Castile, and his son-in-law, Archduke Philip of Burgundy, threatened to take his wife's inheritance by force. Although Philip's death in September 1506 ended the crisis, Henry VII retained his doubts about the advantages of an Anglo-Spanish match.

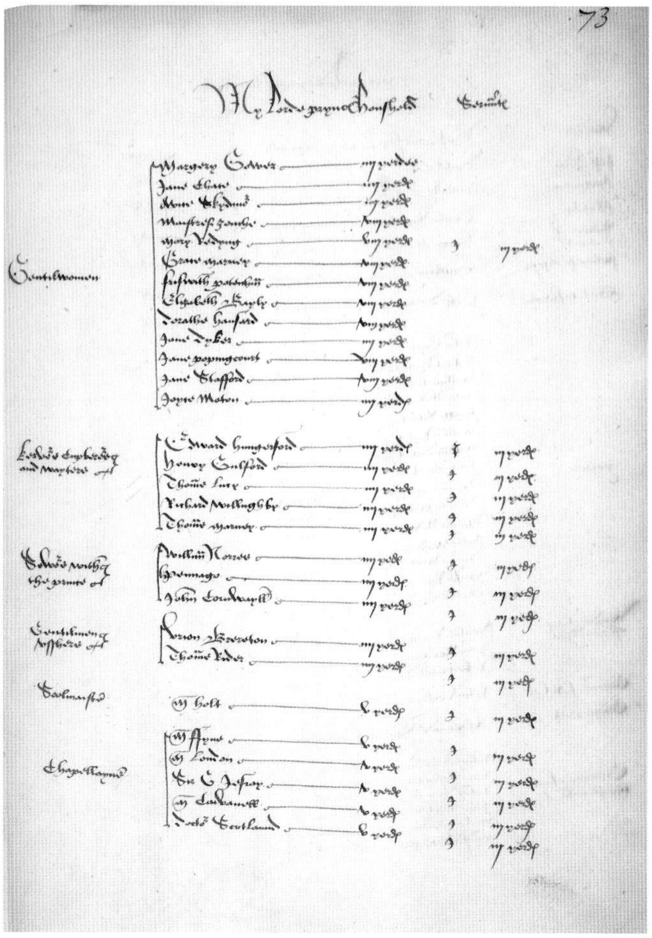

33 Prince Henry's Household

Full listing of Prince Henry's household for 1503 from the Lord Chamberlain's register

The National Archives, Richmond, Kew, Surrey, LC 2/1/1, fol.73 and detail from 73v

The first (and last) full listing of Henry's household when he was Prince of Wales comes from the record of those who were given mourning cloth to walk in the funeral procession of his mother, Elizabeth of York. Most importantly, since the list is headed by thirteen 'Gentilwomen', it shows that, even as Prince and at the age of twelve, Henry was still being brought up with his sisters. But the list also points to change as well, especially in Henry's education. His old, all-purpose tutor, John Skelton, had been dismissed, and replaced by a series of professionals: Henry's 'Scolmaister', 'Mr Holt', who taught him advanced Latin; Giles Duwes, a musician from French-speaking Flanders, who taught Henry both the lute and French; another musician 'Guillam', who was his 'scolmaister at pipes' and taught Henry to play wind instruments; and, finally, his 'master at Axes', Thomas Simpson, who supervised Henry's physical education and began to introduce him to knightly lore.

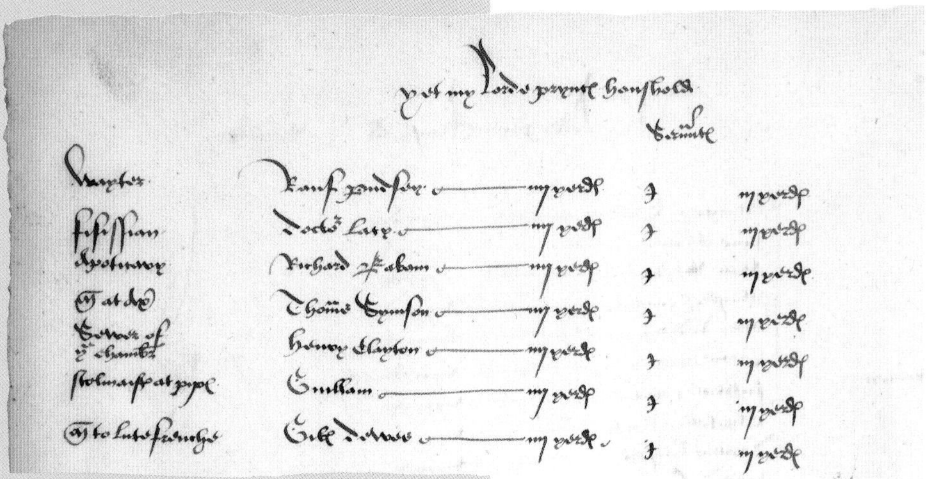

Eighteen months later, this independent household was dissolved as his father took him to live at court: another, very different, sort of education had begun. (DS)

LITERATURE: Starkey, *Henry: Virtuous Prince*

34 A Schoolbook for Prince Henry?

John Holt, *Lac puerorum* (Mylke for chyldren), 1508

British Library, C.33.b.47, title page and A iii^{v}–A iv

These pages are from *Lac puerorum* (Children's milk), the innovative Latin grammar written by Henry's second tutor, John Holt. It is a mnemonic, or memory aid, and is intended to help the student remember Latin parts of speech and word forms with the help of the finger and joints. In contrast to Henry's first teacher, Skelton, Holt was the consummate professional. He went to Oxford; became a junior fellow of Magdalen College, which pioneered the new approaches to Latin, and was appointed usher, or assistant master, of Magdalen College School. He was a great success and was poached to teach the boys in Cardinal Morton's household at Lambeth. Here, probably, he met and was befriended by Thomas More. And it was More, almost certainly, who recommended him to succeed Skelton when Henry's education was revamped following Arthur's death. But Holt himself died only two years later in 1504.

Lac puerorum, written for the boys of Morton's household and dedicated to More, was almost certainly used by Henry as well. His copy does not survive. But other schoolbooks of his do, including Skelton's *Speculum principis* (Mirror for a Prince). (DS)

LITERATURE: Starkey, *Henry: Virtuous Prince*

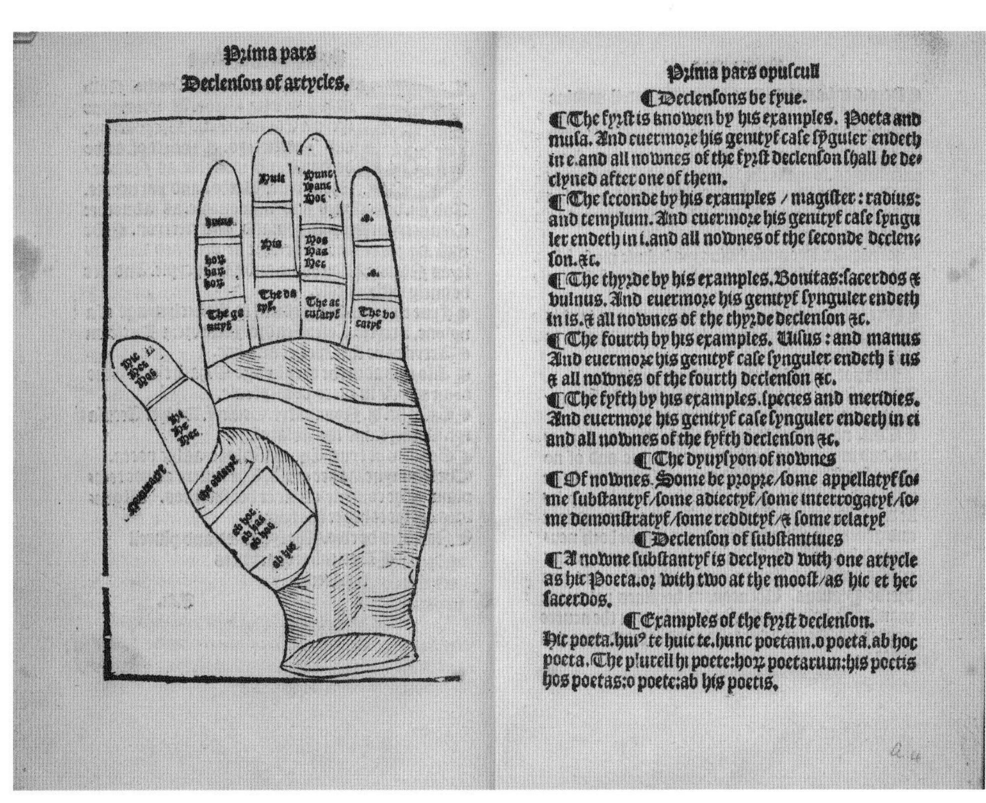

Prima pars

Declenson of artycles.

Prima pars opusculi

Declensons be fyue.

The fyrst is knowen by his examples. Poeta and musa. And euermore his genityf case syguler endeth in e. and all nownes of the fyrst declenson shall be declyned after one of them.

The seconde by his examples / magister: radius: and templum. And euermore his genityf case synguler endeth in i. and all nownes of the seconde declenson. &c.

The thyrde by his examples. Bonitas: sacerdos & vulnus. And euermore his genityf synguler endeth in is. & all nownes of the thyrde declenson &c.

The fourth by his examples. Usus: and manus And euermore his genityf case synguler endeth i us & all nownes of the fourth declenson &c.

The fyfth by his examples. species and meridies. And euermore his genityf case synguler endeth in ei and all nownes of the fyfth declenson &c.

The dyuysyon of nownes

Of nownes. Some be propre / some appellatyf / some substantyf / some adiectyf / some interrogatyf / some demonstratyf / some reddityf / & some relatyf

Declenson of substantiues

A nowne substantyf is declyned with one artycle as hic Poeta. or with two at the moost / as hic et hec sacerdos.

Examples of the fyrst declenson.

Hic poeta. hui^{9} te huic te. hunc poetam. o poeta. ab hoc poeta. The plurell hi poete: hor poetarum: his poetis hos poetas: o poete: ab his poetis.

35 Henry's Youthful Religion

Ushaw College, Durham, MS 29

The real nature of Henry's religious beliefs has always been a problem, as, in less than a decade, he went from being the most loyal son of the Church to schismatic-in-chief. Had he always harboured doubts? Or did he undergo some form of conversion? This 'bede' (prayer roll), which has never been publicly exhibited before, settles the matter beyond doubt, as it was owned and used by Henry himself when Prince of Wales.

The roll, which is made of narrow strips of parchment stitched together end to end, is some 4 metres long and over 12 cm wide. It was designed in this way in order to make it readily portable, as it was intended to be both used and read. For it is as much talismanic, liturgical and magical as it is religious. In the centre of the roll is a series of illuminations – of the Trinity, the Crucifixion, the different elements of Christ's Passion and several saints – while on either side are prayers (in Latin) and rubrics or instructions (in English). The latter explain how the devotions are to be performed and what rewards the faithful might expect, such as remission of time in Purgatory, protection against illness, accident and assault, and (for women) safe delivery in childbirth.

And it is under the central image of Christ's Passion that Henry writes his inscription. It is addressed to William Thomas, a favourite groom of his Privy Chamber as both Prince and (briefly) as King. 'Willyam Thomas,' it reads, 'I pray yow pray for me your lovyng master: Prynce Henry'. Were prince and groom praying together before the roll? Was Henry giving it to Thomas? In any case, the inscription makes it certain that, as a young man, Henry practised the devotions characteristic of the late medieval popular piety that, with the Reformation, he would later come to reject. *Why* is another story. (DS)

LITERATURE: Starkey, *Henry: Virtuous Prince*

36 The Marriage that Made the Habsburg Empire

Albrecht Dürer (1471–1528)

Woodcut engraving from The Triumphal Arch

British Museum, London, E, 2.334

The marriage, in 1496 of Philip the Fair (1478–1506) and Joanna ('the Mad') (1479–1555), laid the foundations of the power of the house of Habsburg. Philip had inherited the Netherlands from his mother, Mary of Burgundy (1457–1482), and was expected to inherit Austria from his father Maximilian von Habsburg (1459–1519); while from her parents, Isabella of Castile and Ferdinand of Aragon, Joanna was heiress of Spain, the New World and much of Italy. The couple had six children. This woodcut shows their betrothal. Philip is receiving the arms of Castile, Leon, Aragon, Sicily and Granada from Joanna.

Philip was declared adult in 1494 and took over the rulership of the Netherlands from his father, who had been acting as regent. Then in 1504, Joanna's mother, Isabella of Castile, died. As the union of Castile and Aragon was only a personal one, Philip immediately claimed Castile as Joanna's right and in January 1506 the couple embarked for Spain to make good her title. The voyage began as a splendid seaborne pageant. But, halfway along the Channel, violent storms broke up the fleet and drove Philip and Joanna ashore in England. There they were in effect prisoners, though Henry VII disguised the fact by laying on a lavish welcome for his unwilling guests. (DS)

LITERATURE: Edwards, *Ferdinand and Isabella*; Cunningham, *Henry VII*

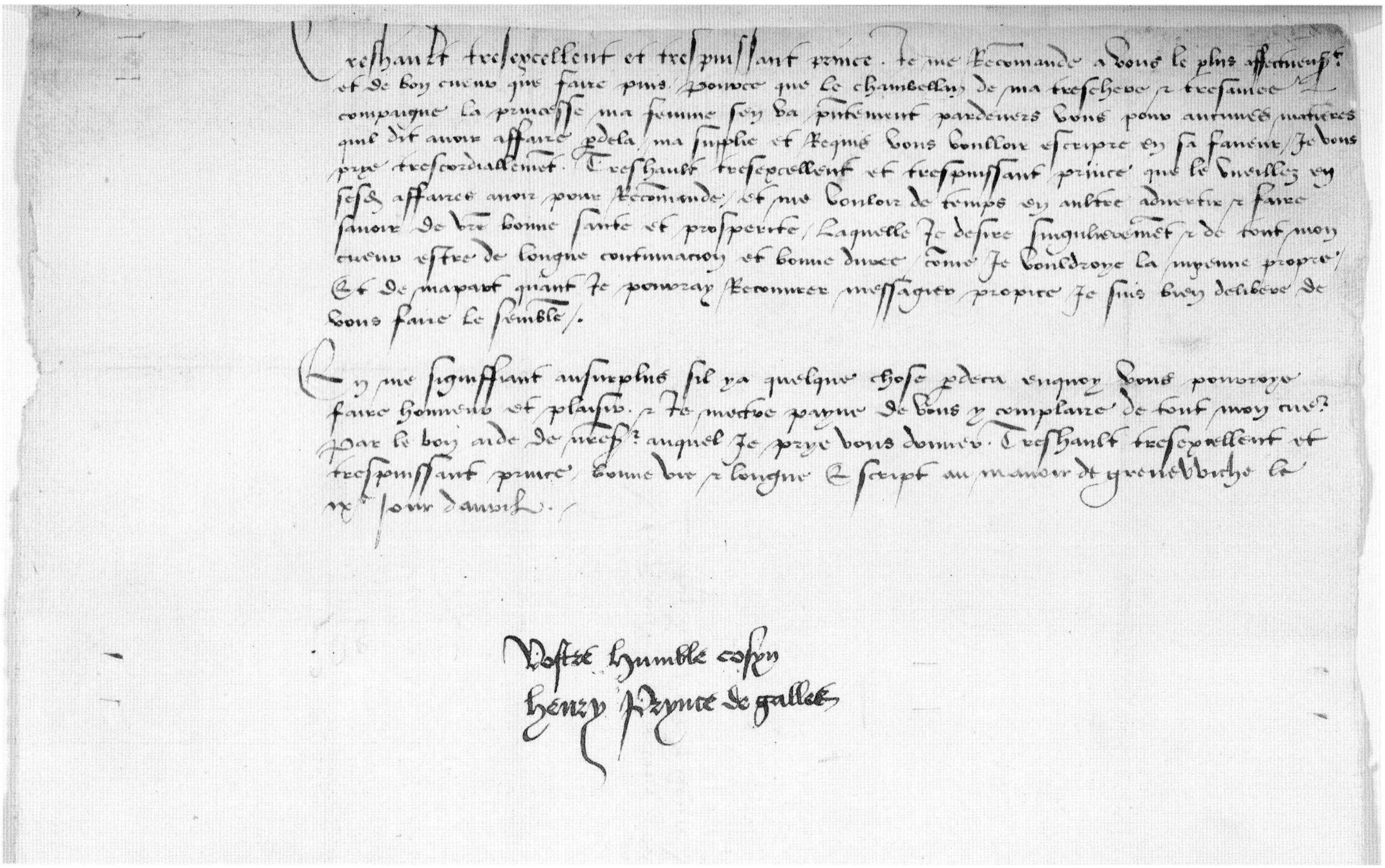
Treshault tresexcellent et trespuissant prince. Je me recommande a vous le plus affectueusement et de bon cueur que faire puis. Pource que le chambellain de ma treschiere et tresamee compaigne la princesse ma femme sen va presentement pardevers vous pour aucunes matieres quil dit avoir affaire pardela, ma supplie et requis vous vouloir escripre en sa faveur. Je vous prie tres cordiallement. Treshault tresexcellent et trespuissant prince que le vueillez en ses affaires avoir pour recommande, et me vouloir de temps en aultre advertir et faire savoir de vostre bonne sante et prosperite, laquelle je desire singulierement et de tout mon cueur estre de longue continuacion et bonne duree comme je vouldroye la myenne propre. Et de ma part quant je pourray recouvrer messagiers propices je suis bien delibere de vous faire le semblable.

En me signiffiant aussurplus sil ya quelque chose pardela envers vous pourroye faire honneur et plaisir, et je mectrai payne de vous y complaire de tout mon cueur par le bon ayde de nostre seigneur auquel je prye vous donner. Treshault tresexcellent et trespuissant prince, bonne vie et longue. Escript au manoir de Grenewiche le ixe jour davril.

Vostre humble cosyn
Henry Prynce de Galles

37 Henry's Role-model?

Letter from Henry, Prince of Wales, to Archduke Philip, Greenwich, 9 April 1506

British Library, Additional MS 21404, fol.9

This letter, written by Henry to Philip the Fair, is the first of Henry's to survive. Henry, now in his fifteenth year, acted as Philip's co-host throughout his visit to England. He met him at Winchester, whose Arthurian associations were invoked once more as the two princes inspected the Round Table in the Great Hall of Winchester Castle. Then Henry escorted Philip to meet Henry VII at Windsor and sat in on the confidential discussions.

It was Henry's first summit conference and it established a lasting taste for the genre. Even more important perhaps was the personal impression made by Philip. Henry VII maintained the utmost magnificence. But, partly because of age and partly to preserve his dignity, he did not take part in jousts or other active sports. Philip did – taking on and beating the champion English tennis player, Thomas Grey, the Marquess of Dorset. Henry found Philip's example seductive and it seems to have provided – along with historical or pseudo-historical antecedents, such as King Arthur and Henry V – an important model for his own kingship.

Having paid for his entertainment by agreeing to a profoundly unequal trading treaty, the *Intercursus Malus*, and surrendering the Yorkist claimant, Edmund de la Pole, Earl of Suffolk, Philip was allowed to resume his journey to Spain in late March. Henry's letter, dictated in his fluent French and signed in his own sprawling hand 'Henry, Prynce des Galles', was dated 9 April 1506, while Philip and Joanna were still waiting for favourable winds at Falmouth. It asked for favour for an official of Katherine of Aragon, Joanna's sister and Henry's nominal wife; it also requested Philip to correspond with Henry and promised to write in return. It was almost as though Henry was asking Philip to be his pen-pal. Five months later, Philip was dead. (DS)

LITERATURE: Starkey, *Henry: Virtuous Prince*

38 Henry and Katherine's Marriage Contract

Archivo General de Simancas, Patronato Real, Caja 53, Doc. 1

In order to preserve the Anglo-Spanish alliance, Arthur's widow Katherine was offered as a bride for Prince Henry, the new heir to the English throne, and a treaty of marriage was concluded at Richmond on 23 June 1503. This is the ratification of that treaty, signed by Henry VII on 3 March 1504 and decorated with the royal arms and the red roses of Lancaster. The treaty stipulated that the union of Henry, aged twelve, and Katherine, seventeen, should be solemnized when Henry turned fourteen on 28 June 1505, by which time Katherine's parents were expected to have paid the second instalment of the marriage portion. The treaty also recognized that a papal dispensation would be necessary for Katherine to marry Henry, as canon law forbade a man to marry his brother's widow, even though years later Katherine would deny that her union with Prince Arthur had been consummated. (AC)

LITERATURE: Starkey, *Henry: Virtuous Prince*; Starkey, *Six Wives*; Mira y Delva (eds), *A La Búsqueda del Toisón de Oro*

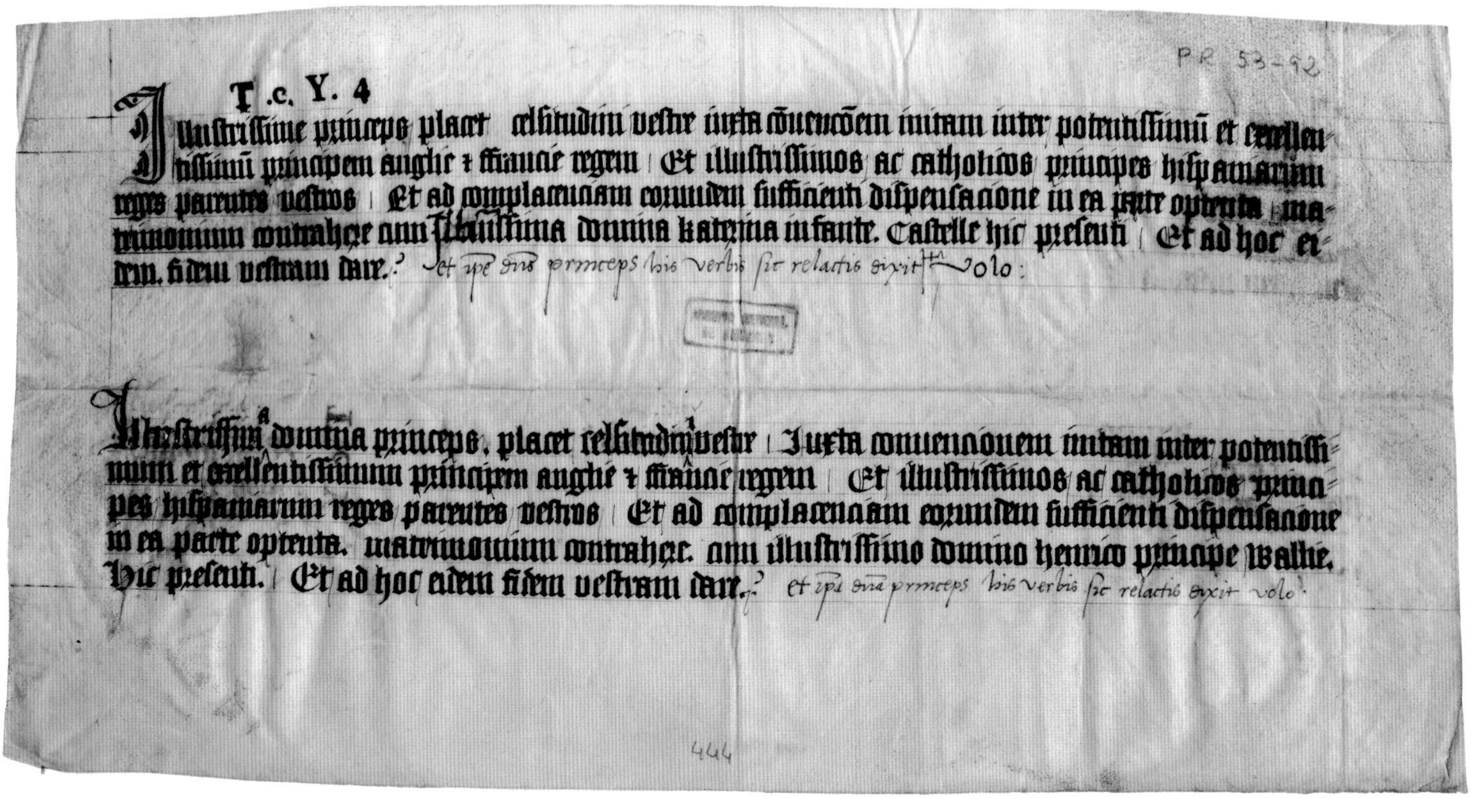

39 Marriage *per verba de praesenti*

Archivo General de Simancas, Patronato Real, Caja 53, Doc. 92

The marriage treaty also required that, once the necessary papal dispensation was granted, a marriage *per verba de praesenti* should take place between Katherine and Henry. This undated document bears witness that the proxy marriage duly took place. It records that Henry and Katherine were asked in turn if it was 'their will to fulfil the treaty of marriage concluded by their parents and, as the Pope had issued a dispensation to allow their marriage, take each other as their lawful spouse'. The handwritten addition notes that both Henry and Katherine responded *'volo'* (I will). When Henry turned fourteen, however, Henry VII refused to allow the marriage to be solemnized. This was partly because of Ferdinand's failure to pay the remainder of Katherine's marriage portion and also because of the death of Queen Isabella in 1504, which deprived Ferdinand of his title as King of Castile and greatly reduced his power. Henry VII now felt that other more advantageous alliances might be found. (AC)

LITERATURE: Starkey, *Henry: Virtuous Prince*; Starkey, *Six Wives*; Scarisbrick, *Henry VIII*

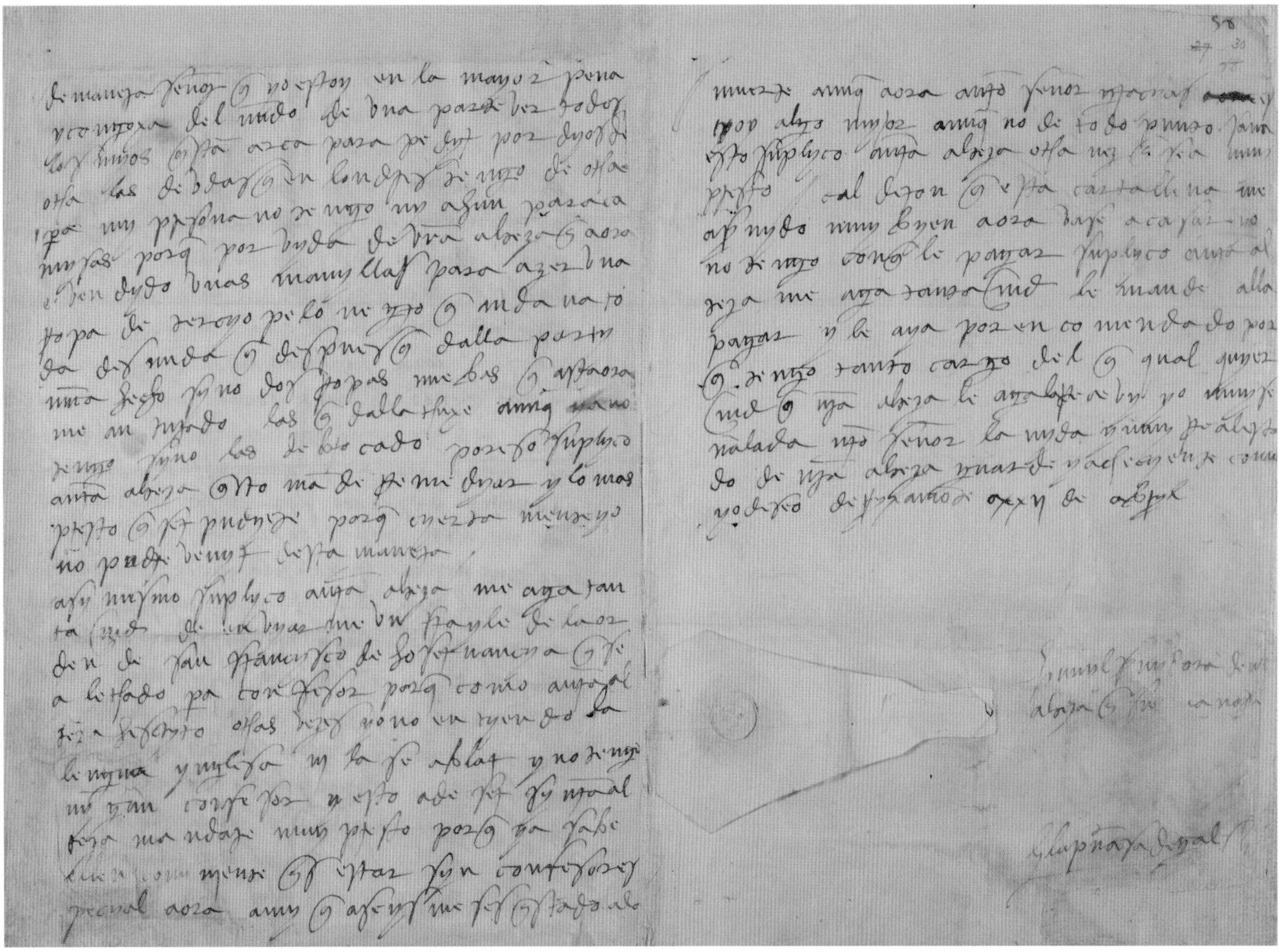

40 A Miserable Widow

Autograph letter from Katherine of Aragon to her father Ferdinand, Richmond, 22 April 1506

British Library, Egerton MS 616, fols 29v–30

After Arthur's death on 2 April 1502, Katherine spent seven impoverished years as the Dowager Princess of Wales while Henry VII refused to allow her to marry Prince Henry. This is one of several pitiful letters that Katherine wrote to her father during this time, describing her trials and begging him for money to pay her servants. Here, Katherine tells Ferdinand 'I am in debt in London and this not for extravagant things … but only for food'. The King of England, she continued, would not pay for anything, even though she had pleaded with him and his Council with tears in her eyes. Katherine reported that she was 'in the greatest trouble and anguish in the world' and had to resort to selling items from her dower plate because she had no decent clothes to wear and not even enough money to buy a new chemise so that she 'was all but naked'. (AC)

LITERATURE: Starkey, *Six Wives*; Mattingly, *Catherine of Aragon*; Mumby, *The Youth of Henry VIII*

VENUS AND MARS (1509–13)

Steven Gunn

Henry VIII's reign opened with high expectations, but also great uncertainty. For the first 44 hours or so after the death of his father, Henry VII, on 21 April 1509, it was not even clear that Henry was king, as the old King's courtiers pretended he was still alive until practical arrangements for the succession were in place. Large questions remained thereafter. How far would Henry repudiate the men and measures of his father's reign? Not yet eighteen years old, would he really govern in person? And how would the ruling dynasty, now hanging by the slender thread of a single unmarried adolescent, perpetuate itself?

Many welcomed Henry VIII as a change from his father. Noblemen arrested under suspicion of plotting were set free. Edmund Dudley and Sir Richard Empson, the most notorious of his father's fiscal agents, were locked up and executed. Many debts were cancelled and commissioners were sent out to invite complaints. Yet the changing of the guard was only partial. Among the leading councillors of the new reign, it soon emerged, were not only great lords and churchmen who had served Henry VII, but also some of the lawyers and bureaucrats who had given the old regime its edge of rapacious efficiency. Many debts to the Crown were judged to be justified and rigorous auditing was restored. The Council put real constraints on the new King, counter-signing his warrants and letters as though he were a minor or an incompetent.

Henry's decision to marry Katherine does seem to have been his own. They married at Greenwich on 11 June 1509 and, on Sunday, 24 June, went together to Westminster Abbey for the coronation. Henry swore the traditional oath to preserve the laws, protect the Church and be just to his subjects. It was a day to remember for both the King, who later commissioned a mural of it for Whitehall Palace, and the crowds, who cut up the processional carpet for souvenirs.

At court the King was more able to influence matters than in the Council. Henry excelled in the aristocratic pastimes of his day. He hunted, he jousted, he shot the longbow, he played tennis; he danced, he sang, he played and composed music. He chose the friends with whom he followed this hectic lifestyle

◀ Detail from cat. no. 59

and on whom he increasingly conferred the rewards at his disposal. The Queen was caught up in this courtly whirl, but also had serious dynastic work to do. Her first known pregnancy ended in a miscarriage on 31 January 1510, but, on 1 January 1511, everything went according to plan and she gave birth to a son. The guns of the Tower of London shot off celebratory salvoes and towns from Newcastle to Dover and Plymouth staged 'triumphs' with bonfires, bell-ringing and barrels of beer. Henry himself held the grandest tournament of the reign to date from 12 to 13 February. On 22 February the young prince died. Further unsuccessful pregnancies followed.

Henry's duty was to breed a line of kings who would bring domestic peace by uniting the warring claims of the red and white roses. He also felt called to a more personal kind of glory, matching himself with the warrior kings of the nation's past and with the great princes of Europe. His military ambitions were evident by 1511, with new ships, attacks on Scottish pirates and expeditions to Spain and the Netherlands. In November he agreed a Holy League against France with the Pope, the Venetians and his father-in-law Ferdinand of Aragon.

Papal involvement highlighted another uncertainty. Just how would Henry discharge his duty to the Church as a Christian prince? His father had extorted money from the Church and cut back its jurisdiction, yet been blessed by successive pontiffs. Henry ruled the Church with a strong hand, prompting mutterings from Archbishop Warham about Thomas Becket, but promoted his war as a blow for Rome against the schismatic Louis XII of France (r.1498–1515).

At first the war did not go well. In 1512 Henry's fleet raided the coasts of Brittany but lost a capital ship in a devastating explosion. An attempt to begin the re-conquest of English France with Gascony, the last province to fall in 1453, failed because Ferdinand did not co-operate. Henry's men drank to excess, mutinied and came home. In spring 1513 Henry's admiral, Sir Edward Howard, was killed attacking the French galley fleet from puny English row-barges.

Everything now rested on Henry's own campaign in northern France in the summer of 1513, leading a force more than 30,000 strong, twice the size of any English army in the Hundred Years' War. On 16 August a French supply column was surprised and took flight so fast that the encounter was dubbed the Battle of the Spurs. Henry's artillery bombarded first Thérouanne, then Tournai into submission. On 25 September the conquering King, in armour, rode into Tournai beneath a silken canopy, to hear Mass at the cathedral, knight 49 of his captains and bow graciously from the town hall steps to his rather sullen new subjects.

Tournai was a substantial centre of trade and manufacture and the seat of a major bishopric. Its conquest marked Henry out as a leading player in

European politics and the reputation of the English was higher than it had been for three generations. Yet uncertainty hovered even over this achievement. Was Tournai, far inland and expensive to maintain, really worth the effort put into its capture? Events in England in Henry's absence begged the question. James IV of Scots, allied to France, invaded Northumberland and met the English at Flodden on 9 September 1513. Desperate fighting lasted from four in the afternoon till after dark. Next morning James himself, ten earls, thirteen barons and perhaps 10,000 Scots lay dead. Katherine, whom Henry had left behind as governor of the realm, rather rashly put this victory on a par with Henry's.

Victories over the Scots did not register in Europe, or in Henry's imagination, like victories in France. But his war had cost around a million pounds, driving up taxes and consuming the personal fortune that Henry had inherited from his father. The population under his rule was perhaps a third that of Spain, a sixth that of France. His wager had gained him a modicum of glory and a seat in the councils of Europe. But would his resources, his greatness of mind and his good fortune enable him to continue to play the role he had won?

A NEW KING

Henry VII died on Saturday, 21 April 1509, at Richmond Palace, but his intimate courtiers kept the death a secret for two days. Perhaps they wanted to prevent a pretender making a claim to the throne; perhaps too they wanted to mount a coup against the old King's unpopular ministers. If so, they were successful on both counts. Henry VII's only surviving son – the seventeen-year-old Henry VIII – was the first king since 1421 to succeed peacefully as a crowned monarch rather than to take the throne by conquest or usurpation. His father's ministers, Edmund Dudley and Sir Richard Empson, were imprisoned in the Tower of London and later executed.

41 Henry VII on his Deathbed

Wriothesley's Heraldic Collections, vol.1: *Book of Funerals*

British Library, Additional MS 45131 fol.54

Though he may not have been actually present, the Garter King of Arms, Sir Thomas Wriothesley (d.1534), wrote a detailed account of the proceedings surrounding the death of Henry VII and drew this picture of the King on his deathbed. The dying King is in his Privy Chamber, surrounded by his most intimate courtiers and household (clockwise round the bed): Richard Fox, Bishop of Winchester (d.1528); George, Lord Hastings (d.1544); Richard Weston, Esquire of the Body (a household officer in constant attendance on the king) and Groom of the Privy Chamber (d.1541); Richard Clement, Groom of the Privy Chamber (d.1538); Matthew Baker (or Basquer), Esquire of the Body (d.1513); John Sharpe and William Tyler, Gentlemen Ushers; Hugh Denys, formerly Groom of the Stools and the King's most intimate attendant; and William Fitzwilliam, Gentleman Usher (d.1542), who holds a wand of office and closes the King's eyes. Also present are two tonsured clerics and three physicians holding urine bottles. It was possible to keep Henry's death a secret, as he was out of the public eye, and it was Weston who is described by Wriothesley as keeping up the pretence that the old King was still alive until 23 April. (AA and SD)

LITERATURE: Gunn, 'The Accession of Henry VIII'; Howard de Walden, *Banners Standards and Badges from a Tudor Manuscript*; Marks and Payne (eds), *British Heraldry*

42 Henry VII's Tomb

Cast by Domenico Brucciani, after Pietro Torrigiano Torrigiani

Electrotype of effigy in Westminster Abbey, London, 1512–18

National Portrait Gallery, London, NPG 290

Believing himself to be the heir of the Lancastrian kings, Henry VII planned for his tomb to be placed next to Henry V's chantry in the new royal chapel he had started building in Westminster Abbey. He also intended that Henry VI's remains (then buried at Windsor) would be moved to Westminster Abbey, but the reburial never took place. On Henry VII's death, the new chapel was still incomplete, and it was only in October 1512 that the Florentine sculptor Pietro Torrigiani was awarded the commission to design the tomb. Torrigiani, one of a number of Italian sculptors who were working at Henry VIII's court, had just completed the tomb of Henry's grandmother Margaret Beaufort. At this time Henry VIII also discussed with Torrigiani costs for a double tomb for himself and his wife, Katherine of Aragon, to be placed in the chapel. It was, of course, never built. (SD)

LITERATURE: Strong, *Tudor and Jacobean Portraits*; Starkey (ed.), *A European Court in England*; Tatton-Brown and Mortimer, *Westminster Abbey*

A ROYAL WEDDING AND CORONATION

Within days of his accession, Henry VIII announced his intention to marry Katherine of Aragon. He claimed that he was fulfilling a deathbed promise to his father, but in truth he wanted an alliance with her father, Ferdinand of Aragon, against France. The marriage took place on 11 June 1509 in the Queen's Closet or Oratory at Greenwich, and two weeks later the couple were crowned by the Archbishop of Canterbury in Westminster Abbey.

43 The Young Henry VIII

Anonymous

Portrait, *c.*1513

Berger Collection at the Denver Art Museum, TL-17964

This portrait of Henry in his early twenties is much less well known than the later depictions by Holbein, but is still recognizable as the King with his auburn hair, grey-blue eyes, bump in his long nose and rosebud mouth. It can be compared to the portrait of Henry processing to Parliament in 1512, especially in the long, flowing hairstyle, clean-shaven face and shape of his bonnet. The Venetian ambassador described Henry in 1515 as 'the handsomest potentate I ever set eyes on … his complexion very fair and bright, with auburn hair combed straight in the French fashion; and a round face so very beautiful that it would become a pretty woman, his throat being rather long and thin'. In this depiction the King holds a rose, which may be a symbol of the Tudor dynasty; but the flower held in this way is typically a reference to betrothal or marriage, so possibly this gesture borrows from an earlier marriage portrait. (TS)

LITERATURE: Fletcher, 'A Group of English Royal Portraits'; String, *Art and Communication in the Reign of Henry VIII*

44 The Young Katherine of Aragon

Michael Sittow (1469–1525)

Portrait, *c.*1504–5

Kunsthistorisches Museum, Vienna, Inv. Nr.GG5612

The youngest child of Ferdinand and Isabella of Spain, Katherine came to England at the age of sixteen to marry Henry's elder brother Prince Arthur in 1501. Only several months into their marriage, and at the age of just fifteen, Arthur died. Following protracted negotiations, Katherine eventually married Henry, who was five-and-a-half years her junior, in 1509. In this portrait, thought to be of the young Katherine, she is represented as demure and pretty. A 'C' for 'Catalina' (her Spanish name) is embroidered on her dress but 'K' for Katherine, the name used in England, is on the necklace together with the red and white Tudor roses. (AC and SD)

LITERATURE: Starkey, *Six Wives*; Mattingly, *Catherine of Aragon*; Starkey, *Henry: Virtuous Prince*

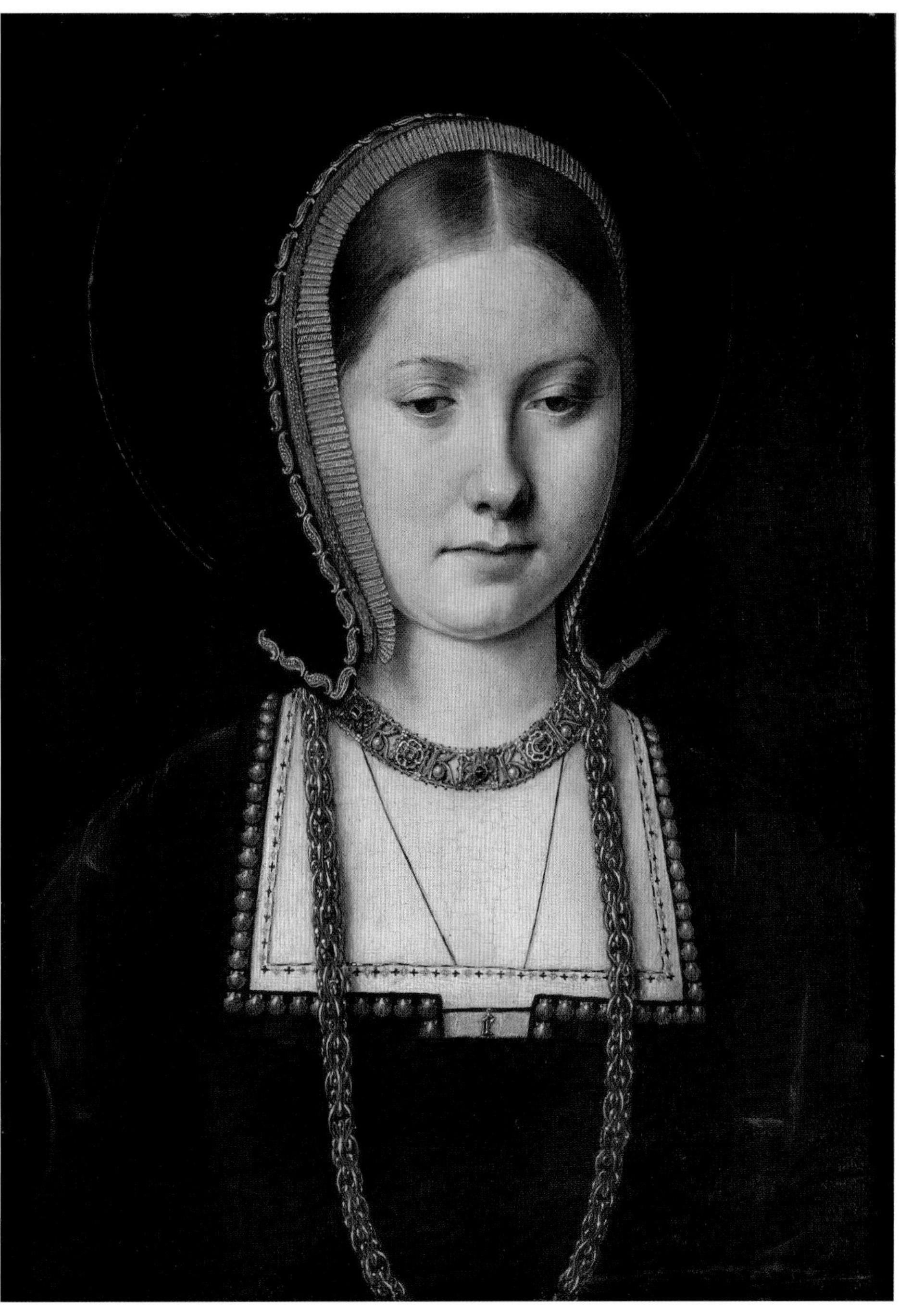

45 The Marriage of Henry VIII and Katherine of Aragon

Draft licence for the marriage of Henry and Katherine, 8 June 1509

Lambeth Palace, London, CM 51/115

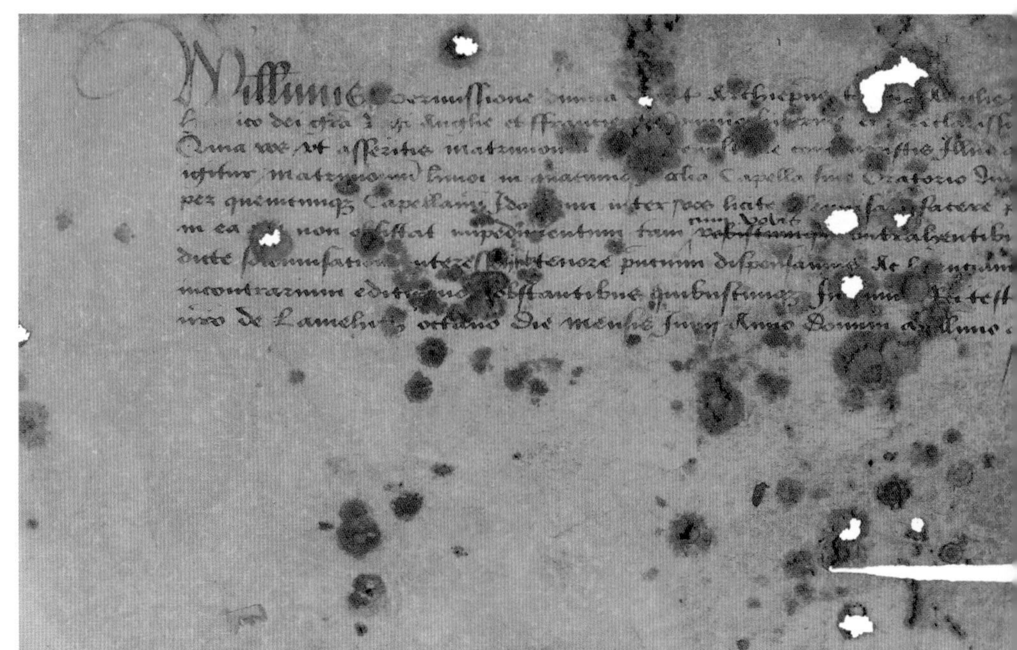

For seven years following the death of Prince Arthur, Katherine of Aragon was used as a pawn by Henry VII in his complex diplomatic manoeuvrings. Shortly after his father's death, Henry VIII made it known that Katherine was to become his wife. The draft of Archbishop Warham's licence for the marriage of Henry and Katherine dispensed with the normal requirement for three readings of the banns and merely insisted that they be published once. It also authorized the marriage to take place in any chapel or church. Three days later, on 11 June 1509, the marriage was performed by the Archbishop in a private ceremony in the Queen's Closet (private chapel) at Greenwich. (AC)

LITERATURE: Starkey, *Six Wives*; Scarisbrick, *Henry VIII*; Starkey, *Henry: Virtuous Prince*

46 A Wedding Gift

Guilelmus de Saliceto, *De salutate corporis* and Johannes de Turrecremata, *De salutate animae*

British Library, C.37.f.8, title page

Inscribed: *Per te rosa toluntur vitia, Per te datur mestis Leticia*

In hoc Libro hec continentur. Salus corporis Salus anime. Pius contra venereos yliada Homeri.

Dated 12 December 1509, this was the first printed book to celebrate the royal marriage. Commissioned by Piers de Champagne, Esquire of the Body to Henry VIII, it was dedicated to both Henry and Katherine. The woodcut on the title page incorporates Henry's arms, the Beaufort portcullis, and his supporters, dragon and greyhound; Katherine's arms appear on the verso. The words on the scroll – 'Through you, o rose, sins are removed, Through you, the sorrowing rejoice' – link the Tudor rose, which it surrounds, with the Virgin Mary. The printer, Richard Facques, took over the printing business of his relative, William Faques, who had been the first printer in England to designate himself as *regius impressor*, and used his type and ornaments in this volume. The 'No. 864' on the title page refers to the inventory number in the Westminster catalogue of 1542. (JC)

LITERATURE: Neville, 'Richard Pynson, King's Printer (1506–1529)'; Carley, *The Books of King Henry VIII and his Wives*

47 The Coronation of Henry VIII and Katherine of Aragon

Stephen Hawes (c.1474–before 1529)

A ioyfull medytacyon to all Englonde of the coronacyon of our moost naturall soueraynе lorde kynge Henry the eyght, 1509

Printed by Wynkyn de Worde

Cambridge University Library, Sel. 5–55

The joint coronation of Henry and Katherine took place at Westminster Abbey on 24 June 1509 – Midsummer's Day – a fortnight after their marriage. The previous day, the royal couple had processed through the City to Westminster, Katherine dressed in white with her hair loose in traditional style and Henry magnificent in garments studded with precious gems. In the religious ceremony, the crowns used were thought to have belonged to Edward the Confessor and his wife.

In this title page to Stephen Hawes's *A ioyfull medytacyon* (1509), celebrating the coronation in verse, prelates are shown crowning the couple in what was seen as the union of the Tudor rose and the pomegranate. The pomegranate (*granada* in Castilian) was Katherine's personal emblem, possibly because she had been present as a small child at the ceremonial taking of the city from the Moors; ironically the pomegranate also symbolized fertility. (SD)

LITERATURE: Katherine of Aragon, *Oxford DNB*; Wooding, *Henry VIII*; Hoak (ed.), *Tudor Political Culture*

48 John Skelton's Celebration of Henry VIII's Accession and Coronation

John Skelton

'A Lawde and Prayse Made for Our Sovereigne Lord the Kyng'

The National Archives, Kew, Richmond, Surrey, E 36/228, fol.7

Henry's former tutor, the poet John Skelton, greeted Henry's accession with this ballad-like English effusion in verse. It begins with the conceit of the Tudor rose, conjoining the red and the white of Lancaster and York in one, and confidently expecting Henry to be 'sage', 'just', and a protector of the common people. Its banality as verse complements the poverty of the manuscript copy in which it survives, hardly fit for a king! It is in Skelton's own handwriting, undecorated or minimally so, written out on a pair of paper sheets, nested one within the other, then folded and folded and folded again, and endorsed like a letter, on the outside, 'A Lawde and Prayse Made for Our Sovereigne Lord the Kyng.' It is possible that the copy is a working-document for household-officers engaged in staging accession-ceremonials. The poem may have been recited on the occasion, or, as happened with other verse of Skelton's, it may have been set to music and sung. (DC)

LITERATURE: Streitberger, 'John Skelton: The Entertainments, Plays and Revels at Court'; Waite, 'Approaching the Poet's Language'; Croft, *Autograph Poetry in the English Language*

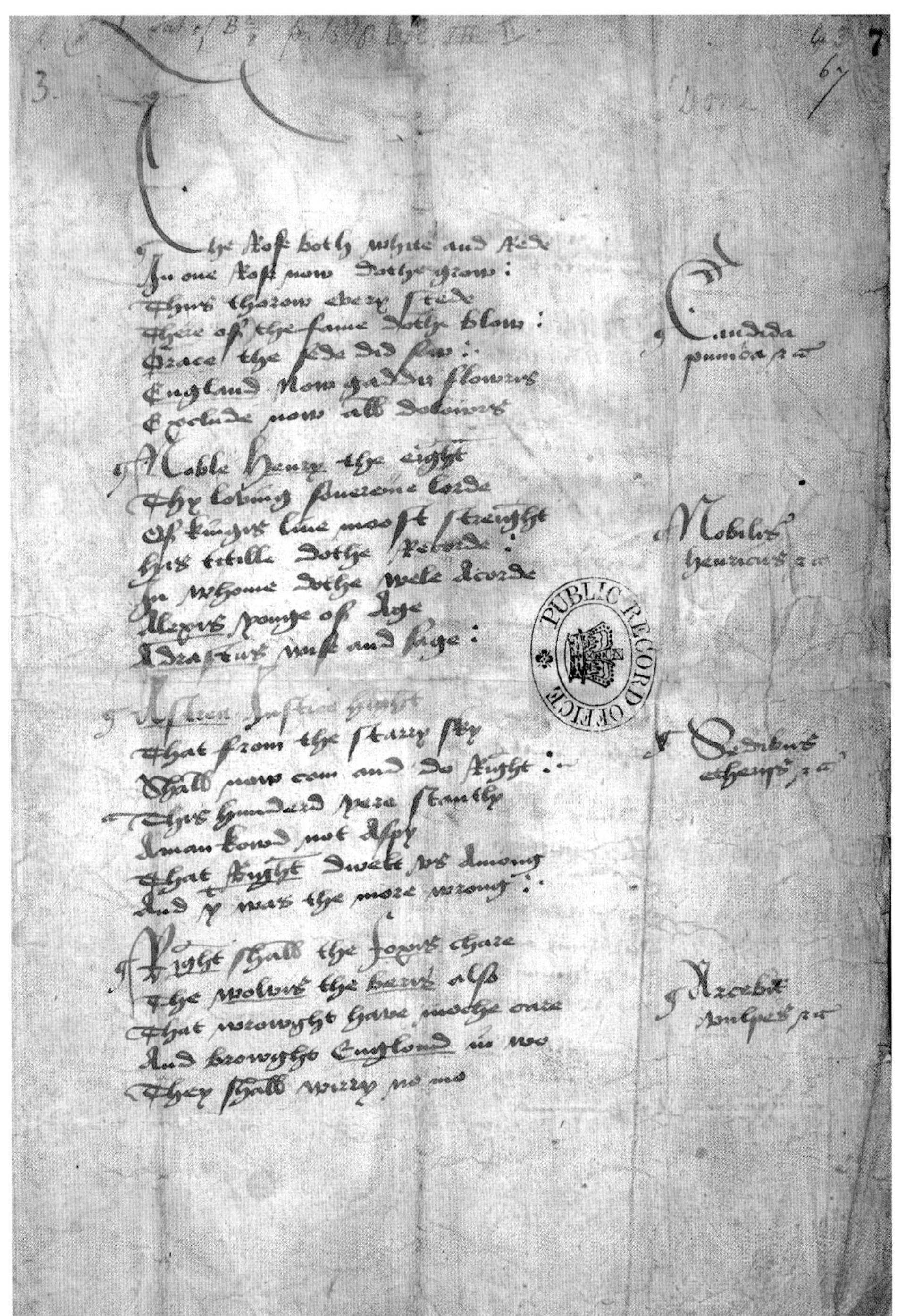

The Rose both white and rede
In one rose now dothe grow:
Thus thorow every stede
Thereof the fame dothe blow:
Grace the sede did sow:
England now gaddir flowris
Exclude now all dolowrs

Noble Henry the eight
Thy lovinge sovereine lorde
Of kyngis line most streight
His titille dothe recorde:
In whome dothe wele acorde
Alexis yonge of age
Adrastus wise and sage:

Astrea Justice hight
That from the starry sky
Shall now com and do right:
This hunderd yere scantly
A man kowd not aspy
That right dwelt us among
And yt was the more wrong:

Right shall the foxis chare
The wolvis the beris also
That wrought have moche care
And browght England in wo
They shall wurry no mo

Candida punica &c

Nobilis Henricus &c

Arcebit vulpes &c

PUBLIC RECORD OFFICE

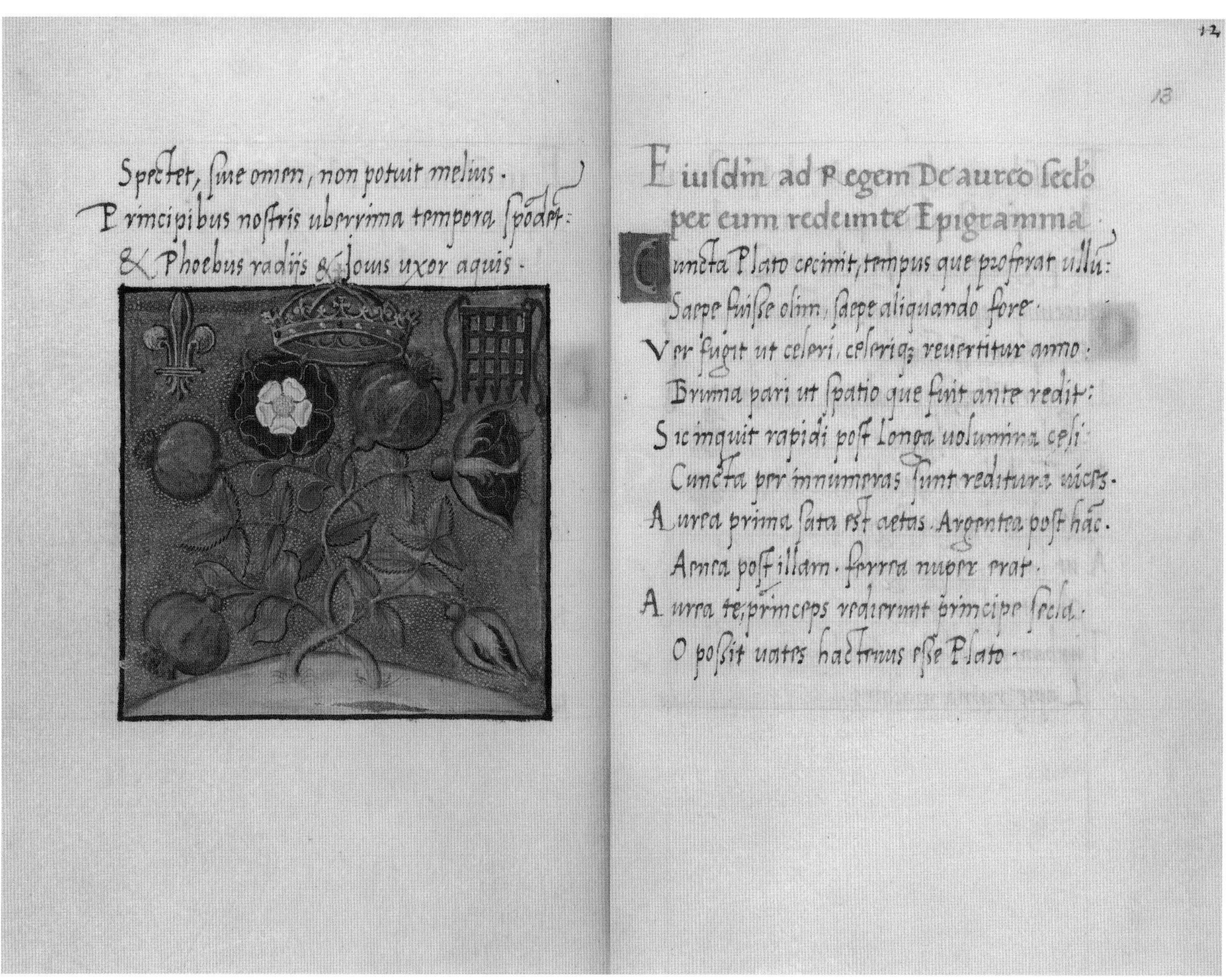
Spectet, sine omen, non potuit melius.
Principibus nostris uberrima tempora spondet:
& Phoebus radiis & Jovis uxor aquis.

12
13
Eiusdem ad Regem De aureo seclo
per eum redeunte Epigramma
Cuncta Plato cecinit, tempus que proferat ullu:
Saepe fuisse olim, saepe aliquando fore.
Ver fugit ut celeri, celerique revertitur anno:
Bruma pari ut spatio que fuit ante redit:
Sic inquit rapidi post longa volumina celi
Cuncta per innumeras sunt reditura vices.
Aurea prima sata est aetas. Argentea post hac.
Aenea post illam. ferrea nuper erat.
Aurea te, princeps redierunt principe secla.
O possit vates hactenus esse Plato.

49 Thomas More's 'Coronation Suite'

British Library, Cotton MS Titus D iv, fols 12v–13

'Heaven smiles, earth rejoices; all is milk and honey and nectar,' wrote William Blount, Lord Mountjoy, to Erasmus upon Henry VIII's accession. Though English affairs did not turn out always as hoped, the accession was certainly perceived as bringing opportunities for a younger humanist generation that had been excluded from royal benefaction in the later part of the reign of Henry VII. Erasmus' close friend Thomas More was one of those who welcomed the accession. More composed a 'coronation suite' of Latin poems for presentation to the new King in the form of this de luxe manuscript presentation copy. The decoration incorporates the Tudor rose, the pomegranate of Granada, the fleur-de-lis and the Beaufort portcullis badge. The poems were later republished in print, as an addendum to the famous 1518 Froben edition of *Utopia.* (DC)

LITERATURE: Rundle, 'A New Golden Age? More, Skelton and the Accession Verses of 1509'; Carlson, *English Humanist Books*

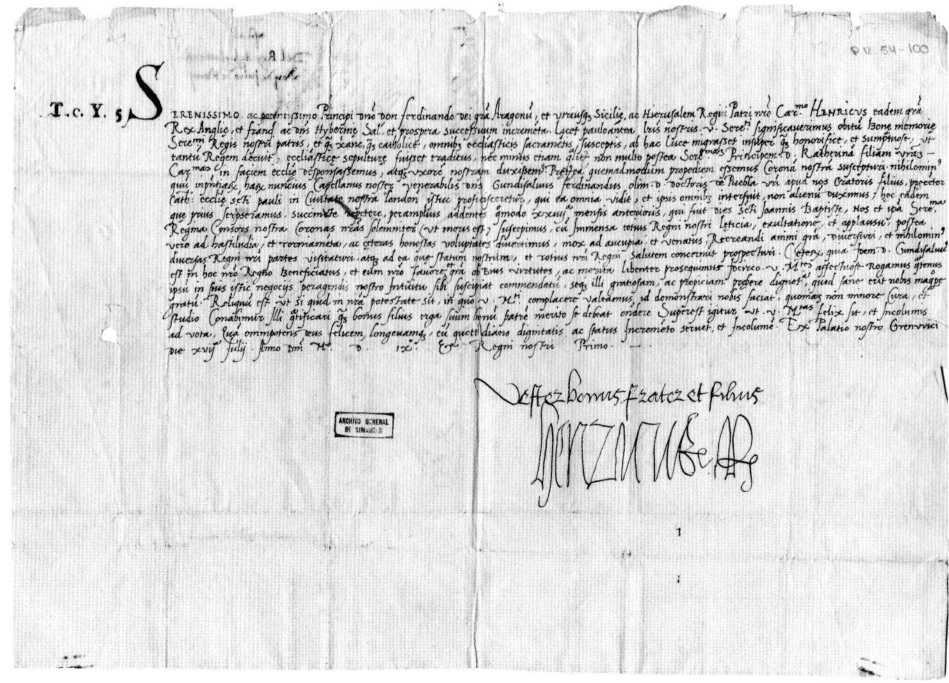

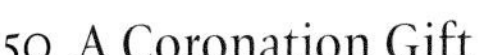

50 A Coronation Gift

Pewter plate

British Museum, London, Prehistory and Europe, 1900, 2–12, 1

This pewter dish, one of two engraved with the crown and feather badge of the Prince of Wales, is thought to have been presented to Henry VIII on the occasion of his coronation by the Worshipful Company of Pewterers, which was established in 1478 to take control of England's expanding pewter trade. The dishes are rare examples of high-quality medieval dining pewter and probably formed part of a set of pewter tableware. (AC)

LITERATURE: Michaelis, *British Pewter*; Michaelis, *Antique Pewter of the British Isles*

51 Early Days of Married Life

Autograph letter from Henry VIII to Ferdinand of Aragon, 17 July 1509

Archivo General de Simancas, Patronato Real, Caja 54, Doc. 100

This is one of several letters that Henry wrote to Ferdinand of Aragon in July 1509. Henry informs his new father-in-law that he and Katherine were solemnly crowned on 24 June, the feast day of St John the Baptist. Proudly, Henry reports that they were greeted by great multitudes of people cheering and applauding them. Since then, Henry tells Ferdinand, he has been 'diverting himself with jousting, hawking, hunting and other innocent and honest pastimes' and visiting different parts of his kingdom with his new Queen. Henry presented himself as genuinely in love with Katherine. In another letter to Ferdinand, dated 26 July, he declared that 'as for that entire love which we bear to the most serene Queen, our consort – day by day do her inestimable virtues more and more shine forth, flourish and increase, so that even if we were still free, it is she, nevertheless, that we would choose for our wife before all other'. (AC)

LITERATURE: Starkey, *Henry: Virtuous Prince*; Mattingly, *Catherine of Aragon*

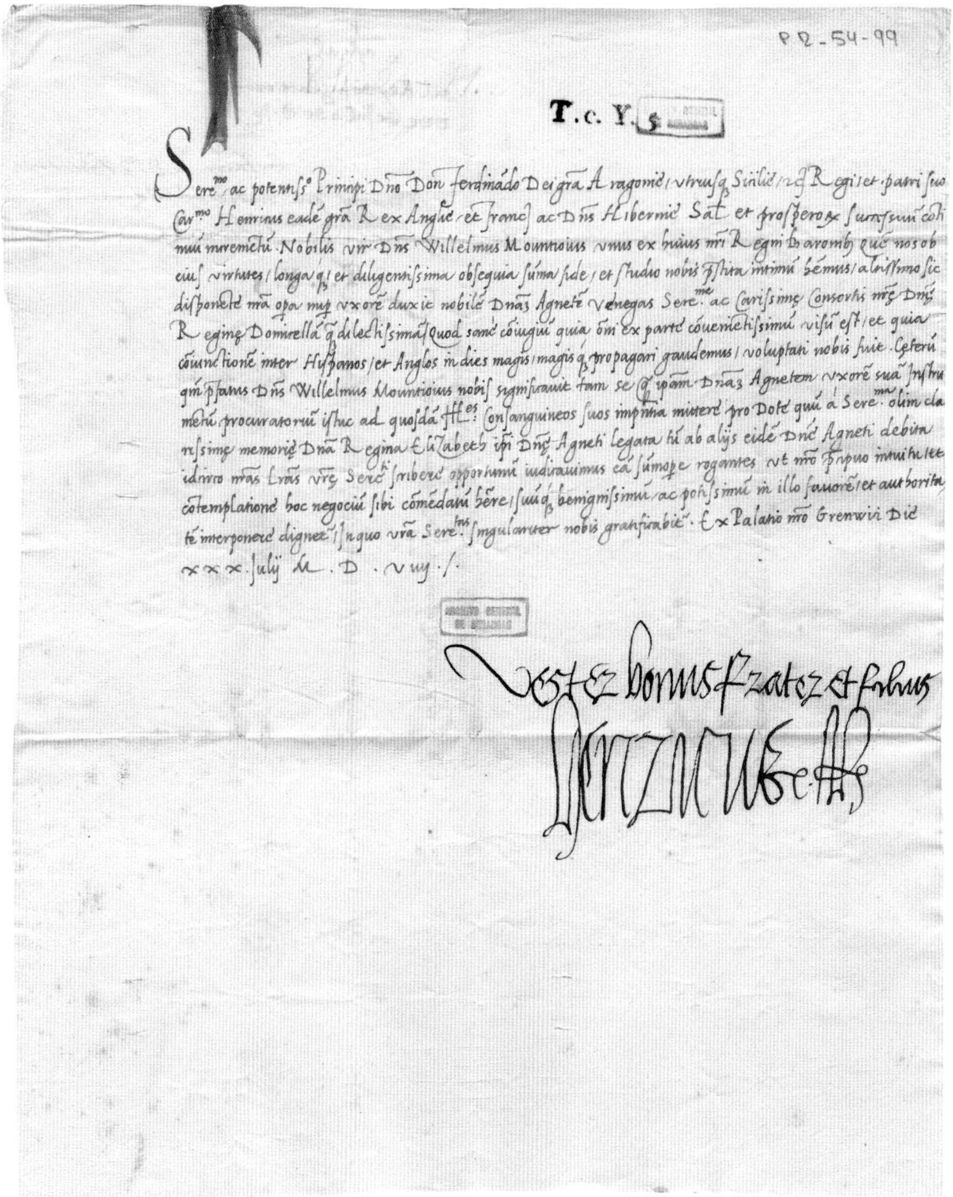

52 Henry VIII Seeks a Favour from his Father-in-Law

Autograph letter from Henry VIII to Ferdinand of Aragon, 30 July 1509, from Palace of Greenwich

Archivo General de Simancas, Patronato Real, Caja 54, Doc. 99

In this letter, Henry writes to Ferdinand on behalf of his former academic mentor, William Blount, Lord Mountjoy, who had recently married Iñez de Venegas, one of Queen Katherine's Spanish ladies. Henry warmly endorsed Mountjoy as 'one of his barons whom he holds in high esteem' and sought Ferdinand's support for the new Lady Mountjoy's claim to a legacy from Queen Isabella. Henry's willingness to conclude the letter in his own hand, despite his dislike of writing, reveals the deep affection that he felt for Mountjoy. In May 1512 the baron was appointed Lord Chamberlain to Queen Katherine, a promotion that reflected the King and Queen's interest in learning and humanism. Mountjoy's patronage of Erasmus had drawn him into the humanist circle that included Thomas More and John Colet (1467–1519); Henry was keen to appoint men of learning to high office, believing that their presence would draw attention to his own erudition. (AC)

LITERATURE: Starkey, *Henry: Virtuous Prince*; Blount, William, *Oxford DNB*

HENRY'S PLEASURES AND PASTIMES

As a young man Henry was naturally athletic. He loved to hunt and hawk, both in the parks around Westminster and during his summer 'progresses'. Unlike his father, he participated in tournaments, jousting and tilting, at least until he suffered severe concussion after a fall in 1536. These pursuits displayed his courage, strength and resourcefulness, all virtues valued in a prince, particularly when he entered battle. Additionally, Henry enjoyed music: he played several instruments, sang from sight and composed and arranged music.

53 Henry's Love of Hunting

William Twiti, *The Art of Hunting*, 1327

Edward of Norwich, 2nd Duke of York, *The Mayster of Game*, mid-15th century

British Library, Cotton MS Vespasian B xii, fols 3v–4

This is one of a number of manuscripts which Henry VIII inherited from his father's library and which he no doubt read and enjoyed as a small boy. The Middle English manuscript, produced in East Anglia in the middle of the 15th century, contains both William Twiti's *The Art of Hunting* (shown here) and a second manual on hunting by Edward, 2nd Duke of York (d.1415), known as *The Mayster of Game*.

Henry was passionate about hunting and, during the early years of his reign, it often took priority over business. In 1520, Richard Pace, in a letter to Thomas Wolsey, commented that 'the King rises daily, except on holy days, at 4 or 5 o'clock, and hunts till 9 or 10 at night. He spares no pains to convert the sport of hunting into a martyrdom'. Henry no doubt took great delight in the illustrations of several animals (fox, hare, hart, marten, otter, wild boar, wildcat, wolf) at the beginning of Twiti's book. (JH and AC)

LITERATURE: Scott, *Later Gothic Manuscripts, 1390–1490*; Carley, 'The Royal Library as a Source for Sir Robert Cotton's Collection'; Boffey and Edwards, *A New Index of Middle English Verse*

54 A Song Composed by Henry VIII: 'Pastyme with good companye'

British Library, Additional MS 31922, fols 14v–15

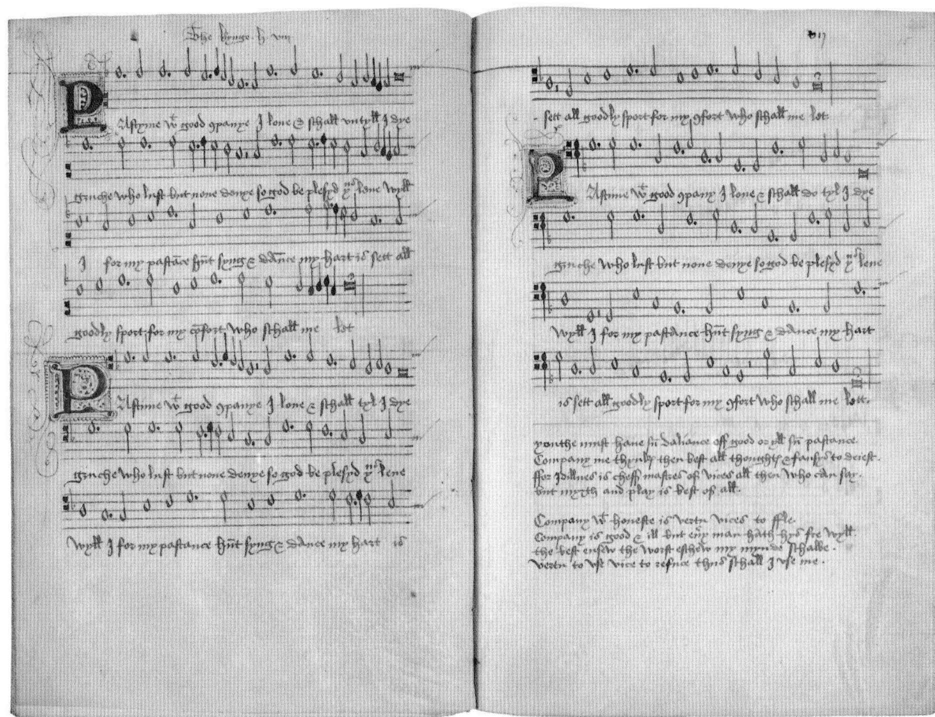

Henry was held in high regard as a musician and composer. This manuscript, known as the Henry VIII Songbook, was probably compiled around 1518, and includes twenty songs and thirteen instrumental pieces ascribed to 'The Kynge H. viij'. The anthology also contains 76 pieces by other musicians associated with the court, including William Cornysh and Robert Fayrfax, as well as some foreign composers, but there are more pieces attributed to Henry than to any other composer. Some of the King's pieces are musical arrangements, but there are also many original compositions. It is most likely that he composed this music while still a prince, though some pieces may date from the early years of his reign. This famous song, 'Pastyme with good companye', extols all the virtues of the princely life, including hunting, singing and dancing. The manuscript was produced for someone close to the court, possibly Sir Henry Guildford (1489–1532), the Controller of the Household and Master of the Revels. (NB)

LITERATURE: Stevens, *Music at the Court of Henry VIII*; Stevens, *Music and Poetry in the Early Tudor Court*; Fallows, 'Henry VIII as a Composer'

55 Motet, 'Celeste beneficium'

Jean Mouton (1459–1522)

British Library, Royal MS 8 G vii, fols 2v–3

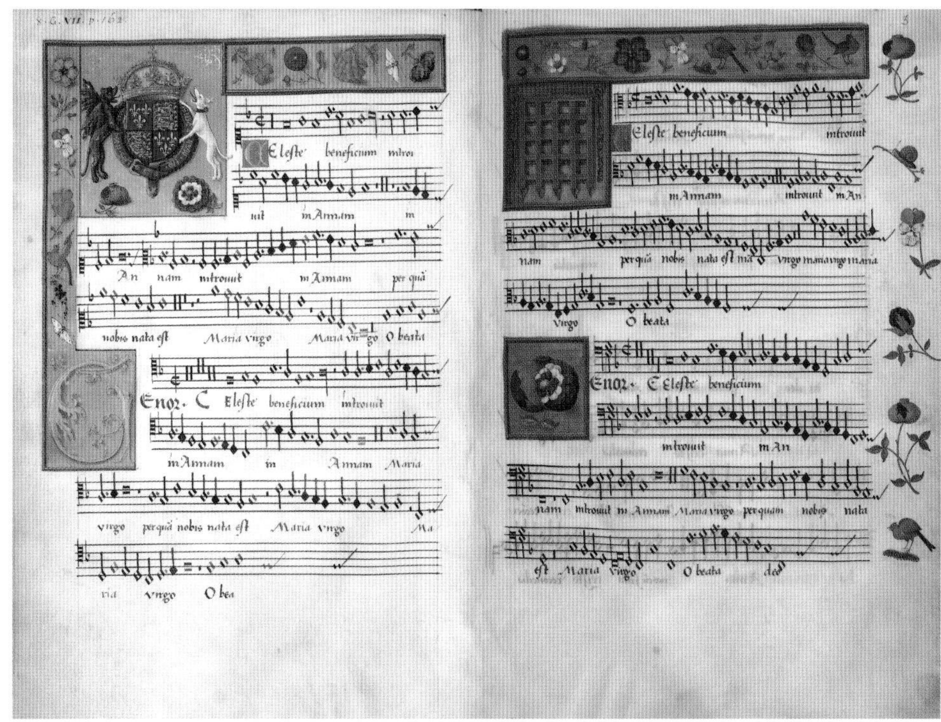

This magnificent choirbook contains 28 motets by Josquin des Prez, Pierre de la Rue and others, together with an extraordinary series of five different settings of Dido's lament from Virgil's *Aeneid*. This first opening is the most richly decorated, with various Tudor symbols as well as Katherine of Aragon's pomegranate. This piece, 'Celeste beneficium', was originally composed for Anne of Brittany and Louis XII of France, and calls upon St Anne, mother of the Virgin Mary, to bring forth children, a matter of particular concern for Henry VIII and Katherine. The book was compiled sometime between 1513 and 1525, but the circumstances of its presentation to the King are not known. It was produced in the workshop of Petrus Alamire, a famous Flemish music scribe who made several similar choirbooks for other European courts. He also acted as a spy, informing Henry of the movements of Richard de la Pole, exiled pretender to the English crown. (NB)

LITERATURE: Kellman, *Renaissance Music in Facsimile*, vol.9; Kellman (ed.), *The Treasury of Petrus Alamire*

56 The Tournament of 1511

Jousting tournament challenge

British Library, Harley Ch. 83 H. 1

To celebrate the birth of his son, Prince Henry, in 1511, the King proclaimed an allegorical tournament of the sort developed in the previous century at the court of the Dukes of Burgundy. This challenge, issued on 12 February and signed by the King, lists the rules to be followed and explains the background story. Queen 'Noble Renown' of the kingdom of 'Noble Heart', rejoicing at the happy event, had sent four knights, Ceure Loyall, Vailliaunt Desyre, Bone Voloyr and Joyous Panser, to joust in England against all comers. Their shields appear in the margin. In reality they were Henry and three of his leading courtiers, Sir Thomas Knyvet, Lord William Courtenay and Sir Edward Neville. Other courtiers signed up to answer the challenge. The tournament that followed was a great spectacle of expensive pageantry. The challengers first arrived inside a movable forest topped by a castle made of golden paper and the Great Wardrobe was ordered to produce all manner of splendid trappings, such as the new banners to hang from the royal trumpeters' instruments. The whole occasion was commemorated in a painted roll preserved at the College of Arms, London. Sadly, however, Prince Henry was dead within ten days. (SG)

LITERATURE: Anglo (ed.), *The Great Tournament Roll of Westminster*

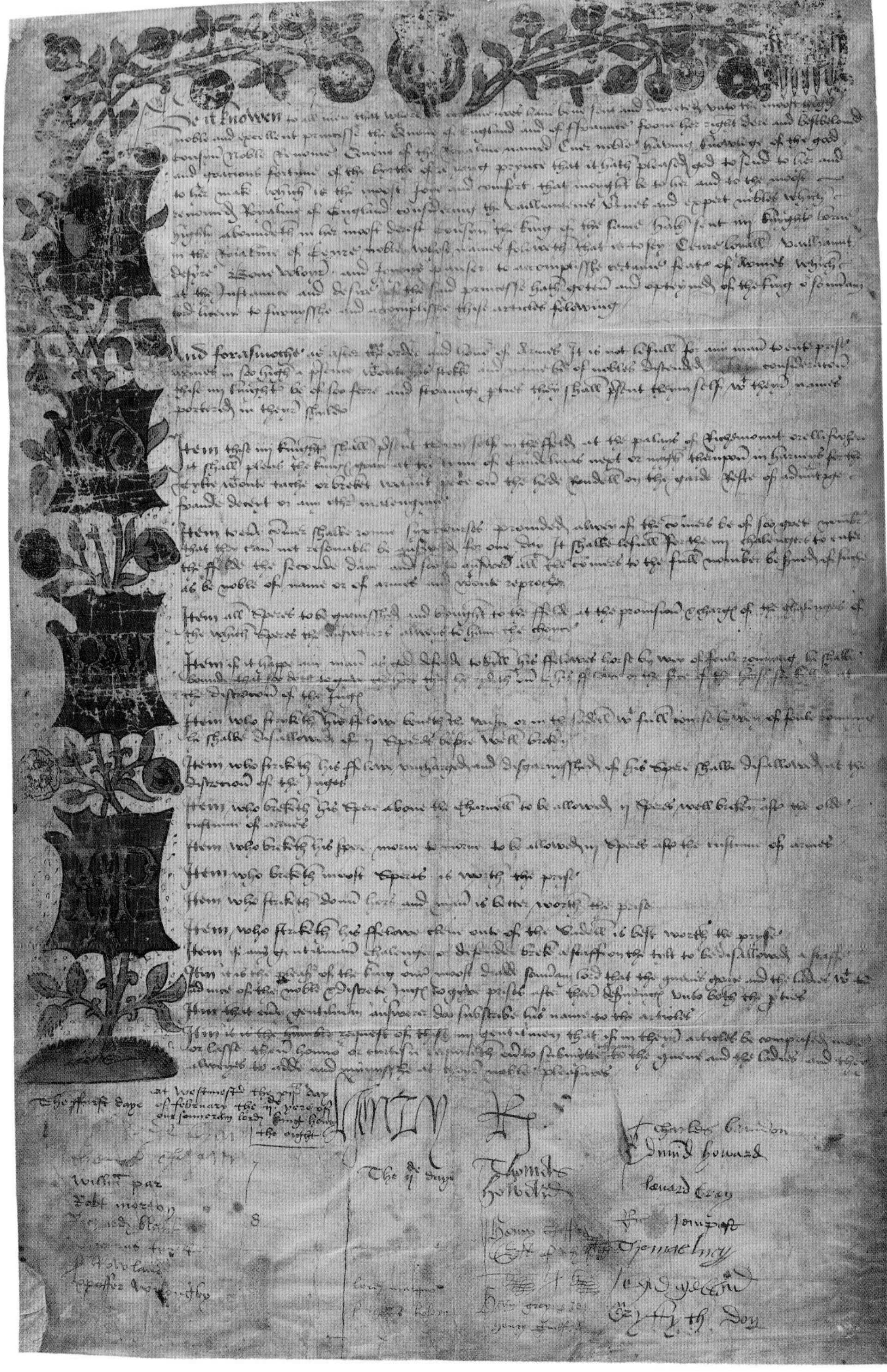

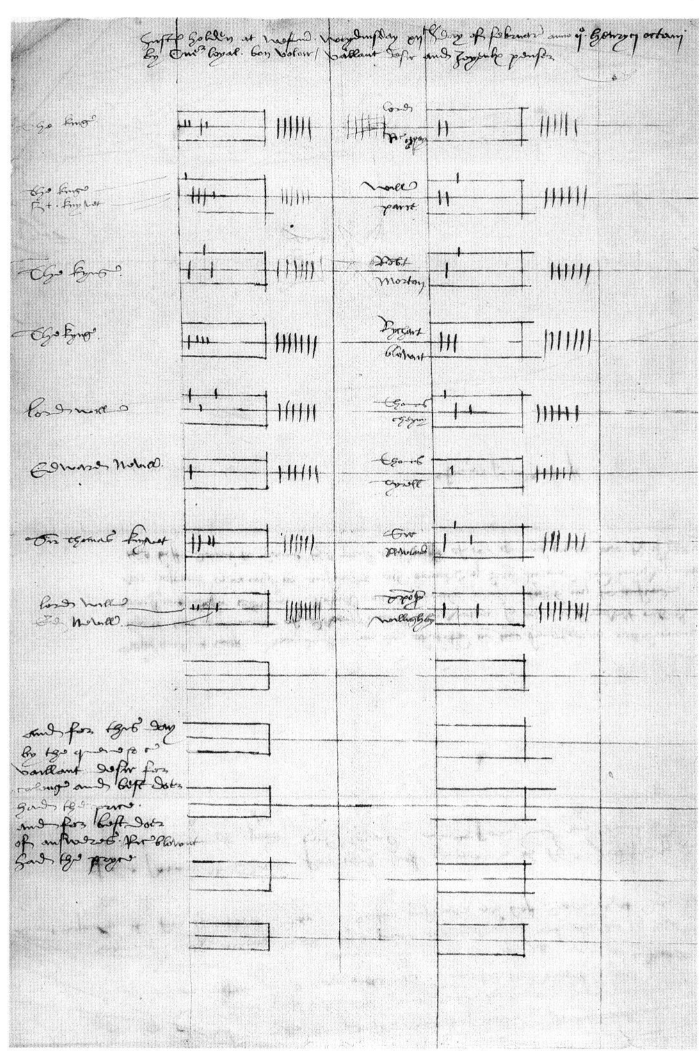

57 Score Cheque for the First Day of the Westminster Tournament

College of Arms, MS Tournament Cheque 1a

This, the score cheque for 12 February 1511, the first day of the tournament to celebrate the birth of Prince Henry, records the performance of the contestants, rather as in boxing. And it shows that Henry, on this occasion at least, let his enthusiasm outrun his skill.

The score cheque follows the usual pattern: the names of the challengers ('the home team') form the column on the left; the answerers ('the away team') the column on the right. By each name is a parallelogram with strokes: a mark above the upper line is a blow ('attaint') to the head; above the middle line, to the body. If the stroke bisects either line, the lance has been broken. The strokes outside the parallelogram indicate the number of courses run.

Contemporary accounts wax lyrical about Henry's performance; the notation tell a soberer story. Henry hogged the limelight by running 25 courses – far more than anybody else. In these he broke four lances and made three attaints to the body. But Sir Thomas Knyvet (Vailliaunt Desyre), running in half the number of courses, did better with five broken lances and three attaints and was declared 'best doer' by Queen Katherine and 'had the price (prize)'. (DS)

LITERATURE: Anglo, 'Archives of the English Tournament'

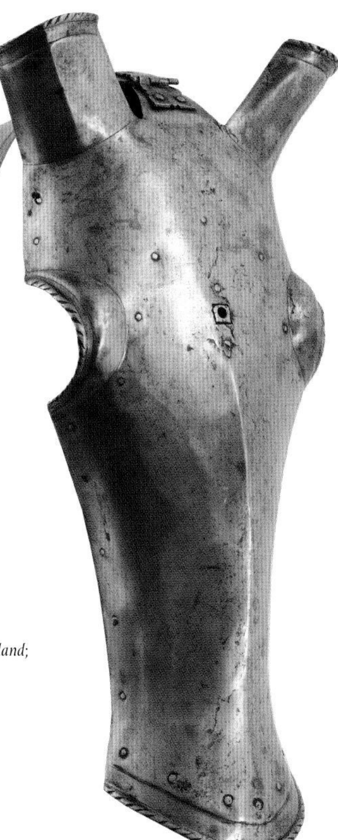

58 Shaffron

Probably Flemish, *c.*1520

Lent by the Board of Trustees of the Armouries, VI.37

This shaffron – a head defence for a horse – was the type used on a battlefield, but similar specialised armour was used in tournaments. This piece is one of a group of surviving elements of armour for man and horse from Henry's armoury at the Tower of London. The inventory of Henry VIII's possessions, drawn up after his death in 1547, also lists among 'Thodde harnesse for horsemen' at Hampton Court 'great Shaffrons cccxvj' and 'Demi Shaffrons xiij'. (TR)

LITERATURE: Starkey (ed.), *Henry VIII: A European Court in England*; Starkey (ed.), Inventory nos. 8467, 8468

WARFARE AGAINST FRANCE

Henry VIII sought glory on the battlefield and aimed to emulate his namesake, Henry V, who had won the celebrated victory at Agincourt. At the outset of his reign, the King's military and political objective was to win back Aquitaine and Normandy, England's ancestral lands in France that had been lost during the previous century. The opportunity to declare war came in 1511, when King Louis XII of France challenged papal power and was declared a schismatic. Henry now had allies and a justification for taking up arms. In January 1512 Parliament voted Henry a subsidy to finance an invasion, and in April war was formally declared. Then, in June 1513, Henry led a large army into northern France. The victories he achieved at Thérouanne and Tournai were the first successes for the English against the French since the 1440s.

59 Robert de Balsac, 'Manual on Warfare for the Instruction of a Prince'

British Library, Cotton MS Vespasian A xvii, fol.13v

Robert de Balsac was a French nobleman, who composed a military treatise in the 1490s for the instruction of the King of France. Just two manuscript copies are known to survive, one in the Biblioteca Nacional in Madrid (lacking the author's epilogue) and the other in the British Library. This last-named contains the arms of England on its opening page, flanked by the traditional Tudor supporters. At one time it was thought to have been made for Henry VII, but it clearly belonged instead to his son, since the pomegranate motif of Katherine of Aragon is found on the same page, and is entwined with the Tudor rose at the end. The illustrations typically depict English troops overcoming their French adversaries: the miniature here shows the King of England, mounted on a white stallion, chasing the fleeing King of France, a neat reversal considering the treatise's original intended audience. (JH)

LITERATURE: Contamine, 'The War Literature of the Late Middle Ages'

60 John Lydgate's Siege of Troy

British Library, Royal MS 18 D vi, fol.4

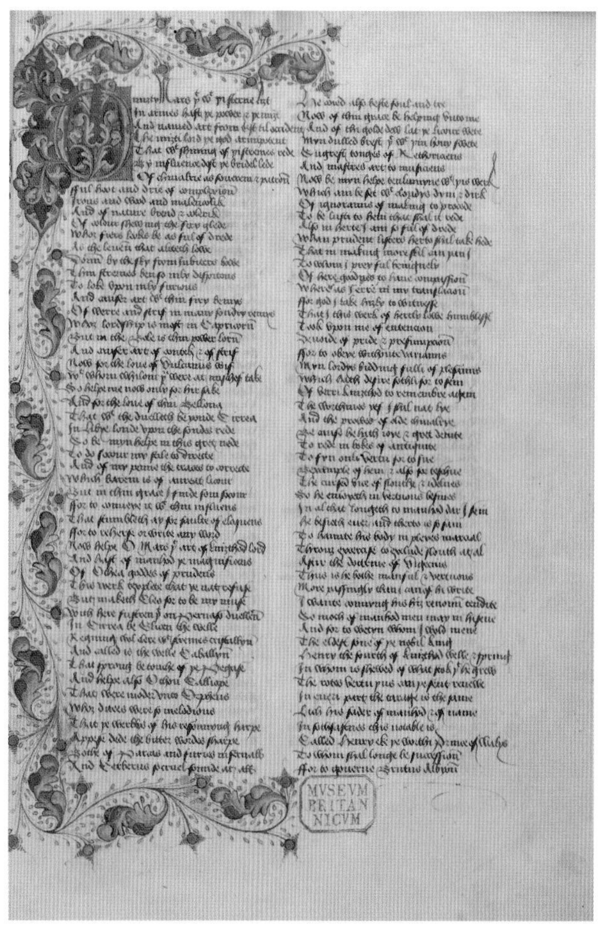

This verse translation by John Lydgate (*c*.1370–*c*.1450) of Guido delle Colonne's account of the siege of Troy was originally written for Henry V before he came to the throne. This copy was presented to Henry VIII by John Touchet, 8th baron Audley, no doubt in gratitude for restoration in blood and honours in 1512. English kings took pride in their heritage as descendants of the Trojan stock through the line of Brutus. Audley enclosed his own flattering verses, written in rhyme royal, with the gift. Among other accomplishments he complimented Henry on his scholarship: 'For whate man of so high parence wolde so studye and muse / To take half suche paynes the trwe knolege to be hadde / As yowre grace hathe done'. One year later, in the context of the campaigns against Scotland and France, Henry commissioned the King's Printer, Richard Pynson (*c*.1449–*c*.1530), to print Lydgate's *Siege of Troy*, also known as *The Troy Book*, as a reminder of England's glorious military past. It was a shrewd piece of propaganda. (JC)

LITERATURE: Ward, *Catalogue of Romances*; Neville, 'Richard Pynson, King's Printer (1506–1529)'

61 *The Gardyners Passetaunce*, *c*.1512

Alexander Barclay ? (*c*.1484–1552)

Westminster Abbey Library, London, C E 3, sig Aii

The Gardyners Passetaunce was one of the most accessible of the large number of items published as propaganda for Henry VIII's first war with France. It is a poem of 30 rhyme royal stanzas, recycling the arguments of a learned Latin tract written to justify the war by the canon lawyer Dr James Whytstons. The eponymous gardener notices how, in contrast to the fair rose representing England and Henry and the noble pomegranate standing for Katherine, the lily, representing France, is proud and foul-smelling. These qualities match the actions of the French King, Louis XII, in defying Pope Julius II and tyrannizing other princes, offences that should justly be punished. The poem was printed in at least two editions, one by the King's Printer, Richard Pynson (*c*.1449–*c*.1530), and the other by Hugh Goes and Henry Watson. Each survives in a unique copy in Westminster Abbey Library, the second having been discovered among fragments of bookseller's waste inside a 16th-century binding. (SG)

LITERATURE: Williams Jr (ed.), *The Gardyners Passetaunce*

In a gardeyn booth goodly and pleasaunt
Walkynge a loone deuysyng on the flourys
Whiche were right fayre delycious & fragraũt
Moste delicatly redolent after ẏ swete shourys
The red Rose chase I.and toke in amours
Howbeit the lyle was growen soo hye
That he thought hym self moost pleasaunt to the Iye

The cause me mouynge to chese the red Rose
Was for his fresshenesse and moost pleasaunt odour
Whiche to the syght and also to the nose
Surmounteth the lyle in vertue smell and colour
And yet the haulte lyle lyke a prowde Empour
Groweth for the tyme aboue all floures other
Presumptuously thynkyng to haue no make ne brother

And though in apparaunce his colours be right fayre
With whyte ẏ flowre garnysshed with grene leef & stalke
Yet well enserched he hath no pleasaunt ayre
But noyeth the smellers as they by hym walke
Of whoys foundry propties farther to talke
It were superfluous/but the trowth is this
His apparaunce is better/than hym self is/

The lilye by the craft sufferaunce and subtilitie
Hath vppon all princes vsurped with puyssaunce
Surmysynge that it is for theyr vtilitie
All that he doeth to theyr extreme noyssaunce
Entendyng to brynge vnder his obeysaunce
The Churche themptre and all princes cristened
Whiche dampnable ambicion must nedely be extinyned
A.ii.

62 The French Campaign of 1513

Albrecht Dürer

Woodcut, *c.*1526

British Museum, London, Department of Prints and Drawings, 1895,0122.720

In June 1513 Henry's forces laid siege to the northern French town of Thérouanne, about 50 miles from Tournai. Little progress had been made by early August when Henry and the Emperor Maximilian arrived with reinforcements. The situation was then transformed. A French relieving force was put to flight during a minor skirmish, 'the Battle of the Spurs' on 16 August. Thérouanne surrendered six days later, while Henry went on to besiege and take the far more important town of Tournai. This woodcut probably derives from a sketch map or 'plat' made by German soldiers during the siege of Thérouanne. It forms part of the massive printed 'triumphal arch' created for Maximilian in 1515. The foreground shows Maximilian meeting Henry on 10 August. Behind is 'the Battle of the Spurs' and in the background are Tournai (left) and the siege of Thérouanne. The woodcut was the source for a painting, now in Hampton Court, that was probably commissioned by Charles V for Henry in about 1526, together with a painting of the Battle of Pavia. (PB)

LITERATURE: Millar, *The Tudor, Stuart and Early Georgian Pictures in the Collection of Her Majesty The Queen*; Schauerte, *Die Ehrenpforte für Kaiser Maximilian*; Barber, 'Cartography, Topography and History Painting'

63 The Parliamentary Procession Roll of 1512 (see opposite)

Vellum roll

British Library, Additional MS 22306

This 17th-century copy of a contemporary roll shows Henry on the way to open Parliament for the second time on 4 February 1512. The procession, accompanied by heralds, was led by the mitred abbots, followed by the bishops. Next came the King, carrying a sceptre, under a canopy decorated with a Tudor rose, then the secular peers in their parliamentary robes. Most lords are identified by their name and coat of arms. Two high-ranking or specially favoured peers carried a cap of maintenance and a sword of state before the King, on this occasion Edward Stafford, Duke of Buckingham (1478–1521), and either his brother Henry Stafford, Earl of Wiltshire (*c.*1479–1523), or Charles Somerset, Lord Herbert (*c.*1460–1526). Such parliamentary processions displayed Henry's majesty to his subjects at a time of solemn governmental action and the roll perpetuated that magnificence. (SG)

LITERATURE: Hoak (ed.), *Tudor Political Culture*; Wagner and Sainty, 'The Origin of the Introduction of Peers in the House of Lords'

64 Warrior King

Letter from Henry VIII to Maximilian Sforza, Duke of Milan, 24 September 1513

British Library, Egerton MS 2014, fol.2

It was no surprise that Henry made his international debut as a warrior against France in the summer of 1513 for he had long dreamed of restoring the reputation of English arms, covering himself in military glory and establishing an international reputation as a warrior king. In this letter to Maximilian Sforza, Henry's pride is almost palpable as he informs the Duke of his victories at Thérouanne and Tournai, assuring him that 'from the time he entered France he has always had the better of his enemies, of whom he has captured many of the noblest'. Henry also reports that the King of Scots, 'unmindful of his affinity' had sided with the French and sent 10,000 troops into England. The English army, which numbered just 1,000 men, 'slayed a great number of the Scots and put the rest to flight'. (AC)

LITERATURE: Cruickshank, *Henry VIII and the Invasion of France*; Richardson, 'Eternal Peace, Occasional War: Anglo-French Relations under Henry VIII'

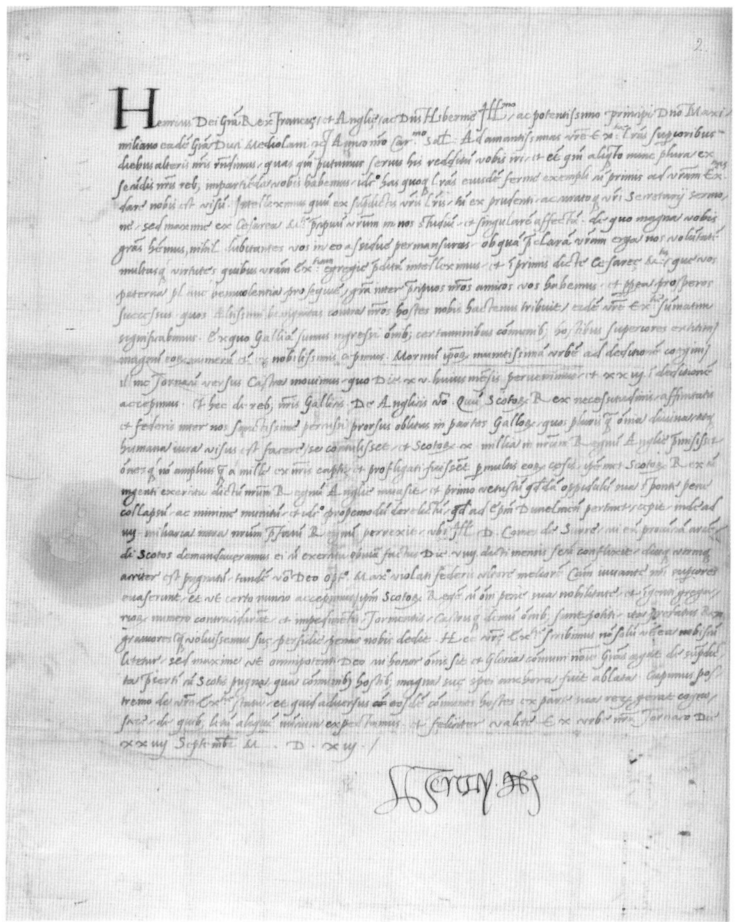

65 Erasmus' Translation of Plutarch's *De discrimine adulatoris et amici*

Cambridge University Library, Additional MS 6858, fol.3

In 1513, while he was at Cambridge, Erasmus dedicated to Henry VIII his translation from Greek into Latin of Plutarch's *De discrimine adulatoris et amici* (How to Tell a Flatterer from a Friend). Written by a professional scribe, this manuscript is almost certainly a presentation copy. It lacks illumination, but stubs suggest that there may originally have been a leaf containing the royal arms and another with a decorated title page. In the dedicatory letter Erasmus expressed his hope that the treatise would be useful to the King and it is likely he was trying to warn Henry against following the advice of flattering councillors who had advocated the war against France. Prudently, since he was writing to a patron, he also observed that the art of admonishing friends requires tact as well as devotion 'in case we undermine friendship itself even while we clumsily try to cure our friend's fault'. Henry apparently at first forgot about the gift but later on paid Erasmus 60 angels as a reward. (JC)

LITERATURE: Clough, 'A Presentation Volume for Henry VIII'; Garrod, 'Erasmus and his English Patrons'

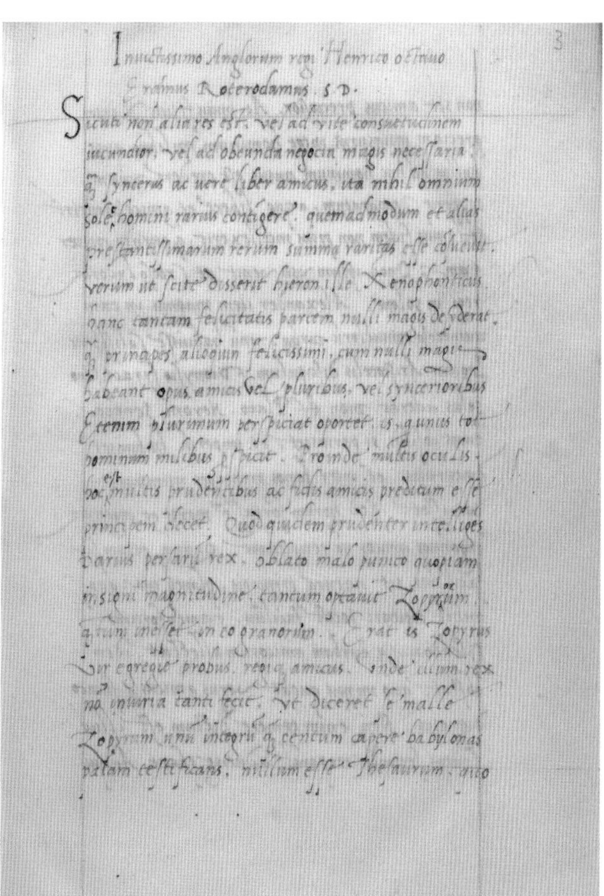

Invictissimo Anglorum regi Henrico octavo
Erasmus Roterodamus S.D.
Sicuti non alia res est, vel ad vitae consuetudinem
iucundior, vel ad obeunda negocia magis necessaria

SCOTLAND

On Henry's accession, he and his brother-in-law King James IV of Scotland (1473–1513) swore oaths to preserve the peace between the two realms. However, as war loomed between England and France, Henry became concerned that James would respect Scotland's Auld Alliance with France and invade England. His clumsy attempts to secure Scotland's neutrality failed. In 1513 James sent his herald to declare war on Henry, who was then besieging Thérouanne, and followed it up with an incursion into Northumberland. At the Battle of Flodden Field the Scots were roundly defeated by Thomas Howard, the Earl of Surrey (1473–1554), whom Henry had left as his lieutenant to defend the border. James himself was killed, leaving a one-year-old son as his successor.

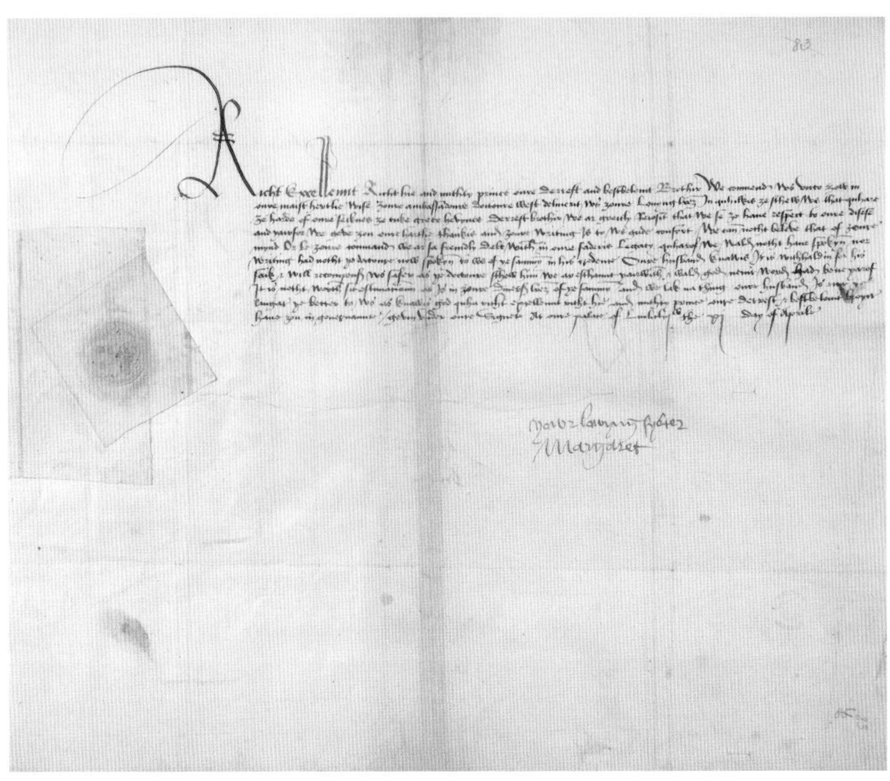

66 A Search for Peace

Autograph letter from Margaret Queen of Scotland to Henry VIII, 11 April 1513

British Library, Cotton MS Caligula B vi, fol.83

In a final effort to secure a promise from James IV that he would not invade England while the English were fighting in France, Henry sent an English ambassador, Dr Nicholas West, to Scotland. Following instructions, West told Margaret, Queen of Scotland and Henry's sister, that, if James promised to refrain from siding with France, she could have her father's legacy (Henry had withheld it from her for four years). On 11 April Margaret wrote this letter to Henry, diplomatically stating 'we can nocht beleve that of youre mynd or be youre command we are sa sriendly delt with in oure faderis Legacy'. More defiantly, she continued: 'Oure husband knawis it is withhaldin for his saik, and will recompens us … we lak na thing; our husband is evir the langer the better to us'. The letter is signed 'your lowynn syster Margaret' and sealed with a small personal seal she used for private communications. (AC)

LITERATURE: Perry, *The Sisters of Henry VIII*; Mackie, *King James IV of Scotland*

67 Preparing for War

Autograph letter of James IV to Henry VIII, 24 May 1513

British Library, Cotton MS Caligula B vi, fol.76

In May 1513, Louis XII offered James IV incentives of victuals, 50,000 francs and, ultimately, the English crown if he committed to invading England as soon as Henry set sail for France. War was now imminent, but, on 24 May, James sent this half-hearted attempt at reconciliation to Henry, suggesting that they both enter into the truce that the Kings of France and Aragon had arranged on 1 April. Then, in a move bound to infuriate Henry, James made reference to the loss of the English Admiral, Sir Edward Howard, in a recent encounter between an English and French fleet off the coast of Brittany. He wrote, 'we think mair lose is to you of yowre lait admirall, quha decessit [who deceased] to his grete honour and laude, than ye avantage micht have bene of the vynnyng [winning] of all ye Franche galeis, and thair equippage'. Henry made no response to his brother-in-law's letter, and, days later, James decided to send a fleet of ships to aid France. (AC)

LITERATURE: Mackie, *King James IV of Scotland*; Perry, *The Sisters of Henry VIII*

68 The Battle of Flodden Field, 9 September 1513

Holograph letter from Katherine of Aragon to Henry VIII in France, 16 September 1513

British Library, Cotton MS Vespasian F iii, fol.33

When Henry departed for France he made Katherine the Governor of the Realm and Captain-General of the forces. He also left Thomas, Earl of Surrey, in the north to protect the border against James IV. James invaded England in late August, and, on 9 September, the Scottish and English armies engaged in bloody battle at Flodden. Henry lived on the fame of his victory at the Battle of the Spurs but Surrey's victory at Flodden, which left James IV and 10,000 Scots dead, was far more significant. In this letter, Katherine, writing as Henry's 'humble wif and true servunt', informs him of the victory, stating 'this batell hath bee to your grace and al your Reame the grettest honor that coude bee, and more than ye shuld wyn al the crown of ffraunce'. Katherine adds, rather ghoulishly, that she will send Henry James IV's blood-stained coat to be made into banners. (AC)

LITERATURE: Mattingly, *Catherine of Aragon*; Scarisbrick, *Henry VIII*

69 Bernard André on the Victories of 1513

Bernard André, Poet Royal (*c.*1450–*c.*1522)

'The Famous Victory of our Invincible King Henry VIII over the French and the Scots'

Collection of the Most Hon. the Marquess of Salisbury, Hatfield House, Hertfordshire, Cecil Papers MS 277/1, fol.1

Henry's victories in France and northern England occasioned an extraordinary verse-outpouring: a John Skelton poem rushed into print for popular consumption had to be revised and reprinted within days. Among other poems were those written by Bernard André, Thomas More, Alexander Barclay, Andrea Ammonio, James Whitstones, Pietro Carmeliano and Camillo Paleotti. André – a blind Austin friar – had come to England from northern France, just after the Tudor victory at Bosworth Field, and, in addition to holding various offices, including the tutorship of Prince Arthur, had installed himself as the early Tudor court's literary arbiter. He stayed at court after Henry VIII's accession, but in increasing isolation and infirmity; this Latin poem invokes the 'deities of land and sea, whose care it is to guard the English crown' and declares, 'For nor plunder nor bloodshed is the aim of his arms; rather is sought but return of dominions rightly due his sway'. (DC)

LITERATURE: Hobbins, 'Arsenal MS 360 as a Witness to the Career and Writings of Bernard André'; Carlson, 'The Writings of Bernard André'; Scattergood, 'A Defining Moment: The Battle of Flodden and English Poetry'

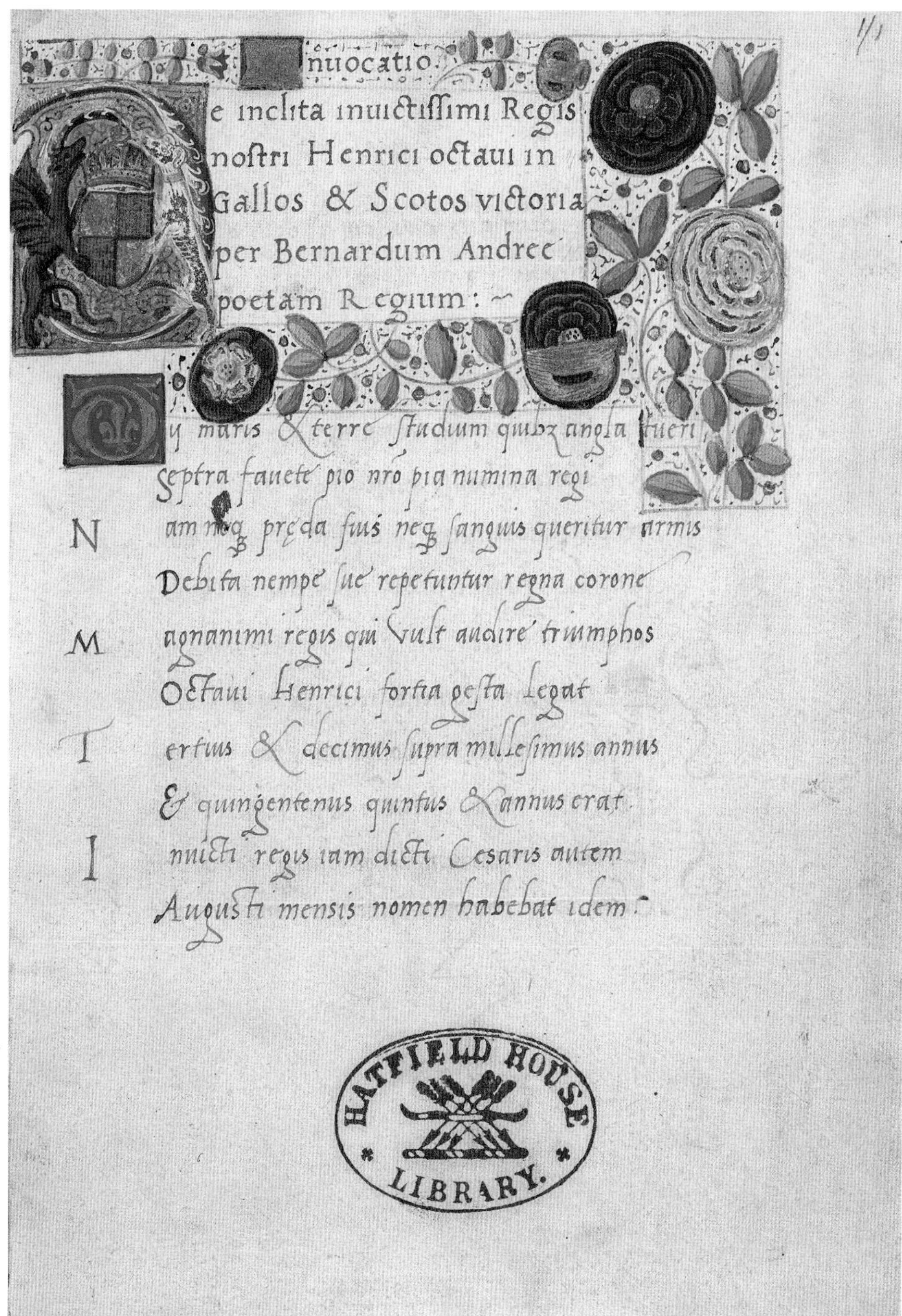

1/1

nuocatio

e inclita inuictissimi Regis
nostri Henrici octaui in
Gallos & Scotos victoria
per Bernardum Andree
poetam Regium :~

y maris & terre studium quibz angla fuerit
Septra fauete pio nro pia numina regi
N am neq preda suis neq sanguis queritur armis
Debita nempe sue repetuntur regna corone
M agnanimi regis qui vult audire triumphos
Octaui Henrici fortia gesta legat
T ertius & decimus supra millesimus annus
Et quingentenus quintus & annus erat
I nuicti regis iam dicti Cesaris autem
Augusti mensis nomen habebat idem.

THE TRIUMPH OF PEACE? (1514–27)

Glenn Richardson

The young Henry VIII had come to the throne of England in 1509 with a burning ambition to make his name as a European prince. This ambition focused foremost on war with France and he longed to repeat the deeds of Henry V. Yet it was not until 1513 that Henry finally had the opportunity to test himself in battle against King Louis XII. With allies in Ferdinand of Aragon and the Holy Roman Emperor Maximilian, Henry invaded France. There was no second Agincourt, but he did take the city of Tournai and the town of Thérouanne.

When his allies deserted him at the end of that year's campaign, Henry found himself isolated in Europe once more. Guided by his Chancellor, Cardinal Thomas Wolsey, who had overseen the logistics of the French campaign, Henry achieved a diplomatic triumph. He suddenly made peace with his erstwhile enemy, Louis. The French King committed himself to paying Henry an annual pension that Henry regarded as 'tribute' for 'his' kingdom of France. In October 1514 Louis married Henry's sister Mary. The English King was once again a key player in European dynastic politics. Unfortunately for Henry, Louis XII died almost three months later, on 1 January 1515. He was succeeded by Francis I, the young and glamorous scion of the House of Valois. Worse still for Henry, in September 1515, Francis achieved a major military triumph by conquering the Duchy of Milan.

Francis's clever diplomacy soon left Henry isolated again in Europe, but help came from an unexpected quarter. In 1517 Pope Leo X announced plans for an international peace and alliance between virtually all the major European states, ostensibly as a prelude to joint action against the Ottomans. The desirability of peace (at least between Christians) was an important theme in much public discourse of the time. Erasmus of Rotterdam published his treatise, *The Education of a Christian Prince*, in 1516. He argued that princes should avoid war wherever possible as antithetical to the calling of a true Christian ruler and, although he recognized the concept of a 'just war', Erasmus considered that very few conflicts of his time truly deserved the title.

◀ Detail from cat. no. 87

Cardinal Wolsey's view was more practical. It was he who finally took the initiative to organize the papal peace agreement and put it under Henry's aegis. To induce him to participate in the scheme, Francis was given the opportunity to buy back the city of Tournai, lost to England in the war of 1513. He accepted the deal and an Anglo-French alliance crowned the much wider European peace agreement enshrined in the Treaty of London, which was signed in October 1518. Henry was once more star of the show as the apparent arbiter, under papal authority, of international disputes. He and Francis first met in June 1520 at the Field of Cloth of Gold, where they personally affirmed the peace and alliance between them. Before and after that event, Henry also met his nephew, the newly elected Holy Roman Emperor, Charles V, presenting the encounter as part of his efforts to ensure European peace under the terms of the Treaty of London. It seemed that an Erasmian peace had indeed triumphed.

But neither Henry nor Wolsey (nor, indeed, Francis I or Charles V) was interested in peace for its own sake. For Henry, peace was primarily a way of curbing Francis I's ambitions. Francis, meanwhile, expected that peace would restrain Charles V without restricting his own freedom to pursue his 'just' dynastic claims in Italy and elsewhere. In 1521, seeing conflict with Charles as almost inevitable and wishing to fight sooner rather than later, Francis launched a covert and pre-emptive attack on imperial territory. Open war with Charles soon ensued. Acting as the apparent defender of international peace, Henry summoned a conference at Calais in the summer of 1521 presided over by Wolsey. Yet, almost immediately, Henry made a secret alliance with Charles, the likely victor in the Habsburg-Valois conflict. An Anglo-imperial force invaded France in 1523 but poor coordination of aims and tactics meant that the allies had no significant victory in northern France.

Two years later, however, on 24 February 1525, Charles *was* victorious in northern Italy. An imperial army broke the French siege of the town of Pavia, defeating and capturing Francis I himself. Henry VIII was overjoyed and urged that France be immediately partitioned between Charles V and himself. However, the Emperor ignored these pleas, seeing in Pavia a God-given opportunity to settle his own dynastic rivalry with Francis permanently. Henry was thus, for a second time, abandoned, apparently on the brink of victory, by an unreliable Habsburg ally.

Henry's subsequent repudiation of Charles was as dramatic as his volte face of 1514, although it had greater long-term significance. In April 1527 Henry and Francis agreed to an Anglo-French 'eternal peace', secured by annual French payments of 100,000 crowns. In May 1527 rebellious imperial troops sacked Rome, threatened Pope Clement VII and effectively made him the prisoner of an embarrassed Emperor. In July, Wolsey travelled to France and, in August, under the Treaty of Amiens, amplified the Anglo-French peace into a full alliance, ostensibly for the Pope's benefit. Its primary intent was to enable Francis to escape the terms of the Treaty of Madrid of 1526 which had required him to surrender to Charles the Duchy of Burgundy and his claims in Italy. With the offer of help for the Pope went Henry's demand for an annulment of his marriage to Katherine of Aragon.

Peace with Francis gave Henry his only major ally in Europe during the following two decades as he broke from Rome and implemented religious change in England. For Francis, peace kept Henry and Charles apart, thereby increasing his own freedom of movement against them both, at least until 1542, when they once more made an alliance and attacked France for a third and final time. Thus, ironically, the 'eternal' Anglo-French peace of 1527 presaged war in Europe for the next twenty years, as well as laying the diplomatic foundations for the English Reformation.

THE ANGLO-FRENCH PEACE OF 1514

Henry VIII wanted to continue the war against France after his successful 1513 campaign, but his allies reached a separate agreement between themselves to make peace and he did not have the resources to continue fighting alone. Anglo-French peace negotiations began in June, and two months later a treaty was signed between Henry and Louis XII. According to its terms, Henry was to keep Tournai and receive an annual pension from Louis. A dynastic marriage was also arranged between Henry's young sister Mary and the fifty-two-year-old French King. To Henry's annoyance – but Mary's obvious relief – the new Queen of France was widowed just eleven weeks after the wedding.

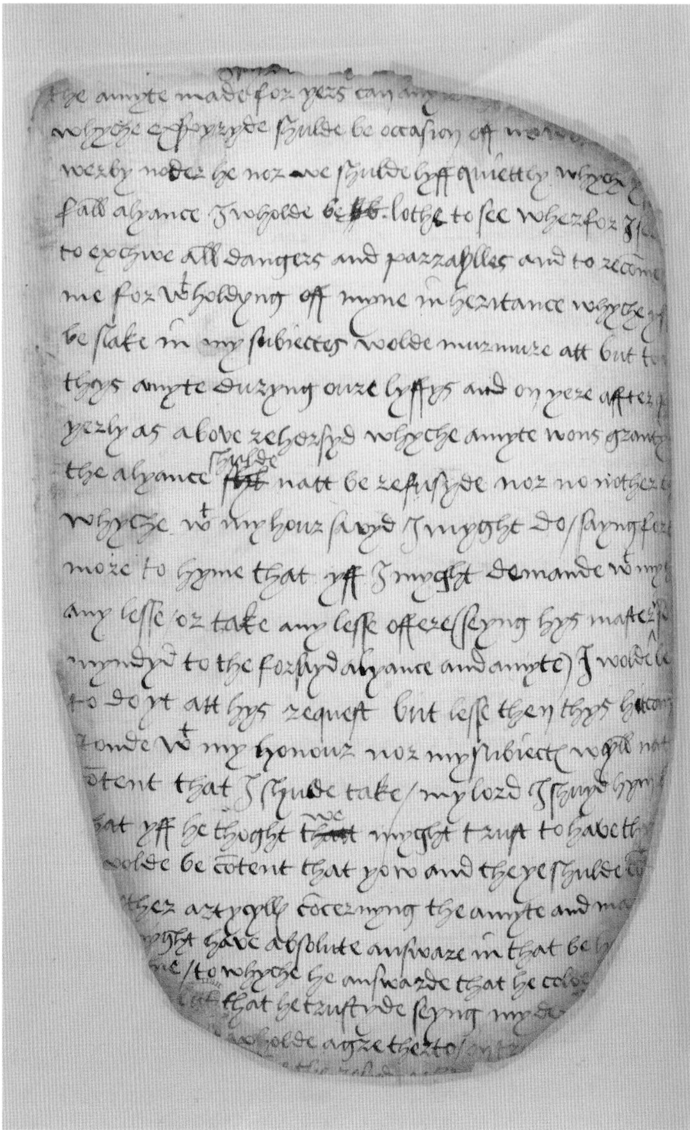

70 Prospects of Peace

Holograph letter from Henry VIII to Thomas Wolsey, 1514

British Library, Cotton MS Caligula D vi, fol.121v

Full letter transcribed by Rymer before letter was damaged; Rymer also transcribed address: 'To my Lorde Lyncolne' Rymer XIII, p.403

This is one of many important documents from Robert Cotton's library which were damaged in a fire at Ashburnham House in 1731. It is a fragment of a letter that Henry wrote to Thomas Wolsey in 1514 discussing French overtures for an alliance. Henry tells Wolsey that, for peace and an alliance, the French must pay 100,000 crowns annually as a pension 'to recompense me for witholdyng of myne inheritance', that is, the crown of France, which he claims as his own. The letter is a rare piece of evidence of Henry's initiative in foreign affairs and his view of how 'peace' worked. As he explains earlier in the letter, the 'amyte shulde no lenger contynw then the payment off money'. This was indeed the basis on which Henry finally made peace with Louis XII in 1514 and thereafter with his successor, Francis I. For Henry, peace with France, based on payment of an annual 'tribute', was honourable, demonstrating his own power and high international status. (GR)

LITERATURE: Scarisbrick, *Henry VIII*; Richardson, 'The French Connection'; Baumgartner, *Louis XII*

71 Mary Tudor as Queen of France

Pierre Gringore (*c*.1475–*c*.1538)

De la reception et entrée de la illustrissime dame et princesse Marie d'Angleterre (fille de Hen. VII) dans la ville de Paris, le 6. Nov[emb]re 1514. Avec belles peintures.

British Library, Cotton MS Vespasian B ii, fol.15

This is the only manuscript edition of six surviving descriptions of Mary Tudor's ceremonial entry to Paris after her marriage to Louis XII, and features seven illuminations of the pageants that greeted her on her journey to the Palais Royal. This folio illustrates the pageant presented at the end of her entry. At the highest level was a representation of the Annunciation. Below this were the royal arms of Louis and Mary linked by lovers' knots and supported by a porcupine (Louis's badge) and a lion of England. The main space of pageant displayed 'the garden of France' with figures representing the King and Queen, flanked by Justice holding a sword and Truth holding a symbol of peace. At their feet flowers grow and shepherds and shepherdesses 'sing musically'. The message is clear: as peace between God and humanity came through the Virgin Mary, so Mary in marriage brings peace between England and France. (GR)

LITERATURE: Baskervill (ed.), *Pierre Gringore's Pageants for the Entry of Mary Tudor into Paris*; Giry-Deloison, 'Mary Tudor's Marriage to Louis XII'; Perry, *The Sisters of Henry VIII*

72 A Letter between Royal Siblings

Holograph letter from Mary to her brother Henry VIII from Paris, 15 November 1514

British Library, Cotton MS Vespasian F iii, fol.50

Mary's letter was written nine days after her entry into Paris as Queen of France on 6 November 1514, just as the English ambassadors who had escorted her were preparing to return home. In it she explained that the Lord Chamberlain (Charles Somerset, Earl of Worcester), who headed the delegation, would tell Henry 'how luffyngly the kyng my husband delyth w'me'. What the 'good counsell' was that Henry had offered Mary, which she promises to follow 'every day', is not known precisely. It probably concerned how to make the best of her dynastic marriage to Louis, which she had not sought, and perhaps her prospects after his death. The resemblance between her handwriting and her brother Henry's is striking, almost certainly because she too had been taught to write by their mother, Elizabeth of York. (GR)

LITERATURE: Gunn, *Charles Brandon, Duke of Suffolk*; Perry, *The Sisters of Henry VIII*; Scarisbrick, *Henry VIII*

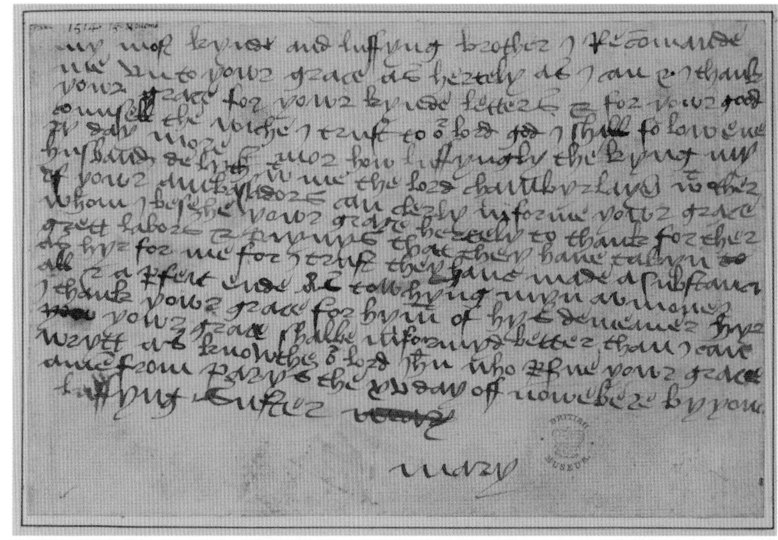

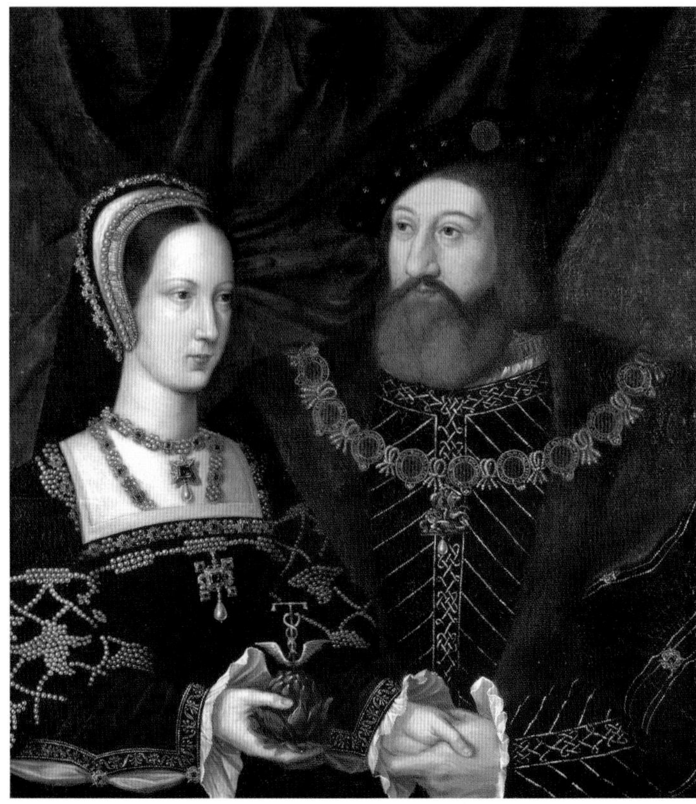

73 Charles Brandon and Mary Tudor

Letter from Charles Brandon, Duke of Suffolk, to Henry VIII, from Montreuil, France, 22 April 1515

British Library, Cotton MS Vespasian F xiii, fol.153

Charles Brandon (*c*.1484–1545) rose the highest and the fastest of all Henry's courtiers, from esquire to duke in under five years. Yet, in April 1515, he was fighting for his life. Sent to France to bring back Mary, the widowed Queen of France, he had married her, in direct contravention of his promise to Henry. Charles and Mary tried to appease the furious King by surrendering her jewels and plate. They also appealed to Thomas Wolsey, the rising star on the council, for help. But when they reached Montreuil, on the way to Calais, their fate was still uncertain. Henry's other councillors wanted Brandon executed or imprisoned, Charles wrote to the King, but he knew it was not in Henry's nature to let them 'caus you to dysstru me for ther malles'. He was right. Henry met the pair at Birling in Kent and, for a healthy slice of his sister's French dower income, pardoned them. Brandon lived on to serve the King for three more decades. (SG)

LITERATURE: Gunn, *Charles Brandon, Duke of Suffolk*; Richardson, *Mary Tudor, the White Queen*

74 A Marriage Portrait

Anonymous portrait of the Duke and Duchess of Suffolk

His Grace the Duke of Bedford and the Trustees of the Bedford Estates

After making their peace with the King, Charles Brandon, Duke of Suffolk, and Mary Tudor were married publicly at Greenwich, in the presence of the court, on 13 May 1515. Afterwards, they spent much of their time on Suffolk's landed estates in East Anglia, and Mary only occasionally came to London. Nonetheless, her relationship with Henry seems to have remained affectionate, until his decision to annul his first marriage drove a wedge between them. Mary was close to Katherine of Aragon and disapproved of Anne Boleyn.

This double portrait was probably painted at the time of Suffolk and Mary's marriage. He is wearing the order of St George round his neck and a badge depicting an allegorical figure in his hat. Her dress is richly embroidered with pearls and in her hand she holds an artichoke, the emblematic significance of which is elusive. The union of the Suffolks produced two sons who died young and two daughters, Frances (1517–59) and Eleanor (*c*.1520–47). Their granddaughter was Lady Jane Grey (1537?–54), who claimed the throne on Edward VI's death in 1553. (SD)

LITERATURE Gunn, *Charles Brandon, Duke of Suffolk*; Perry, *The Sisters of Henry VIII*

RIVALS FOR POWER: HENRY VIII, FRANCIS I AND CHARLES V

On his death in January 1515, Louis XII was succeeded by his twenty-year-old cousin Francis I. Like Henry, Francis sought glory on the battlefield and spent large amounts of money on lavish building projects at his court, so the two men were natural rivals. The following year, Ferdinand of Spain died, leaving his sixteen-year-old grandson, the Habsburg Archduke Charles of Burgundy, as his heir. When, in February 1519, the Emperor Maximilian I died, it seemed likely that his grandson Charles would be elected as Holy Roman Emperor in his place; and, indeed, after paying out huge sums to the German Electors, Charles prevailed over the other candidates, who included Francis I and Henry VIII. The stage was set for intense rivalry, even war, between the three monarchs.

75 Francis I, King of France

Unknown artist, probably early 16th century

Society of Antiquaries of London, Scharf XXIX

Inscribed: 'FRANCICVS I REX FRANCORX'

Francis I (1494–1547), King of France between 1515 and 1547, was the son of Charles of Orléans, Count of Angoulême, and Louise of Savoy. He became Duke of Valois in 1499 after his second cousin, Louis of Orléans, succeeded to the French throne as Louis XII. He married Louis's elder daughter, Claude, in 1514 and succeeded him as King on 1 January 1515. The dating of the wooden panel indicates that the portrait was done some time between 1499 and 1531. The painting has obvious similarities with 15th-century Netherlandish portrait types. This fact, together with the style of the King's clothing, suggests that it was made quite early in his reign. Francis I is much better known from the work of more skilled French and Italian artists, chiefly Jean Clouet and Titian, who painted far more dynamic and flattering portraits of the King in the 1520s and 1530s. (GR)

LITERATURE: Knecht, *Renaissance Warrior and Patron*; Cox-Rearick, *The Collection of Francis I*; Châtelet, *Early Dutch Painting*

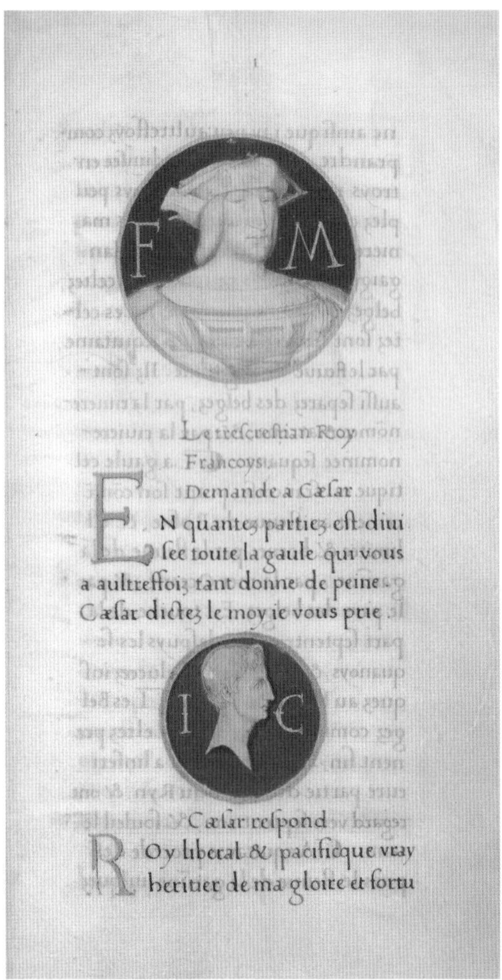

F M

Le treſcreſtian Roy
Francoys
Demande a Cæſar
EN quantes parties eſt diui
ſee toute la gaule qui vous
a aultreffois tant donne de peine
Cæſar dictes le moy ie vous prie

I C

Cæſar reſpond
ROy liberal & pacificque vray
heritier de ma gloire et fortu

76 Francis I: the Warrior King

François du Moulin (d.*c.*1526) and Albert Pigghe (*c.*1490–1542), illuminated by Godefroy Le Batave (fl.1515–24)

Les Commentaires de la guerre gallique, vol.2, 1519

British Library, Harley MS 6205, fol.3

This commentary on the Gallic wars was commissioned by Francis I or his mother Louise of Savoy not long after the King's great victory over a large veteran Swiss army at the Battle of Marignano in September 1515. The battle took place south-east of Milan and resulted in the French occupation of the Duchy. At a stroke Francis had established his credentials as a great warrior-king, far surpassing the minor achievements of Henry VIII in 1513 and arousing considerable envy in the English King. This page is designed to compare the French King with Julius Caesar, the conqueror of Gaul. A cameo of Francis is placed above that of Caesar, and in the text Caesar recognizes Francis as the heir to his glory and fortune. (SD)

LITERATURE: Meyer, 'Marguerite de Navarre and the Androgynous Portrait of François Ier'; Knecht, *Francis the First*

77 Archduke Charles of Burgundy

Flemish School, *c.*1514–16

Born in 1500, Charles (1500–56) was the grandson of Ferdinand and Isabella of Spain on his mother's side and Mary, Duchess of Burgundy, and the Emperor Maximilian I of the House of Habsburg on his father's. As such, he inherited vast territories across Europe, including the Netherlands, Spain, Austria and the County of Burgundy. Here he is shown holding a sprig of rosemary (for remembrance) in his left hand. Around his neck he wears the insignia of the chivalric Burgundian Order of the Golden Fleece. His hat badge features an image of the Virgin Mary and is inscribed 'SANCTA MARIA ORA PRO NOBIS' (Holy Mary, pray for us). The painting, owned by Henry VIII, was catalogued in both the 1542 Whitehall inventory and that taken at his death in 1547. Quite possibly it was the portrait sent to Henry's sister Mary towards the end of her betrothal to Charles (1507–14); if so, it was mentioned in a letter of 30 June 1514 as the likeness 'where he is very badly painted'. It is certainly not very flattering to the adolescent Charles. With his prominent lower jaw and chin fully emphasized, it verges on a caricature of the future Emperor. (GR and SD)

LITERATURE: Campbell, *The Early Flemish Pictures in the Collection of Her Majesty the Queen*; Soly (ed.), *Charles V 1500–1558 and his Time*; Tracy, *Emperor Charles V, Impresario of War*

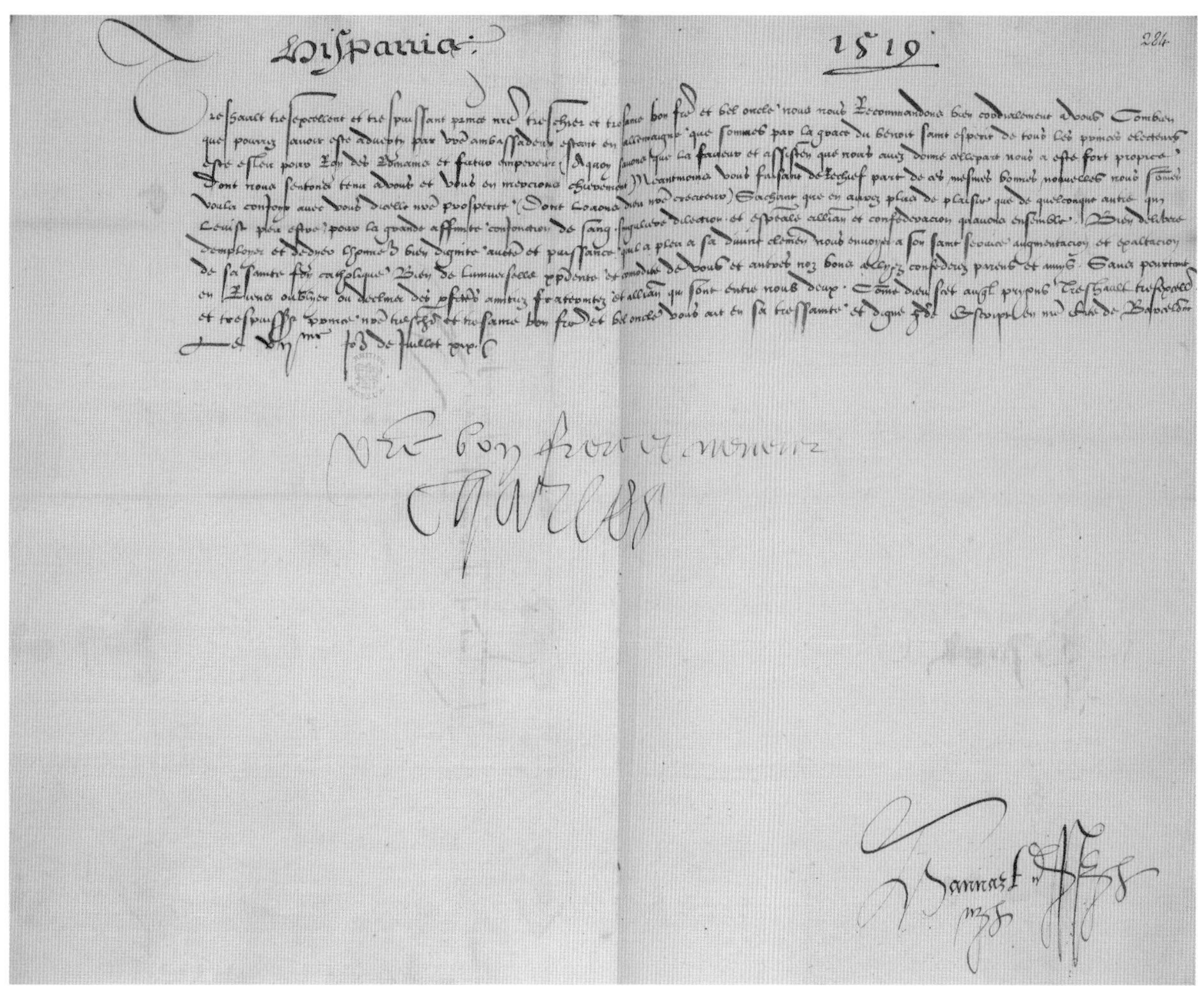

Hispania 1519 284

78 Charles V: the New Holy Roman Emperor

Letter from Charles V to Henry VIII, from Barcelona, 7 July 1519

British Library, Cotton MS Vespasian C i, fols 283v–284

In this letter written in French after he was elected as 'king of the Romans and future emperor', Charles thanks Henry for favouring his election and says that he wishes the English King to share his good fortune because of the family link between them: Charles was Katherine of Aragon's nephew. He promises to work for the advancement of the Catholic faith and the security of his friends and allies. He ends the letter personally, 'your good brother and nephew Charles'. Henry had been a candidate for the elective German Imperial throne in May 1519, but he gave limited public support to Charles to ensure that his greatest rival, Francis I of France, also a candidate, would be unsuccessful. In 1530 Charles was eventually crowned as Holy Roman Emperor Charles V in Bologna by Pope Clement VII. (GR)

LITERATURE: Richardson, *Renaissance Monarchy*; Tracy, *Emperor Charles V, Impresario of War*; Blockmans, *Emperor Charles V, 1500–1558*

79 Charles V

Giovan Pietro Birago (fl.1470–1513) and Gerard Horenbout of Ghent (1465–1541)

Sforza Hours

British Library, Additional MS 34294, fol.213

To mark Charles V's recent election, a gold oval medallion of the new Holy Roman Emperor was added in 1520 to the bottom border of this folio within the 'Sforza Hours', a Book of Hours owned by Charles's aunt, Margaret of Austria, the Regent of the Netherlands. The medallion is flanked by the fourfold monogram K.I., standing for 'Karolus Imperator', and a pair of painted gilt glass vases whose feet cast an illusionistic shadow over the edge of the border. The folio marks the beginning of the Seven Penitential Psalms and is directly opposite a miniature of King David in penitence. Most of the decoration on the folio is by Giovan Pietro Birago, who painted the original Book of Hours around 1490. However, Margaret's court painter, the Flemish illuminator Gerard Horenbout, added the medallion during the time that he was working to complete the Book of Hours, which had been left unfinished after sixteen folios were stolen from Birago. (SD)

LITERATURE: Evans, *The Sforza Hours*; Kren (ed.), *Renaissance Paintings in Manuscripts*

80 Henry VIII

Miniature attributed to Lucas Horenbout (also known as Hornebolt; d.1544)

Watercolour on vellum on card, *c.*1526–7

Fitzwilliam Museum, Cambridge, PD.19-1949

This tiny portrait depicts Henry's head and shoulders within a gold-lined circle. His beardless head is shown in three-quarters profile. Fashionably dressed, the monarch wears a black cap sporting a gold ensign, doubled gold neck chain, blue-grey doublet and fur-trimmed gown. To the left and right of Henry's head inscriptions provide his name and age. Outside the central circle two pairs of angels hold tassels of the cords that link the initials of Henry and Katherine. In its small scale, parchment support and painting technique, the portrait follows the traditions of manuscript illumination. Contemporary and later sources record similar miniature portraits, both as independent works within books, and as items of fashionable apparel worn by European noblemen and women. Such portraits were exchanged as diplomatic gifts, for example, between Henry VIII and the future Margaret of Navarre during preliminary talks to the Treaty of Amiens, which took place from 1526 to 1527. (SMcK)

LITERATURE: Marks and Williamson (eds), *Gothic: Art for England 1400–1547*

THOMAS WOLSEY AND DIPLOMACY

Thomas Wolsey (b.1470/1471–1530) was nearly forty years old when Henry VIII came to the throne. Over the next twenty years he was by the King's side, advising Henry on policy, implementing royal decisions and participating prominently in ceremonial occasions. His pre-eminence was largely the result of his exceptional ability and energy as an administrator and diplomat. He earned the King's trust because, in the words of his near contemporary, the biographer George Cavendish, 'he was most earnest and readiest among all the Council to advance the King's only will and pleasure without any respect to the case'. After the war against France, Wolsey used his diplomatic skill to bolster Henry's reputation by transforming the English King into the leading peacemaker of Europe. In 1518, he negotiated the Treaty of London and a series of alliances between England and France. They brought prestige to his master, not least by making his capital the centre of international diplomacy.

The Treaty of London marked the pinnacle of Wolsey's success as a diplomat and earned Henry the admiration of humanists for bringing peace to a war-torn Europe and achieving the unity of Christendom.

81 Cardinal Thomas Wolsey

Unknown British School, probably late 16th century, of Wolsey in 1520s

National Portrait Gallery, London, NPG 32

Inscribed: 'CARDINAL/WOOLSEY'

Born in 1470 or 1471, Wolsey rose from modest beginnings to become Henry's most powerful minister and prelate in the early part of his reign. He lived up to his role as the King's principal minister by indulging his lavish tastes, and, in 1514, he acquired and rebuilt Hampton Court as a palace in the style described in Paolo Cortese's 1510 manual for cardinals. The Venetian ambassador Sebastian Giustinian, who worked closely with Wolsey between 1514 and 1519, described him as 'very handsome, learned, extremely eloquent, of vast ability, and indefatigable'. Yet, apart from a manuscript drawing in the *Bibliothèque d'Arras*, no contemporary portraits of Wolsey appear to exist. This portrait is almost certainly after an earlier lost image and shows him in profile wearing his cardinal's robes. The arched top might indicate that the picture was originally designed as part of a wider decorative scheme within an Elizabethan domestic space. (TC and SD)

LITERATURE: Strong, *Tudor and Jacobean Portraits*; Gwyn, *The King's Cardinal*

82 Wolsey's Coat of Arms, 1515

Arms of the Sovereign and Peers Spiritual and Temporal in the Parliament Roll

British Library, Additional MS 40078

Wolsey's meteoric rise brought him ecclesiastical as well as secular promotion: in February 1513 he was made Dean of York; on 6 February 1514 he became Bishop of Lincoln and Tournai. Just six months later, Wolsey was appointed Archbishop of York, making him the second most senior person within the Church in England after William Warham, Archbishop of Canterbury. The roll of arms of the Lords spiritual and temporal, who sat in the Parliament held at Westminster on 5 February 1515, displays the personal and official arms of 'Th[e] archbishopp of yorc the lord Thomas Wulcy' impaled beneath a mitre. In 1515, he was created Cardinal by Pope Leo X and succeeded Archbishop Warham as Lord Chancellor. He was appointed *legate a latere* (an extraordinary representative of the Pope) in 1518. (AC)

LITERATURE: Eden, 'Heraldic Parliament Rolls'; *Heralds' Commemorative Exhibition 1484–1934*; Wagner and Sainty, 'The Origin of the Introduction of Peers in the House of Lords'

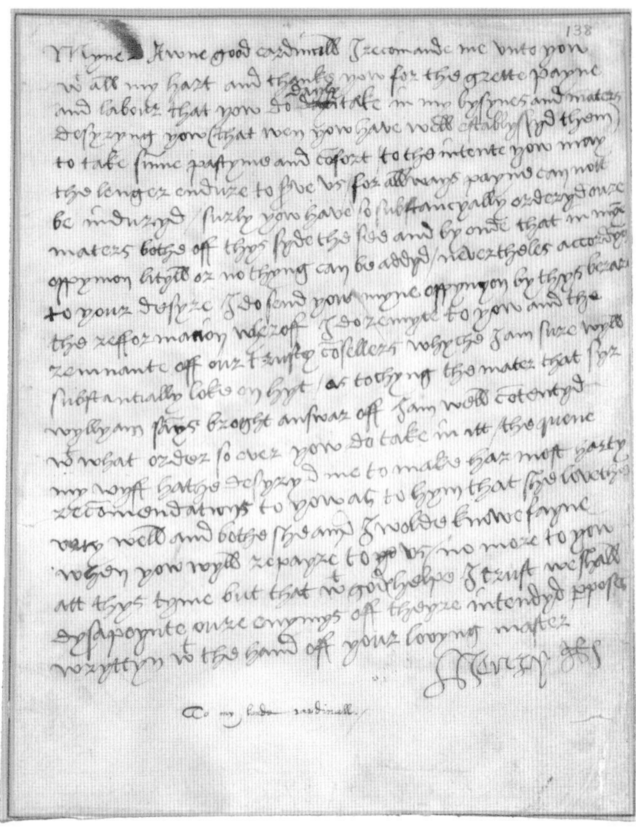

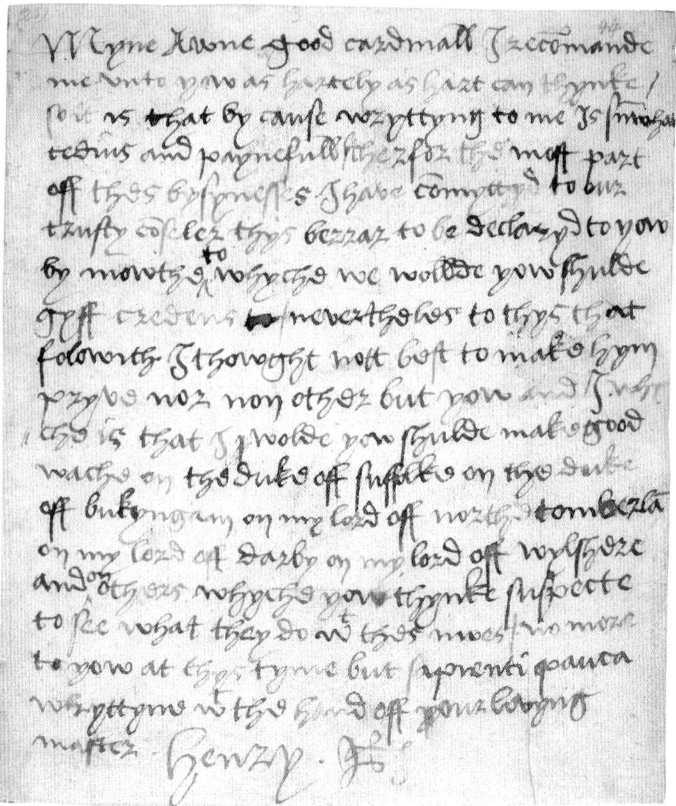

83 Henry VIII's Relationship with Wolsey

Holograph letter from Henry VIII to Wolsey, *c.*1520

British Library, Cotton MS Vespasian F xiii, fol.138

This letter, written in Henry's own hand, provides the clearest evidence of Wolsey's favour with the King and the freedom of executive power he enjoyed until the late 1520s. The maintenance of that royal trust was to be the entire foundation and purpose of Wolsey's career. Although undated, the letter was probably written around 1520. The King thanks Wolsey for all his labours and 'pains' and urges him to take some rest so that he might 'the longer endure to serve us'. In response to a matter referred to him by Wolsey, Henry simply replies: 'I am well contented with what order so ever you do take in it'. Queen Katherine sends greetings and both long to know when Wolsey will visit them. Henry trusts that with Wolsey's help he will 'disappoint our enemies of their intended purposes' and signs 'with the hand of your loving master'. (GR)

LITERATURE: Starkey, *The Reign of Henry VIII*; Gwyn, *The King's Cardinal*

84 Conspiracy at Court

Holograph letter from Henry VIII to Wolsey, undated

British Library, Additional MS 19398, fol.44

In this secret, undated note to Wolsey, it is evident that the King puts his absolute trust in his minister. Henry confesses that he found writing 'somewhat tedius and paynefull' but the matter about which he writes could not be made privy to the messenger 'nor non other but yow and I'. He proceeds to warn Wolsey about a noble conspiracy and urges him to 'make good wache on the duke off suffolke on the duke off bukyngam on my lord off northetomberla[nd] on my lord off darby on my lord off wylshere and on others whyche yow thynke suspecte'. The letter was probably written in 1519 or 1520 when Henry's relationship with Edward Stafford, the 3rd Duke of Buckingham (1478–1521) was particularly strained, but his anxiety also sprang from a general sense of insecurity because of his lack of a legitimate male heir, coupled with childhood memories of Yorkist pretenders. Henry's suspicions of Buckingham proved well founded. Resenting Wolsey's prominence and disliking Henry's pro-French foreign policy, Buckingham allowed his discontent to spill into treasonous words, and, on 17 May 1521, he was executed after a short trial. (SD)

LITERATURE: Starkey, *The Reign of Henry VIII*; Scarisbrick, *Henry VIII*; Harris, *Edward Stafford, Third Duke of Buckingham, 1478–1521*

THE FIELD OF CLOTH OF GOLD

After the signing of the Treaty of London, preparations began for a meeting between Henry VIII and Francis I. Charles V was keen not to be excluded from this personal diplomacy and came over to England in May 1520 to meet Henry and his aunt, Queen Katherine. Soon after Charles had departed, Henry set off for France accompanied by over 5,000 people. His meeting with the French King between 7 and 24 June 1520 at 'The Field of Cloth of Gold' between the English headquarters at Guînes and the French town of Ardres was a glittering occasion. However, the friendship proclaimed between the two Kings was shallow: during the proceedings their rivalry was palpable and two years afterwards they were at war.

85 The Embarkation of Henry VIII at Dover

S.H. Grimm (*c*.1733–94)

Watercolour, 1779

Society of Antiquaries of London, Scharf ADD 70

This picture was associated directly with the meeting between Henry VIII and Francis I on 31 May 1520, but anomalies of costume and other details mean that art historians today are not certain that it necessarily represents Henry's crossing that year. The King is seen setting sail for Calais with his Queen and a vast retinue of nobles, servants and horses. Dover Castle is visible on the top left of the picture and the coast of France in the distance. Henry, surrounded by courtiers, trumpeters and yeomen of the guard, stands on the deck of a four-masted ship (probably intended to represent the *Henry Grâce-à-Dieu*). This watercolour, commissioned by the Society of Antiquaries of London, is a copy of the large painting of the same subject in the Royal Collection, now at Hampton Court Palace. The minutes of the meeting of the Society on 13 May 1779 record that Samuel H. Grimm was paid £70 for 'a tinted Drawing' of the scene. (GR and SD)

LITERATURE: *Making History: Antiquaries in Britain 1707–2007*; Roberts, *George III and Queen Charlotte*; Topham, 'A Description of an Antient Picture in Windsor Castle'

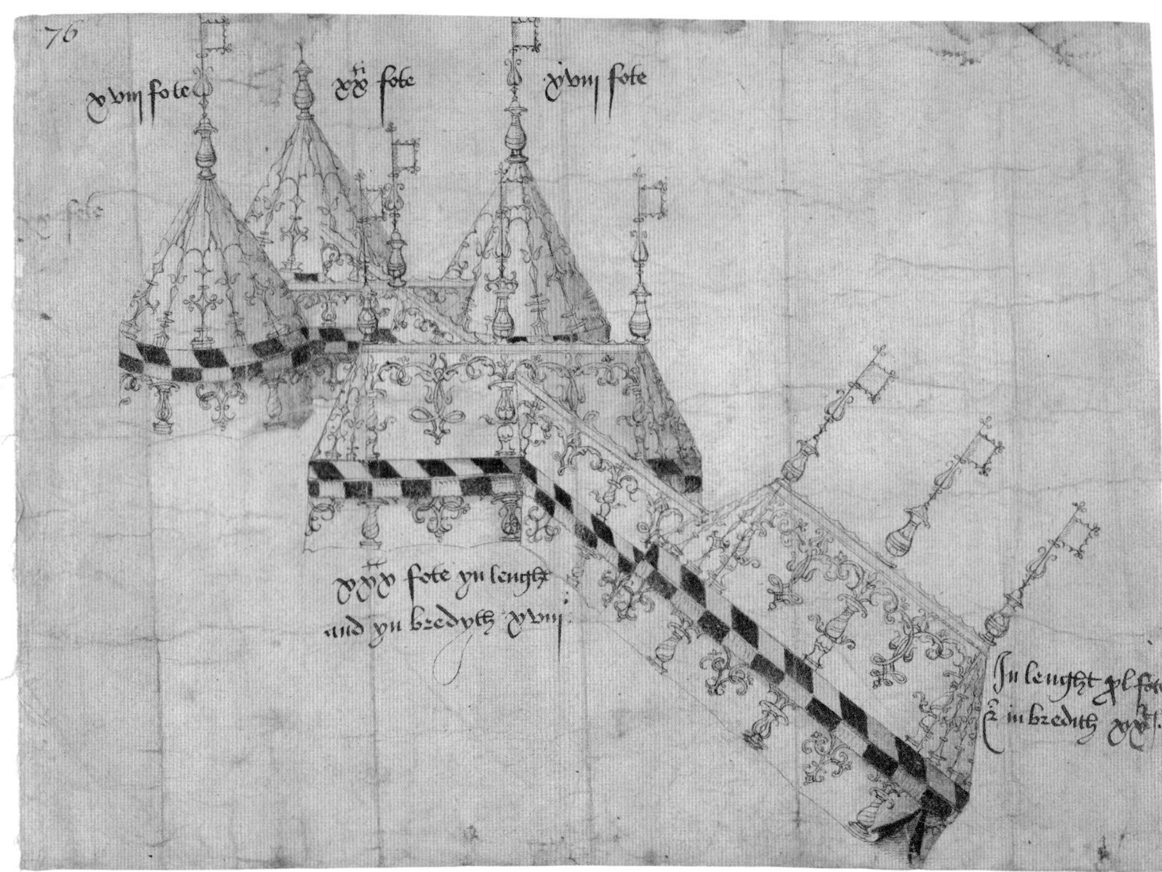

86 Designs for Tents for the Field of Cloth of Gold (see between pages 96–7)

British Library, Cotton MS Augustus III, fols 11, 18, 19; Cotton MS Augustus I.ii.76

In material and arrangements the tents drawn here closely resemble those depicted in the near contemporary painting of the Field of Cloth of Gold, and it is therefore safe to assume that they were the original designs for the structures. They reveal the impressive size and splendour of the temporary accommodation erected for Henry's court during his meeting with Francis I in June 1520. Each design features a series of tents connected to the next via galleries, together making up a pavilion. The layout of the pavilions followed as far as possible the arrangements in Tudor palaces. Larger spaces could be divided using hangings of rich cloth, and reception rooms, private apartments and chapels could be arranged enfilade or with galleries connecting them. The canvas tents were dressed with rich fabrics, usually cloth of gold and velvet.

On folio 11, each tent is dressed with blue cloth, decorated with gold. The tents are fringed under the eaves with the Tudor livery colours of white and green. The gold painted ridgeboards at the top of the roofs support carved fleurs-de-lis.

Folio 18 is the most complex of the designs, featuring a series of four principal tents, each of which has two small round tents on either side of it. The tents are dressed in red cloth with Renaissance candelabra and 'grotesque' decoration. At the eaves is a running frieze bearing the royal mottoes 'DIEU ET MON DROIT' and 'SEMPER VIVAT IN ETERNO', under which is a fringe of gold. The ridgeboards here are painted gold and decorated with carved Tudor roses interspersed with fleurs-de-lis along their length. On top of the tent poles are 'King's beasts' (lions, greyhounds, dragons, harts and heraldic antelopes) holding standards topped either with the closed crown imperial or a fleur-de-lis and flying square pennants of fleurs-de-lis, Beaufort portcullises, royal arms and Tudor roses. At the extreme left end, above the entry flap, is a vase structure, out of which arises a standard of the Tudor rose, topped by a fleur-de-lis.

The design on folio 19 features tents in the green and white Tudor livery colours: one large tent followed by one smaller one and linked by galleries, flanked on each side and intersected by ten smaller rectangular and circular tents. The ridgeboards carry carved fleurs-de-lis painted gold; plate-like stands can be seen with poles or spikes onto which 'king's beasts' or other decorative devices could be set. They are fringed at the eaves in blue, red and gold – the colours of the royal arms.

Folio 76 shows a pavilion of tents, also in green and (discoloured) white livery colours. It features a cluster of three tents with a central set of two large tents linked by galleries. All are decorated with Renaissance candelabra, arabesque and foliage motifs.

The ridgeboards are relatively plain, and the pennants flying are square and undecorated. The drawing, intended to convey three-dimensionality, is annotated with measurements down the page:

> xviij foote; xx fote; xviij fote (18 foot; 20 foot; 18 foot)
>
> xxx fote yn length and yn bredyth xviij (30 foot in length and in breadth 18)
>
> In length XL fote and in bredth xix fote (In length 40 foot and in breadth 19 (GR)

LITERATURE: Marks and Payne (eds), *British Heraldry from its Origins to c. 1800*; Russell, *The Field of Cloth of Gold*

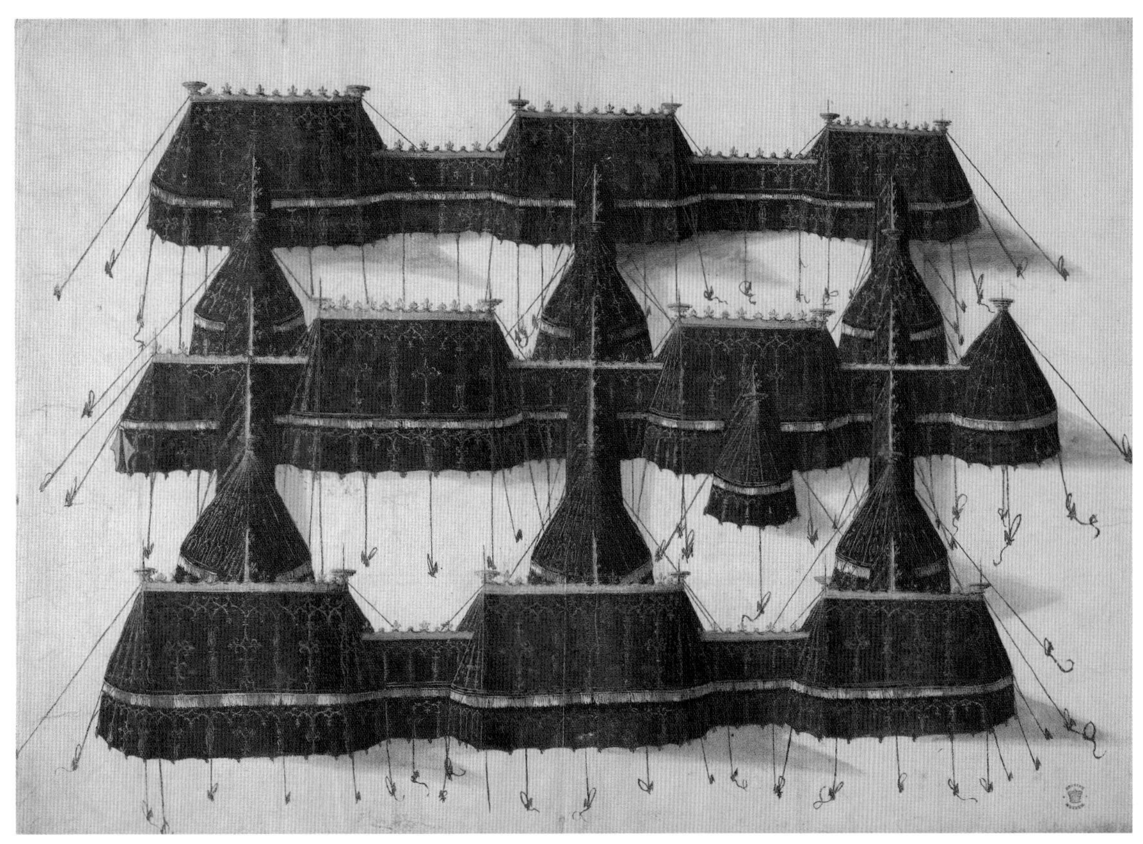

87 The Field of Cloth of Gold

'The Meeting of Henry VIII, King of England and the French King Francis I between Guines and Ardres in the month of June 1520'

Edward Edwards (1738–1806)

Watercolour, 1771

The Royal Collection © 2009 Her Majesty Queen Elizabeth II, RCIN 452771

Like the Grimm watercolour, which was executed a few years later, this watercolour was commissioned by the Society of Antiquaries of London and is a copy of the larger original also at Hampton Court Palace. Unlike the Grimm, though, it was presented to George III and thereby came into the Royal Collection. James Basire (c.1730–1802) produced engravings of both watercolours that were published in 1781 in the series *Historical Prints*.

The Field of Cloth of Gold watercolour accurately reproduces the overall scheme of the original painting and also renders, with great precision and clarity, many of the details not easily observed in the much larger original. Henry's magnificent temporary palace can be seen in the forefront on the right. Henry is shown in procession and beside him rides Wolsey on a mule; on the extreme left, behind the King, is Charles Brandon, Duke of Suffolk. The meeting of Henry and Francis takes place in a tent of cloth of gold in the centre, and the tournaments are shown top right. (GR and SD)

LITERATURE: Millar, *The Tudor, Stuart and Early Georgian Pictures in the Collection of Her Majesty The Queen*; Turner (ed.), *The Dictionary of Art*; Roberts, *George III and Queen Charlotte*

88 Tapestry of 'The Triumph of Chastity over Love'

Flemish tapestry, early 16th century

Victoria and Albert Museum, London, 440-1883

Contemporaries commented upon the magnificence of the tapestries exhibited in the temporary palace erected at Guînes in 1520, and this 'Triumph of Chastity Over Love' may well have been one of those hanging in Wolsey's rooms. In the 1522 inventory of Wolsey's possessions a set of tapestries called the 'Triumphs of Petrarch' is listed, while the date '1520' is inscribed on another tapestry in that series (which is also in the Victoria and Albert Museum). The design was inspired by Petrarch's poem *I Trionfi* and reflects Wolsey's taste for humanist themes. To the left of the scene can be seen Cupid falling from a triumphal car fitted with flaming torches of love, drawn by four winged white horses. His left arm is grasped by Chastity mounted on a unicorn and carrying the column symbolizing strength or fortitude. In the centre, a bound Cupid sits at the feet of the triumphant Chastity as part of a procession going towards the virginal goddess, Diana. (SD)

LITERATURE: Marks and Williamson, *Gothic: Art for England 1400–1547*; Campbell, *Henry VIII and the Art of Majesty*

DIPLOMACY 1522–28

Henry VIII's role as a European peacemaker proved to be fragile because of the underlying conflict between Francis I and Charles V. As the Venetian ambassador reported in September 1520, 'these sovereigns are not at peace; they adapt themselves to circumstances, but hate each other very cordially'. During 1521 it became obvious that war between the two men was imminent.

Henry initially tried to settle their disputes but soon chose to throw in his lot with Charles. In coordination with his ally, Henry sent a large army into France in 1523 under the command of the Duke of Suffolk. The campaign, however, was a disappointing failure. Although he came within 50 miles of Paris, Suffolk was forced to retreat with no territorial gains.

Charles's war proved far more successful: two years later at the Battle of Pavia his army won Milan and captured the French King. Now Henry wanted to share in the spoils of his ally's victory. His ambassadors presented to the Emperor a 'grand design' whereby Charles and Henry would mount a joint invasion of France in order to partition the realm. To pay for this projected campaign, Henry requested an 'Amicable Grant' from his subjects. However, they strongly objected and successfully resisted its payment. To make matters worse, Charles refused to cooperate and satisfy Henry's ambitions; he even broke off his betrothal to Henry's daughter.

Humiliated and furious at this 'betrayal', Henry immediately made moves to reach an agreement with France. That summer he signed the Treaty of the More, in which he promised to work for Francis's release from captivity; and in 1526 he signed a treaty with the newly liberated Francis, pledging not to make a separate peace with the Emperor. Finally, in 1527, the two kings agreed to the Treaty of Amiens, committing them to an 'eternal peace'. This Anglo-French alliance lasted over a decade and successfully sustained Henry during his annulment crisis and break with Rome.

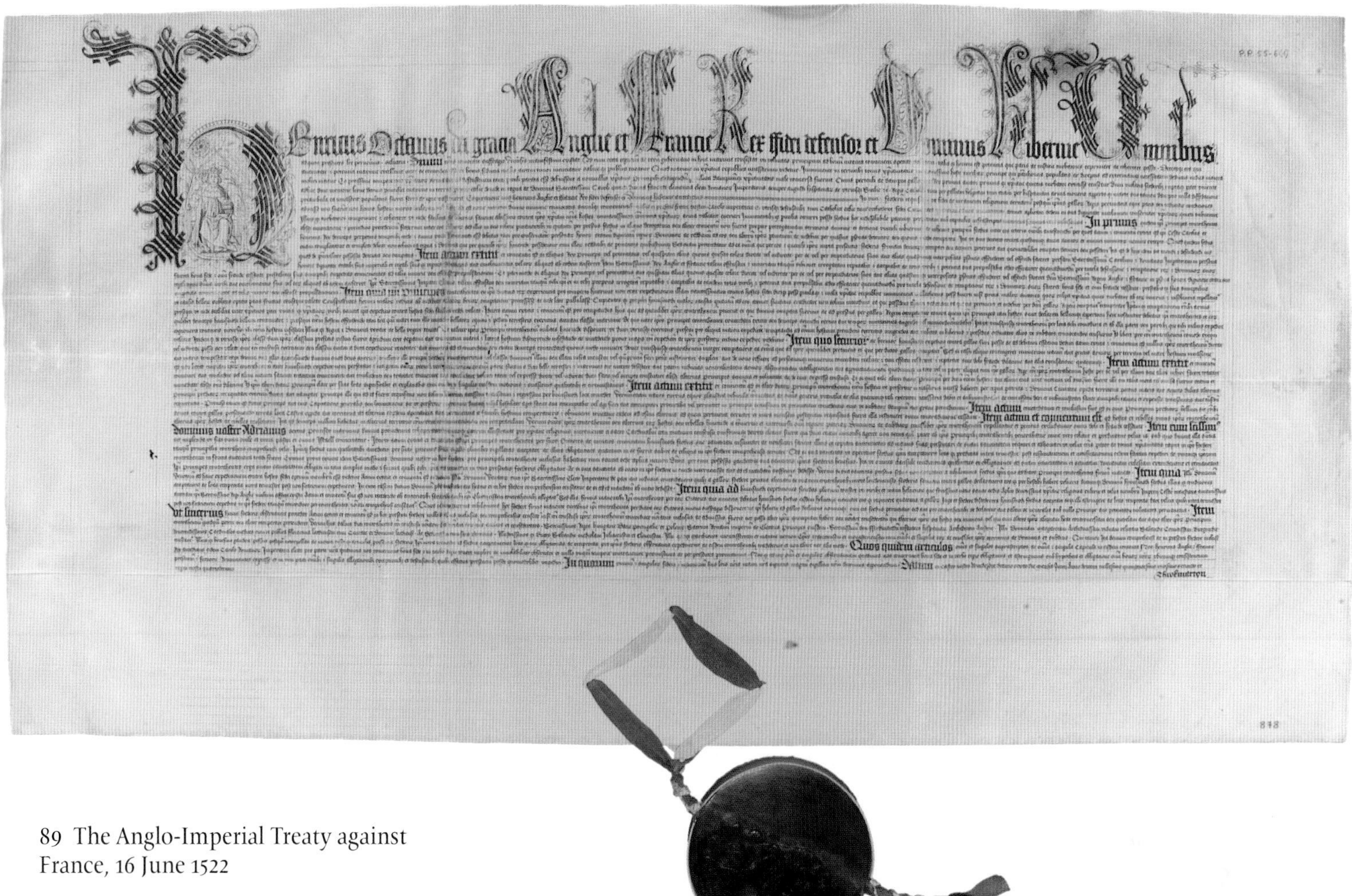

89 The Anglo-Imperial Treaty against France, 16 June 1522

Archivo General de Simancas, Patronato Real, Caja 55, Doc. 6(1)

After the Treaty of London, England's role as arbiter of Europe depended on the continued balance of power between the rival great powers of Francis I and Charles V. Both Henry and Wolsey did their best to uphold the Treaty of London, but, as relations between France and the Empire grew more acrimonious, Henry increasingly inclined towards the Empire. On 26 May 1522 Charles V arrived in England on a state visit to mark the signing of a new Anglo-imperial alliance. The treaty, which displays a fine penwork initial 'H' with an enthroned Henry, provided for concerted Anglo-imperial attacks on France to 'defend their present possessions but also to re-conquer from the King of France all their former dominions which have been wrested from them'. A secret treaty, concluded on 19 June, sealed the alliance with the betrothal of Charles to Princess Mary. (AC)

LITERATURE: Scarisbrick, *Henry VIII*; Gwyn, *The King's Cardinal*

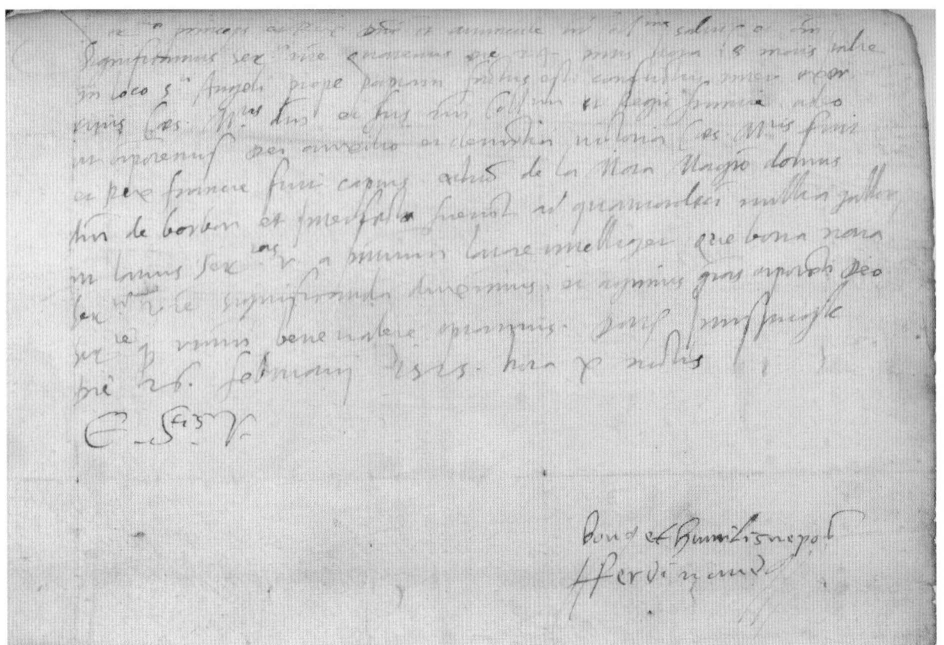

90 Charles V's Victory at Pavia, 24 February 1525

Letter from Archduke Ferdinand of Austria to Henry VIII from Innsbruck, 26 February 1525

British Library, Cotton MS Galba B viii, fol.160

In this letter, Ferdinand of Austria (1503–64), the younger brother of Charles V, conveys to the English King the good news (*bona nova*) of the imperial victory in a battle at St Angelus near Pavia in northern Italy on the eighteenth hour (11 am) of 24 February 1525. The French King, Ferdinand writes, was captured by De la Mota, the *maître d'hotel* of the Duke of Bourbon, and some 14,000 Frenchmen were slain. The news of Charles's great victory reached Henry early on 9 March. His delight was evident, not least because the last Yorkist prince Richard de la Pole, who was fighting on the French side, was killed in the battle. Bonfires were lit and Wolsey sang a High Mass at St Paul's. (SD)

LITERATURE: Blockmans, *Emperor Charles V*; Scarisbrick, *Henry VIII*; Konstam, *Pavia 1525*

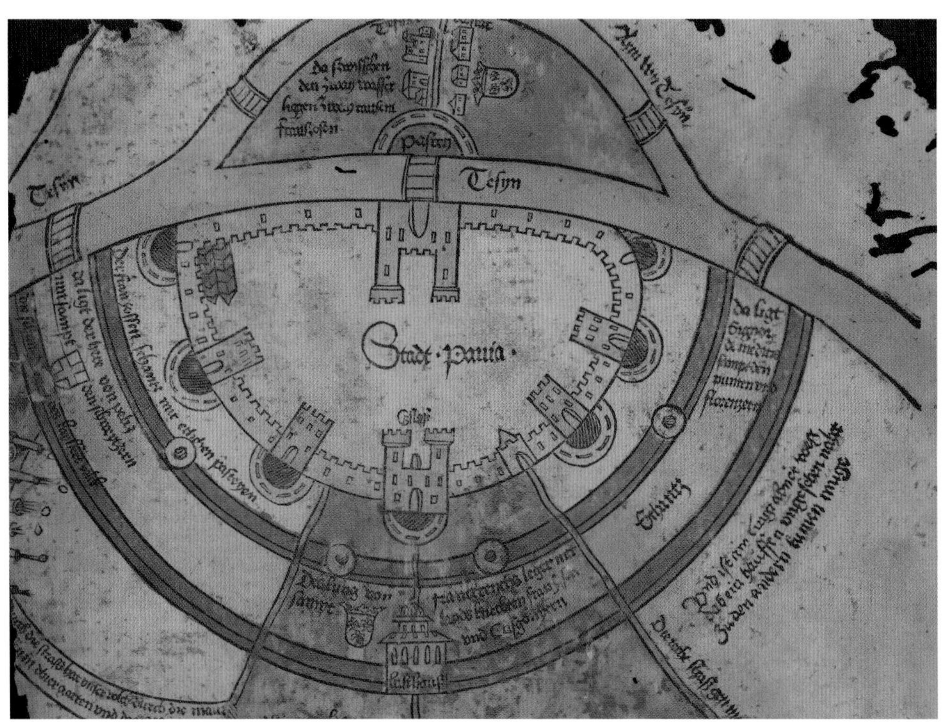

91 Spreading the News

Anon.

Plan of the siege and Battle of Pavia, Basel (?), 1525

British Library, Maps cc.5a.257

The Battle of Pavia created a sensation throughout Western Europe. The most widely reported battle of the Italian Wars, it spawned commemorative tapestries, medals, drawings, woodcuts and numerous paintings. Henry possessed at least two paintings, including *The Table of the Siege of Pavie*, a gift from the victorious Charles V, which is now in the Royal Armouries Museum in Leeds. Most depictions seem to derive from this woodcut plan, which only came to light, together with eleven other examples, in the 1990s, when it was found in the binding of a Basel book of 1529. Based on a sketch plan drawn and annotated on the spot, perhaps by a Swiss mercenary, it is one of the earliest known battle plans. It was sent to be printed in Basel and probably illustrated a news sheet. (PB)

LITERATURE: Sinistri and Casali, 'Il Ritrovamento della più antica pianta di Pavia'; Meuschel, *Antiquariat Achtzigster Katalog*; Barber, 'The Maps, Town-Views and Historical Prints in the Columbus Inventory'

92 The Amicable Grant

Letter from Archbishop William Warham to Cardinal Thomas Wolsey, 5 April 1525

British Library, Cotton MS Cleopatra F vi, fol.271

The crushing defeat of Francis I at Pavia revived Henry's martial ambitions. In order to finance an invasion of France, Henry asked his subjects to make what was called an 'Amicable Grant', a remarkably heavy financial demand not sanctioned by Parliament. Noblemen, leading gentry and churchmen were appointed as commissioners in the counties. In this letter written to Wolsey very soon after the demand was first made, Archbishop Warham, commissioner in Kent, reported considerable difficulties. The people spoke 'cursedly', complaining that they should have no rest from payments. Criticisms were being voiced of the King's foreign policy: all the sums that Henry had spent on invading France till then had not won a foot of land there. Warham regretted that 'this practesing with the people for soo greate sommes' had not been postponed until after the summer. In the event Henry backed down, claiming falsely that he had no knowledge of the level of its exaction. (GB)

LITERATURE: Bernard, *War, Taxation and Rebellion in Early Tudor England*; Gwyn, *The King's Cardinal*; Kelly, 'Canterbury Jurisdiction and Influence'

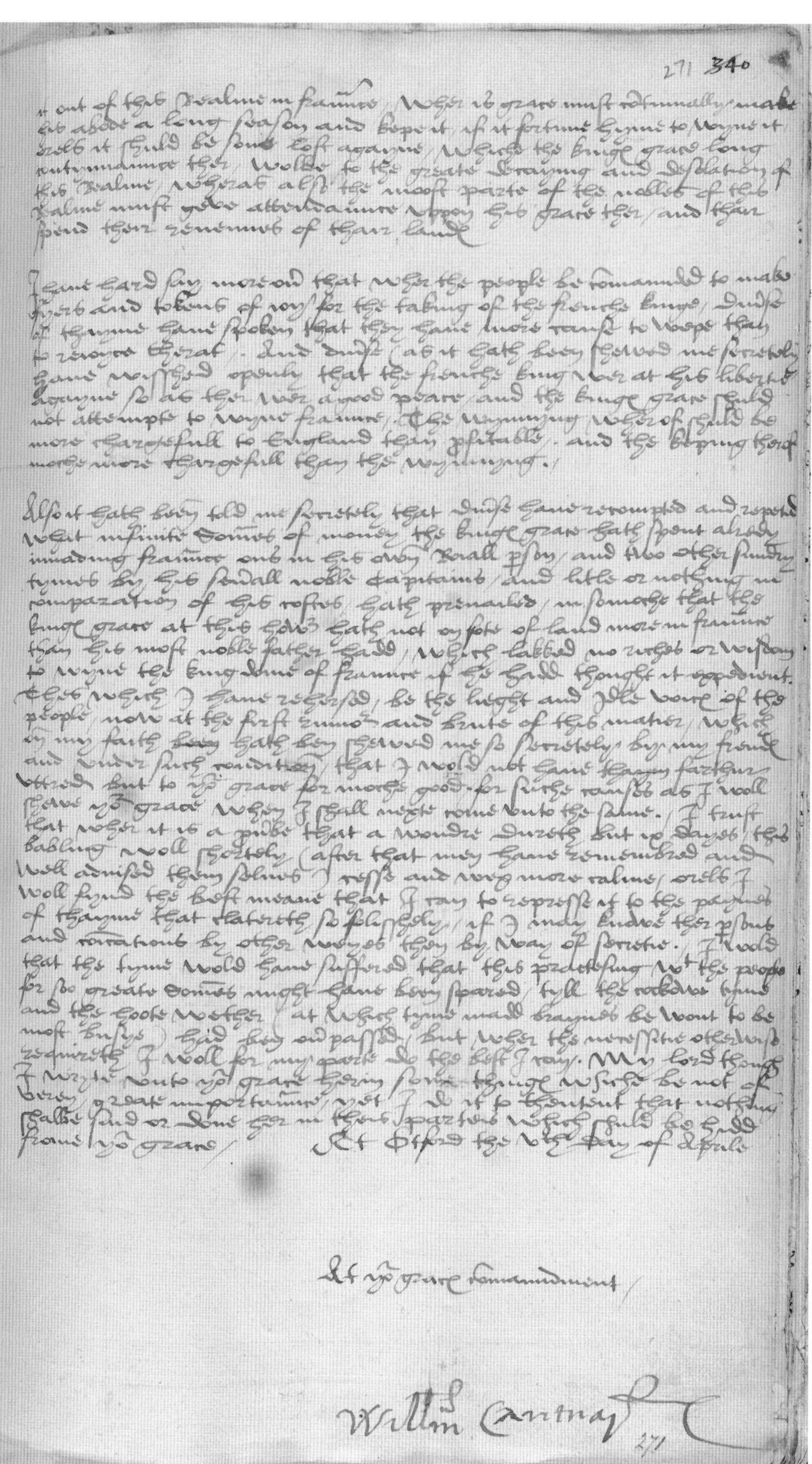

93 The Treaty of Amiens, 18 August 1527

The National Archives, Kew, Richmond, Surrey, E30/1109

This is the final confirmation of a series of agreements made in April and August 1527, which, together, constituted the 'eternal' or 'perpetual' peace made between Henry VIII and Francis I that year. It was brought to England in October by an embassy led by Anne de Montmorency, the *Grand Maître* of France. The illumination shows a portrait of Francis closely modelled on a painting of him made by Jean Clouet in 1526. It also features two examples of the King's badge, the salamander amid flames spitting water, and Francis's motto *'Nutrisco et extinguo'*. At the foot of the page the French royal arms are encircled by the collar of the chivalric Order of Saint-Michel, surmounted by a closed crown imperial and supported by two angels. With its pendant golden 'bulla' or seal in French Renaissance style, the treaty is arguably the finest diplomatic document preserved in the National Archives. (GR)

LITERATURE: Orth, 'A French Illuminated Treaty of 1527'; Mellen, *Jean Clouet*; Richardson, 'Eternal Peace, Occasional War: Anglo-French Relations under Henry VIII'

DEFENDER OF THE FAITH

Religion and war were the main concerns of princes during the 1520s. In 1517 Martin Luther (1483–1546), an Augustinian friar from Saxony, wrote 95 theses that objected to the sale of indulgences. Over the next three years Luther extended his attacks on the Church, criticizing many existing Church practices, denying the spiritual authority of the papacy and enunciating the theology of justification by faith alone. In January 1521 Pope Leo X (1475–1521) excommunicated Luther. The following year the heretic appeared before the Emperor Charles at Worms and was told to recant. When he refused, he was declared an outlaw and forced into hiding. Henry's support for the papacy and condemnation of Luther's doctrines earned him the title of *Fidei defensor*.

Numina cœlestem nobis peperere Lutherum,
Nostra diu maius secla videre nihil.
Quem si Pontificum crudelis deprimit error,
Non feret iratos impia terra Deos.

IHESVS.

MARTINVS LVTHERVS
August. Hermanno Tulichio suo
Salutem.

VELIM, nolim, cogor indies eruditior fieri, tot tantisq; magistris certatim me urgentibus & exercentibus. De indulgentijs ante duos annos scripsi: sed sic, ut me nunc mirum in modum pœniteat editi libelli. Herebam enim id temporis magna quadam superstitione Ro. tyrannidis, unde & indulgentias non penitus reijciendas esse censebam, quas tanto hominum consensu cernebam comprobari. Nec mirum: quia solus tum voluebã hoc saxũ. At postea, beneficio Syluestri & fratrum adiutus qui strennue illas tutati sunt, intellexi eas aliud non esse, quam meras adulatorum Romanorum imposturas, quibus & fidem dei, & pecunias hominum perderẽt. Atq; utinam a Bibliopolis queam impetrare, & omnibus qui legerunt persuadere, ut uniuersos libellos meos de indulgentijs exurant, & pro omnibus quæ de eis scripsi hanc propositionem apprehendant.

INDVLGENTIAE
sunt adulatorũ Romanorũ nequitiæ.

Post hæc, Eccius & Emser cum coniuratis suis, de primatu Papæ me erudire cœperunt. Atq; hic etiam, ne hominibus tam doctis ingratus sim, confiteor me valde promouisse eorum opera. Nempe, cum Papatum negassem diuini, admisi esse humani iuris. Sed ut audiui & legi subtilissimas subtilitates istorum Trossulorum, quibus suum idolum fabre statuunt (est enim mihi ingeniũ in his rebus non usquequaq; indocile) scio nunc & certus sum, Papatum esse regnum Babylonis, & potentiam Nimroth robusti venatoris. Proinde & hic, ut amicis meis omnia prosperrime cedant, oro librarios, oro lectores, ut ijs quę super hac re edidi exustis, hanc propositionem teneant.

PAPATVS EST ROBUSTA venatio Ro. Episcopi. Probatur, ex rationibus Eccianis, Emseranis, & Lipsensis Lectoris Biblici.

a ij

94 Martin Luther

Martin Luther, *De Captivitate Babylonica Ecclesiae* (On the Babylonian Captivity of the Church), 1520

British Library, 697.h.21, sig aii

On the Babylonian Captivity of the Church was the most incendiary of the three major reforming pamphlets written by Martin Luther in 1520. Addressed in Latin to the clergy, it challenged the traditional seven sacraments of the Church, claiming that only those proven by Scripture to have been instituted by Christ were true sacraments. This reduced the seven to three – Baptism, Eucharist and (with reservations) Penance. Luther went further in radically redefining the nature of these, most controversially of the Eucharist: he called for the laity to share the chalice, rejected transubstantiation and insisted that the Mass was a spiritual communion with Christ, rather than a sacrifice by the priest.

Luther's message spread quickly, with at least seven Latin and five German editions of the pamphlet published in 1520 alone. Both supporters and opponents recognized that the aggressive style and undermining of key Catholic doctrines made a breach with Rome inevitable. (SR)

LITERATURE: English text at: http://www.ctsfw.edu/etext/luther/babylonian/babylonian.htm; Bainton, *Here I Stand;* Edwards, *Printing, Propaganda and Martin Luther*

95 Henry VIII, *Assertio septem sacramentorum*, 1521

Biblioteca Apostolica Vaticana (Vaticano), Memb. III. 4, fol.2

Henry's elegant and lightly learned rebuttal of Martin Luther's *On the Babylonian Captivity of the Church* (1520) was composed by the King – with a little help from his friends – in the spring of 1521. It was printed in July and 30 copies were sent to Rome; one, richly bound in cloth of gold and with a handsomely illuminated title page, was intended for Pope Leo. Inside Henry ascribed a personal message to the Pope in Latin verse:

> Henry, King of the English, sends Leo the Tenth
>
> This work as witness of his faith and friendship.

The additional copies were intended for the cardinals and, like the one here shown, were signed by Henry. The work was formally presented to Leo X on 2 October 1521. In recognition of this contribution to the Church's campaign against Luther, Henry was awarded the title 'Defender of the Faith', thus fulfilling a longstanding ambition of his to have a sacred title to rival the 'Catholic King' of Spain and the 'Most Christian King' of France. (RR)

LITERATURE: Vian, 'La presentazione e gli esemplari Vaticani della Assertio Septem Sacramentorum di Enrico VIII'; Rex, 'The English Campaign against Luther in the 1520s'

SANCTISSIMO DOMINO NOSTRO
domino Leoni.X.pont.max. Henricus dei gra=
tia rex Angliæ, et Franciæ, ac domi=
nus Hyberniæ perpetu=
am felicita=
tem.

VVM PARTIM BEL=
licis, partim alijs longe diuer=
sis studijs, rei publicæ causa,
adolescentiam nostram insu=
euerimus, miraturum te bea=
tissime pater non dubitamus,
ꝙ eius nunc hominis partes
nobis sumpserimꝰ, qui omnē
potius ætatem consumpsisset in literis, ut grauem sci=
licet hæresim pullulantem cōprimamus. Sed desinet
(opinor) tua sanctitudo mirari postq̄ causas expen=
derit, quæ nos subegerunt, ut hoc scribendi onus (q̄q̄
nō ignari q̄ sumus impares) subierimus. Vidimus si=
quidem in messem domini iacta zizaniæ semina, pul=
lulare sectas, hæreses in fide succrescere, et tātam per
orbem totum christianum seminatam discordiæ ma=
teriam, ut nemo qui syncæra mēte christianus sit, hęc
tanta mala tam late serpētia, ferre diutius possit, quin
et studium cogatur, et uires qualescunq; possit, oppo=
nere. Mirum igitur uideri non debet, si nos quoq;, ta=
metsi potestate non maximi, fide tamen ac uolūtate
nemini secundi, in opus tam pium, tam utile, tam ne=
cessarium

ASSERTIO SEPTEM SA=
cramentorum aduersus Martin.
Lutherū, ædita ab inuictis=
simo Angliæ et Fran=
ciæ rege, et do. Hy=
berniæ Henri=
co eius no
minis
o=
ctauo.

96 Henry VIII, *Assertio septem sacramentorum adversus Martinum Lutherum*, 1521

British Library, 9.a.9, title page

Henry's *Assertio* was a best-seller, running to over a dozen editions in Latin and German by the end of 1524. Although printed by the middle of July 1521, it was kept under strict embargo until the work had been presented to the Pope, upon which presentation copies were circulated to select princes and prelates around Europe. Some later editions included the speech with which John Clerk, Henry's ambassador to Rome, had presented the book to the Pope, as well as the papal bull granting Henry his title 'Defender of the Faith'. Henry's was one of the few Catholic attacks to catch the eye of Luther himself, eliciting from him a bad-tempered response in the spring of 1522. In the 1530s, of course, the *Assertio* became an embarrassment, but while Henry claimed that he had been manoeuvred into writing it by his conniving bishops, it is revealing that he was unable to disown it entirely. (RR)

97 *Fidei Defensor*

Hans Schwartz (fl.1518–25)

Lead medal

British Museum, London, Department of Coins and Medals, M.6787 and M.6788

This unique lead medal of Henry VIII, made around 1524, has been attributed to the German medallist Hans Schwartz. It shows a bearded Henry in profile, wearing a hat with drapery looped under the brim, a cloak and a riband, from which a jewel or a medal would have hung around his neck. The reverse of the coin displays the Tudor rose and bears a double inscription in Latin: 'Its smell is like frankincense', and 'Defensor fidei', Henry's new papal title, which he was given as a reward for writing *Assertio septem sacramentorum*. (AC)

LITERATURE: Hawkins, Franks and Grueber, *Medallic Illustrations of the History of Great Britain and Ireland*; Hill and Pollard, *Medals of the Renaissance*

ANNA BOLLINA
VXOR HEN

THE TURNING POINT (1527–29)

Eric Ives

The year 1527 was the most decisive of Henry VIII's reign for three reasons. First, he started the process of having his marriage to Katherine of Aragon annulled by the Pope. Second, he claimed the annulment on the grounds that, in allowing him to marry Katherine, Pope Julius II had exceeded his authority. Third, at long last he secured from Anne Boleyn a promise that when he was free she would marry him. These three steps set the stage for the rest of his reign and the repercussions continued to be felt for the rest of the century.

In 16th-century aristocratic society, marriage was distinct from emotional/sexual satisfaction. Some couples found happiness but it was not expected. Marriage was concerned with property and producing legitimate offspring. Until 1527 Henry held this conventional view and, although he was not the sexual athlete he liked to imagine, he is known to have had two mistresses: Elizabeth Blount, who, in 1518, gave him his only illegitimate child, Henry Fitzroy, later Duke of Richmond; and Mary, the daughter of the courtier, Sir Thomas Boleyn.

However, at the end of 1521, Mary's younger sister Anne returned from nine years in the households of Margaret, Archduchess of Burgundy, and then of Claude, the Queen of France, courts recognized throughout Europe as the height of sophistication. Coupled with a sharp intelligence and a feisty personality, Anne, who had absorbed much of the continental style, took the provincial English court by storm. The initial plan was to marry her to the son of an Irish earl, but it came to nothing, possibly because of her attachment to Henry Percy, the Earl of Northumberland's son. It took until 1525 to force Percy to abandon Anne.

Other gallants such as Thomas Wyatt were also part of Anne's circle and, increasingly, the King, who made a coded announcement of his serious intentions at the Shrovetide festivities of 1526. The story of his growing passion is documented in a series of letters written by Henry to Anne, which are remarkable because they came from a man who disliked the chore of writing and because they revealed the King's intimate feelings. Anne resisted; she was determined to have a proper

◀ Cat. no. 105

aristocratic marriage, not the candle-flame life of a royal mistress. But the decision to replace Katherine changed everything. Henry realized that, by offering Anne marriage, he would resolve at a stroke his desire to sleep with her and his need for a second wife to give him the vital legitimate heir.

Henry had been concerned for some time by the lack of a male heir. Katherine might have believed that their daughter Mary would inherit, but Henry thought differently. In his view, England had never had a queen regnant; government was man's business and Mary's marriage would almost certainly lead to England becoming part of whatever continental power block supplied the husband. Time was not on Henry's side. In 1527 Katherine was past child-bearing age and he was thirty-six. In the most optimistic scenario – a new marriage that produced a son in 1528 or 1529 – he would be in his mid-fifties when the boy reached the age of eighteen. And would Henry survive that long? He had already outlived one grandfather, the other died at forty-one and his own father at the age of fifty-two. Being succeeded by a minor was becoming a very real possibility, and 'woe to the kingdom whose king is a child'. Something had to be done, and Henry took the first step in May 1527 by having Cardinal Wolsey call him to answer the charge that he was living in sin with the widow of his elder brother Arthur.

Marrying a brother's widow was contrary to Church law. Therefore, in order for Henry and Katherine to marry, a dispensation had to be obtained from the Pope. To annul the marriage, that dispensation had to be set aside. There were precedents for the Pope obliging rulers who had succession problems, but Henry did not take the usual route of exploiting some technicality. Instead, he sought an annulment on the grounds that Julius II had had no power to grant the 1509 dispensation in the first place. Marrying a deceased brother's widow was contrary to divine law as declared in the Bible (Leviticus 20: 21) and no Pope could ignore that. Why Henry decided to challenge papal power is explained by his psychological make-up. Deeply religious, he was convinced that as long as he devoutly served God – which he understood as believing creeds and observing Church rituals – God would look kindly on him. Yet, despite his devotion, he had no son, so he must have offended God in some way. Leviticus gave him the answer because it promised that if a brother and sister-in-law married, they would be childless, a term which one Hebrew scholar assured him meant 'sonless'. Only an annulment which recognized that initial sin could put him right with God, and only then could he expect a son.

In August 1527 Henry applied to Rome for a dispensation to allow him to marry Anne when he was free, despite his earlier relations with her sister. The couple clearly expected to marry within months, and emotional and sexual frustration explains the increasing bitterness of a struggle that actually took five years and more.

The emotional hold that Anne had on Henry was also important for another reason. Anne was deeply religious, but not as Henry was. At the French court, she had been strongly influenced by the prevailing atmosphere of evangelical reform which sought to promote a religion of personal experience, and back in England she kept in touch with these developments by collecting the works of French reforming divines. Evangelical reform was not openly – or even covertly – schismatic (as was Lutheranism). Instead, its emphasis was on Bible reading and personal piety. Nevertheless, it inevitably marginalized the importance of the Church machine, liturgical observance and papal authority. The result was that, as the Pope frustrated her marriage to Henry, Anne became a conduit for alternative ideas and strategies. In particular, soon after its publication in 1528, she introduced the King to William Tyndale's *The Obedience of a Christian Man*, which argued that 'one king, one law is God's ordinance in every realm'. Henry's reaction was 'this book is for me and all kings to read'.

Although Anne was in touch with radical ideas, initially she and Henry happily left prosecuting the annulment to Cardinal Wolsey. With a European reputation, he was the obvious choice. Anne's letters to the minister were full of confidence and the promise of reward, and progress did seem to be made. In the spring of 1528, Clement VII issued a commission empowering two legates, Wolsey and Lorenzo Campeggio, the Cardinal Protector of England, to hear the case. However, Clement's priority was Italy where Charles V, Katherine's nephew, was dominant after his army had sacked Rome in May 1527. Rome also believed that Henry's case was weak in law and, anyway, that the problem would go away when he got tired of Anne. Hence the Pope reserved the final decision and instructed Campeggio to delay. Anne, however, decided that Wolsey was playing a double game. The legatine court opened at Blackfriars on 31 May 1529 but got nowhere, and Campeggio abruptly adjourned it on 31 July.

Anne and her allies thereupon submitted to Henry a dossier of the Cardinal's misdeeds, but Henry was still under his spell and refused to act. The only positive step was a decision to mobilize international support by consulting the universities of Europe. During the summer, however, King and minister did fall out over how best to proceed. Wolsey struggled on for some weeks, but again the vultures gathered and in October 1529 he was charged with *praemunire* – infringing royal authority – dismissed as Lord Chancellor and put under house arrest. His fall marked the end of the first phase of the campaign to annul the Aragon marriage – what Henry called 'his Great Matter'. It had achieved nothing, but it did leave Anne even more firmly positioned to influence Henry. The time was ripe for radical thinking.

THE PROBLEM OF THE SUCCESSION

By 1525 Henry VIII was becoming very worried about the succession. Although Queen Katherine had been pregnant at least six times, she had suffered three stillbirths, as well as the death of two sons very soon after their births, in 1511 and 1513. Only Princess Mary, born in 1516, survived infancy. While Katherine groomed her to be a queen, Henry grew increasingly anxious at the prospect of a female succession. With his wife middle-aged and time running out, he even began to consider the possibility of making his illegitimate son, Henry Fitzroy, his heir, although he continued to treat Princess Mary as next in line for the throne. Two years later another solution presented itself to him – divorce and remarriage.

98 Concerns about the Succession

Salve radix: canon in honour of Henry VIII

British Library, Royal MS 11 E xi, fols 2v–3

Inscribed: 'Hail, root, bringing forth stems of different colours from your shoot, among which one stands out, from whose top there gleams a scarlet rose, where peace and justice stand enclosed and harmonious.'

This grand manuscript was prepared for Henry in 1516 by a successful Flemish merchant named Petrus de Opitiis. His son Benedictus wrote one of the motets found later in the volume, and became Henry's court organist in the same year. The six compositions are carefully chosen to reflect Henry's most pressing concern at the time, which was to ensure the perpetuation of the Tudor dynasty through the birth of a male heir. The first two pieces are tributes to Henry as the Tudor rose, symbol of the union of the Houses of York and Lancaster, and the four remaining motets all refer to the theme of childbirth. This piece is a canon (or round) for four voices: two voices sing the music as written and another two sing the same melody a perfect fourth higher, beginning when the first singers reach the points marked with a sign. (NB)

LITERATURE: Bell, *Music for King Henry*; Dumitrescu, *The Early Tudor Court and International Musical Relations*

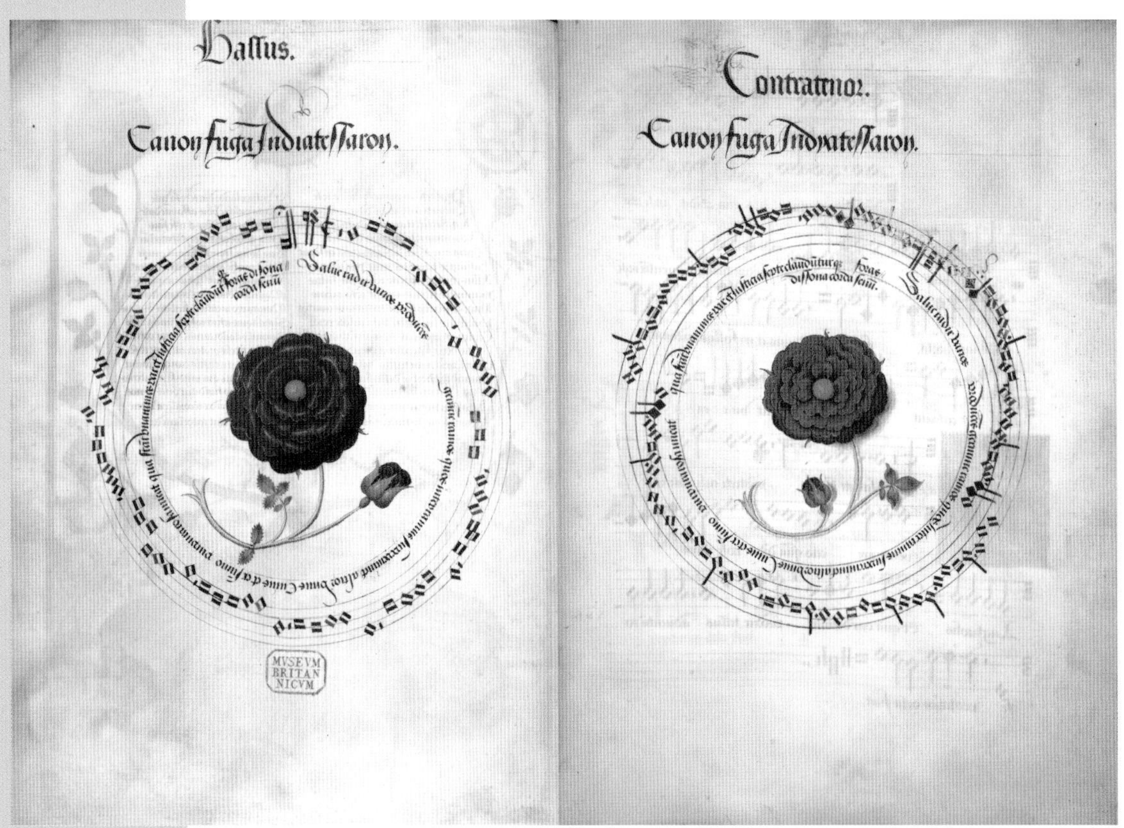

99 Hopes of a Male Heir Revived

Letter from Henry VIII to Thomas Wolsey, June 1518

British Library, Cotton MS Vespasian F iii, fol.73

Though disappointed at the sex of his new child, Princess Mary, born on 18 February 1516, Henry told the Venetian ambassador that he and Katherine were both young and that, by the grace of God, sons would follow. In this letter, written to Wolsey in June 1518, Henry confides that 'I trust the quene my wyffe be with chylde'. Henry explains that it was partly due to Katherine's 'dangerus tymes' that he was reluctant to allow her to travel to London from Woodstock, where they were staying. No doubt remembering past unhappy experiences, Henry adds: 'my lord I wrytt thys unto [you], nott as a ensuryd thyng, but as a thyng wherin I have grette hoppe and lyklyodes'. In November 1518, Henry's hopes for a legitimate male heir to ensure the Tudor succession were once again crushed when Katherine gave birth to a still-born girl. (AC)

LITERATURE: Wooding, *Henry VIII*

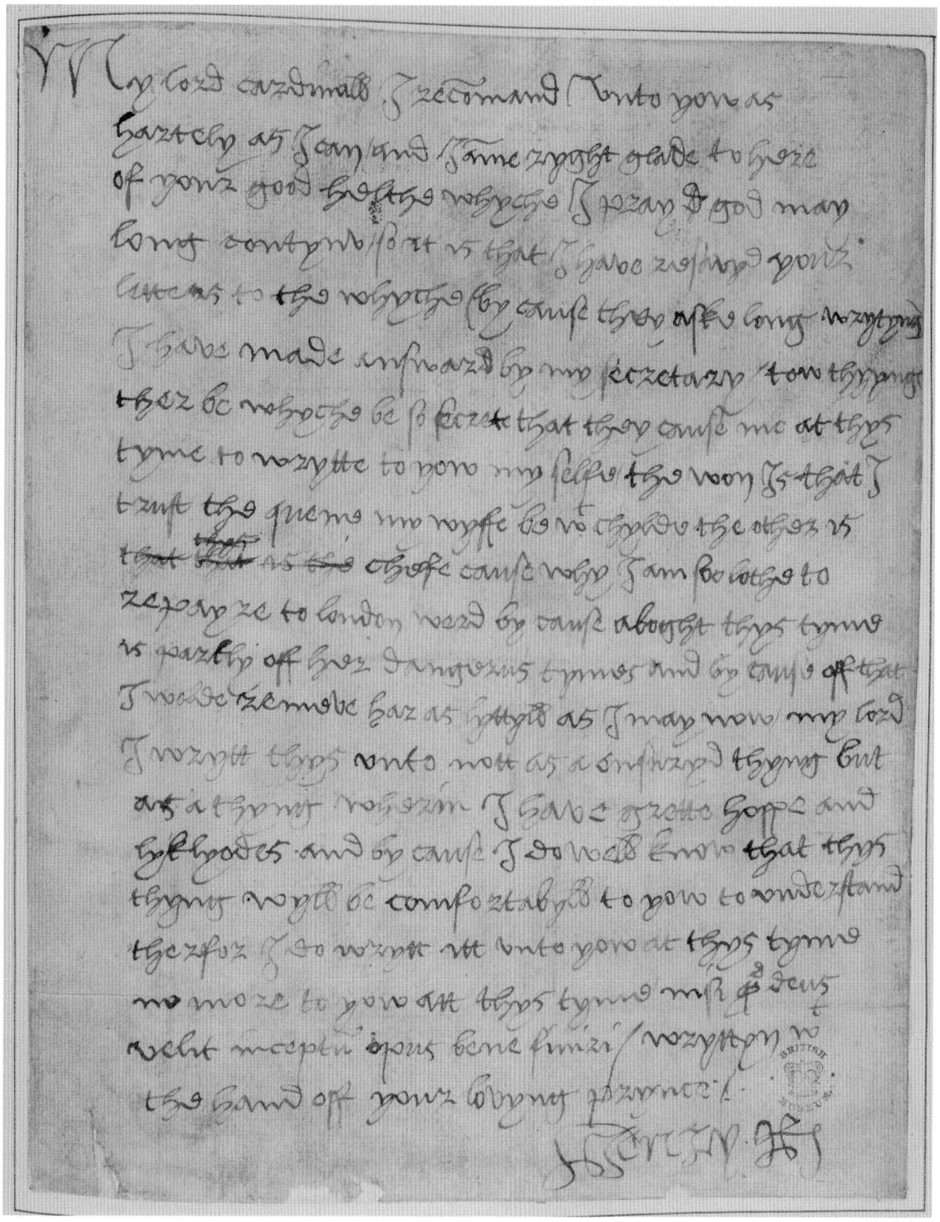

My lord cardinall I recomand unto you as
hartely as I can and I am ryght glade to here
of your good helthe whyche I pray God may
long contynew. So it is that I have resayvyd your
lettres to the whyche by cause they aske long wrytyng
I have made answard by my secretary. Tow thyngs
ther be whyche be so secrete that they cause me at thys
tyme to wrytte to you my selfe. The won is that I
trust the quene my wyffe be with chylde. The other is
the chefe cause why I am so lothe to
repayre to London ward by cause abought thys tyme
is partly off her dangerus tymes and by cause off that
I wolde remeve her as lyttyll as I may now. My lord
I wrytt thys unto nott as a ensuryd thyng but
as a thyng wherin I have grette hoppe and
lyklyodes and by cause I do well know that thys
thyng wyll be comfortabyll to yow to understand
therfor I do wrytt itt unto yow at thys tyme.
No more to yow att thys tyme nisi quod Deus
velit inceptum opus bene finiri. Wryttyn with
the hand off your lovyng prince.
Henry R.

100 Henry's Natural Son: Lord Henry Fitzroy (1519–36)

Letter from Henry Fitzroy, Duke of Richmond, to Cardinal Thomas Wolsey, from Sheriff Hutton Castle, Yorkshire, 4 March [1526?]

British Library, Cotton MS Vespasian F iii, fol.44

Although Henry's marriage produced no male heir, his short liaison with Elizabeth Blount resulted in the birth of a son. Called 'Lord Henry Fitzroy' to signify his blood relationship with the King, the child lived in the household of his godfather Wolsey until 1525. Then Fitzroy's life changed: he was raised to the peerage on 18 June 1525 and soon afterwards sent to Sheriff Hutton Castle in Yorkshire as head of his own household and the King's Lord Lieutenant. Henry was probably considering the possibility of making him his legitimate heir in the future. In any case, the child's titles – Richmond and Somerset – had once been held by Henry VII and Margaret Beaufort's father respectively. In the north until 16 June 1529, Fitzroy wrote regularly to his father. This letter to Wolsey was probably a writing exercise, as he says 'a demonstracion off thys my proceding in writinge'. (SD)

LITERATURE: Murphy, *Bastard Prince*

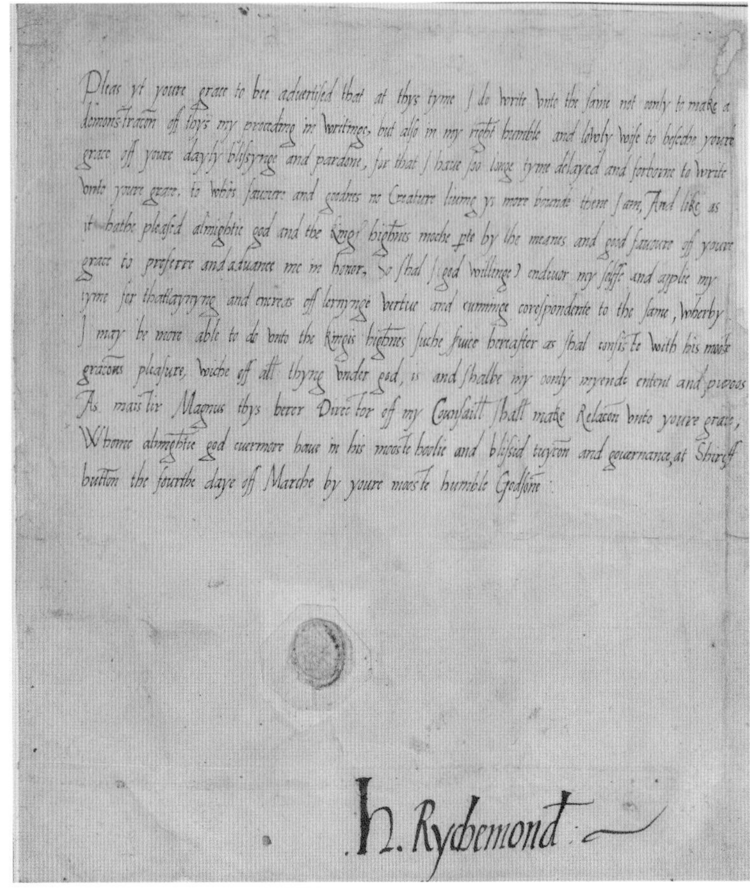

Pleas yt youre grace to bee aduertised that at thys tyme I do write vnto the same not oonly to make a demonstracon off thys my proceding in writinge, but also in my right humble and lowly wyse to beseche youre grace off youre dayly blissynge and pardone, for that I haue soo longe tyme delayed and forborne to write vnto youre grace, to whos fauour and goodnes no Creature liuing ys more bounde then I am, And like as it hathe pleased almightie god and the kings highnes moche pte by the meanes and good fauoure off youre grace to preferre and aduance me in honor, So shal I (god willinge) endeuor my selffe and applie my tyme for thattaynynge and encreas off lernynge vertue and cunninge corespondente to the same, wherby I may be more able to do vnto the kingis highnes suche suice hereafter as shal consiste with his moost gracous pleasure, whiche off all thynge vnder god, is and shalbe my oonly myende entent and puroos As maister Magnus thys berer Director off my Counsaill shall make Relacon vnto youre grace, Whome almightie god euermore haue in his mooste hoolie and blissid tuycon and gouernance, at Shirefhutton the fourthe daye off Marche by youre mooste humble Godsone

h. Rychemond

101 Henry's Legitimate Daughter: Princess Mary

Letter from Katherine of Aragon to Princess Mary, October 1525

British Library, Cotton MS Vespasian F xiii, fol.140

Soon after Fitzroy was sent north, the nine-year-old Princess Mary was taken to live at Ludlow Castle, Shropshire. This move was intended to signal that she, like previous Princes of Wales, was being prepared as a future ruler of England. Clearly, Henry had not yet made up his mind about the succession. Although Katherine was pleased at this recognition of Mary's status, this intimate letter indicates her maternal distress at their separation. The move meant Mary acquired a new tutor, Richard Featherstone, apparently a good choice as he held that position for some eight years, and Mary's Latin was agreed to be sound. Katherine had previously supervised her daughter's Latin studies herself, and wanted to continue to see examples of her work. That is a reminder that Henry's first, and Spanish, Queen was reputedly the first laywoman in England to be well educated in Latin. At the end of the letter written on a Friday night, Katherine prays 'you to my Lady of Salisbury'; Margaret Pole, Countess of Salisbury, had been recently appointed Mary's governess. (JR and SD)

LITERATURE: Richards, *Mary Tudor*; Loades, *Mary Tudor*; Elston, 'Transformation or Continuity'

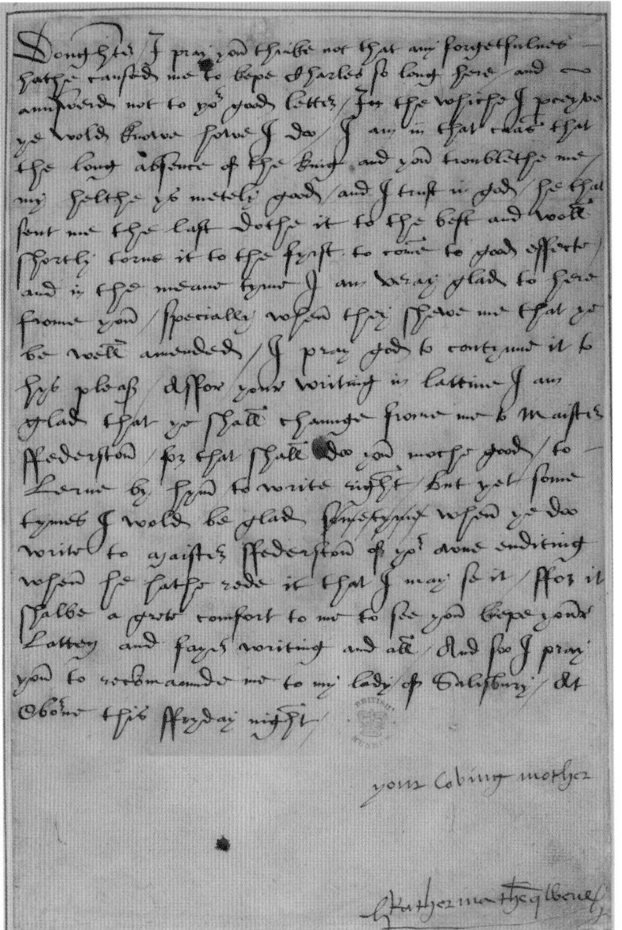

Doughter I pray you thinke not that any forgetfulnes hath caused me to kepe Charles so long here and answered not to your good letter / In the which I perceyve ye wold know howe I do / I am in that case that the long absence of the king and you troublethe me / my helthe is metely good / and I trust in god he that sent me the last dothe it to the best and woll shortly torne it to the first to come to good effect / and in the meane tyme I am very glad to here frome you / specially when they shew me that ye be well amended / I pray god to contynue it to his pleasure / As for your writing in lattine I am glad that ye shall change frome me to maister Federston / for that shall do you moche good to lerne by hym to write right / but yet some tymes I wold be glad when ye do write to maister Federston of your owne enditing when he hathe rede it that I may se it / ffor it shalbe a gret comfort to me to se you kepe your lattyn and fayr writing and all / And so I pray you to recommande me to my lady of Salisbury / At Woborn this ffryday night

Your loving mother

Katherina the qwene

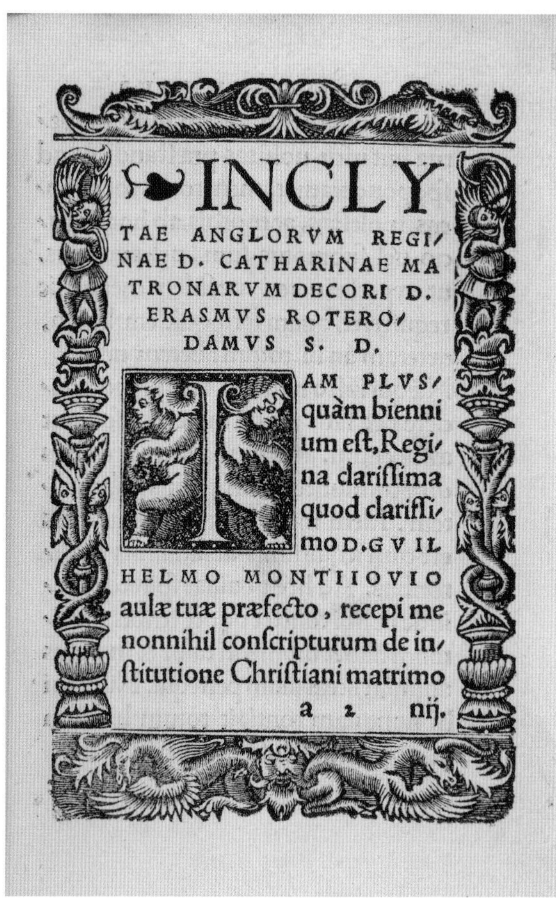
INCLY
TAE ANGLORVM REGI-
NAE D. CATHARINAE MA
TRONARVM DECORI D.
ERASMVS ROTERO-
DAMVS S. D.
IAM PLVS-
quàm bienni
um eſt, Regi-
na clariſſima
quod clariſſi-
mo D. GVIL
HELMO MONTIIOVIO
aulæ tuæ præfecto, recepi me
nonnihil conſcripturum de in-
ſtitutione Chriſtiani matrimo
a 2 nij.

102 On Christian Marriage

Erasmus, *Christiani matrimonii Institutio*, 1526

British Library, G.12018, sig a2

In 1524 Erasmus promised William Blount, Lord Mountjoy, the Queen's Chamberlain, that he would compose something on Christian marriage, presumably to complement the *De institutione feminae Christianae* (*The Education of a Christian Woman*) written by Juan Luis Vives for Princess Mary's instruction and published in that year. According to a letter written early in 1526, he was hard at work on the tract that had been requested by Katherine herself, 'a woman both pious and learned'. Dedicated to her, he considered her union to be 'the perfect model of a most holy and blessed marriage'. Displaying a remarkable knowledge of marriage law, *Christiani matrimonii Institutio* anticipates later debates when it maintains that union with one's sister-in-law is not grounds for the dissolution of a marriage. Although Thomas More claimed that Katherine was well pleased with the *Institutio*, she forgot to send Erasmus any reward for his efforts until he discreetly reminded her to do so in 1528. By then the annulment proceedings were underway. (JC)

LITERATURE: Sowards, 'Erasmus and the Education of Women'; Carley, *The Books of King Henry VIII and his Wives*

103 Katherine of Aragon in Middle Age

Unknown British School, probably late 16th or early 17th century

Merton College, Oxford, MCP065

At forty-two-years old, Katherine was past child-bearing age when Henry began proceedings to annul their marriage in 1527. Although she continued to live in the royal apartments for several years afterwards, her relationship with Henry became increasingly acrimonious, for she refused to co-operate with his plans. She claimed her marriage to Henry did not contravene the laws of affinity because she had never had sexual intercourse with his brother. Additionally, she would not enter a convent to allow Henry to marry again. On 11 July 1531 Katherine saw her husband for the last time. She was then described as being 'rather small' and 'somewhat stout' but 'always with a smile on her countenance'. Several double portraits, showing her alongside Henry, existed in the 16th century – one even recorded among Katherine's possessions at her death – but all have apparently been lost. This portrait, showing the Queen wearing a large jewelled cross and stiff English jewelled hood, was probably once part of a larger set portraying kings and queens of England and Wales produced in the late Elizabethan or early Jacobean periods. It derives from an earlier image now lost. (TC and SD)

LITERATURE: Strong, *Tudor and Jacobean Portraits*; Kelly, *The Matrimonial Trials of Henry VIII*

ANNE BOLEYN

When Anne Boleyn (1501?–36), the daughter of Thomas Boleyn and niece of the 3rd Duke of Norfolk, arrived at court from France she attracted a lot of attention. Among her admirers were Henry Percy (later Earl of Northumberland) and the poet Thomas Wyatt. Some time in 1526 Henry fell in love with her, and, after she refused to follow her sister Mary's example of becoming a royal mistress, he sought to marry her. By this time he had ceased to have sexual relations with Katherine, and now he hoped for a son with Anne. It was probably in January 1527 that Anne agreed to be his wife. In the spring of the same year, Henry revealed his doubts – his 'scruple of conscience' – about the validity of his first marriage.

104 Acts of the Apostles and Book of Revelation

Collection of the Most Hon. the Marquess of Salisbury, Hatfield House, Hertfordshire, Cecil Papers MS 324, fol.4

This fine manuscript was produced for Henry VIII in the final years of his marriage to Katherine. Its opening page includes his heraldic arms and devices: the crowned arms of England, supported by a red dragon and white greyhound; two Tudor red-and-white roses over sunbursts; the linked initials H and K; a large gold fleur-de-lis on a blue ground and the Beaufort badge of the portcullis. The initials and portcullis are set on dimidiated ground of the Tudor livery colours of green and silver (here white). A lavishly painted illustration of St Luke, the supposed author of the Acts of the Apostles, heads the beginning of two parallel Latin texts. In the left-hand column is the Vulgate of St Jerome and, in the right, the translation of Acts by Erasmus. Apparently made to complete a New Testament begun for John Colet, this large and opulent manuscript was, like its companions, intended for the lectern, to be displayed and read out loud. (SMcK)

LITERATURE: Trapp, *Erasmus, Colet and More*; Kren and McKendrick, *Illuminating the Renaissance*

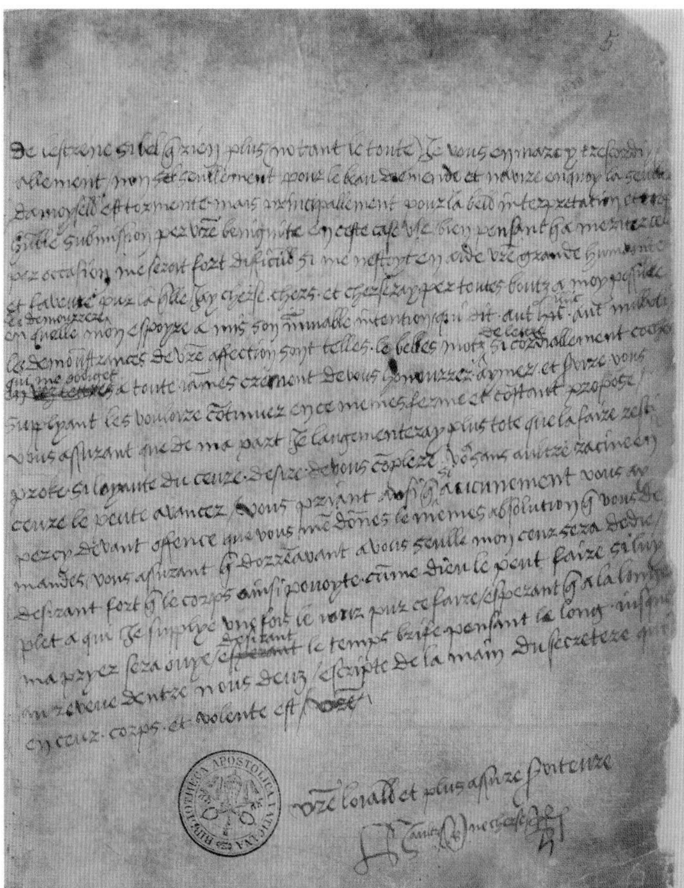

105 Anne Boleyn

Unknown British School, 17th century

Dean and Chapter of Ripon Cathedral

Inscribed: *'Anna Bolina Vxor Henrici-Octa'* [Anne Boleyn, wife of Henry VIII]

This painting is an example of the standard likeness of Anne and probably belonged to one of the sets of royal portraits that English gentry liked to display in order to demonstrate loyalty. The likeness corresponds to the only contemporary likeness of Anne, a portrait medal in the British Museum, London, and is confirmed by comparison with a tiny enamel of her, owned by Elizabeth I, now at Chequers. Thus this portrait must ultimately derive from a lost original taken from life. Other examples of the standard likeness give Anne a more sallow complexion, something noted by her contemporaries, so indicating that this portrait has been somewhat 'glamorized', a process that is taken further in subsequent copies. Anne's allure came from her personality, education and style, not from her good looks. (EI)

LITERATURE: Ives, *The Life and Death of Anne Boleyn*

106 A Love Letter from Henry VIII to Anne Boleyn, 1527

Biblioteca Apostolica Vaticana (Vaticano), Vat. Lat. 3731A, fol.5

Henry VIII hated having to write. His seventeen letters to Anne Boleyn are thus an index of his passion and his relentless pursuit of her over, perhaps, eighteen months. Some are in English, the rest (as here) in French. How they ended up in the Vatican we do not know, though probably it was as (damning) evidence against his divorce suit. In this climactic letter, Henry erupts in gratitude at a signal from Anne that at long last she is ready to marry him. She had sent a specially made trinket: a ship (no doubt, in enamel), tossing on waves and crewed by a single girl, with a diamond (presumably a pendant). The meaning was transparent. The ship was a centuries-old symbol of protection; a diamond spoke of steadfastness. Henry replied: 'The proofs of your affection are such … that they constrain me ever truly to honour, love and serve you'. But when did Henry and Anne pledge their troth? Like the others in the series, this letter is undated. But the fact that Anne's gift was 'une étrenne' – a New Year's Day gift – pins it down to January 1527. A few weeks later, Henry launched the first trial of his marriage before Cardinal Wolsey and he and Anne clearly expected to be free to wed within months. Neither could guess that it would take more than five years. (EI and DS)

LITERATURE: Starkey, *Six Wives*

107 Henry VIII's Writing Desk

Victoria and Albert Museum, London, W.29:1– 9–1932

This beautifully decorated portable writing desk is one of the few luxury items to have survived from Henry's court. Made of walnut and covered with painted and gilded leather, the desk displays the royal arms, supported by putti and flanked by Mars, the Roman god of war, and Venus, the goddess of love, with her son Cupid. Henry and Katherine's initials and the pomegranate of Granada and arrow-sheaf of Aragon, both personal symbols of Katherine, also form part of the decoration. The various drawers and compartments in the desk would have been used to store the King's writing equipment, although, as he once confessed to Wolsey, he found writing letters 'tedious and painful' and therefore reserved it for matters of great importance. Made before 1527, this desk may well be the one that Henry used to write his love letters to Anne Boleyn.

As he grew older, and became more deeply involved in the detail of policy, Henry wrote more and more, and writing desks, pens, pencils and spectacles were to be found in quantity in all his principal palaces. (AC and DS)

LITERATURE: Starkey (ed.), *Inventory*

108 Messages between Henry VIII and Anne Boleyn

Book of Hours, *c.*1528, Southern Netherlands (Bruges)

British Library, Kings MS 9, fols 231v (right), 66v (above)

Henry and the court regularly attended Mass in the royal chapel, sometimes more than once a day. The King often used the time before the consecration to transact business, but this manuscript shows him using a book of prayers to send a flirtatious message to Anne Boleyn instead. He wrote in French: 'If you remember my love in your prayers as strongly as I adore you, I shall hardly be forgotten, for I am yours. Henry R. forever.' Presenting himself as lovesick, he wrote his note on a page depicting the man of sorrows. Anne replied with a couplet in English:

> Be daly prove you shall me fynde
> To be to you bothe lovynge and kynde.

And, with deliberate enticement, she chose to write her message below a miniature of the Annunciation, the angel telling the Virgin Mary that she would have a son. (EI)

LITERATURE: Ives, *The Life and Death of Anne Boleyn*; Carley, *The Books of King Henry VIII and his Wives*

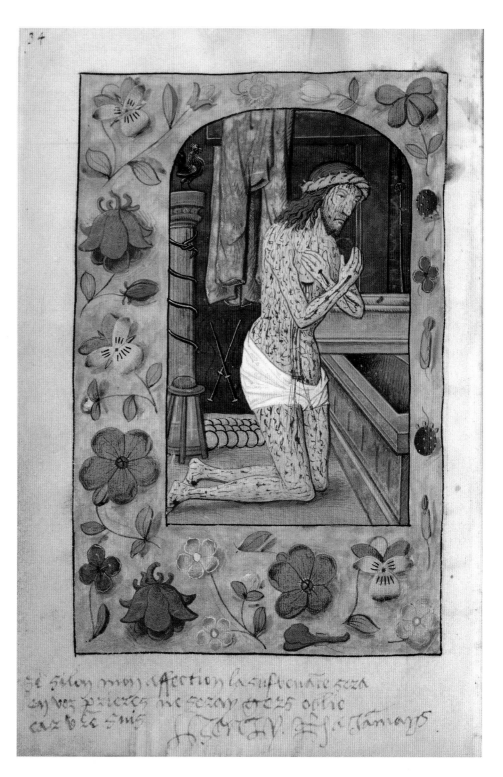

THE STRUGGLE FOR THE ANNULMENT

In May 1527 Cardinal Wolsey began proceedings for the annulment of Henry VIII's marriage to Katherine. Wolsey and Archbishop Warham presided over a secret court that charged the King with cohabiting with his brother's widow in contravention of Scripture. Henry's hopes for a quick annulment were dashed, however, when Katherine's nephew Charles V sacked Rome and held the Pope prisoner. Pope Clement VII could not now be trusted to confirm the verdict of Wolsey's legatine court were Katherine to appeal to Rome. Consequently, over the next two years, Wolsey tried to secure an agreement from the Pope that English judges could make the final decision on the case. At the same time, Wolsey gathered evidence in support of the annulment.

At last, on 18 June 1529, a legatine court opened at Blackfriars to consider Henry's matrimonial case. Wolsey was one of the presiding judges; the other was the papal legate, Cardinal Campeggio. At the first session, Katherine announced her appeal to Rome, and at the second she called upon Henry to withdraw the case or let it be heard in Rome; she did not reappear again. On 31 July, Campeggio adjourned the case until 1 October. However, before the court could reconvene, the Pope transferred the case to Rome.

109 A Commentary on Leviticus

British Library, Royal MS 1 E iv, fol.159v

One of the manuscripts brought to the Royal Library during these years was a 13th-century glossed copy of the Book of Leviticus from St Augustine's Canterbury which contains an interpolated passage in 18: 16 to the effect that 'Nobody may marry his brother's wife'. This passage, marked by a manicule in the margin, was much debated by contemporary scholars: those supporting Katherine pointed out that it did not appear in the Hebrew and Greek texts, while those in the other camp argued that it formed part of the Arabic tradition. John Stokesley, future Bishop of London, one of the compilers of the collection of arguments submitted at the Blackfriars trial under Henry's own name, made much of the fact that the Pope had overstepped his authority by condoning a marriage which transgressed divine law as articulated in these words. This 'ancient' manuscript was later stored at Westminster and has the characteristic inventory number, No. 982. (JC)

LITERATURE: Carley, *The Libraries of King Henry VIII*; Chibi, *'Turpitudinem uxoris fratris tui non revelavit'*

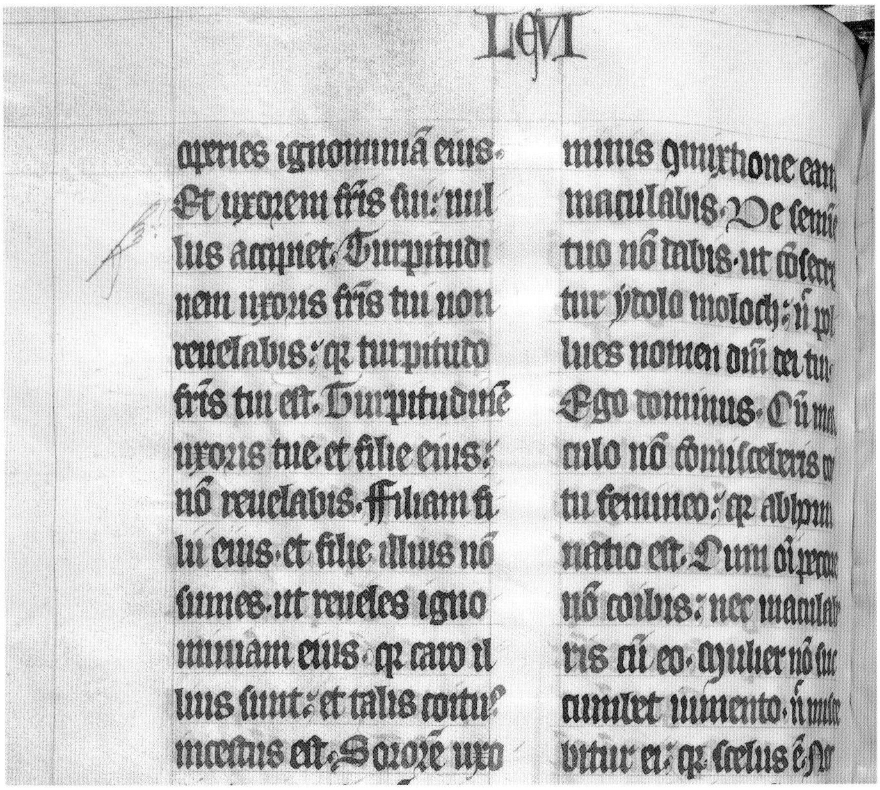

LEVI

aperies ignominiã eius.
Et uxorem fr̃is tui: nul
lus accipiet. Turpitudi
nem uxoris fr̃is tui non
reuelabis: q͛ turpitudo
fr̃is tui est. Turpitudinẽ
uxoris tue et filie eius:
nõ reuelabis. Filiam fi
lii eius. et filie illius nõ
sumes. ut reueles igno
miniam eius. q͛ caro il
lius sunt: et talis coitu͛
incestus est. Sororẽ uxo

minis commixtione eam
maculabis. De semi
tuo nõ dabis. ut consecre
tur ydolo moloch: n̄ pol
lues nomen dñi dei tui.
Ego dominus. Cũ ma
sculo nõ commisceberis co
itu femineo: q͛ abhomi
natio est. Cum oĩ pecore
nõ coibis: nec maculabe
ris cũ eo. Mulier nõ suc
cumbet iumento. n̄ misce
bitur ei: q͛ scelus ẽ. Ne

110 Wolsey's Efforts to Obtain an Annulment

Letter from Anne Boleyn to Cardinal Wolsey, *c.*1528–9

British Library, Cotton MS Vespasian F xiii, fol.141

When Anne Boleyn and Henry agreed to marry, they turned to Wolsey to secure from the Pope a decree annulling Henry's marriage to Katherine of Aragon. Outstandingly able and renowned as a diplomat, the Cardinal was the obvious person on whom to rely. He in turn sought to keep on the right side of Anne and inform her of progress. In this reply, from early in the proceedings, she gives Wolsey 'humble thankes for the gret payn and travell that your grace doth take' and promises him favour in the future: 'I assewer you that after this matter is brought to pas you shall fynd me, as I am bownd in the meane tym, to owe you my servyse, and then looke what thyng in this woreld I can in magen to do you pleasor in you shall fynd me the gladdyst woman in the woreld to do yt.' The language shows how at the start Anne saw herself as the suppliant and Wolsey as the benefactor. (EI)

LITERATURE: Ives, *The Life and Death of Anne Boleyn*; Gwyn, *The King's Cardinal*; Wooding, *Henry VIII*

141

My lord after my most humble recomendacions this shall be to gyve unto yor grace as I am most bownd my humble thankes for the gret payn and travell that yor grace doth take in sterdyeng by yor wysdome and gret dylygens howe to bryng to pas honerably the gretyst welth that is possyble to com to any creator lyvyng and in especyall remembryng howe wretchyd and unworthy I am in comparyng to his hyghnes and for you I do knowe my self never to have deservyd by my desertes that you shuld take this gret payn for me yet dayly of yor goodnes I do perceyve by all my frends and though that I hade nott knowlege by them the dayly proffe of yor deds doth declare yor words and wrytyng toward me to be trewe nowe good my lord yor dyscressyon may consyder as yet how lytle it is in my power to recompence you but all onely wt my good wyll the whiche I assewer you that after this matter is brought to pas you shall fynd me as I am bownd in the meane tym to owe you my servyse and then looke what thyng in this woreld I can in magen to do you pleasor in you shall fynd me the gladdyst woman in the woreld to do yt and next unto the kynges grace of one thyng I make you full promes to be assewryd to have yt and that is my harty love unfaynydly deveryng my lyf and beyng fully determynd wt godds grace never to change thys purpos I make anend of thys my rude and trewe meanyd letter prayng owre lord to send you moche incres of honor wt long lyfe wrytten wt the hand of her that besechys yor grace to except this letter as prosydyng from one that is most bownd to be

From Mrs Anne Bullen before her Mariadg to the King

yor humble and obedient servant

anne boleyn

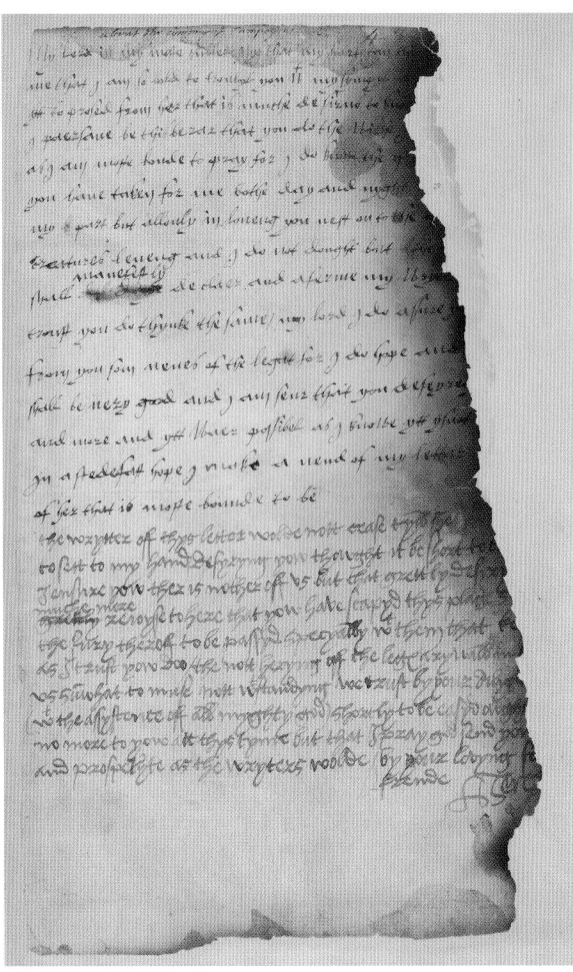

111 Awaiting Cardinal Campeggio's Arrival at the Legatine Court

Letter from Anne Boleyn and Henry VIII to Cardinal Wolsey, August 1528

British Library, Cotton MS Vitellius B xii, fol.4

This autograph letter (partially burned) was written at the start of August 1528, when the ending of the epidemic of sweating sickness allowed Anne to rejoin Henry. In the upper part Anne sent good wishes to Cardinal Wolsey, expressed her debt to him and asked for news about the progress of Cardinal Campeggio, the papal legate who (with Wolsey) was to hear Henry's suit for the annulment of his marriage. Anne then handed the letter to Henry and nagged him to complete it: 'The wrytter of thys letter wolde nott cease tyll she [had caused me likewise] to sett to my hand; desyryng yow, thowght it be short, to [take it in good part].' The King also made clear that the couple were worried because no news had reached England about Campeggio even arriving in France. The joint letter clearly demonstrates that Henry's second marriage was based on mutual affection, a rarity among royal marriages, which were almost always with foreign brides for diplomatic reasons. (EI)

LITERATURE: Ives, *The Life and Death of Anne Boleyn*

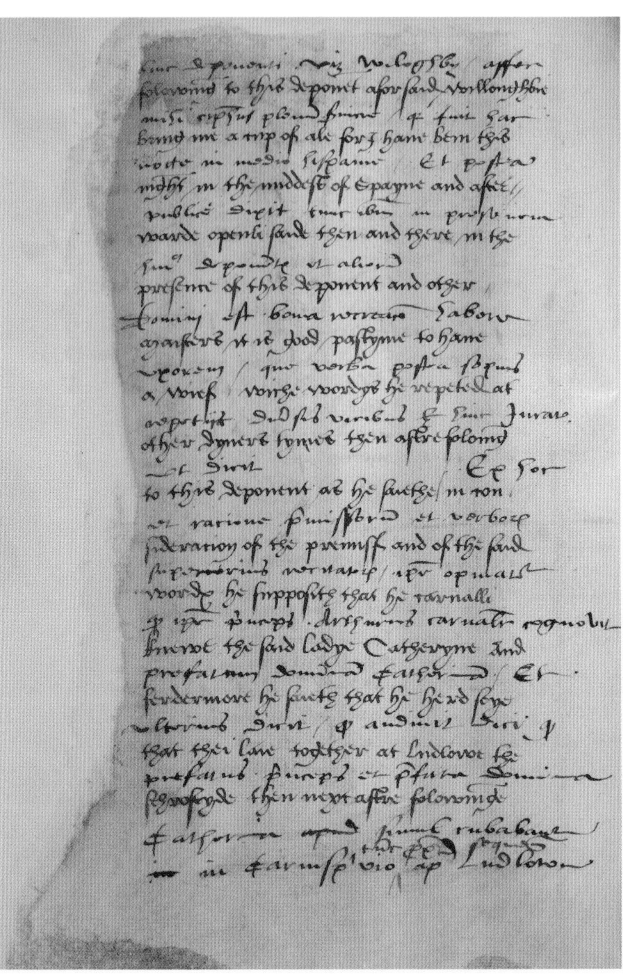

112 Was Katherine's First Marriage Consummated?

British Library, Cotton MS Vitellius B xii, fol.85v

In preparation for the legatine tribunal, a series of depositions were collected from those who had looked after Prince Arthur on his wedding night in order to provide evidence that his marriage to Katherine had been consummated and thus demonstrate that the original papal dispensation that permitted Henry and Katherine's marriage to take place was invalid. This testimony belongs to Sir Anthony Willoughby, a body servant of Arthur's, who stated that the following morning the newly wed prince ordered him to 'bring me a cup of ale, for I have ben this night in the middest of Spayne' and then declared to all present 'Maisters, it is good pastyme to have a wief'. Katherine always denied that her marriage to Arthur had been consummated and, in his deposition, Nicholas West, Bishop of Ely, who was present at the marriage of Arthur and Katherine, stated that the Queen had often told him on the testimony of her conscience, *'quod [non] fuit carnaliter a dicto Arthuro cognita'*. (AC)

LITERATURE: Kelly, *The Matrimonial Trials of Henry VIII*; Starkey, *Henry VIII: The Virtuous Prince*

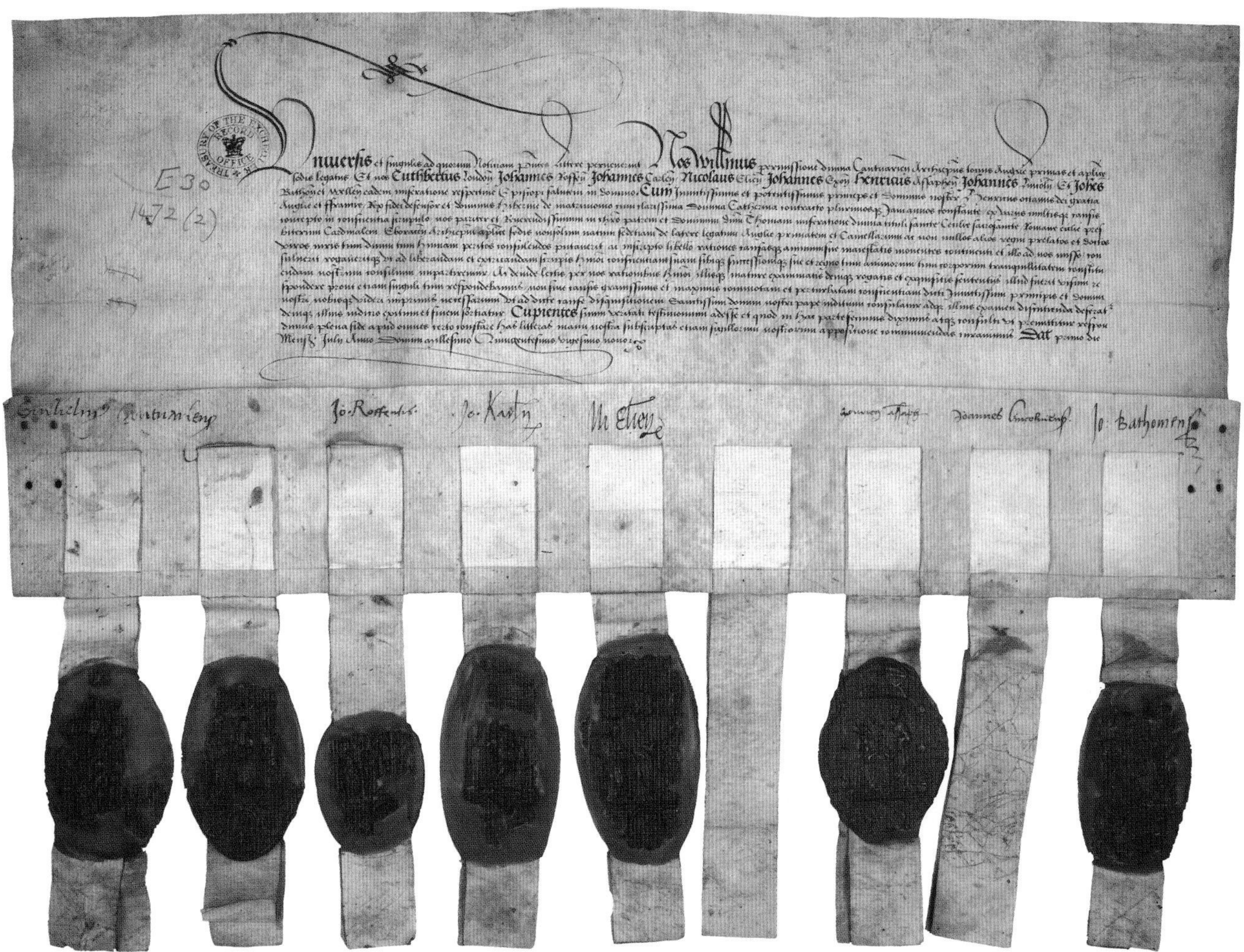

113 Henry VIII's 'Scruple of Conscience'

The National Archives, Kew, Richmond, Surrey, E30/1472/2

This is Henry's registration of his 'scruple of conscience', dated 1 July 1529 and listed among the documents exhibited at the legatine court. The document states that the undersigned prelates – Archbishop Warham, Bishops Tunstall, West, Standish, Fisher, Clerk, Voysey, Kite and Longland – had been consulted about the validity of Henry's marriage to Katherine, agreed that the King had cause for concern and that he should seek the Pope's judgement on the matter. According to George Cavendish's 'Life of Wolsey', the licence caused considerable controversy during the legatine trial when John Fisher, Bishop of Rochester, and one of the Queen's counsellors, claimed that his seal and signature (third from the left) had been forged. Although Henry dismissed Fisher's protest with the words, 'Well, it shall make no matter. We will not stand on argument herein, for you are but one man,' Fisher succeeded in raising questions about the integrity of Henry's advisers. (AC)

LITERATURE: Kelly, *The Matrimonial Trials of Henry VIII;* Bernard, *The King's Reformation*

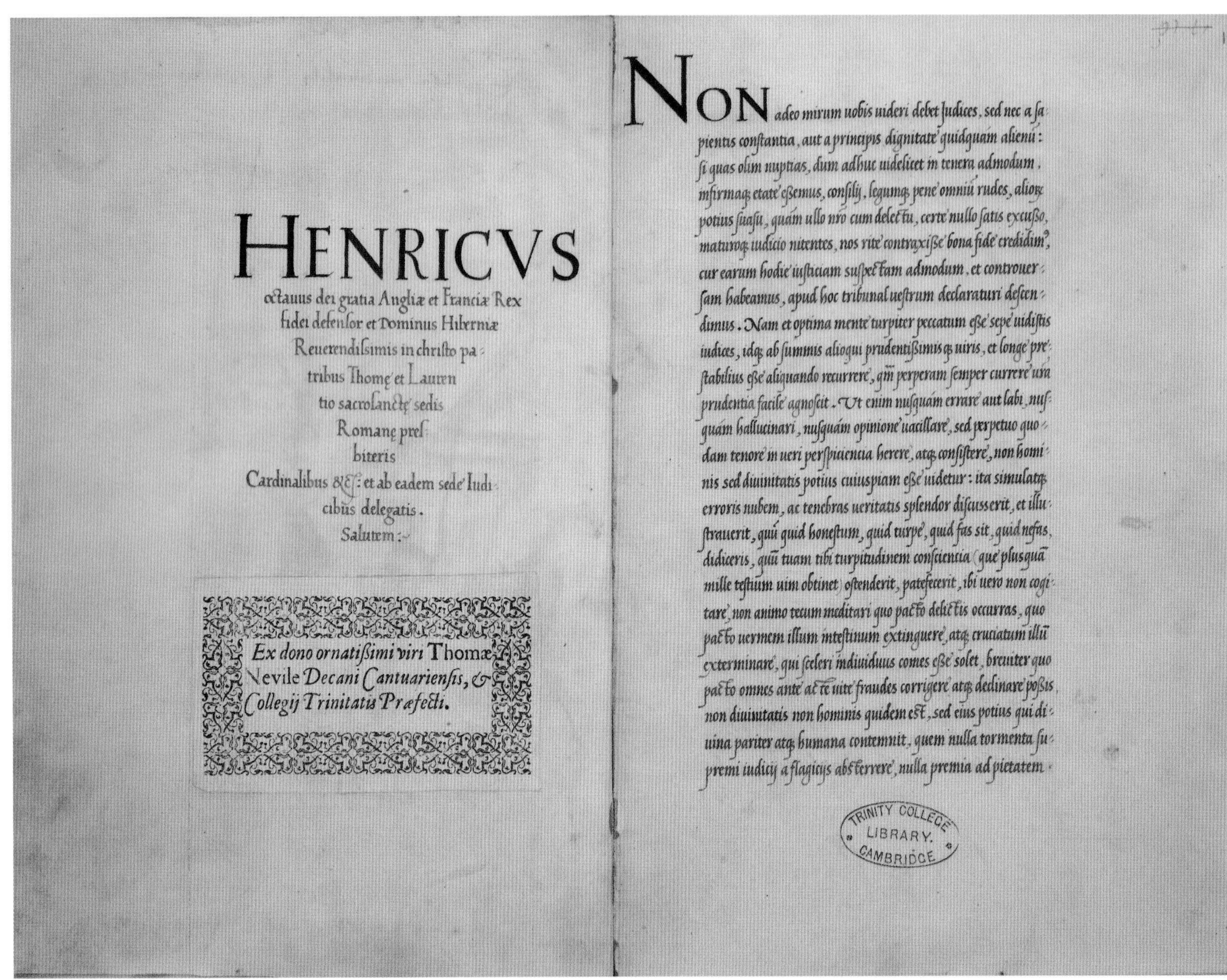

HENRICVS
octauus dei gratia Angliæ et Franciæ Rex
fidei defensor et Dominus Hiberniæ
Reuerendissimis in christo pa-
tribus Thome et Lauren
tio sacrosancte sedis
Romane pres
biteris
Cardinalibus &c: et ab eadem sede Iudi-
cibus delegatis.
Salutem:-

Ex dono ornatissimi viri Thomæ
Nevile Decani Cantuariensis, &
Collegij Trinitatis Præfecti.

NON adeo mirum uobis uideri debet Iudices, sed nec a sa-
pientis constantia, aut a principis dignitate quidquam alienu:
si quas olim nuptias, dum adhuc uidelicet in tenera admodum,
infirmaq; etate essemus, consilij, legumq; pene omniu rudes, alioru
potius suasu, quam ullo nro cum delectu, certe nullo satis excusso,
maturoq; iudicio nitentes, nos rite contraxisse bona fide credidim,
cur earum hodie iusticiam suspectam admodum, et controuer-
sam habeamus, apud hoc tribunal uestrum declaraturi descen-
dimus. Nam et optima mente turpiter peccatum esse sepe uidistis
iudices, idq; ab summis aliogui prudentissimisq; uiris, et longe pre-
stabilius esse aliquando recurrere, qm perperam semper currere ura
prudentia facile agnoscit. Ut enim nusquam errare aut labi, nusquam hallucinari, nusquam opinione uacillare, sed perpetuo quo-
dam tenore in ueri perspiciencia herere, atq; consistere, non hominis sed diuinitatis potius cuiuspiam esse uidetur: ita simulatq;
erroris nubem, ac tenebras ueritatis splendor discusserit, et illu-
strauerit, quu quid honestum, quid turpe, quid fas sit, quid nefas,
didiceris, quu tuam tibi turpitudinem consciencia (que plusqua
mille testium uim obtinet) ostenderit, patefecerit, ibi uero non cogi-
tare, non animo tecum meditari quo pacto delictis occurras, quo
pacto uermem illum intestinum extinguere, atq; cruciatum illu
exterminare, qui sceleri indiuiduus comes esse solet, breuiter quo
pacto omnes ante acte uite fraudes corrigere atq; declinare possis,
non diuinitatis non hominis quidem est, sed eius potius qui diuina pariter atq; humana contemnit, quem nulla tormenta su-
premi iudicij a flagicijs absterrere, nulla premia ad pietatem

114 Henry VIII's Case for the Annulment

Epistola Regis ad Cardinales (royal letter to the cardinals), 1529

Trinity College, Cambridge, MS B.15.19, title page and fol.1

This manuscript, written in a fine italic hand and bound in gold-tooled leather by 'King Henry's Binder', was presented in Henry's name at the legatine trial of 1529. It is the earliest complete 'king's book' to have survived and the first formal and public statement of the King's position in England. The text begins with an address from Henry to Wolsey and Campeggio and then presents Henry's case for the annulment of his marriage, focusing on the Levitical argument. A letter written by John Stokesley (1475–1539) to Thomas Cromwell in 1535 reveals that the legatine treatise was assembled by Stokesley, Edward Fox (1496–1538) and Nicolas de Burgo, working under Henry's personal direction. The book has a Westminster inventory number that, like the binding, indicates its importance. (AC)

LITERATURE: Surtz and Murphy (eds), *The Divorce Tracts of Henry VIII*; Murphy, 'The Literature and Propaganda of Henry VIII's First Divorce'

115 Queen Katherine's Appeal to the Court of Rome

Document submitted by Queen Katherine to the Legatine Court, June 1529

British Library, Cotton MS Vitellius B xii, fol.192

On 18 June, Katherine appeared before the legatine court at Blackfriars and read aloud a written protestation against the jurisdiction and competence of the Cardinals. Katherine then produced further written appeals and asked for them to be registered in the acts of the courts. This is the first page of one of her appeals, written in Latin and signed 'Katherine Regina' by the Queen at the top and bottom of each page. In the appeal, Katherine asserts that her union with Henry was valid, that the papal dispensation of 1503 had removed all impediments, and as such she had been Henry's true and lawful wife for twenty years. Insisting that she would not receive a fair trial in England, Katherine repeats her appeal for the case to be heard in Rome. (AC)

LITERATURE: Kelly, *The Matrimonial Trials of Henry VIII*; Hughes, *The Reformation in England*

116 The Court Closes

Letter from Henry VIII to William Benet, Sir Gregory Casale and Peter Vannes, 23 June 1529

British Library, Cotton MS Vitellius B xi, fol.169

This letter, signed by Henry to his ambassadors at Rome, gives his own account of the events during the Blackfriars trial. Henry's frustration at Katherine's conduct is apparent as he writes that 'the quene, trusting more in the power of the imperiallists then in any iustece of her cause' used 'frustratory allegaciones and delaies to tract and put over the mater to her avantage'. The letter also demonstrates that Henry still refused to believe that the Pope would thwart the will of a model prince and Defender of the Faith, and instead 'like a most loving fader and frende' would 'tender and favour our good, iust and reasonable causes and desires' and not do 'anything hurtefull, preiudiciall, damageable, or displeasant unto us or this our said cause' knowing 'how inconvenient it were this our mater shulde be decided in the courte of Rome, whiche nowe dependethe totally in the Emperor's arbitre'. (AC)

LITERATURE: St Clare Byrne (ed.), *The Letters of King Henry VIII*; Kelly, *The Matrimonial Trials of Henry VIII*

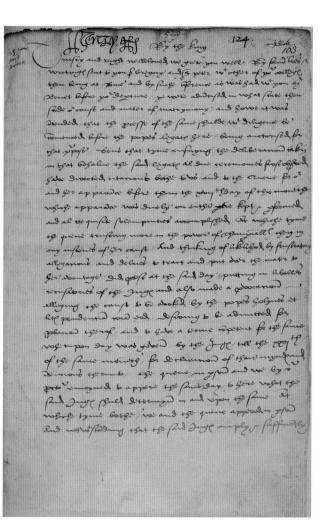

THE FALL OF WOLSEY

With the debacle of the Blackfriars court in July and the signing of a papal-imperial Treaty of Cambrai in August 1529, Wolsey lost Henry and Anne's confidence. Rejecting the Cardinal's diplomatic route, which had failed so miserably, Henry decided to take a more aggressive stance against Pope Clement by attacking Wolsey's legatine powers and the immunities of the Church. Of no more use to Henry and Anne, Wolsey fell from power in October 1529 after fifteen years of serving the King faithfully. The following autumn he was accused of treason, and he died at Leicester on 29 November 1530 while on his way down from York to a trial and certain execution in London.

117 Wolsey's Dismissal from Office, October 1529

George Cavendish, 'Life of Cardinal Wolsey', 1578

Bodleian Library, Oxford, Douce MS 363, fols 70v–71

In early October 1529, Wolsey was indicted before King's Bench for *praemunire*; implicit in the charge was the illegality of his legatine authority from the Pope. Shortly afterwards, the Dukes of Norfolk and Suffolk ordered Wolsey to surrender the Great Seal, the symbol of his office as Lord Chancellor. That dramatic moment is illustrated in this 1578 manuscript copy of the 'Life of Cardinal Wolsey', written originally by his Gentleman-usher, George Cavendish (1500–61?). Banished from court, stripped of his secular offices and deprived of the Bishopric of Winchester and Abbacy of St Albans, Wolsey no longer seemed to have a future. But Henry allowed him to keep his position as Archbishop of York and packed him off to his northern archdiocese. Perhaps Henry even thought of recalling him at some time in the future. (SD)

LITERATURE: Gwyn, *The King's Cardinal*; Ives, 'The Fall of Wolsey'; Bernard, 'The Fall of Wolsey Reconsidered'

118 Wolsey's Distress

Letter from Thomas Wolsey to Thomas Cromwell, from Esher 'thys Satyrday in the mornyng', 17 December 1529

British Library, Cotton MS Vespasian F xiii, fol.147

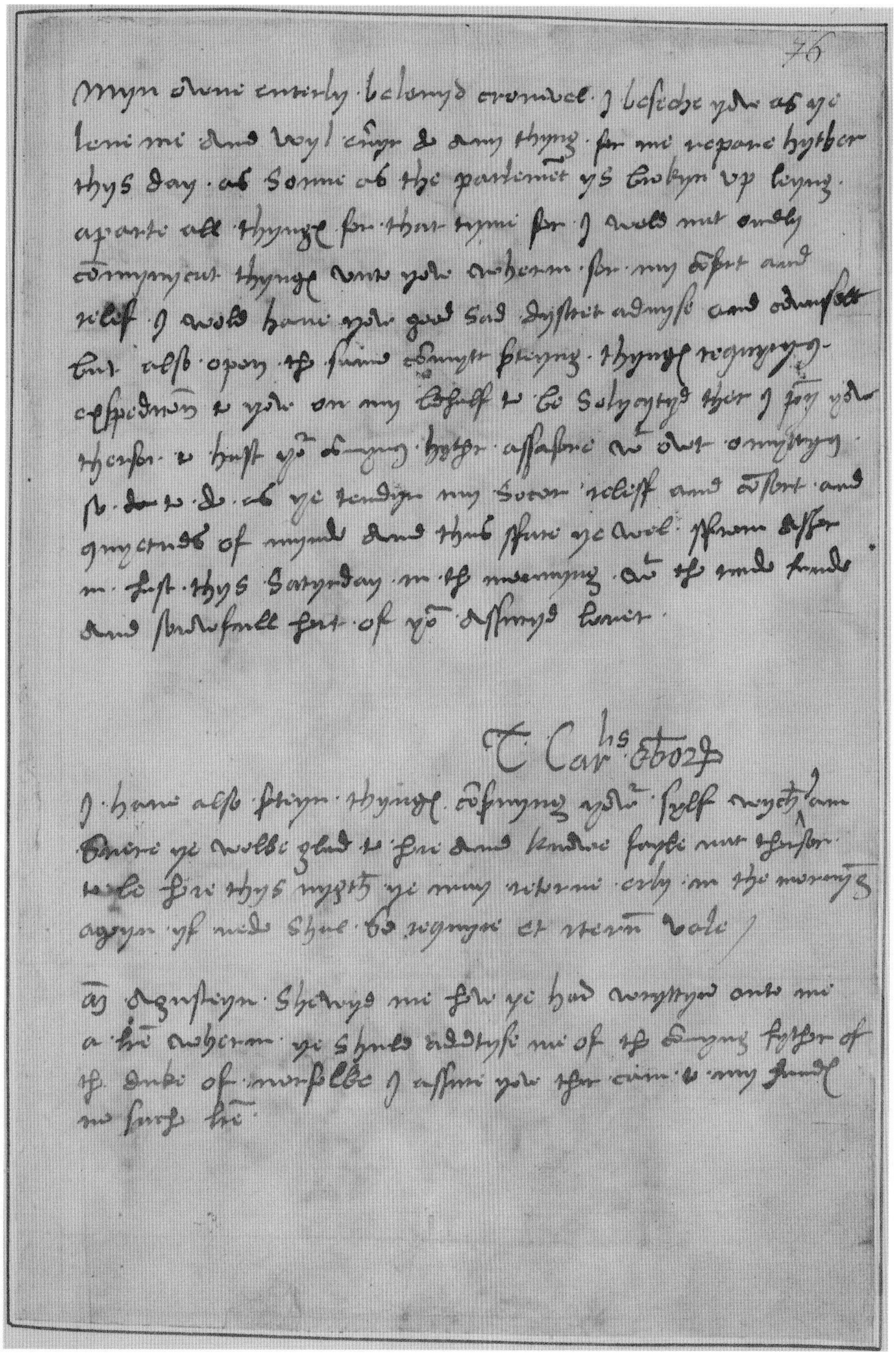

Wolsey remained at his house in Esher from the time of his dismissal from office in October 1529 until he received a pardon from the King the following February. During that time he wrote several letters to his 'belovyd' Thomas Cromwell, his legal adviser who was acting as his chief agent and go-between with the court. The letters all display Wolsey's great distress at his disgrace and the emotional strain he was under. In this one, written on the last day that Parliament sat before the Christmas recess, Wolsey begs for Cromwell's presence at Esher as soon as Parliament had broken up (Cromwell could not come earlier as he was MP for Taunton). Wolsey seeks Cromwell's 'good, sad, dyscret advyse and cownsell' and also wants to 'commytt serteyng thynges, requyryng exspedicion to yow'. Cromwell did his best for his patron during this difficult time, but he also cast around for new patrons so that he could rebuild his career. (SD)

LITERATURE: Gwyn, *The King's Cardinal*

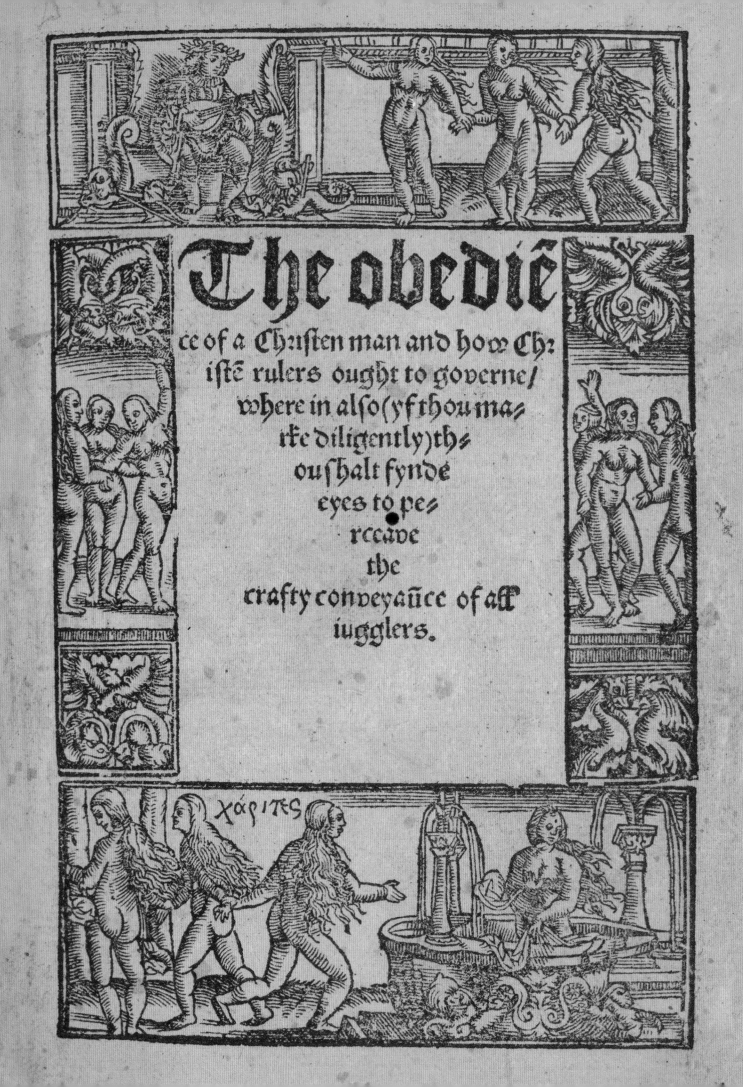

The obediē

ce of a Christen man and how Chr
istē rulers ought to governe/
where in also (yf thou marke diligently) th-
ou shalt fynde
eyes to pe-
rceave
the
crafty conveyaūce of all
iugglers.

THE ROYAL SUPREMACY (1529–35)

Richard Rex

Henry VIII had always had a high sense of his spiritual responsibilities, and had told his subjects in 1527 that it was a particular duty of a Christian king to 'set forth and further the hearts and minds of his subjects in the right religion of God and true faith of Christ'. However, as he told Martin Luther, he also recognized 'how far the estate of a king is inferior' to that of a pope. It was only as his hopes of a papal solution to his matrimonial problem faded that he began to lose his faith in papal authority and to envisage royal supremacy over the spiritual as well as the temporal realm.

The exact genesis of the idea is unclear, but it seems to have originated among the scholars who were scouring libraries for arguments in favour of deciding Henry's matrimonial case in England rather than at Rome. The compilers of the *Collectanea satis copiosa* ('the sufficiently full collections') quarried 'imperial' and 'Gallican' ideas from the treatises and chronicles that recorded medieval disputes that Holy Roman Emperors and Kings of France had had with popes. Thus the French notion that *rex in regno suo est imperator* (a king is emperor within his realm, that is, a king has all the sovereign powers accorded to the emperor in Roman law) surfaced in the resounding words of the Act in Restraint of Appeals of 1553: 'this realm of England is an empire'.

The first public assertion of royal claims over the Church came at the Southern Convocation of 1531, which was called upon to recognize Henry VIII as 'Supreme Head of the Church of England'. The meaning of this grandiose title was obscure – there was no stated intention of repudiating the papacy. But it was as threatening as it was vague, and there were many misgivings. The title was eventually granted with the equally vague but comforting proviso 'as far as the law of Christ allows', and even then some members of Convocation formally registered protests.

The next year the clergy faced a fresh demand, which made the hidden agenda of 'Supreme Head' a little more explicit. Under mounting political pressure – including a petition known as the 'Supplication against the Ordinaries',

◀ Cat. no. 127

a litany of anticlerical grievances, that was put to the House of Commons – Convocation was cowed into undertaking not to pass any spiritual laws without royal assent. It was this 'Submission of the Clergy' that led Lord Chancellor Thomas More to resign the Great Seal into the King's hands the next day (16 May 1532). Despite his own acquiescence in the submission, William Warham, Archbishop of Canterbury, had evident concerns about the tendency of royal policy, and it was therefore not until he died, towards the end of that summer, that the path to a solution finally lay clear.

Work began on drafting the Act in Restraint of Appeals, which would adjust England's legal framework so as to permit Henry's marriage to be annulled without any appeal to Rome. Thomas Cranmer was summoned home from ambassadorial duties at the court of Emperor Charles V in Nuremberg to replace Warham at Canterbury and Anne Boleyn at last welcomed Henry into her embraces. She was pregnant by Christmas, and they got married over the winter, probably on 25 January 1533.

Cranmer annulled Henry's marriage to Katherine in May 1533, and Anne bore Henry a daughter, called Elizabeth, in September of the same year. To resolve any doubts about who might be Henry's heir, Parliament passed in spring 1534 an Act of Succession that confirmed his matrimonial arrangements, debarred Mary from the succession and installed Elizabeth, with any future children of Anne, in her place.

In retrospect, the path to the Royal Supremacy can look smooth. Yet it did not seem so at the time. The politics of 1534 were the politics of bravado, not of assurance. The demand that every adult male in the kingdom swear personal allegiance to the new order speaks volumes for royal insecurity, as does the fate of the first victims of that new order. A Canterbury nun named Elizabeth Barton, and known as the 'Holy Maid of Kent', had for some years been speaking out against Henry's policies. She and her closest aides, declared guilty of treason by Act of Attainder, were executed with the usual cruelty on Monday, 20 April.

The King still felt the need to be reassured that he was in the right, and there were three men, above all others, whose approval he desired: John Fisher, Thomas More and Reginald Pole. All three had enjoyed royal favour in the 1520s, when Henry's reputation as a patron of learning and the Defender of the Faith stood at its height. But all three parted company with him over the divorce and the supremacy. John Fisher was the first, steadfastly defending the King's first marriage in private and in public. Thomas More kept his own counsel on the divorce, in a characteristically eloquent silence, yet still served his King as Lord Chancellor until, in May 1532, he could no longer reconcile such service with his conscience. Reginald Pole had gone so far as to take part in a royal mission to Paris from 1529 to 1530 to lobby the Sorbonne for support for the divorce. Yet, on his return, he became disenchanted with the direction of events, and he retreated to the safety of Italy early in 1532.

Fisher and More were immured in the Tower of London after refusing the Oath to the Succession in April 1534. Later that year two further crucial statutes were passed: the Act of Supremacy, which recognized the King as Supreme Head of the Church of England and defined the jurisdiction he held; and the Act of Treasons, which made it high treason to deny any element of the royal title. News of this reached Fisher and More, and they exchanged views on the significance of the adverb 'maliciously', which had been added during parliamentary debates in an attempt to moderate the statute. Thomas More was dubious about its value, and his doubts were vindicated at Fisher's trial in June 1535. Having by then been induced to disavow the Royal Supremacy, Fisher pleaded that his denial was not malicious, only for the judges to rule that any denial was *ipso facto* malicious. It took perjury rather than trickery to convict More the next month. Benefiting from Henry's double-edged mercy, both men were beheaded, spared the brutalities of hanging, drawing and quartering that had been inflicted earlier that summer on a group of priests and Carthusian brothers indicted for the same offence.

The number of victims of the Royal Supremacy was small, but the impact was enormous. At home, a climate of fear was established in which even a whisper of dissent in an alehouse might come to the ears of the King's chief minister, Thomas Cromwell. Public demonstrations of loyalty were required from those whose sincerity was suspect. Stephen Gardiner, Bishop of Winchester, who had penned the clergy's response to the 'Supplication against the Ordinaries', now wrote his treatise *On True Obedience* to show his allegiance.

Word was sent to Reginald Pole that he too should make clear his loyalty. The result, though, was very different: a searing letter of enormous length, comprising a denunciation of Henry's divorce and remarriage, an indictment of his usurpation of the headship of the Church and a defence of papal primacy. Still more dramatically, Pole acclaimed Henry's victims, Fisher, More and the Carthusians, as martyrs for this cause. His reply to the King was not printed until 1539, but by that time the climate of fear had done its work and Pole's was now a lone voice. Despite the shock of the Pilgrimage of Grace in 1536, and the papal excommunication of the King in 1538, Henry was secure. Dinned into the ears of his subjects by relentless preaching, the Royal Supremacy was becoming part of the English religious landscape.

ORIGINS AND FORMULATION

Henry's decision to obtain an annulment sparked off a lively and wide-ranging debate that focused not only on the validity of the Aragon marriage but also on the nature of papal power. Henry's consistent position was that his marriage to Katherine contravened divine, even natural, law and he denied the Pope's authority to grant a dispensation from scriptural laws and prohibitions. After the fiasco of the Blackfriars court, he also challenged the Pope's right to hear the case at the court in Rome and called for it to be heard in England instead. To convince his subjects and influential people abroad of the justice of his cause, Henry launched a propaganda campaign. Pamphlets were published, while universities at home and on the Continent were canvassed for their views about the annulment, and then pressure was put on them to make a declaration in favour of Henry. Meanwhile, Henry was becoming increasingly anticlerical and convinced that the Pope had no authority within his realm.

119 Archbishop Thomas Cranmer

After Gerlach Flicke, 1545

Lambeth Palace, London

The young Cambridge don, Thomas Cranmer (1489–1556), came to Henry's notice in 1529 when he suggested that the theologians in European universities should be canvassed for their opinions on the annulment case. He then became one of Henry's team writing in support of the annulment and carrying out research to find evidence that the matrimonial case should be held in England, not Rome. As a result of this work, Cranmer came to deny papal authority and embrace evangelical ideas, such as the rejection of clerical celibacy (marrying secretly in 1532).

On Archbishop Warham's death, Henry chose Cranmer for the see of Canterbury. From this position he was able to pronounce Henry's first marriage invalid, support the Royal Supremacy and promote evangelical reform. This portrait of Cranmer – painted when he was fifty-seven – hints at his belief in justification by faith alone, for he is shown reading the Epistles of St Paul, which stresses the importance of faith over works. (SD)

LITERATURE: MacCulloch, *Thomas Cranmer*; *Oxford DNB*

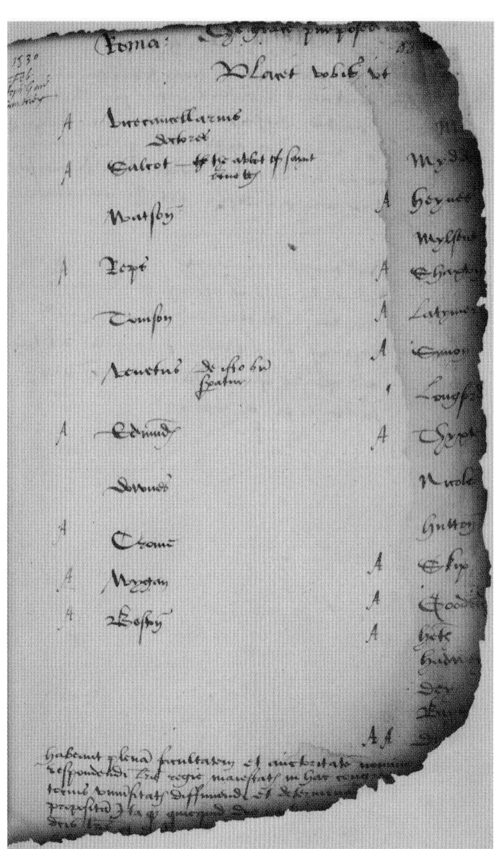

120 Stephen Gardiner

Unknown artist, 17th century?

Trinity College, Cambridge

Originally a scholar in canon and civil law at the University of Cambridge, Stephen Gardiner (*c.*1497–1556), then in Wolsey's household, was sent to Rome first in late 1527 and again in 1528 as one of the envoys charged with justifying Henry's request for an annulment. In 1529 he was appointed as Henry's principal secretary. A strong supporter of the annulment, he used his influence at Cambridge to provide a positive response during the consultation of the universities.

In early March, Cambridge reached the decision that it was forbidden for a Christian to marry the widow of his brother if the first marriage had been consummated. Although this statement implied that marriage to a sister-in-law was perfectly valid if her first marriage was unconsummated, Henry was satisfied. As a reward for his good service, Gardiner received in November 1531 the Bishopric of Winchester (the richest see in England), left vacant since Wolsey's fall. However, the following year Gardiner incurred Henry's displeasure. In Convocation, he led the resistance to Henry's declaration of the Royal Supremacy. As a result, Thomas Cranmer – a mere archdeacon – was elevated above Gardiner to become Primate of England. (SD)

LITERATURE: Redworth, *In Defence of the Catholic Church*; Muller, *Stephen Gardiner and the Tudor Reaction*

121 Stephen Gardiner and the University of Cambridge

Letter from Stephen Gardiner to Henry VIII

British Library, Cotton MS Vitellius B xiii, fol.54, undated

In this letter Gardiner describes the underhand methods he used to secure a statement from the University of Cambridge that Henry's marriage was against human and divine law. When the congregation of the University (about 200 men) convened, so much opposition was expressed that the original plan to hear all views and take a vote was abandoned. The following day, some of the opponents were 'induced' to leave the house, and then congregation agreed to allow a commission of 29 doctors and bachelors to debate and determine the issue by a two-thirds majority. Shown here is a list (appended to the letter) of the doctors and bachelors selected. Gardiner marked with an 'A' the names of those he believed to 'be alredy of your graces opinion' and assured Henry he felt confident that 'with other good meanes' the number of votes 'sufficient for our purpose' would be obtained. (SD and AC)

LITERATURE: Bedouelle and Le Gal, *Le 'Divorce' du roi Henri VIII*

Henrico octauo, Anglię et Francię Regi,
Hybernię Dn̄o et sacro sanctę fidei
Defensori, Frater Jacobus
calchus, Carmelita,
Theologorum minim⁹,
humillimā
salutē.

Rationi plane consentaneū, cum videri debet, Rex Inuictissime, vt cum Diuina prouidentia, celestia simul et ter-
rena vsqadeo moderetur, vt et lilia agri, et terre fenū gra-
to virore adornat, si et hoc quoq religionis christianę inde-
ficiens ouile, non vulgaribus et illiteratis dumtaxat, verum
et sapientibus maxime, atq peritissimis adornare decreue-
rit hominibus, quorum ope, christi oues, per abrupta quan-
doq delirantes, ad veri pastoris caulam, felici auspicio di-
riguntur. Et cum immensa illa Diuinitas, nullius sane per-
fectionis egens, omnem rebus bonitatem largiatur, superce-
les intelligentias, suo ineffabili splendore vberrim illuminans, co-
suffragio, et nos mortales, natura illis et creatione posteriores, as-
siduo illustramur vberrime, atq perficimur. Neq eo angelorum
celesti solum perpotimur patrocinio, verū et sacerdotij munere,

122 Support for the Annulment

Giacomo Calco, 'May a Man Marry the Widow of a Brother who Died without Issue?', 1530

Private Collection, Paris

In March 1530, the Italian Carmelite Giacomo Calco wrote this 34-page treatise in support of Henry's annulment. This was the first work to suggest that a break with Rome might provide a solution to Henry's matrimonial problems. Henry was so impressed that, after the manuscript came into the Royal Library, it was beautifully bound by King Henry's Binder and is perhaps the best of the surviving examples of his work. In gratitude for Calco's advice, Henry offered to make him Bishop of Salisbury, but Calco died before this was possible. The importance of the manuscript was recognized in 2003, when application was made for an export licence; *The Guardian* then described it as 'a little book of theological advice to Henry VIII which helped to change the course of English history'. (JC)

LITERATURE: Nixon and Foot, *The History of Decorated Bookbinding in England*; Carley, 'Misattributions and Ghost Entries in John Bale's *Index Britanniae Scriptorum*'

123 Opposition to the Annulment from Abroad

Declaration of the Universidad de Alcalá de Henares, 21 September 1531

Archivo General de Simancas, Patronato Real, Caja 53, Doc. 95

The University of Alcalá had been founded in 1499 by Cardinal Ximénez de Cisneros, Archbishop of Toledo and High Chancellor of Castile under Ferdinand and Isabella, the parents of Katherine of Aragon. John Fisher's treatise in defence of the validity of her marriage to Henry was published at Alcalá by the university printer, Miguel de Eguia, in August 1530, which was precisely when the university was considering the theological principles raised by the case. The Faculty of Theology reached its conclusions on 4 August, and the university as a whole approved a slightly amended version of them on 21 September. As loyal to the ruling house of Spain as their English counterparts were to the Tudors, the doctors of Alcalá concluded, predictably enough, that 'it is not contrary to natural law to take in marriage the widow of a brother who has died without children' and 'the Supreme Pontiff can issue a dispensation' in such cases. (RR)

LITERATURE: Bedouelle and Le Gal, *Le 'Divorce' du roi Henri VIII*, pp. 161–4

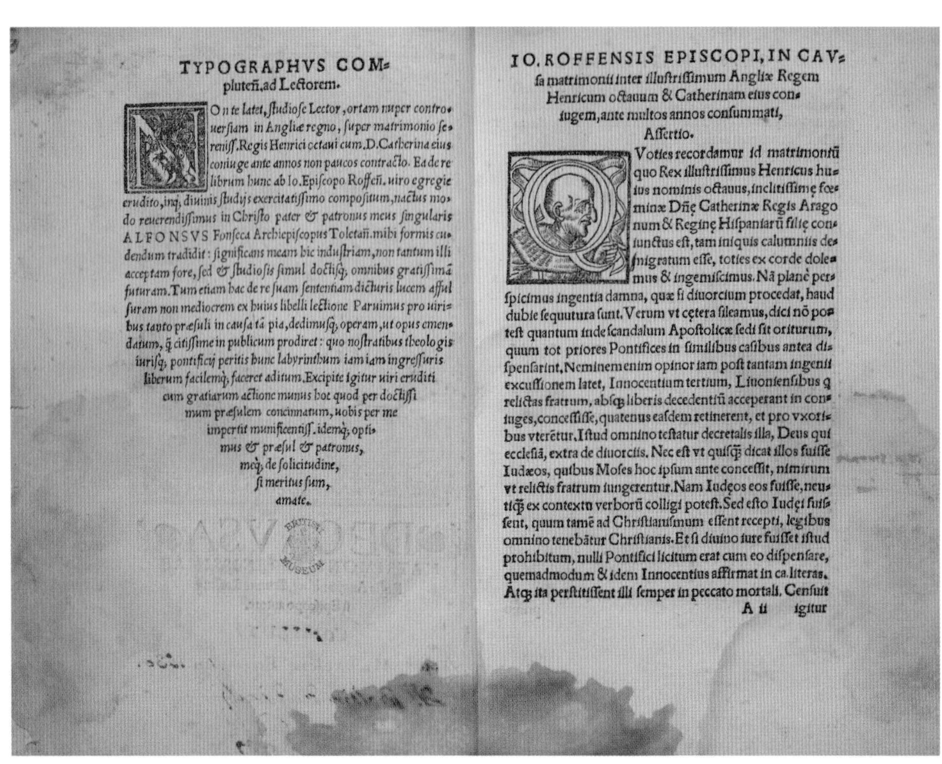

TYPOGRAPHVS COMpluten. ad Lectorem.

NOn te latet, studiose Lector, ortam nuper controuersiam in Angliæ regno, super matrimonio sereniss. Regis Henrici octaui cum D. Catherina eius coniuge ante annos non paucos contracto. Ea de re librum hunc ab Io. Episcopo Roffen. uiro egregie erudito, inq; diuinis studijs exercitatissimo compositum, nactus modo reuerendissimus in Christo pater & patronus meus singularis ALFONSVS Fonseca Archiepiscopus Toletan. mihi formis cudendum tradidit: significans meam hic industriam, non tantum illi acceptam fore, sed & studiosis simul doctisq; omnibus gratissimā futuram. Tum etiam hac de re suam sententiam dicturis lucem allaturam non mediocrem ex huius libelli lectione. Paruimus pro uiribus tanto præsuli in causa tā pia, dedimusq; operam, ut opus emendatum, q̄ citissime in publicum prodiret: quo nostratibus theologis iurisq; pontificij peritis hunc labyrinthum iam iam ingressuris liberum facilemq; faceret aditum. Excipite igitur uiri eruditi cum gratiarum actione munus hoc quod per doctissimum præsulem concinnatum, uobis per me impertit munificentiss. idemq; optimus & præsul & patronus, meq; de solicitudine, si meritus sum, amate.

IO. ROFFENSIS EPISCOPI, IN CAVsa matrimonii inter illustrissimum Angliæ Regem Henricum octauum & Catherinam eius coniugem, ante multos annos consummati, Assertio.

QVoties recordamur id matrimoniū quo Rex illustrissimus Henricus huius nominis octauus, inclitissimę fœminæ Dñę Catherinæ Regis Aragonum & Reginę Hispaniarū filię coniunctus est, tam iniquis calumniis denigratum esse, toties ex corde dolemus & ingemiscimus. Nā planè perspicimus ingentia damna, quæ si diuorcium procedat, haud dubie sequutura sunt. Verum vt cętera sileamus, dici nō potest quantum inde scandalum Apostolicæ sedi sit oriturum, quum tot priores Pontifices in similibus casibus antea dispensarint. Neminem enim opinor iam post tantam ingenii excussionem latet, Innocentium tertium, Liuoniensibus q relictas fratrum, absq; liberis decedentiū acceperant in coniuges, concessisse, quatenus easdem retinerent, et pro vxoribus vterētur. Istud omnino testatur decretalis illa, Deus qui ecclesiā, extra de diuorciis. Nec est vt quisq; dicat illos fuisse Iudæos, quibus Moses hoc ipsum ante concessit, nimirum vt relictis fratrum iungerentur. Nam Iudęos eos fuisse, neutiq; ex contextu verborū colligi potest. Sed esto Iudęi fuissent, quum tamē ad Christianismum essent recepti, legibus omnino tenebātur Christianis. Et si diuino iure fuisset istud prohibitum, nulli Pontifici licitum erat cum eo dispensare, quemadmodum & idem Innocentius affirmat in ca. literas. Atq; ita perstitissent illi semper in peccato mortali. Censuit

A ii igitur

124 John Fisher's Opposition

Alcalá de Henares, *De causa matrimonii serenissimi regis Angliae* (On the matrimonial case of the most serene King of England), 1530

British Library, C.24.a.20, sig Ai^{v}–Aii

John Fisher, Bishop of Rochester and England's premier theologian (1469–1535), was first asked for his opinion on the 'King's Great Matter' in the spring of 1527. For the next six years it was to occupy almost his every waking hour. He said afterwards that he had never worked harder on anything else. His case focused on the text of Deuteronomy, which instructed a man to marry the widow if his brother had died without children. (Henry's case focused on texts in Leviticus.) But Fisher also emphasized the potential challenge that the royal case might pose to papal authority in general. This was the only one of Fisher's many writings on the subject to be printed. Smuggled out to the court of Charles V, it was sent to press by the leading churchman of Spain, the Archbishop of Toledo. Its appearance probably spurred Henry's team to publish its own case, which appeared in 1531 as *Gravissimae censurae*. (RR)

LITERATURE: Rex, *The Theology of John Fisher*; Kelly, *The Matrimonial Trials of Henry VIII*; Bedouelle and Le Gal, *Le 'Divorce' du roi Henri VIII*

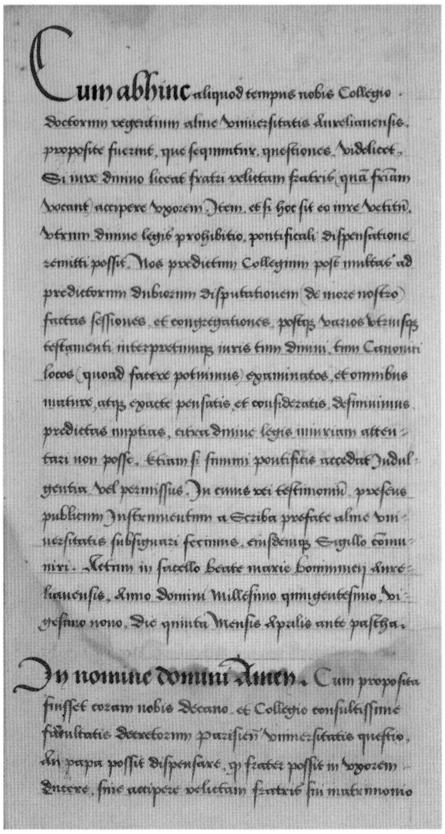

125 The *Gravissimae censurae*, 1531

Gravissimae atque exactissimae illustrissimarum totius Italiae et Galiae academiarum censurae, 1531

British Library, Harley MS 1338, fol.1

The *Gravissimae censurae* was the first major public statement of Henry's case for an annulment of his marriage to Katherine, though it confines its attention to general principles, never once mentioning the King or Queen. The 'weightiest opinions' (*gravissimae censurae*) of the title refer to the favourable opinions that Henry's agents had procured from various European universities by a combination of lobbying and bribery. These judgements had been read out in the Parliament of 1531 before publication, and an English translation by Thomas Cranmer, published as *Determinations of the Universities*, appeared in November that year. The university opinions, however, are only a fraction of the book, the bulk of which is an exhaustive statement of the case, based on the biblical prohibitions on marriage to a brother's wife in Leviticus 18: 16 and 20: 21. (RR)

LITERATURE: Surtz and Murphy (eds), *The Divorce Tracts of Henry VIII*; Kelly, *The Matrimonial Trials of Henry VIII*; MacCulloch, *Thomas Cranmer*

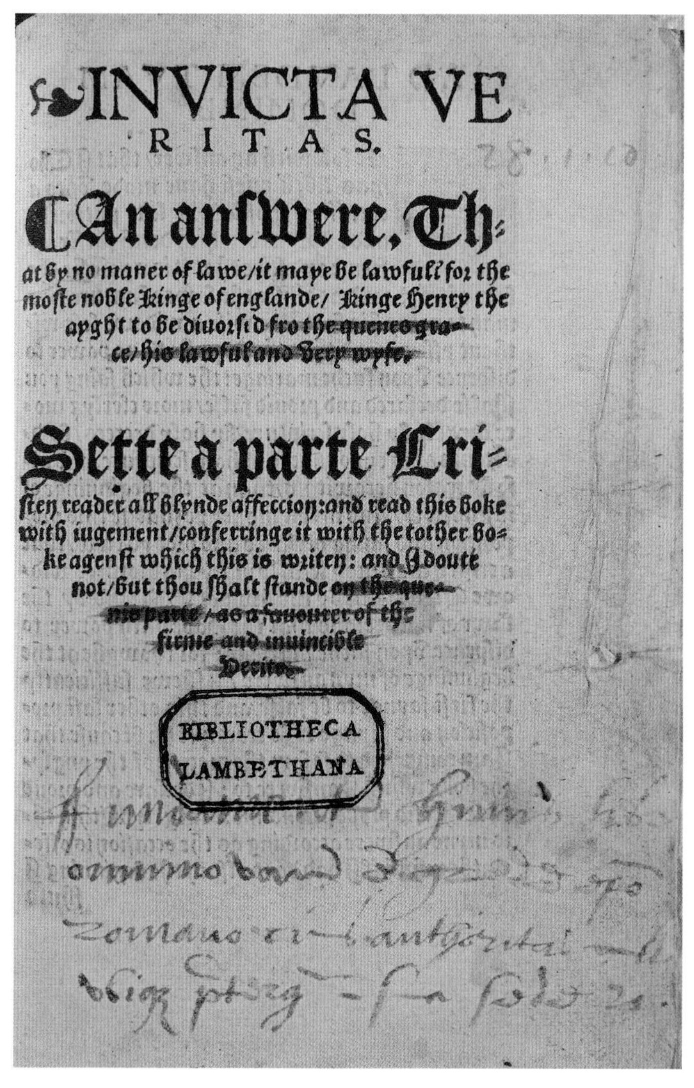

INVICTA VE RITAS.

An answere, That by no maner of lawe/it maye be lawfull for the moste noble kinge of englande/ kinge Henry the aught to be diuorsid fro the quenes grace/his lawful and very wyfe.

Sette a parte Cristen reader all blynde affeccion: and read this boke with iugement/conferringe it with the tother boke agenst which this is writen: and I doutt not/but thou shalt stande on the quenis parte/as a fauourer of the firme and inuincible Verite.

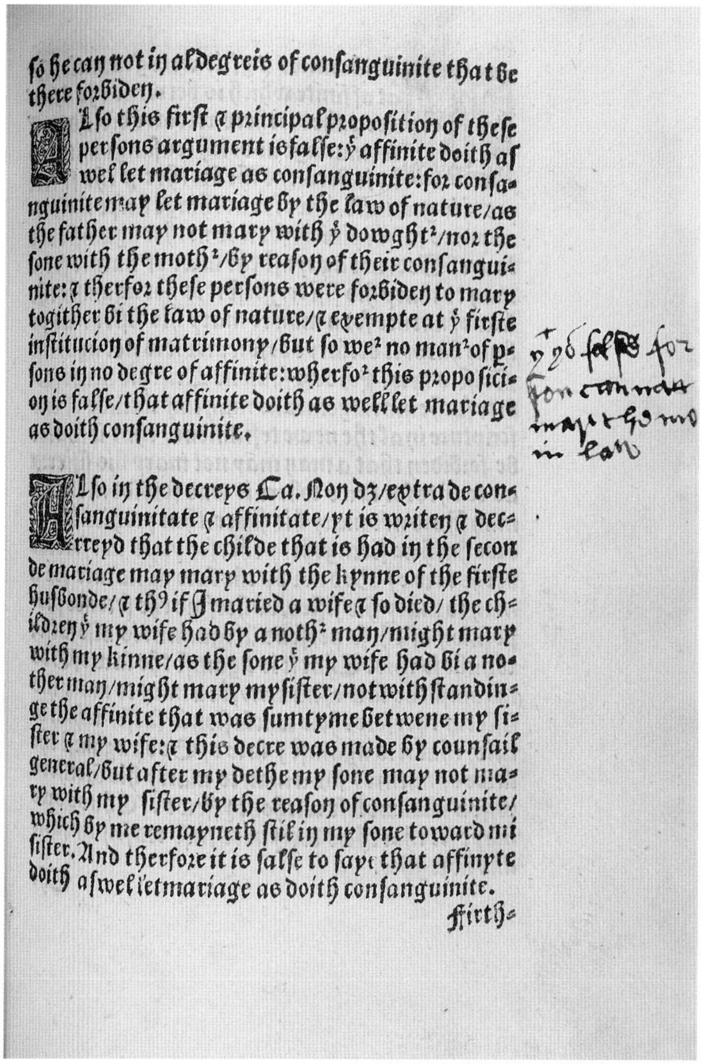

so he can not in al degreis of consanguinite that be there forbiden.

Also this first & principal proposition of these persons argument is false: ye affinite doith as wel let mariage as consanguinite: for consanguinite may let mariage by the law of nature/as the father may not mary with ye dowght[er]/nor the sone with the moth[er]/by reason of their consanguinite: & therfor these persons were forbiden to mary togither bi the law of nature/& exempte at ye firste institucion of matrimony/but so we[re] no man[er] of p[er]sons in no degre of affinite: wherfor this proposicion is false/that affinite doith as well let mariage as doith consanguinite.

Also in the decreys Ca. Non d[e]z/extra de consanguinitate & affinitate/yt is writen & decreyd that the childe that is had in the seconde mariage may mary with the kynne of the firste husbonde/& th[us] if I maried a wife & so died/ the children ye my wife had by a noth[er] man/might mary with my kinne/as the sone ye my wife had bi a nother man/might mary my sister/notwithstandinge the affinite that was sumtyme betwene my sister & my wife: & this decre was made by counsail general/but after my dethe my sone may not mary with my sister/by the reason of consanguinite/ which by me remayneth stil in my sone toward mi sister. And therfore it is false to say that affinyte doith aswel letmariage as doith consanguinite.

Firth-

126 Katherine's Supporters Strike Back

Thomas Abell, *Invicta veritas*, 1532

Lambeth Palace Library, London, 1532.4.01, title page and sig. Q.iiii

In response to the *Determinations of the Universities* (1531), Katherine's chaplain, Thomas Abell, wrote a tract in English, published in Antwerp under a false imprint, called *Invicta veritas* (Unconquered Truth). *An answere, that by no maner of lawe, it may be lawfull for … King Henry the ayght to be divorsed from the Quenes grace.* Drawing on the authority of the Bible, as well as Church Fathers and unwavering in his convictions, Abell challenged the King's position both through citation and logical argument. Henry's personal copy survives and it contains marginalia that bear witness to his violent reaction to Abell's reasoning: 'The whole basis of this book is false. Therefore papal authority is empty save in its own seat.'

One of Abell's crucial points was that affinity (as in the marriage to one's brother-in-law) was not the same as consanguinity (a blood relationship) and that the former did not contravene divine law. In cases of affinity the Pope could therefore provide dispensation. Henry disagreed and noted in the margin that 'yt ys false for the son cannat mari the mo[ther] in law'. (JC)

LITERATURE: Surtz and Murphy (eds), *The Divorce Tracts of Henry VII*; Kelly, *The Matrimonial Trials of Henry VIII*; Carley, *The Books of Henry VIII and his Wives*

127 'This book is for me and all kings to read'

William Tyndale, *The Obedience of the Christian Man and How Christian Rulers Ought to Govern*, 1528

British Library, C.53.b.1, title page

This work by the English Lutheran exile William Tyndale gave voice to Henry's growing conviction that royal authority took precedence over papal authority. *The Obedience of the Christian Man* was written to refute Thomas More's claim that Tyndale and Lutherans like him stirred up rebellion. More held the Establishment view that, by divine decree, Church and State were separate. Popes exercised spiritual authority (which included marriage); kings exercised temporal authority. Tyndale demonstrated from the Bible that 'all men without exception are under the temporal sword'. The papal claim to authority over kings was 'not only a shame above all shames and a notorious thing' but it defied God's order: 'One king one law is God's ordinance in every realm'. The book therefore demonstrated that the Pope had no right to impede Henry. Anne Boleyn quickly obtained a copy, marked passages to show to Henry, whose response was that 'This book is for me and all kings to read'. (EI)

LITERATURE: Ives, *The Life and Death of Anne Boleyn*

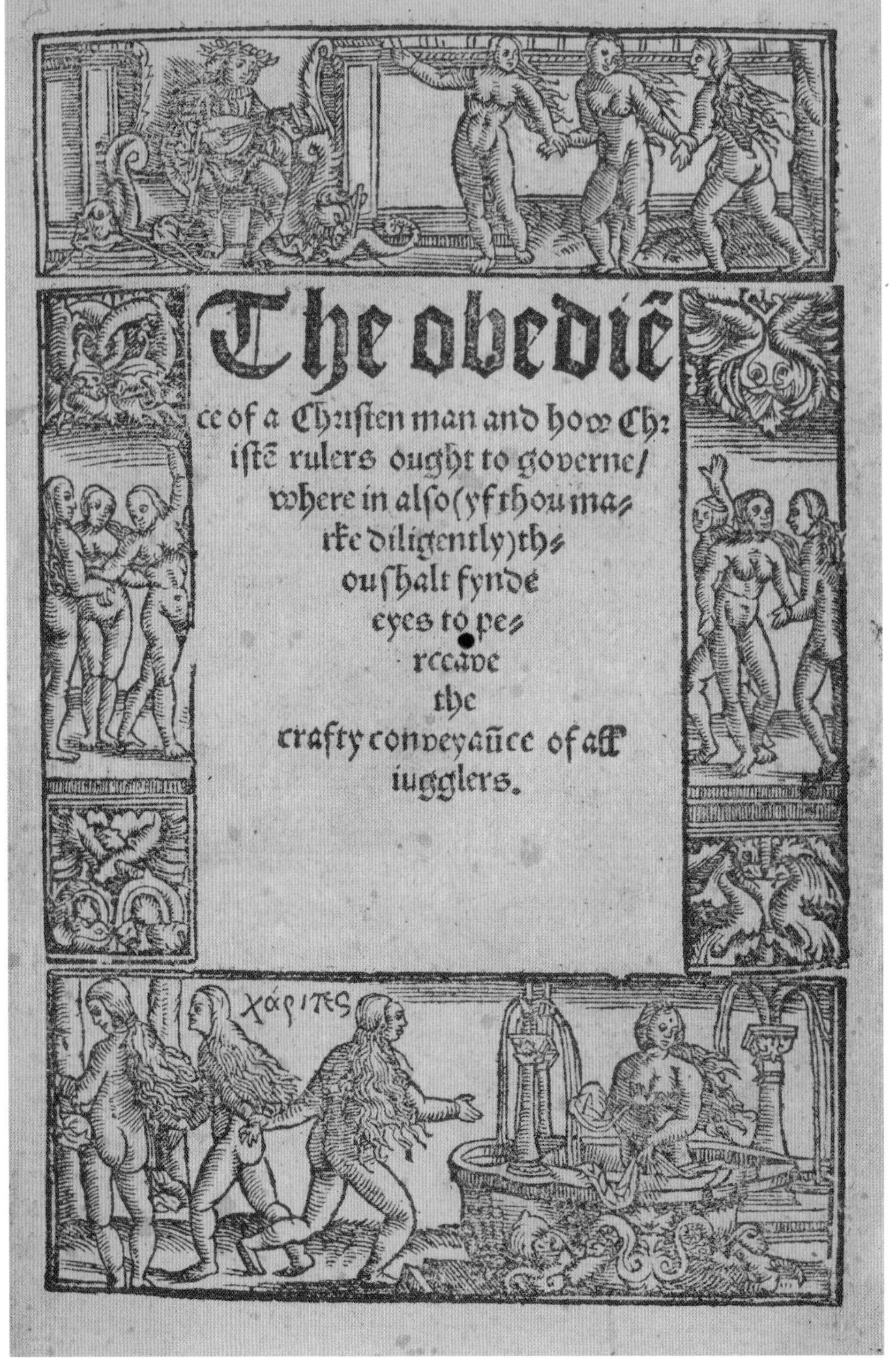

The obedie͂ce of a Christen man and how Christe͂ rulers ought to governe/ where in also (yf thou ma= rke diligently) th= ou shalt fynde eyes to pe= rceave the crafty conveyau͂ce of all iugglers.

TO THE KING OVRE
ſouereygne lorde.

MOſt lamentably compleyneth theyre wofull myſery vnto youre highnes youre poore daily bedemē the wretched hidous monſtres (on whome ſcarcely for horror any yie dare loke) the foule vnhappy ſorte of lepres, and other ſore people, nedy, impotent, blinde, lame, and ſike, that live onely by almeſſe, howe that theyre nombre is daily ſo ſore encreaſed that all the almeſſe of all the weldiſpoſed people of this youre realme is not halfe ynough for to ſuſteine theim, but that for verey conſtreint they die for hunger. And this moſt peſtilent miſchief is comen vppon youre ſaide poore beedmē by the reaſon that there is yn the tymes of youre noble predeceſſours paſſed craftily crept ynto this your realme an other ſort (not of impotent but) of ſtrong puiſſaunt and counterfeit holy, and ydell beggers and vacabundes whiche ſyns the tyme of theyre firſt entre by all the craft and wilineſſe of Satan are nowe encreaſed vnder your ſight not onely into a great nōbre, but alſo ynto a kingdome. Theſe are (not the herdes, but the rauinous wolues going in herdes clothing deuouring the flocke) the Biſſhoppes, Abbottes, Priours, Deacons, Archedeacons, Suffraganes, Preſtes, Monkes Chanons, Freres, Pardoners and Somners. And who is abill to nōbre this idell rauinous ſort whiche (ſetting all laboure aſide) haue begged ſo importunatly that they haue gotten ynto theyre hondes more then the therd part of all youre Realme. The goodlieſt lordſhippes, maners, londes, and territories, are theyrs. Beſides this they haue the tenth part af all the corne, medowe, paſture, graſſe, wolle, coltes, calues, lambes, pigges, geſe, and chikens. Ouer and biſides the tenth part of euery ſeruauntes wages the tenth part of the wolle, milke, hony, waxe cheſe, and butter. Ye and they loke ſo narowly vppon theyre proufittes that the poore wyues muſt be countable to theym of euery tenth eg or elles ſhe gettith not her ryghtes at eſter ſhalbe taken as an heretike. hereto haue they theire foure offering daies. whate money pull they yn by probates of teſtamentes, priuy tithes, and by mennes offeringes to theyre pilgremages, and at theyre firſt maſſes? Euery man and childe that is buried muſt pay ſumwhat for maſſes and diriges to be ſong for him or elles they will accuſe the dedes frendes and executours of hereſie. whate money get they by mortuaries, by hearing of confeſſions (and yet they wil kepe therof no counceyle) by halowing of churches altares ſuper altares chapelles and belles, by curſing of men and abſoluing theim agein for money? what a multitude of money gather the pardoners in a yere? Howe moche money get the Somners by extorcion yn a yere, by aſſityng the people to the commiſſaries court and afterward releaſing thapparaūce for money? Finally, the infinite nombre of begging freres whate get they yn a yere? Here if it pleaſe your grace to marke ye ſhall ſe a thing farre out of ioynt. There are withyn youre realme of Englond .lij. thouſand pariſſhe churches. And this ſtonding that there be but tenne houſhouldes yn euery pariſſhe yet are there fiue hundreth thouſand and twenty thouſand houſhouldes. And of euery of theſe houſhouldes hath euery of the fiue ordres of freres a peny a quarter for euery ordre, that is for all the fiue ordres fiue pens a quarter for euery houſe. That is for all

2 the

A DIALOGE.

HE LAVYERE. Me ſemeth, it is wiſely and truely ſaide, that the right way is euer the nereſt waye: & likewyſe the playne way moſte ſure, to trye al maner of truth by. THE DIVINE. I thynke that it be true, whiche you ſpeke: but you ſpeake ſo obſcurely, that I wotte nere what you meane therby. If you meane it by the imytation of Chriſte, whiche beareth wytneſſe of him ſelfe, ſayeng I am the ryght way, I am the true way, and I am the perfyt lyfe: than are you in the ryghte. And if you meane the playne waye to be moſte ſure, bicauſe that Chriſte ſaieth he is the dore by whiche we muſte entre in, this youre ſayenge canne nat be amended. wherunto god him ſelfe exhorteth vs alſo by his prophete, ſayeng ye chriſten mē loke ye iuge a right. THE LAVYER. The better for my purpoſe. For the cauſe why I ſpeke it, is for the great weightye cauſe of chriſtendome: concernynge the kynges ſeperation fro the quene. It is toſſed and tourned ouer the hye mountaynes, laboured and vexed at Rome,

That our ſauiour Chriſt is the ryght and playne way.

B from

128 Another Book for Kings

Simon Fish, *Supplication of Beggars*, 1529

Printed by Johannes Grapheus?

British Library, C.21.b.45, pp. 1v–2

It is also possible that Anne brought this anti-clerical text to Henry's attention. The author's wife told the Elizabethan martyrologist John Foxe that her husband had sent a copy to Anne, who, after discussions with her brother, George Boleyn, Lord Rochford, passed it on to Henry. The author was Simon Fish, a London lawyer, who had fled abroad after satirizing Wolsey in the Gray's Inn Christmas play of 1526 and also running contraband religious books. From the comparative safety of the Low Countries, Fish flooded London with copies of this petition to Henry which made a searing attack on the out-and-out avarice and shameless immorality of the English clergy. Fish's claim that clerical pretension made nonsense of the King's justice struck a chord with Henry, who pardoned and recalled Fish and subsequently interviewed him. (EI)

LITERATURE: Ives, *The Life and Death of Anne Boleyn*; Freeman, 'Research, Rumour and Propaganda'

129 Royal Propaganda

A Glasse of the Truthe, 1532

Printed by Thomas Berthelet

British Library, Grenville 1237, sig B

Published in September 1532, this book was written in a punchy vernacular to sway public opinion in favour of Henry's divorce. An exercise in royal propaganda, it was released to the press by one of the leading scholars involved in the divorce, Richard Croke (1489–1569), reporting directly to Cromwell. *A Glasse of the Truthe* was the first public sign of a new sense of purpose that marked royal policy from the summer of 1532. It not only makes all the usual arguments against marriage to a brother's wife but also hints at a unilateral solution and urges Englishmen to resist any papal sanctions. A French translation was published in October, presumably for distribution to members of the French court whom Henry and Anne were to meet later that month in Calais. In the preface, it sets out what would become a commonplace in Tudor discussions of the succession, namely the disadvantages of female rule, on the grounds that a woman would inevitably find herself in a state of subjection to her husband. (RR)

LITERATURE: Rex, 'Redating Henry VIII's *A Glasse of the Truthe*'; Warner, *Henry VIII's Divorce;* Murphy, 'The Literature and Propaganda of Henry VIII's First Divorce'

THE *COLLECTANEA SATIS COPIOSA*

For about two years, a team of scholars and royal agents gathered together and studied manuscripts that would provide evidence to buttress Henry's claims that his annulment was justified and that his matrimonial case ought to be determined in England rather than Rome. The manuscripts, which included English and Latin chronicles, Anglo-Saxon laws, Roman law and conciliar decrees, were taken from monasteries and deposited in the Royal Library. They fed into a manuscript compilation called the *Collectanea satis copiosa* ('the sufficiently full collections') that was presented to Henry in the summer of 1530.

The *Collectanea* argued that the Church of England was an autonomous province of the Catholic Church and that Henry had both secular *imperium* and spiritual supremacy in England. In other words, it was the King, not the Pope, who exercised supreme jurisdiction within his realm. It is not surprising that Henry was delighted with the work and wrote approving comments all over the manuscript. Now confident that he had right on his side, he began the campaign to persuade or force his clerics to accept and recognize his imperial pretensions.

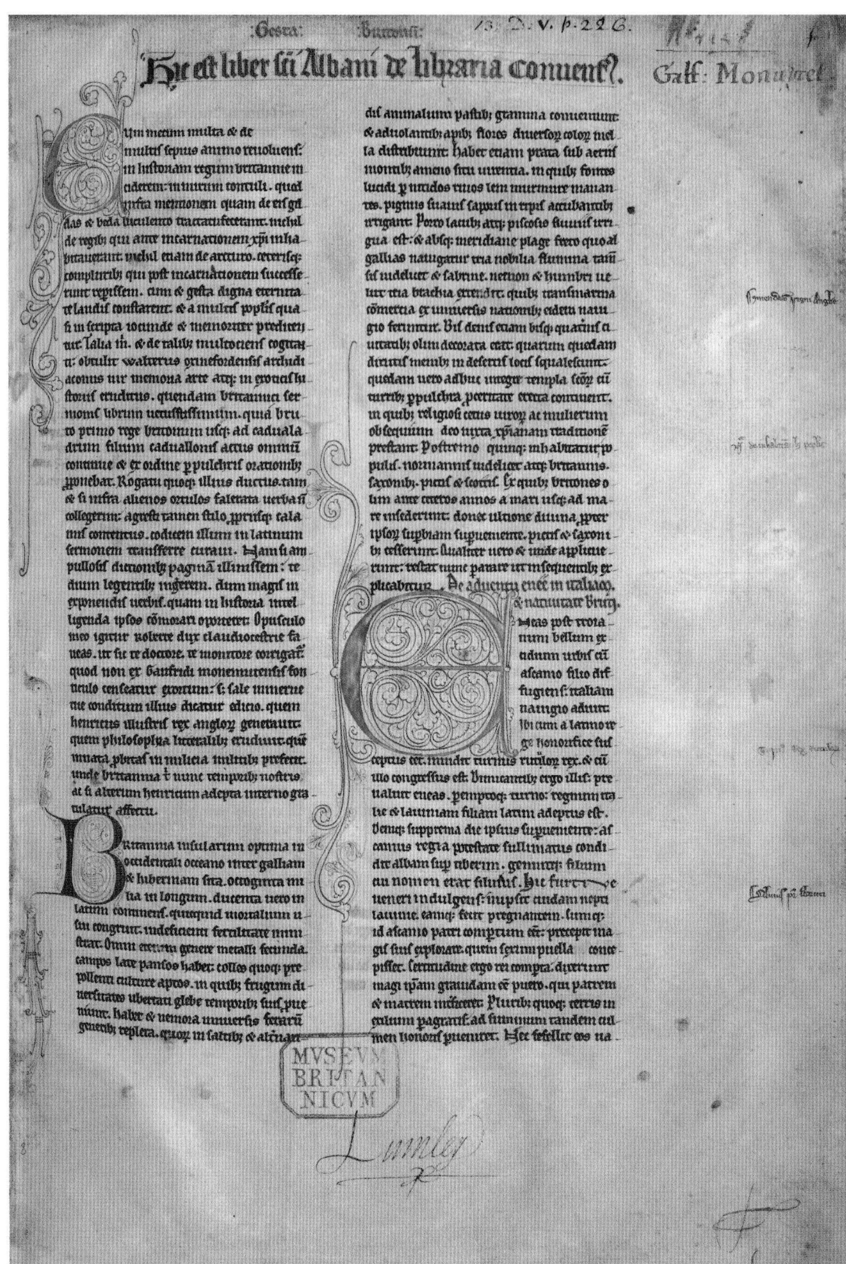

130 Geoffrey of Monmouth, *Historia regum Britanniae*, 1138

British Library, Royal MS 13 D.v, fol.1

During the late 1520s a group of more than 30 medieval manuscripts containing historical and theological texts that might be useful in the debate about Henry's annulment were gathered up and brought to London, where they had an identifying 'TC' monograph inscribed on the first or second folio recto. 'TC' almost certainly stands for Thomas Cardinalis, that is Thomas Wolsey, who was deeply involved in putting together a case for the King, and a significant number of the manuscripts derive from the monastery at St Albans, where Wolsey had been Abbot since 1521. This copy of Geoffrey of Monmouth's *Historia regum Britanniae* (History of the Kings of Britain), a work that glorified Henry's ancestor and imperial precedent King Arthur, had been seen and annotated by the Italian humanist historian Polydore Vergil when it was at St Albans. (JC)

LITERATURE: Carley, 'Sir Thomas Bodley's Library and its Acquisitions'; Carley, 'Marks in Books and the Libraries of Henry VIII'; Carley, *The Libraries of King Henry VIII*

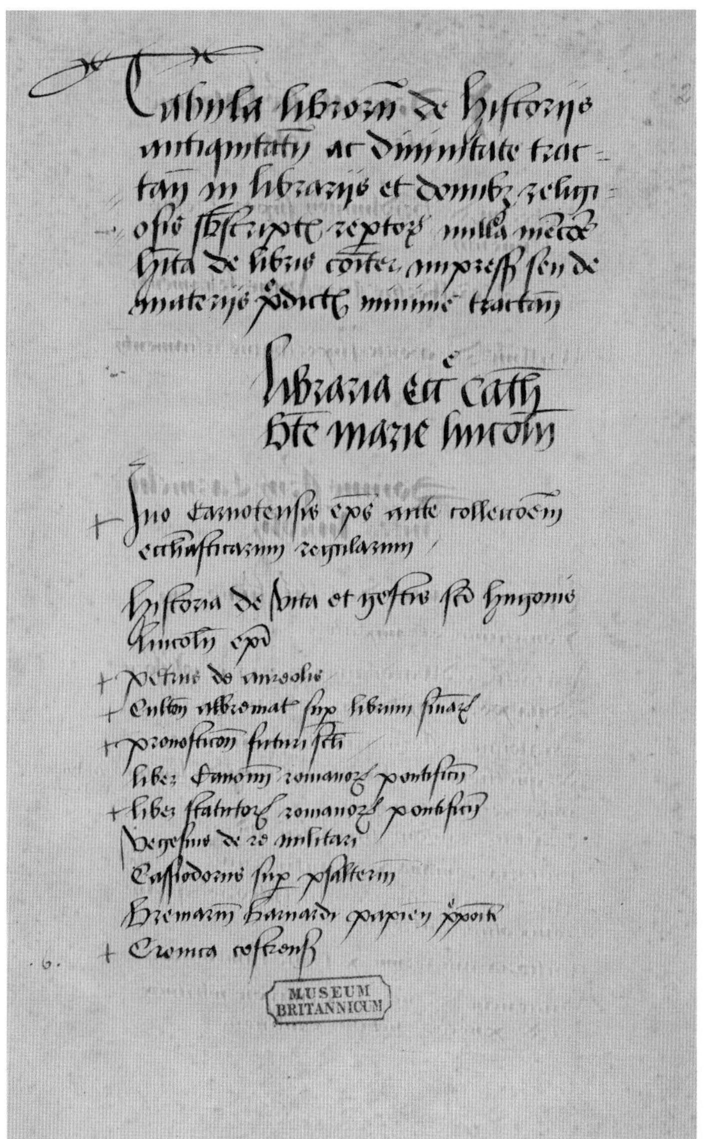

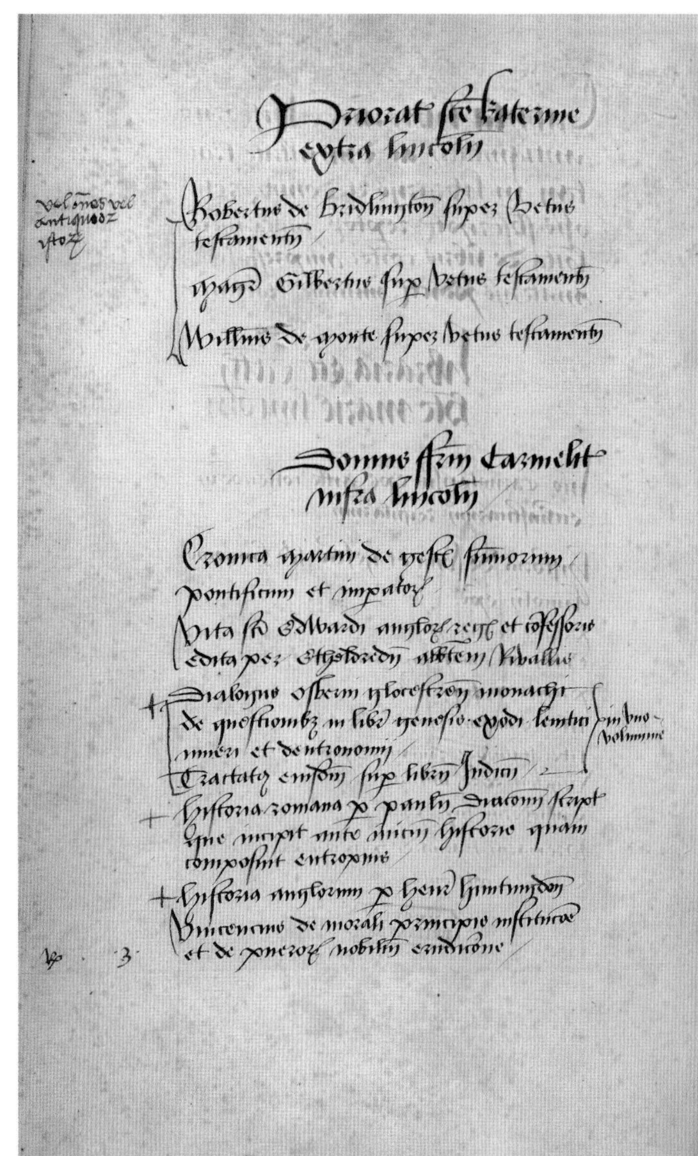

131 The Search for Evidence: the *Tabula librorum*

Tabula librorum de historiis antiquitatum ac diuinitate tractancium in libraries et domibus religiosis (A list of books treating ancient histories and divinity in libraries and religious houses), 1528

British Library, Royal MS Appendix 69, fol.2 r–v

Drawn up in the summer of 1528, when the sweating sickness was raging, this list gives the titles of almost 100 books in religious houses in Lincolnshire that might pertain to Henry's 'Great Matter'. Those books that were to be transported to the Royal Library were marked with a cross. More revealingly, there is a note beside a list of three titles from the Gilbertine priory of St Catherine in Lincoln in Henry's own hand to the effect that all of the books, or at least the older of them, were worthy of examination (*uel omnes uel antiquior istorum*). It is clear that Henry was closely involved in the search for evidence, overseeing what was going on and determining what might be most useful to him. The majority of the manuscripts that were singled out – there were 37 in all – survive in the modern Royal Library, including one from the Lincoln Gilbertines, a glossed copy of books of the Old Testament, misattributed to the medieval theologian William de Montibus, carrying the telltale Westminster Inventory Number, No. 503. (JC)

LITERATURE: Liddell, '"Leland's" List of Manuscripts in Lincolnshire Monasteries'; Carley, 'John Leland and the Contents of the English Pre-Dissolution Libraries: Lincolnshire'

132 William of Malmesbury, *De gestis pontificum*, 12th century

British Library, Harley MS 2, fol.130

Henry's agents brought a copy of the *De gestis pontificum* (History of the English Bishops) by the 12th-century historian William of Malmesbury to the Royal Library from the Augustinian Priory at Thornton-on-Humber in Lincolnshire. Once in London, it was closely examined and passages dealing with councils, the authority of bishops and the Pope, and consanguinity in marriage duly noted. These materials were later to form part of the 'warehouse' of texts known as the *Collectanea satis copiosa*, which was compiled by Henry's scholars in 1530 in order to demonstrate through historical precedents the imperial status of the English monarchy. Indeed, the *Collectanea satis copiosa* quoted directly from a version of the Constitutions of Clarendon of 1164 (Henry II's attempt to define Church-State relations) deriving from William and it is possible the Thornton-on-Humber copy was the very manuscript used by Henry's research team. This manuscript subsequently disappeared from the Royal Collection. (JC)

LITERATURE: Guy, 'Thomas Cromwell and the Intellectual Origins of the Henrician Revolution'

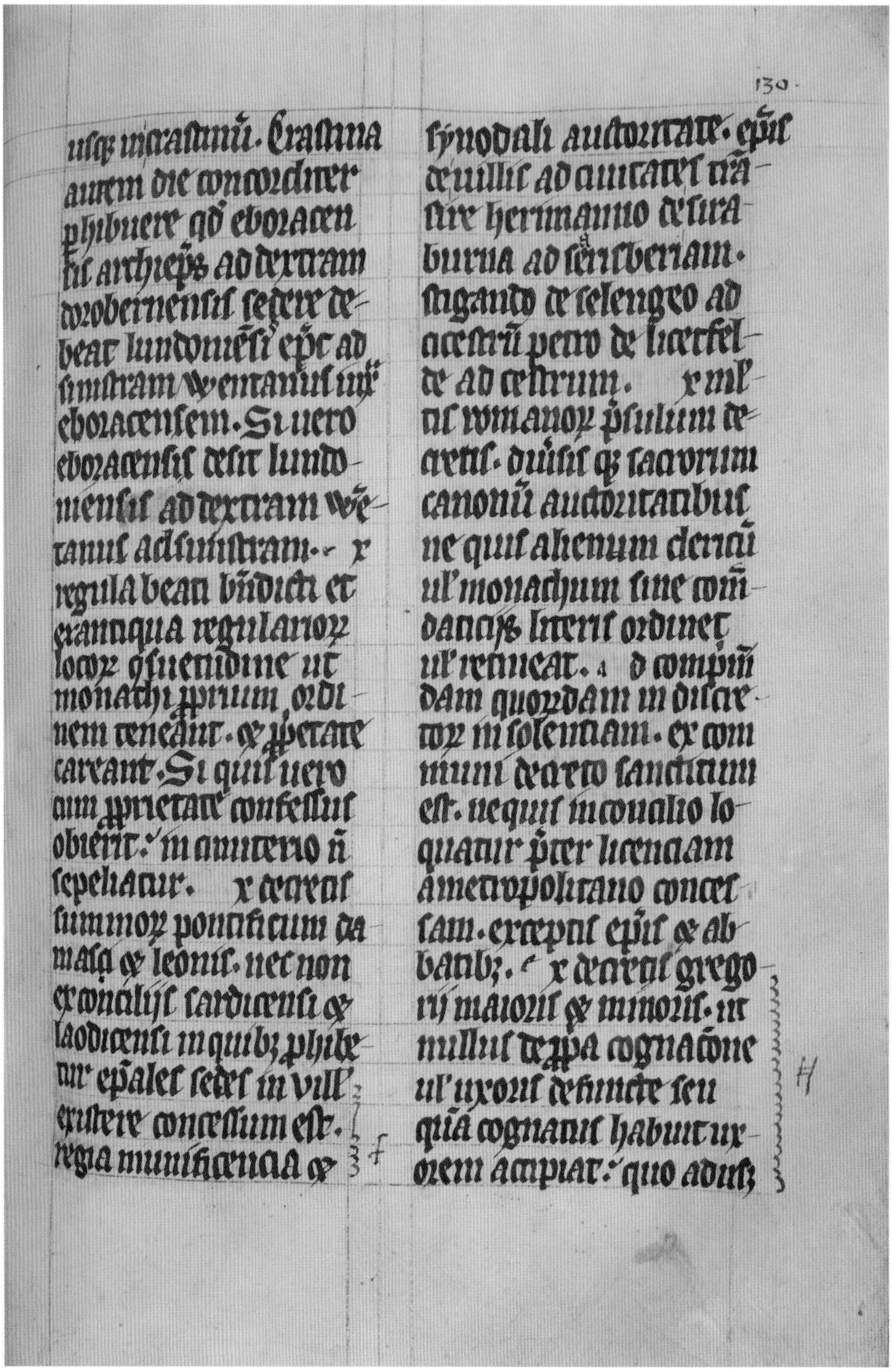

133 The Chronicle of William of Nangis

British Library, Royal MS 13 E iv, fol.444

This Latin *Chronicle* was almost certainly one of the 'divers sundry old authentic histories and chronicles' consulted for the *Collectanea* and mentioned in the Act of Appeals (1533) as supporting royal claims of imperial authority over the Church. The original *Chronicle* was written at St-Denis-en-France by a monk, William of Nangis, also known as Guillaume de Nangis (d.1300), and this fine 14th-century copy came into the possession of Thomas Howard, Duke of Norfolk, who gave it to the King. Henry's political secretaries erased all earlier marginalia and marked many passages for the King's attention, while more than a dozen topical captions were written on parchment to serve as page markers. Henry then perused the volume and wrote fourteen marginal comments. Here he notes that some new papal decrees of 1297 had been first approved by experts in canon and civil law. Following this precedent, Henry set up in 1534 a committee of four legal scholars to approve and codify the laws of the Church in England. (DW)

LITERATURE: Carley, *The Books of King Henry VIII and his Wives*; Bray, *Tudor Church Reform*; Williman, 'Guillaume de Nangis'

134 *Collectanea satis copiosa*

British Library, Cotton MS Cleopatra E vi, fols 37v–38

The *Collectanea satis copiosa* is an arsenal of research material compiled by Henry's scholarly advisers in the early 1530s. The guiding hand was Edward Fox, the King's almoner, but other key members included John Stokesley (Bishop of London) and Thomas Cranmer. The contents of the *Collectanea* bear witness to the gradual shift of focus in royal policy from the marriage to questions about papal jurisdiction in Christian kingdoms, the extent of royal power over the clergy and the very legitimacy of papal authority. The material gathered there was used for many of the propaganda tracts published by Henry's regime in the 1530s, most notably the *Opus eximium, de vera differentia regiae potestatis et ecclesiasticae* (An excellent work on the real difference between royal and ecclesiastical power) that was put out in 1534 to justify the assertion of Royal Supremacy over the Church. (RR)

LITERATURE: Nicholson, 'The Act of Appeals and the English Reformation'; Guy, 'Thomas Cromwell and the Intellectual Origins of the Henrician Revolution'

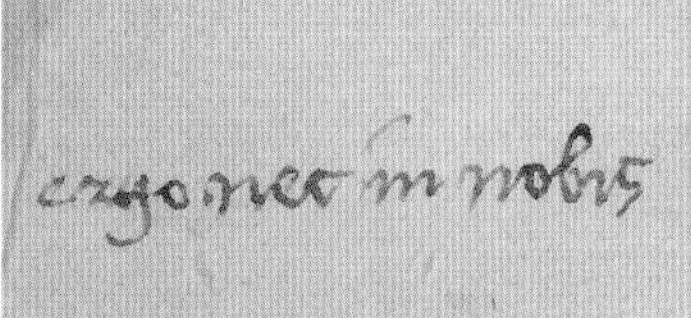

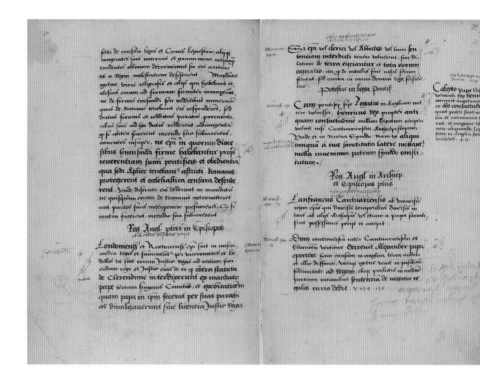

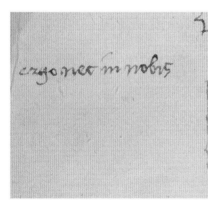

135 Augustinus de Ancona, *Summa de potestate ecclesiastica*, 1475

British Library, IB 3131, fol.193v

Written by the 14th-century theologian Augustinus de Ancona, the *Summa de potestate ecclesiastica* (Summary on ecclesiastical power) emphasized the imperial nature of the papacy. Henry and his advisers, however, turned the arguments on their head and used the *Summa* to posit that lay government within the Church could function independently of Rome. Henry himself read this copy carefully and annotated it at key points: there is a pointing finger beside the discussion on 'Whether or not the pope can exceed in the power of the keys or err'; and he has a note *'de regum correctione'* (concerning the correction of kings), as well as *'de imperatore legum institutione'* (about the imperial institution of laws). Most significantly, beside a passage discussing the practice of bigamy by Old Testament prophets, he observed that it was 'therefore' not against the law in his time either (*ergo nec in nobis*). This is one of the indications that bigamy was seriously considered as a possible resolution to Henry's marital difficulties during the impasse of the late 1520s and early 1530s. (JC)

LITERATURE: Birrell, *English Monarchs and their Books*; Carley, *King Henry's Prayer Book*

136 Bindings

Lambeth Palace Library, London

** H890.A51 [No. 798]; 1488.3 [No. 799]; **H890.T2 [No. 801]

These three books, now held in Lambeth Palace Library, were originally located together in Henry VIII's library at Westminster Palace, where their inventory numbers were nos. 798, 799 and 801. They have retained their original blind-stamped bindings by the London stationer John Reynes and therefore provide a good idea of how sections of the library at Westminster might have looked at the end of Henry's reign. (JC)

LITERATURE: Birrell, *English Monarchs and their Books*; Carley, *King Henry's Prayer Book*

THE END OF A MARRIAGE

Five years after his marriage proposal to Anne, Henry still remained married to his first wife. However, in the autumn of 1532, Henry and Anne had high hopes that the obstacles to their union would soon be removed. Thomas Cranmer, who had consistently supported the annulment and Henry's claims to supremacy, was to be appointed the Archbishop of Canterbury on the death of Warham; and a parliamentary Bill of Appeals was being planned that would prevent judicial appeals going to Rome and so allow Cranmer to make the final judgement on Henry's matrimonial case within England.

Henry therefore decided that Anne should accompany him to France to signal publicly that she would soon be his wife and to obtain the approval of Francis I. So confident were the couple that Anne slept with Henry during their return journey. By the end of December Anne suspected she was pregnant, and, about 25 January, she married Henry secretly. In March 1533 Cranmer was consecrated archbishop and the Act of Appeals cleared Parliament. As a result, in May, the annulment of Henry's first marriage was announced and the legality of his second marriage confirmed.

137 Archbishop William Warham of Canterbury

Unknown artist, after Hans Holbein, early 17th century

Lambeth Palace, London

During the crisis over the annulment, Archbishop Warham (*c.*1450–1532) was supportive of the King and used his influence as Chancellor of Oxford to encourage the University to take Henry's side. He also attempted to silence Bishop John Fisher, who acted for Katherine. However, in March 1532, Warham protested in Parliament against Henry's attacks on papal jurisdiction. Seven weeks later, though, he caved in when Henry attacked Convocation's legislative independence, and was one of three bishops to sign the 'Submission of the Clergy'. It is possible that Warham may have considered resisting further attacks on the independence of the Church, but he died in August of that year.

In this portrait the seventy-year-old Warham is shown in his private chapel with an open prayer book beside him and surrounded by the attributes and insignia of his office: a processional archiepiscopal crucifix to his right and a mitre on his left. His arms and his Latin motto ('my aid is from the Lord') are on the cross. (SD)

LITERATURE: Warham, William, *Oxford DNB*; Strong, *Tudor and Jacobean Portraits*

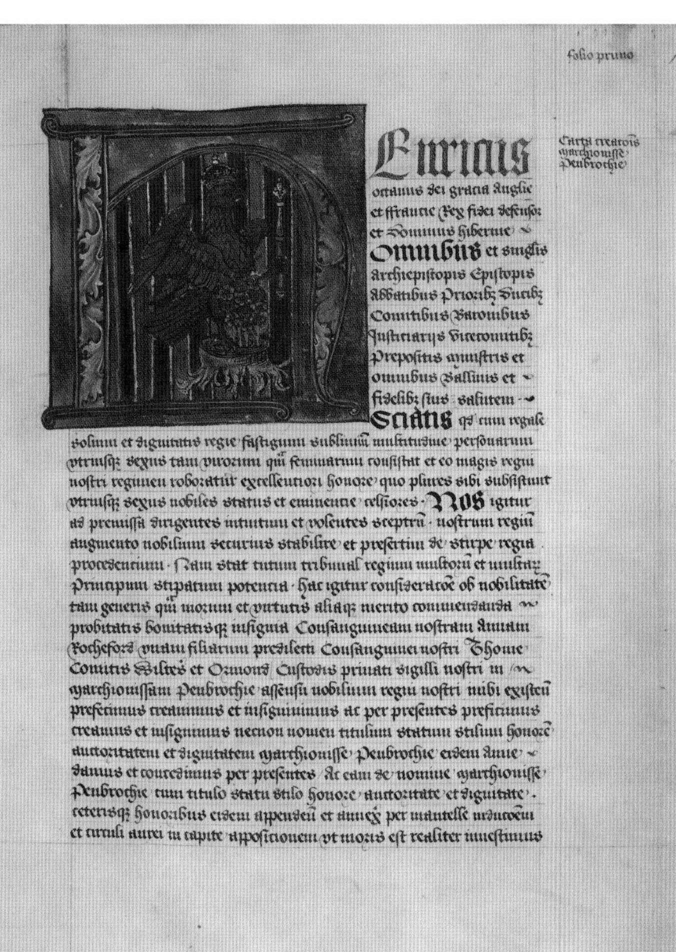

folio primo

Carta creationis marchionisse Penbrochie

Henricus octavus dei gratia Anglie et ffrancie Rex fidei defensor et dominus hibernie Omnibus et singulis Archiepiscopis Episcopis Abbatibus Prioribus Ducibus Comitibus Baronibus Justiciariis Vicecomitibus Prepositis ministris et omnibus Ballivis et fidelibus suis salutem.

138 Anne's Elevation to the Peerage

British Library, Harley MS 303, fol.1

In the autumn of 1532 Anne accompanied Henry to Calais to meet Francis I and cement his support for their marriage. To give Anne the necessary high status for the meeting, on 1 September she had been created Marquis of Pembroke and granted lands worth £1,000 a year. The parchment, silk and gold of this exemplification [record] cost 18 shillings (equivalent to a month's wages for a craftsman). The illuminated 'H' of Henricus incorporates Anne's Boleyn family badge of the white falcon, crowned and sceptred, alighting on a golden tree stump which bursts into a mass of Lancastrian and Yorkist roses, thereby expressing the conviction that Anne will give Henry children. Most unusually, Anne's title was to descend to her son even if he was born outside lawful marriage. This probably indicates that even at this late date Henry was not entirely sure that it would be possible to vindicate the legality of the relationship when he and Anne eventually wed. (EI)

LITERATURE: Ives, *The Life and Death of Anne Boleyn*

139 The Act of Appeals

Draft of the First Act in Restraint of Appeals to Rome, 1533

British Library, Cotton MS Cleopatra E vi, fols 179v–180

Through the autumn of 1532, Henry's Council worked on the legislation that was needed if his matrimonial case was to be brought to a conclusion in England rather than at Rome. The large number of surviving drafts shows just how much effort went into the Act in Restraint of Appeals (enacted in February 1533). Drafting was supervised by Thomas Cromwell, now emerging as the King's chief minister, but Henry himself took a close interest, as can be seen from the suggested amendments here written in his own hand between the lines at the foot of the page. This is a draft of the programmatic opening paragraph, with its portentous claim that 'this realm of England is an Empire', in effect an assertion of full English sovereignty, of independence from any foreign jurisdiction. Henry's angry amendment, defining foreign (that is papal) jurisdiction as 'usurpation', was not adopted in the bill presented to Parliament. Although this idea was to become a commonplace of Henrician propaganda, it was perhaps judged too provocative at this early stage. (RR)

LITERATURE: Elton, 'The Evolution of a Reformation Statute'; Nicholson, 'The Act of Appeals and the English Reformation'; Ullmann, 'This Realm of England is an Empire'

140 Cranmer's Justification for Granting the Annulment

Articuli duodecim, January 1533

British Library, Royal MS 10 B i, fols 4v–5

This treatise *Articuli duodecim* (Twelve articles by which it is completely and plainly proved that a divorce must of necessity be made between Henry VIII, the most unconquered King of England, and the most serene Katherine) was written by Cranmer some time after January 1533. One of only two copies to survive and handsomely bound in purple velvet and gilt edges, this was Henry's personal copy which still bears the Westminster inventory number '935'. The first article of Cranmer's treatise, displayed here, reiterated Henry's conviction that unconsummated, as well as consummated marriages fell under the eternal divine and indispensable ban announced in Leviticus. The treatise also insisted that Arthur had indeed consummated his marriage to Katherine 'because of the many circumstances that attest to it'. Cranmer's treatise would form the background to his findings at the annulment trial at Dunstable Priory later the same year. (AC)

LITERATURE: Kelly, *The Matrimonial Trials of Henry VIII*; Pocock, *Records of the Reformation*; MacCulloch, *Thomas Cranmer*

141 'Divorcing' Katherine

Notification of the sentence of divorce between Henry VIII and Katherine of Aragon, 23 May 1533

The National Archives, Kew, Richmond, Surrey, E30/1025

In April 1533, the Convocation of the ecclesiastical province of Canterbury ruled that the Pope did not have the power to issue a dispensation allowing a man to marry his deceased brother's widow where the original marriage had been consummated. In a further vote, a small group of canon lawyers decided that the consummation of Katherine's marriage to Arthur had been sufficiently proved. On this basis, Archbishop Cranmer obtained permission from Henry to pronounce on his first marriage and convened an ecclesiastical court at Dunstable Priory, a few miles from Ampthill, Bedfordshire, where Katherine was detained. Katherine was cited to appear before the court, but refused to attend. The trial began on the 10 May and, when Katherine did not appear, she was declared contumacious. This document records the sentence of the court, given by Cranmer on 23 March, which found that the King's marriage to Katherine was null and void and prohibited by divine law. (AC)

LITERATURE: Bernard, *The King's Reformation*; Loades, *Henry VIII*; Starkey, *Six Wives*

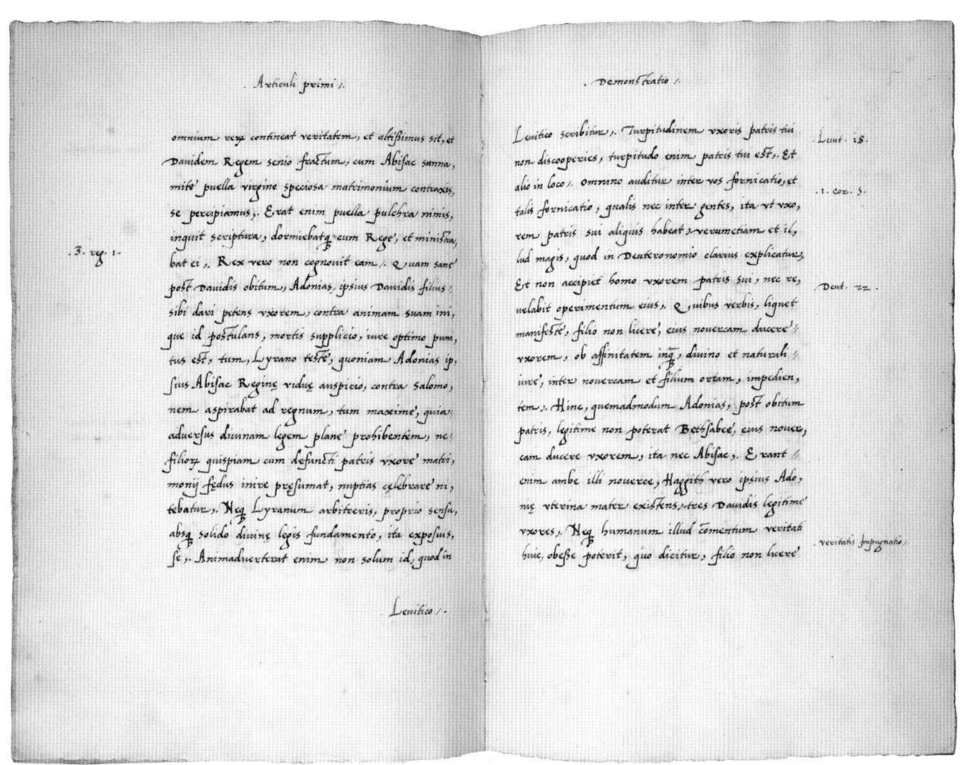

Articuli primi.

omnium verum continet veritatem, et altissimus sit, et
Davidem Regem senio fractum, cum Abisac sunna,
mite puella virgine speciosa matrimonium contraxisse
percipiamus. Erat enim puella pulchra nimis,
inquit scriptura, dormiebatque cum Rege, et ministra-
3. reg. 1. bat ei. Rex vero non cognouit eam. Quam sane
post Davidis obitum, Adonias, ipsius Davidis filius,
sibi davi petens uxorem, contra animam suam ini-
que id postulans, mortis supplicio, iure optimo puni-
tus est, tum, Lyrano teste, quoniam Adonias ipsius Abisac Reginae viduae auspicio, contra Salomo-
nem aspirabat ad regnum, tum maxime, quia
adversus divinam legem plane prohibentem, ne
filiorum quispiam cum defuncti patris uxore matrimonij foedus inire praesumat, nuptias celebrare ni-
tebatur. Neque Lyranum arbitreris, proprio sensu,
absque solido divinae legis fundamento, ita exposuis-
se. Animadverterat enim non solum id, quod in

Levitico.

Demonstratio.

Levitico scribitur. Turpitudinem uxoris patris tui Leuit. 18.
non discooperies, turpitudo enim patris tui est. Et
alio in loco. Omnino auditur inter vos fornicatio, et 1. cor. 5.
talis fornicatio, qualis nec inter gentes, ita ut uxorem patris sui aliquis habeat. Verumetiam et illud magis, quod in Deuteronomio clarius explicatur.
Et non accipiet homo uxorem patris sui, nec re- Deut. 22.
velabit operimentum eius. Quibus verbis, liquet
manifeste, filio non licere, eius novercam ducere
uxorem, ob affinitatem inque, divino et naturali
iure, inter novercam et filium ortam, impedien-
tem. Hinc, quemadmodum Adonias, post obitum
patris, legitime non poterat Bethsabee, eius novercam ducere uxorem, ita nec Abisac. Erant
enim ambae illi novercae, Haggith vero ipsius Ado-
niae uterina mater existens, tres Davidis legitimae
uxores. Neque humanum illud commentum veritati veritatis impugnatio
huic, obesse poterit, quo dicitur, filio non licere

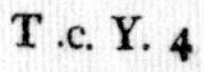

Sententia diffinitiva

Lata per sanctissimum. Dñm Nostrum. D. Clementem. Papã. vij. in sacro Consistorio de Reverendissimorum Dominorum. S. R. E. Cardinalium consilio super validitate Matrimonij inter Serenissimos Henricum. VIII. & Catherinam Anglie Reges contracti.

PRO.

Eadem Serenissima Catherina Angliæ Regina,

CONTRA.

Serenissimum Henricum. VIII. Angliæ Regem.

Clemens Papa. vij.

CHristi nomine invocato in Trono iustitiæ pro tribunali sedentes, & solum Deum præ oculis habentes, Per hanc nostram diffinitivam sententiam quam de Venerabilium Fratrum nostrorum Sanctæ Ro. Ec. Car. Consistorialiter coram nobis congregatorum Consilio, & assensu ferimus in his scriptis, pronunciamus, decernimus, & declaramus, in causa, & causis ad nos, & Sedem Apostolicam per appellationem, per charissimam in christo filiam Catherinam Angliæ Reginam Illustrem a nostris, & Sedis Apostolicæ Legatis in Regno Angliæ deputatis interpositam legitime devolutis, & advocatis, inter prædictam Catherinam Reginam, & Charissimum in christo filium Henricum. VIII. Angliæ Regem Illustrem, super Validitate, & invaliditate matrimonij inter eosdem Reges contracti, & consumati rebusque alijs in actis, causæ & causarum huiusmodi latius deductis, & dilecto filio Paulo Capissucho causarum sacri palatij tunc decano & propter ipsius Pauli absentiam Venerabili Fratri nostro Iacobo Simonetæ Episcopo Pisauricen. unius ex dicti palatij causarum Auditoribus locumtenenti, audiendis instruendis, & in Consistorio nostro Secreto referendis commissis, & per eos nobis, & eisdem Cardinalibus Relatis, & mature discussis, coram nobis pendentibus, Matrimonium Inter predictos Catherinam, & Henricum Angliæ Reges contractum, & inde secuta quecunque fuisse, & esse validum, & canonicum validaque, & Canonica, suosque debitos debuisse, & debere sortiri effectus, prolemque exinde susceptam, & suscipiendam fuisse, & fore legitimam, & præfatum Henricum Angliæ Regem teneri, & obligatum fuisse, et fore ad cohabitandum cum dicta Catherina Regina eius legitima coniuge, illamque maritali affectione, & Regio honore tractandum, & eundem Henricum Angliæ Regem ad præmissa omnia, & singula cum effectu adimplendum condemnandum omnibusque iuris Remedijs cogendum, & compellendum fore, prout condemnamus, cogimus, & compellimus, Molestationesque, & denegationes Per eundem Henricum Regem eidem Catherinæ Reginæ super invaliditate, ac foedere dicti Matrimonij quomodolibet factas, & præstitas fuisse, & esse illicitas, & iniustas, & eidem Henrico Regi super illis ac invaliditate matrimonij huiusmodi perpetuum Silentium imponendum fore, & imponimus, eundemque Henricum Angliæ Regem in expensis in huiusmodi causa pro parte dictæ Catherinæ Reginæ coram nobis, & dictis omnibus legitime factis condemnandum fore, & condemnamus, quarum expensarum taxationem nobis imposterum reservamus.

Ita pronunciavimus .I.

Lata fuit Romæ in Palatio Apostolico publice in Consistorio die. XXIII. Martij. M. D. XXXIIII.

Blosius.

142 *Sentencia diffinitiva*

Copy of Pope Clement VII's pronouncement of validity on Henry and Katherine's marriage, 23 March 1534

Archivo General de Simancas, Patronato Real, Caja 53, Doc. 117 (1)

Cranmer's sentence on the royal marriage directly contravened papal orders forbidding any court to consider the case while it still lay before the Roman tribunals. Six weeks later, therefore, Clement VII excommunicated Cranmer for judging the case and also declared Henry VIII excommunicated unless he left Anne by September and returned to Katherine. Henry's response was to launch a campaign of antipapal propaganda and introduce a series of antipapal laws, including, in December 1533, an order declaring that the Pope should no longer be referred to as the 'Pope' but as 'the Bishop of Rome'.

Unable to ignore such blatant acts of defiance, Clement gave a final judgement on Henry and Katherine's marriage on 23 March 1534. His *Sentencia diffinitiva* found in Katherine's favour, ruling that her marriage to Henry was valid, that she was the King's *legitima coniuge* (legitimate wife) and that Henry should therefore resume living with her. (AC)

LITERATURE: Bernard, *The King's Reformation*; Hughes, *The Reformation in England*

QUEEN ANNE

On Whit Sunday 1533 a visibly pregnant Anne was crowned Queen of England in Westminster Abbey. It was a grand occasion with four days of celebration in London that included processions, pageants and a feast, as well as the religious ceremony. Three months later Anne gave birth to a daughter, much to the disappointment of her parents. While Queen, Anne promoted religious reform. She cannot be labelled a Lutheran, but she was attracted to Christian humanism, especially as it was practised and taught in France. She encouraged Henry to promote reformers in the Church and used her influence to encourage the use of a Bible written in the vernacular.

143 The Birth of Princess Elizabeth

British Library, Harley MS 283, fol.75

Anne and Henry were confident that their first child would be a son and planned to call him Henry or Edward, but, on Sunday, 7 September 1533, Anne was delivered of a daughter. Letters announcing the birth were immediately sent out, some of which (including this one) had been written in advance when a boy was expected. Here God is thanked for sending the Queen good speed in the deliverance and bringing forth of a prince. Hastily an 's' was added to announce the birth of a 'princes'. Of course, the sex of the baby was a grave disappointment to her parents, but they tried to put a brave face on it. A herald announced the arrival of the first of Henry's 'legitimate children' and the Chapel Royal sang the *Te Deum* to thank God for a safe delivery. The baby was named 'Elizabeth' after both her grandmothers and to identify her with the royal dynasty. (SD)

LITERATURE: Ives, *The Life and Death of Anne Boleyn*; Starkey, *Six Wives*

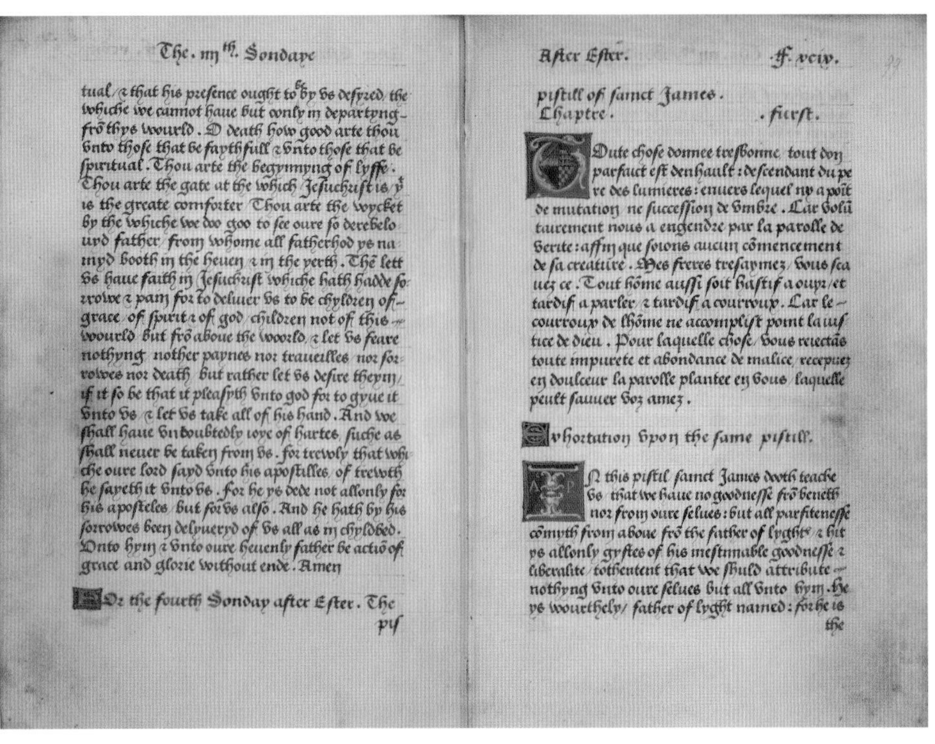

The. iiii^th. Sondaye

tual / & that his presence ought to by us desyred the whiche we cannot haue but onely in departyng fro thys wourld. O death how good arte thou unto those that be faythfull & unto those that be spirituall. Thou arte the begynnyng of lyffe. Thou arte the gate at the which Jesuchrist is ye is the greate comforter Thou arte the wycket by the whiche we doo goo to see oure so derebelouyd father from whome all fatherhod ys namyd booth in the heuen & in the yerth. The lett us haue faith in Jesuchrist whiche hath hadde so trowe & payn for to deliuer us to be chyldren of grace of spirit & of god children not of this wourld but fro aboue the woorld & let us feare nothyng nother paynes nor traueilles nor sorrowes nor death but rather let us desire theym if it so be that it pleasyth unto god for to gyue it unto us & let us take all of his hand. And we shall haue undoubtedly ioye of hartes suche as shall neuer be taken from us. for trewly that whiche oure lord sayd unto his apostilles of trewth he sayeth it unto us. For he ys dede not allonly for his apostelles but for us also. And he hath by his sorrowes been delyueryd of us all as in chyldbed. Unto hym & unto oure heuenly father be actio of grace and glorie without ende. Amen

For the fourth Sonday after Ester. The pis

After Ester. ff. xcix.

pistill of saint James.

Chaptre. first.

Toute chose donnee tresbonne tout don parfaict est denhault: descendant du pere des lumieres: enuers lequel ny a poit de mutation ne succession de umbre. Car volutairement nous a engendre par la parolle de verite: affin que soions aucun cōmencement de sa creature. Mes freres tresaymez vous scauez ce. Tout hōme aussi soit hastif a ouyr/ et tardif a parler & tardif a courroux. Car le courroux de lhōme ne accomplist point la iustice de dieu. Pour laquelle chose vous rejectās toute impurete et abondance de malice receuez en doulceur la parolle plantee en vous laquelle peult sauuer voz amez.

Exhortation upon the same pistill.

In this pistil saint James doth teache us that we haue no goodnesse fro beneth nor from oure selues: but all parfitenesse cōmyth from aboue fro the father of lyght & but ys allonly gyftes of his inestimable goodnesse & liberalite tothentent that we shuld attribute nothyng unto oure selues but all unto hym. He ys wourthely father of lyght named: for he is the

144 Anne Boleyn's Religion

The Pistellis and Gospelles for the LII Sondayes in the Yere, 1532–3

British Library, Harley MS 6561, fols 98v–99

This manuscript – produced between September 1532 and April 1533 – is part copy, part translation of the Epistles and Gospels by the French reformer Jacques Lefèvre d'Etaples that was printed at Alençon from 1530 to 1532. The translator was Anne Boleyn's brother George, Lord Rochford (*c*.1504–36), working on her instructions. Despite water damage, it exemplifies Anne's concern for magnificence (manuscripts ranked above print). It also testifies to the interest that Anne and her brother George showed in the French school of evangelical reform, which saw the Bible as superior to Church tradition. Altogether, Anne and George collected some 40 evangelical books in French or by French printers. As shown here, with the reading for the fourth Sunday after Easter taken from the Epistle of James, this manuscript has the Bible text in French at the top, with the translated commentary below, perhaps reflecting Anne's preference for the Scripture versions to which she had first become accustomed in France. (EI)

LITERATURE: Ives, *The Life and Death of Anne Boleyn*; Carley, *The Books of King Henry VIII and his Wives*

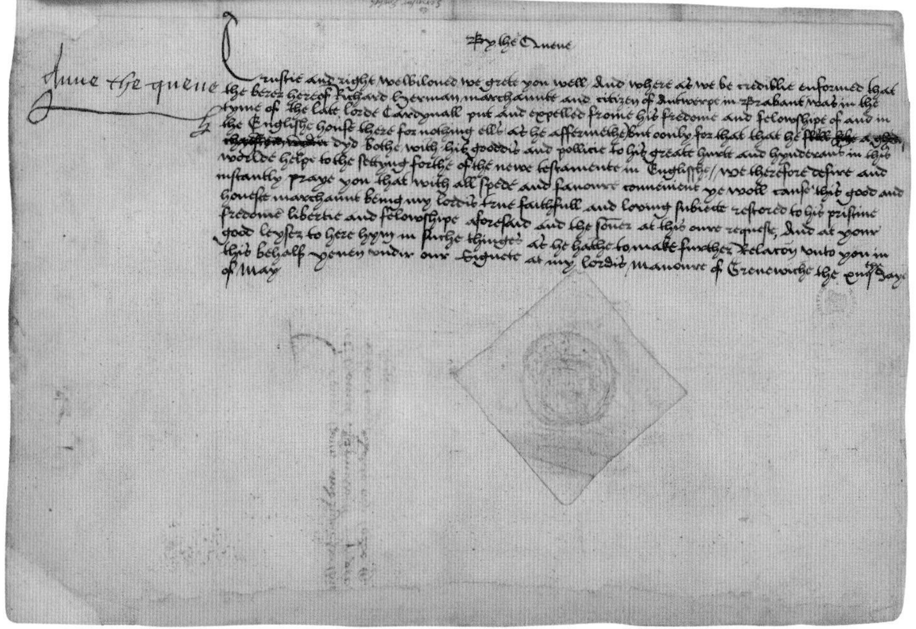

Anne the quene

By the Quene

145 Anne Boleyn's Support for an English Bible

Letter from Anne Boleyn to Thomas Cromwell in support of Richard Herman from Greenwich, 14 May 1534

British Library, Cotton MS Cleopatra E v, fol.350v

Anne Boleyn and her brother were major sponsors of the importation of reformist books published abroad, in particular English Bibles. This letter informs Thomas Cromwell that 'Richard Herman, marchaunte and citizen of Antwerpe in Brabant was in the tyme of the late lorde Cardynall [i.e. Wolsey] put and expelled frome his fredome and felowshipe of and in the Englishe house [that is trading post] there, for nothing ells as he affermethe' but only for that that he 'dyd bothe with his gooddis and pollicie to his greate hurte and hynderans in this worlde helpe to the settyng forthe of the newe testamente in Englisshe'. Anne instructs Cromwell (also a promoter of the vernacular Bible) to have Herman 'restored to his pristine fredome, libertie and felowshipe'. Anne may also have been behind the licensing of a Southwark printer to print Coverdale's Bible in England, and, so long as she was alive, the drafts of the injunctions to the clergy being prepared in 1536, included a clause requiring every parish to set up a Latin and an English Bible in its church, 'for every man that will to look and read thereon'. (EI)

LITERATURE: Ives, *The Life and Death of Anne Boleyn*

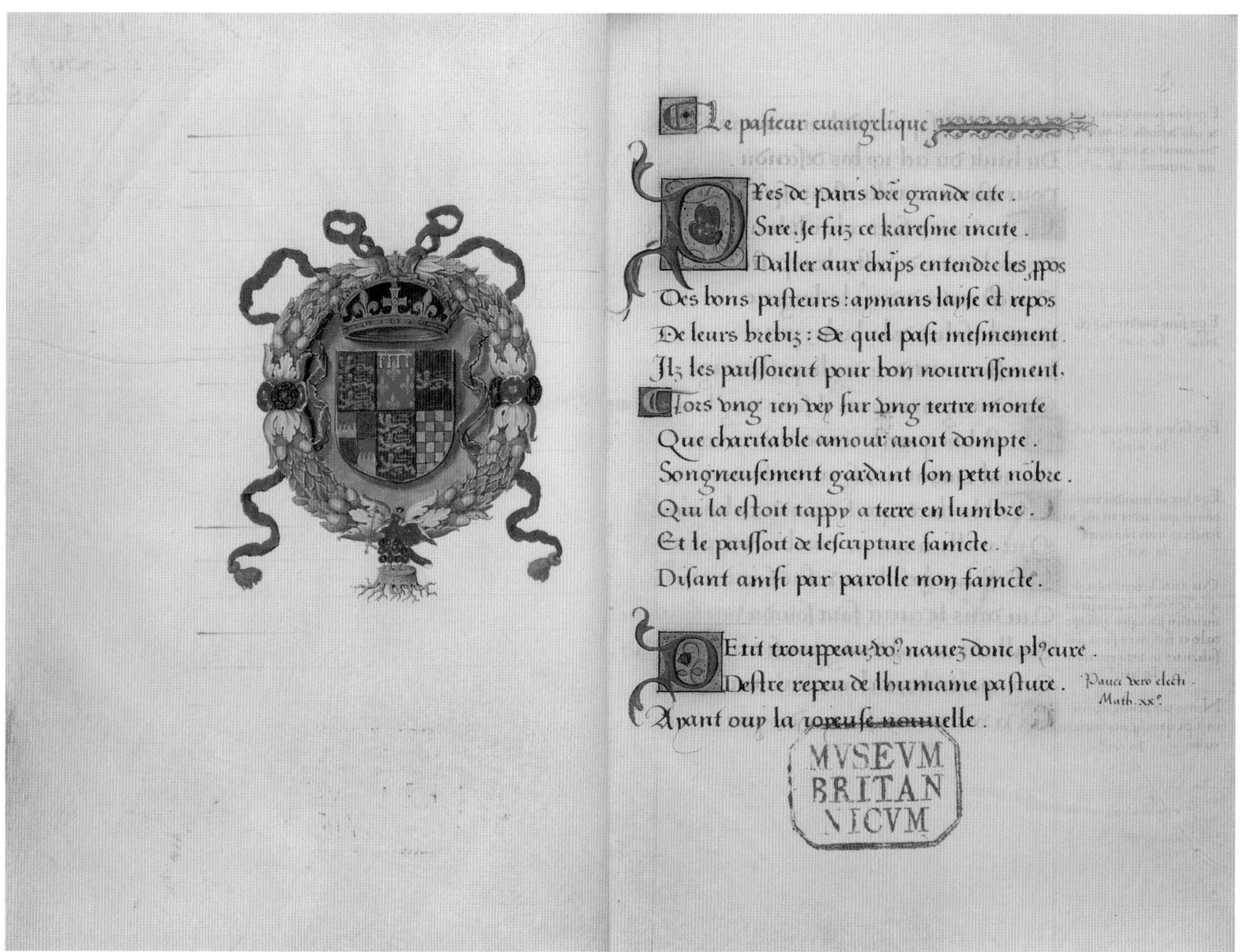

Le pasteur euangelique

Pres de paris vne grande cite .
Sire, Je fuz ce karesme incite .
Daller aux champs entendre les ppos
Des bons pasteurs : aymans lapse et repos
De leurs brebiz : de quel pasi mesmement .
Ilz les paissoient pour bon nourrissement .
Lors vng ien vey sur vng tertre monte
Que charitable amour auoit dompte .
Songneusement gardant son petit nobre .
Qui la estoit tappy a terre en lumbre .
Et le paissoit de lescripture saincte .
Disant ainsi par parolle non faincte .

Petit trouppeau, voꝰ nauez donc plꝰcure .
Destre repeu de lhumaine pasture . Pauci vero electi . Math. xx°.
Ayant ouy la ~~ioyeuse nouuelle~~ .

146 *Le Pastor evangélique*

Clément Marot (1496–1544)

British Library, Royal MS 16 E xiii, fols 1v–2

This is an elite copy of *Le Pastor evangélique* presented to Anne Boleyn, possibly by Jean de Dinteville the French ambassador, on the occasion of her coronation. The major French poet and religious reformer, Clément Marot, customized an existing poem with lines celebrating Henry as a religious reformer and added a final prophecy that the Good Shepherd [Christ] would give Anne a son in Henry's image, whom the couple would live to see grow into manhood.

> Oh Anne my lady, Oh incomparable queen
> This Good Shepherd who favours you
> will give you a son who will be the living image
> of the king his father, and he will live and flourish
> until the two of you can see him reach the age
> when a man is mature.

The manuscript demonstrates the strength of Anne's links with French religious reformers. The falcon pendant to Anne Boleyn's arms was originally silver but is now oxidized. (EI)

LITERATURE: Ives, *The Life and Death of Anne Boleyn*; Dowling, 'Anne Boleyn and Reform'; Ives, 'Anne Boleyn and the Early Reformation in England'

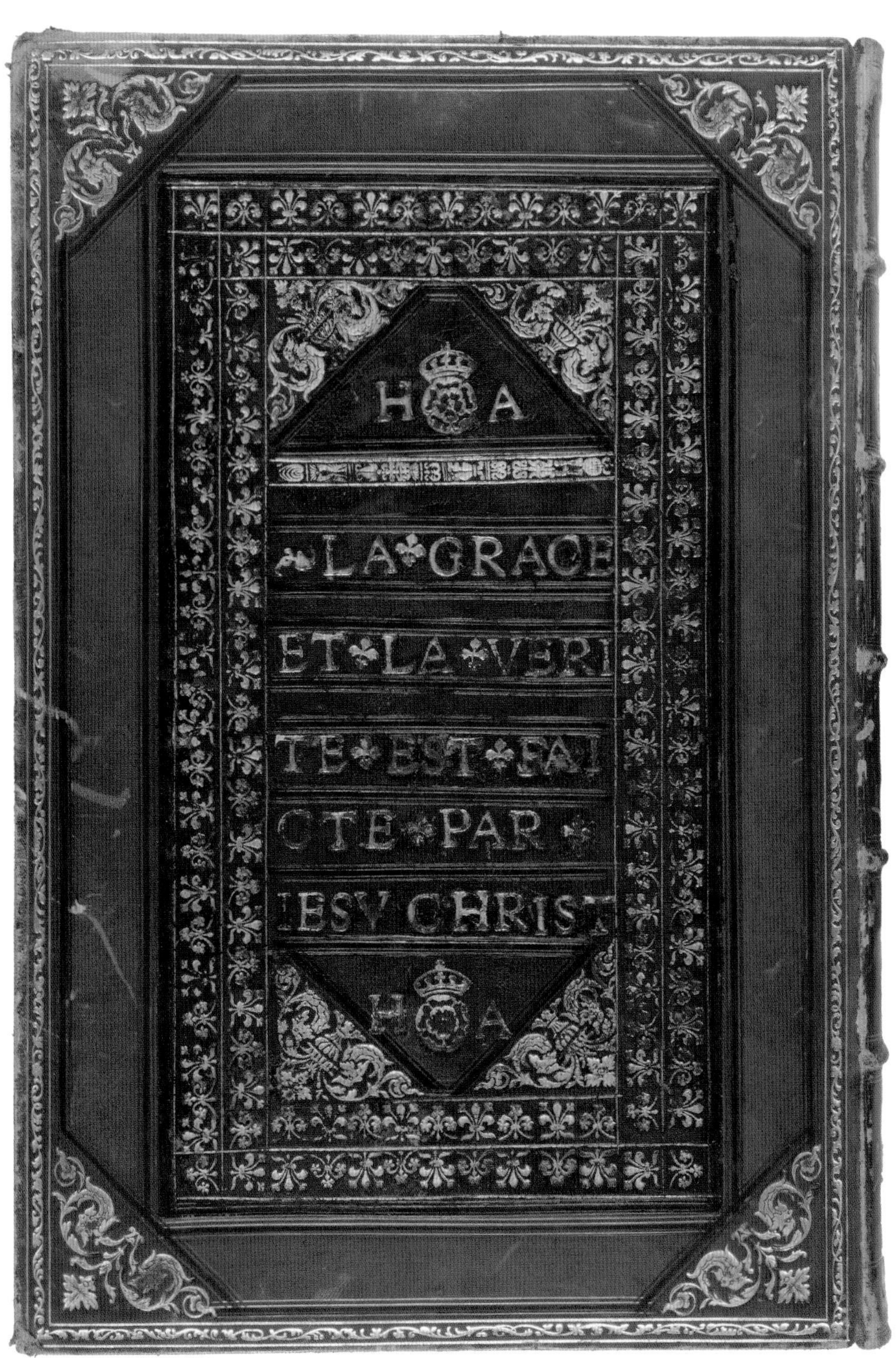

147 Evangelical Writings

Translation of the Bible into French by Jacques Lefèvre d'Etaples, 1534

British Library, C.18.c.9, binding

This translation of the Bible into French, a revised version of the text originally undertaken slightly earlier by Jacques Lefèvre d'Etaples (*c*.1445–1536), the reformist scholar patronized by Francis I and his sister Marguerite de Navarre, is one of a group of evangelical writings, some translations from Luther, that can be associated with Anne Boleyn and her circle. The printer was the Frenchman Martin Lempereur (d.1536), resident in Antwerp, who also published in the same year Willam Tyndale's New Testament, of which Anne was a promoter and financial backer. It has been bound in two volumes by King Henry's Binder. There is an 'H' and an 'A' flanking a Tudor rose at top and bottom of the cover, with text in the form of biblical quotations in French of the sort favoured by the reformers. On Volume II the first half of John I: 17 appears on the front, 'For the law was given by Moses', while the second half, 'but grace and truth came by Jesus Christ', is stamped on the back, as shown here. Even the binding of Henry's books had a political agenda. (JC)

LITERATURE: Carley, 'French Evangelical Books at the Court of Henry VIII'; Carley, 'Henry VIII's Library and Humanist Donors'; Ives, *The Life and Death of Anne Boleyn*

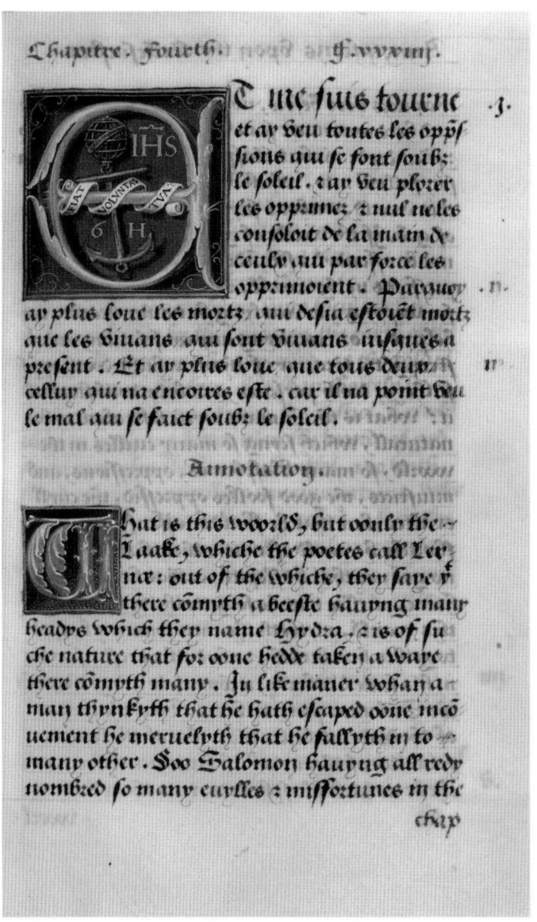

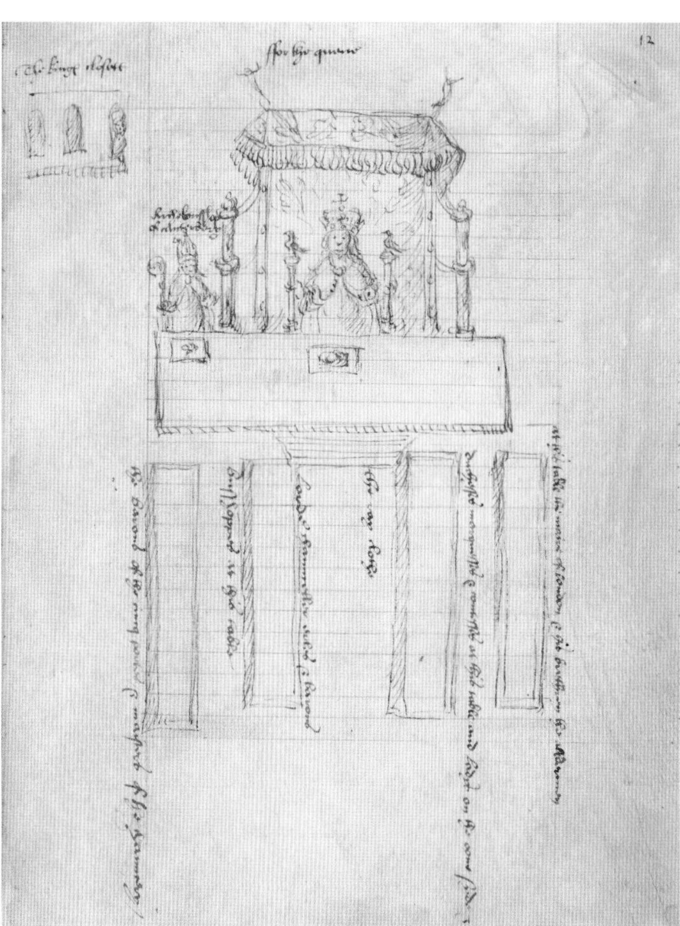

148 The Ecclesiastes

Collection of His Grace the Duke of Northumberland, Percy MS 465, fol.34

Later than *The Pistellis and Gospelles*, this second hybrid translation by George Boleyn is of the text and commentary by Jacques Lefèvre d'Etaples on the Old Testament book, Ecclesiastes. It is illuminated throughout with Anne Boleyn's badges and symbols referring to her. The historiated 'E' at the start of chapter 4: *Et me suis* has a double meaning. The horizontal bears the motto *Fiat voluntas tua* (Thy will be done) – the anchor means commitment and the celestial sphere, constancy. The 'IHS' is the monogram for Jesus and hence the design points to obedience to, and faith in, Christ, which is the theme of Lefèvre's commentary. In the lower half is the Greek letter sigma, s, or 'S', which, in royal monograms, means 'Sovereign'. Hence 's H' means 'Sovereign Henry, so the design points to obedience to, and faith in, Henry VIII. And the 's H' is below the 'IHS', because Henry is the Supreme Head 'under Christ'. Hence Christ's will and Henry's will are one and the same. The celestial sphere makes the design specific to Anne because she used it as a personal symbol, as would her daughter. (EI)

LITERATURE: Ives, *The Life and Death of Anne Boleyn*

149 Anne's Coronation, Sunday, 1 June 1533

British Library, Harley MS 41, fol.12

A grand feast was the final event on Anne's coronation day. This sketch of the seating plan reads top left – 'the kinges closett'; top centre – 'ffor the quene'; next to Anne – 'Archebusshop of Canterbury'. The legends by the tables read (from the right): 'at this table the maire of london & his brethren the alldermen'; 'duchesses marquesses and contesses at this table and ladys on the oone syde &c'; 'the ray clothe'; 'lorde chauncelleer erles & barons'; 'busshoppes at this table'; 'the barons of the cincq portes & maisters of the chauncery'. Anne, six months pregnant, occupied the great marble royal throne, sitting on a specially made inner seat. Two noblewomen stood either side (not shown) who held up a cloth if Anne wished 'to spit or do otherwise'. Two gentlewomen (not shown) sat under the table to do her bidding. Henry watched from the royal closet with the French and Venetian ambassadors. (EI)

LITERATURE: Ives, *The Life and Death of Anne Boleyn*; Wooding, *Henry VIII*; Starkey, *Six Wives*

THE ROYAL SUPREMACY

The break with Rome and Henry's headship of the Church of England were formally recognized in the Act of Supremacy of 1534. The statute, which was the culmination of the antipapal legislation of the previous two years, gave statutory recognition to Henry's title of 'Supreme Head of the Church of England' and set out the vast powers he enjoyed in this capacity. In 1535, a Treasons Act was passed that prescribed legal penalties, beginning with imprisonment and confiscation, and ending with death, for 'maliciously' denying the Royal Supremacy.

150 The Act of Supremacy, 1534

The National Archives, Kew, Richmond, Surrey, C65/143, m.5, no 8

This is the formal entry in the Parliament Roll of the Act of Supremacy. This, the most revolutionary statute of the Reformation Parliament, was also one of its shortest. A single paragraph sufficed to place the King, instead of the Pope, at the pinnacle of ecclesiastical hierarchy and jurisdiction. The Act was careful to emphasize that it was not conferring power upon the King, but merely recognizing a power already his by right. This legal pretence highlighted the uncomfortable gap between the convenient theory of a supremacy that was conferred by God in the Bible and the inconvenient truth that the taming of the medieval Church could be achieved only through statute law and Parliament. (RR)

LITERATURE: Rex, *Henry VIII and the English Reformation*; Bernard, *The King's Reformation*; Elton, *The Tudor Constitution*

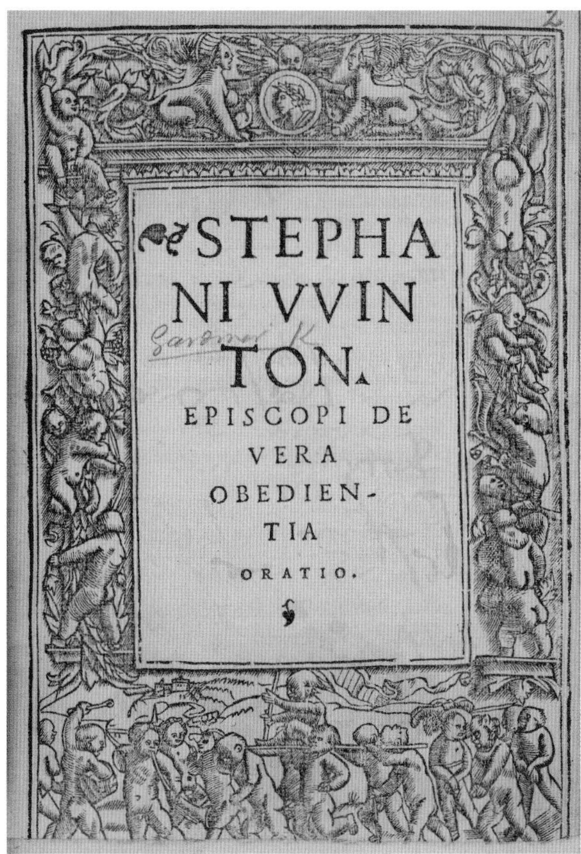

STEPHA
NI VVIN
TON.
EPISCOPI DE
VERA
OBEDIEN-
TIA
ORATIO.

151 Stephen Gardiner, *De Vera Obedientia*, 1535

British Library, T.811(2), title page

De vera obedientia (Of true obedience) is the best-known and most accomplished defence of the Royal Supremacy produced under Henry. Written by Stephen Gardiner, Bishop of Winchester, in the summer of 1535, just after the executions of John Fisher and Thomas More, the book constructed a theory of obedience and defended the Royal Supremacy. The true Christian, Gardiner wrote, was one who never failed in his obedience to God and so had to obey God's representative on earth, namely the prince. Gardiner also argued that, since the time of Solomon, the prince had had an *imperium* in his realm with the authority to determine temporal and spiritual affairs in his kingdom. Consequently, in calling himself the Supreme Head on earth of the Church of England, Henry was doing nothing new or against God's law. This Latin tract helped restore Gardiner to royal favour after his earlier defence of the liberties of the Church had raised doubts about his loyalty. It was reprinted several times both in England and reformed centres on the Continent. (SD)

LITERATURE: Fox and Guy, *Reassessing the Henrician Age*; Hughes, *The Reformation in England*; Guy, 'The Henrician Age'

152 The Oath of Supremacy, 1535

British Library, Additional. Ch. 12827

Once the Royal Supremacy had been enacted, the Supreme Head of the Church of England sent out 'visitors' (agents) to exact an oath to his new title from every member of every ecclesiastical corporation in England, including the universities. Cambridge was duly visited in October 1535. This document, renouncing any allegiance to the 'Bishop of Rome', was signed on 23 October 1535 in the name of the entire University by the Vice-Chancellor, the Proctors and nearly twenty other senior figures, including many heads of colleges. There was no trouble: the former Master of Michaelhouse, Dr Nicholas Wilson (d.1548), was at that moment in the Tower of London for having refused the Oath to the Succession. The execution of Cambridge's former Chancellor, John Fisher, in June 1535 provided the ultimate deterrent to any thoughts of recalcitrance, and the university had since shown its goodwill by electing Cromwell as his successor. (RR)

LITERATURE: Logan, 'The First Royal Visitation of the English Universities, 1535'; Leader, *A History of the University of Cambridge*, vol.1; Porter, *Reformation and Reaction in Tudor Cambridge*

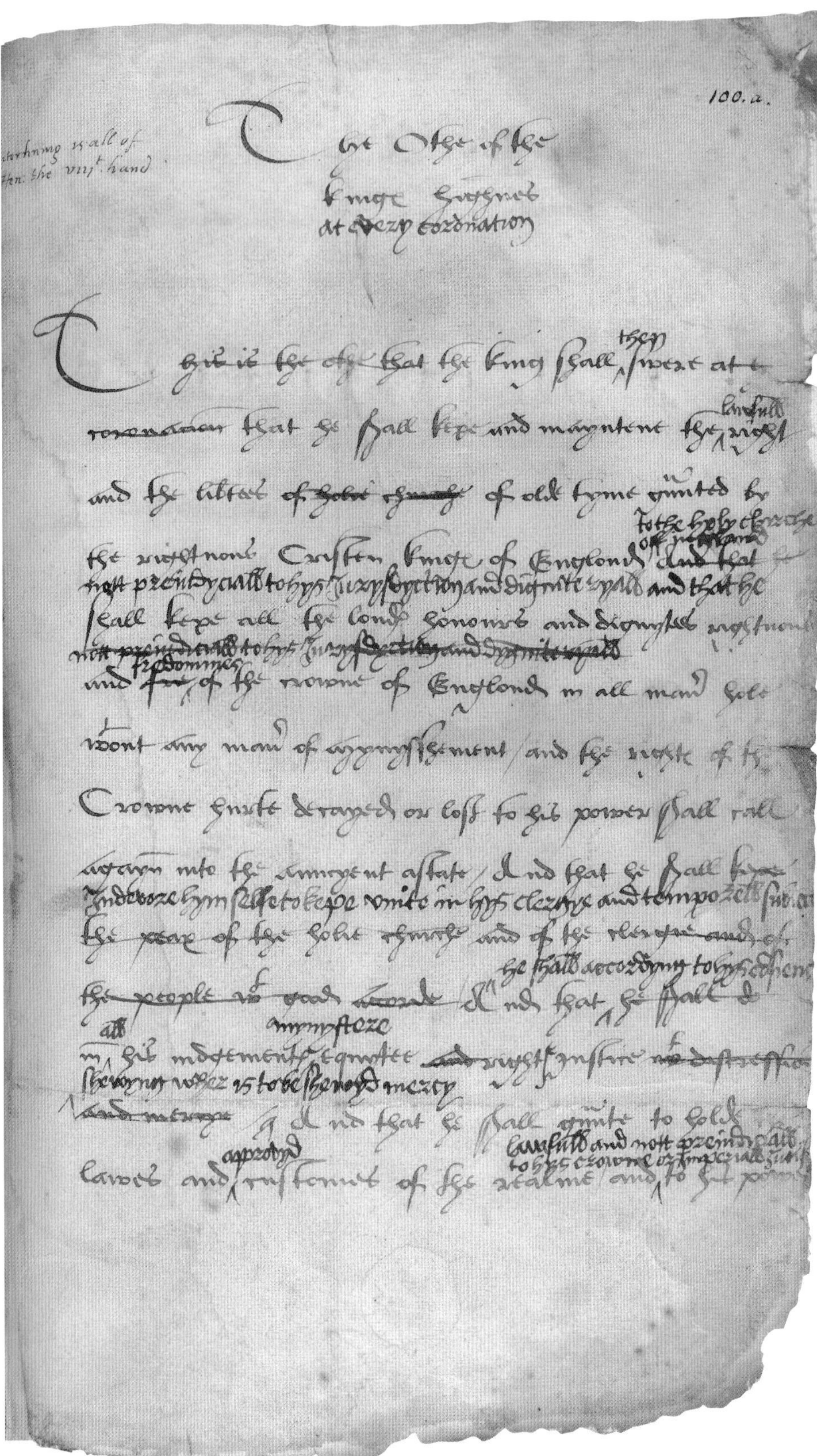

153 Henry VIII's Coronation Oath

British Library, Cotton MS Tiberius E viii, fol.89

On acceding to the throne, monarchs were crowned in a magnificent and elaborate ceremony in which the new king swore to observe the laws and defend the Church. At his own coronation in 1509, Henry took the traditional oath. But probably in the 1530s he made, as his unmistakable hand shows, several significant revisions to the oath which fundamentally changed its meaning. Instead of swearing to maintain the rights and liberties of 'holy churche', the King would now swear to maintain those of 'the holy churche off ingland' – but with the crucial qualification, 'nott preiudyciall to hys Iurysdyction and dignite ryall'. Precisely when Henry introduced this modification is unknown, but it may have been at the time when he was planning Jane Seymour's coronation or after the birth of his son and heir. Henry's version of the oath was never used. Nonetheless, his manuscript alterations provide a clear indication of his commitment to the Royal Supremacy over the Church, as well as showing his awareness that, by assuming it, he had broken his own original coronation oath. (GB and SD)

LITERATURE: Hoak (ed.), *Tudor Political Culture*; Wickham Legg (ed.), *English Coronation Records*; Loach, 'The Function of Ceremonial in the Reign of Henry VIII'

VICTIMS

Henry could not brook disagreement or opposition to his second marriage and the Royal Supremacy. He seems to have been especially rattled by Elizabeth Barton, an uneducated nun known as the 'Holy Maid of Kent', who had predicted Henry's death if he married Anne Boleyn. Accused of treason, Barton was condemned by a parliamentary Act of Attainder, forced to recant publicly and executed in 1534.

Thomas More and John Fisher also incurred Henry's anger. Neither man endorsed Henry's policy towards the Church (Fisher spoke out in opposition while More remained silent) and in 1534 they were both imprisoned for refusing to take the Oath to the Succession, an oath recognizing the legitimacy of Henry's marriage to Anne Boleyn and renouncing papal power. By 1535 Henry had had enough of their defiance. Fisher was put on trial and beheaded for denying the Royal Supremacy; More was tried and executed for denying the validity of the Act of Succession. Other victims of Henry's demand for compliance were some of the monks based at the Charterhouse in London and at Sheen. Although a majority acknowledged the Royal Supremacy, eighteen of them died as a result of their refusal to take the oath: these Carthusians were either starved to death in prison or else hanged, drawn and quartered.

154 Sir Thomas More

Hans Holbein the Younger (1497/8–1543)

Chalk drawing, *c.*1526

Inscribed: 'Sier Thomas Mooer' in an unknown near-contemporary hand

This drawing is the working sketch for the figure of Sir Thomas More in Holbein's family-group portrait which is now lost, though the preliminary sketch for it was sent as a gift to Erasmus by Margaret Roper and is now in Basel. It is a world apart from Holbein's other drawing of him, the cartoon for the portrait in the Frick Collection, New York, in which Thomas poses in his official dress as 'the king's good servant'. Here Thomas appears more at ease, more open; the hat is softer and reveals more of his forehead. His long hair flows out freely from beneath it. His expression is animated, unguarded, enquiring, more vulnerable than in the Frick portrait, less remote, and there is a disarming hint of mirth and the suppressed smile of someone who finds the whole idea of posing for his portrait pleasantly ridiculous. He looks here as Erasmus described him: 'always friendly and cheerful, with something of the air of one who smiles easily, and (to speak frankly) disposed to be merry rather than serious or solemn'. The wash in the hat is not from Holbein's hand, and some of the outlines have also been retouched. (JG)

LITERATURE: Parker and Foister, *The Drawings of Hans Holbein the Younger in the Collection of Her Majesty The Queen at Windsor Castle*; *Holbein and the Court of Henry VIII*; Guy, *A Daughter's Love*

155 Sir Thomas More and Henry VIII

Letter from Sir Thomas More to Henry VIII, Chelchith (Chelsea, London), 5 March 1534

British Library, Cotton MS Cleopatra E vi, fols 176v–177

More resigned as Lord Chancellor on 16 May 1532 and Henry had allowed him to live as a private citizen. However, in 1533 More incurred the enmity of Anne and Henry by refusing to attend Anne's coronation and by publishing *The Apology of Sir Thomas More*, a defence of the old Catholic order in which he advised every good Christian to stand firm to the old faith. Attempting to win More's compliance to his second marriage and to his growing belief that he was Head of the Church of England, Henry grew increasingly impassioned and vindictive as he realized he was likely to fail. In late February 1534, he decided to add More's name, along with Fisher's, to the Bill for the Attainder (for treason) of Elizabeth Barton.

In this, the last of his six extant letters to Henry, More began by giving an account of his resignation, saying that Henry, then, had promised 'that for the service which I byfore had done you (which it than lyked your goodnes far above my deserving to commend) that in eny suit that I should after have un to your Highnes ... I should fynd your Highnes good and graciouse lord un to me'. Now, taking Henry up on his offer, More accordingly petitioned the King not to listen to such 'sinistre information' as might have been given against him. He protested his honesty and sincerity in Barton's case, and urged that, if the King, after reconsidering the matter, still suspects him to be 'a wreche of such a monstrouse ingratitude', then his only comfort would be that 'I shold onys mete with your Grace agayn in hevyn, and there be mery with you.' (JG)

LITERATURE: Rogers (ed.), *The Correspondence of Sir Thomas More*; Elton, *Policy and Police*; Guy, *A Daughter's Love*

156 A Badge of Office

Private Collection, London

Livery chains were ubiquitous in the first half of Henry VIII's reign and Sir Thomas More famously wears one in Holbein's portrait of him. Livery collars began in the late 14th century: ordinary folk wore their lord's symbol or badge and his colours in their clothing; knights and the higher ranks wore their lord's collar. This applied especially to the king's followers, who included the greatest in the land. The Lancastrian collar was a chain of letters of 'S' (for 'Souverayne'). Edward IV of York replaced this with a chain of white roses alternating with sun-bursts with a pendant lion; Richard III replaced the lion pendant with his own badge of the boar. Henry VII, who claimed to be the heir of Lancaster, reverted to the chain of S's but closed it with two portcullises (the badge of his mother's family, the Beauforts), with his own badge of the Tudor rose suspended from them.

This chain did not actually belong to More. From its provenance and the fineness of its gold it is thought to have been made in the last year or two of Henry VIII's reign. With knots (as in the Garter collar) placed between the S's, it is suggested that it was given to Sir Edward Montagu, Chief Justice of Commons Pleas from 1546 to 1553, and subsequently handed down to his successors as a badge of office. (DS)

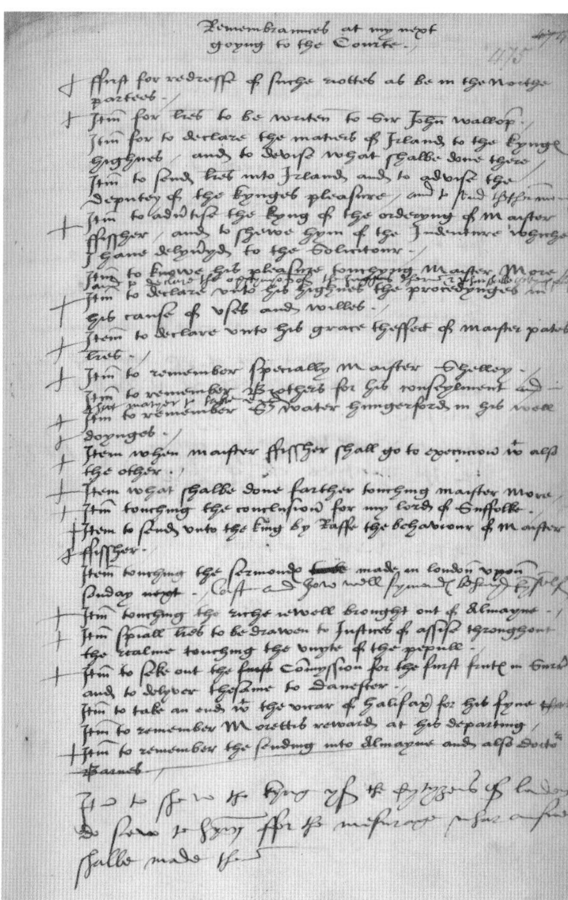

157 What to Do about Sir Thomas More?

'Remembraunces at my next goying to the Courte', June 1535

British Library, Cotton MS Titus B i, fol.475

This document must, from internal evidence, be dated before 22 June 1535 (Bishop John Fisher's execution) and after 17 June (Fisher's trial). Written out by a clerk, but corrected in Cromwell's own hand, the text relates to a meeting between Cromwell and Henry at Windsor, where the court had moved on 12 June. Cromwell noted: 'Item, to knowe his [Henry's] pleasure touchyng Maister More, [adding, in his own hand] and to declare the oppynyon of the Judges theron and what shalbe the kynges plesure.' Twelve lines below is the note: 'Item, what shalbe done farther touching Maister More.' One of several notes concerning Fisher asks: 'Item, when Maister Fisshher shall go to execucion with also the other.' It follows that More's conviction and execution must have been a foregone conclusion, decided by Henry and implemented by Cromwell. In this connection, another entry, 'Item, to remember S[i]r Wa[l]ter Hungerford in his well doynges' is suggestive, as Hungerford had been the foreman of the jury that convicted Prior Houghton and was a juror at Fisher's trial. (JG)

LITERATURE: Guy, *A Daughter's Love*; Elton, *Policy and Police*; Trapp and Schulte Herbrüggen (eds), *'The King's Good Servant'*

158 Bishop John Fisher

Unknown British School, after Hans Holbein the Younger, 16th century (*c*.1527)

National Portrait Gallery, London, NPG 2821

John Fisher had been the spiritual adviser of Henry's grandmother, Margaret Beaufort, and through her influence gained advancement both in the University of Cambridge and as Bishop of Rochester in 1504. He was a patron of humanism, a friend of Erasmus, a preaching bishop, a church reformer and a dedicated opponent of the Lollard and Lutheran heresies. However, Fisher opposed the King's annulment from the start, writing scholarly tracts against it and speaking out for Katherine at the Blackfriars court. He also led resistance to the Royal Supremacy. For his refusal to take the Oath to the Succession, he was imprisoned. He was afterwards put on trial and executed on charges of denying the Royal Supremacy.

This remarkable drawing is an artist's working pattern, produced for the purpose of making other versions of Fisher's portrait, and provides highly unusual evidence of 16th-century artistic practice. It probably dates from Mary's reign, but derives directly from Hans Holbein's drawing of *c*.1532–4 made towards the end of Fisher's life.
(SD and TC)

LITERATURE: Fisher, John, *Oxford DNB*; Strong, *Tudor and Jacobean Portraits*; Foister, *Holbein in England*

159 John Fisher Answers Questions in the Tower, 1535

British Library, Cotton MS Cotton Cleopatra E vi, fols 165v–166r

When the King's Council learned in 1535 that Fisher had been exchanging secret letters in the Tower with Thomas More, both men were questioned closely. Fisher's answer to the fifth 'Interrogatorie' is shown here with his usual signature, 'Io Roffs' (short for 'Ioannes Roffensis', John of Rochester) to authenticate it. He recalls telling More what his brother, Robert Fisher (MP for Rochester), had told him, namely that the House of Commons had added the word 'maliciousle' to the Act of Treasons that made it high treason to deny any part of the King's title – such as the Royal Supremacy. Fisher surmised that therefore 'it shulde be no daunger' to give honest answers to questions about the Royal Supremacy provided that it was not done 'maliciousle'. This line of defence was brusquely dismissed by the King's Justices when it came to the trials in June. Any denial of the Royal Supremacy, it transpired, was malicious. (RR)

LITERATURE: Dowling, *Fisher of Men*; Reynolds, *Saint John Fisher*

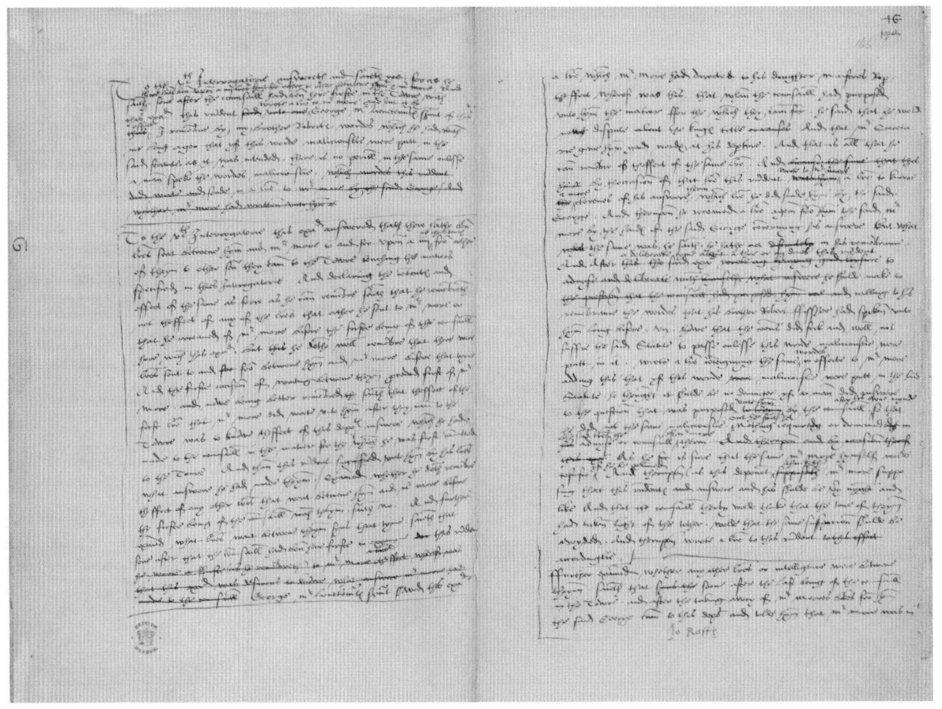

160 The Martyrdom of English Carthusian Monks, 1535

Probably Nicholas Beatrizet (1507/15–65) after Niccolò Circignani (c.1530/5–c.1590)

Uncatalogued engraving

Lambeth Palace Library, London

Pio ac catholico lectori (To the pius and catholic reader) is inscribed on this broadside made in Rome in 1555 and depicting in vivid detail the various stages in the martyrdom of the English Carthusians who were executed from 1535 to 1540. The text names the martyrs, recounts their suffering and gives the details and dates of their deaths, beginning with the three priors who were drawn through the streets on hurdles (plate 2) to Tyburn, where they were hung (plates 3 and 4), then drawn and quartered (plate 5) and their vital organs boiled in oil (plate 6) on 4 May 1535. Henry had hoped that the example would serve to warn others of the terrible fate awaiting those who refused to subscribe to the Acts of Succession and Supremacy. (AH)

LITERATURE: Dillon, *The Construction of Martyrdom in the English Catholic Community*

Nottyngham

Veri et Annuales Valores omn et singlorum dominiorum Maneriorum terrarum et tenemen ac aliarum possessionum quarumcumque spiritualium Necnon decimarum Oblacionum pensionum porcionum ac aliorum proficuorum quorumcumque spiritualium in dicto Com Nott aliis quam separalibus Com subscript existen quibuscumque Abbathiis Monasteriis Prioratibus et domibus religiosis Hospitalibus Archidiaconatibus Decanatibus Collegiis ecclesiis collegiatis Rectoriis Vicariis Cantariis liberis Capellis et aliis promocionibus quibuscumque spiritualibus in per totum Com Nott pertinen siue spectan vnacum deductionibus et allocacionibus eorundem pro decimis inde domino Regi nunc Henrico Octavo et Successoribus suis Annuatim soluend inferius conscribuntur

videlicet

Decanatus Nottyngham

Archidiaconatus
Nottingham Cuthbertus Marshall archidiaconus ibidem

Valet per annum in Sinodalibus et procuracionibus receptis de ecclesiis infra Decanatus subscriptos viz Decanatus Ruralem de Nottingham Decanatus Ruralem de Byngham Decanatum de Retford Decanatum Ruralem de Newarke cum Sinodalibus receptis de Sinodis post festum Pasche et Sancti Michaelis de decanis Decanatuum predictorum annuatim lxxxiiij li iiij s Inde soluta annuatim pro feodo Johannis Plumptre Senescalli Archidiaconatus predicti liij s iiij d pro procuracionibus expositis in [illegible] viij s viij d Et pro visitacione Archidiaconatus annuatim xxxvj s viij d Et remanet clare — lxx li xvij s viij d

Decima inde — c xlj s ix d

THE CRISIS OF 1536

Peter Marshall

The year 1536 defined and tested Henry's rule like no other in his 38-year reign. It began with the King's determination to use his new Royal Supremacy to engineer dramatic change in the English Church, and ended in an explosion of popular protest that might have cost the King his throne. Along the way, a princess was broken and humiliated, and a queen lost her head.

The policy that really brought home to the English people what Henry's Royal Supremacy might mean for them was the dissolution of the monasteries. The groundwork for this had been laid the previous year when Thomas Cromwell was appointed the King's Vice-Gerent in Spirituals (or Vicar-General in Church matters). Cromwell arranged for a general ecclesiastical visitation to demonstrate royal authority (no religious order was exempt from inspection) and to calculate the taxable wealth of the Church of which the King was now Supreme Head. It is unlikely that either Henry or Cromwell had decided from the outset to close the 800 or so monasteries, friaries and nunneries in England and Wales. However, in the course of the visitation process these venerable institutions – upholders of a thousand-year-old tradition of prayer, work and learning – suddenly became vulnerable. The comprehensive survey of the Church's wealth compiled in 1535, the *Valor Ecclesiasticus*, showed that the religious houses were collectively extremely wealthy, with an income equal to, or greater than, that of the Crown itself. At the same time, the commissioners (handpicked by Cromwell) who visited the monasteries over the autumn and winter of 1535–6 produced highly negative reports, harping on about sexual delinquency and 'superstition' (by which they meant the possession of suspect relics).

This was an opportunity not to be lost. A compilation of monastic misdemeanours (the *Compendium compertorum*, or collection of complaints) was placed before Parliament in March 1536 along with a bill proposing the closure of all monasteries with an annual income of less than £200, on the grounds of the 'manifest sin, vicious, carnal, and abominable living' of the small abbeys.

◀ Cat. no. 164

The closures began in the autumn, though only 243 of 419 houses assessed at £200 were actually closed. The others were (temporarily) exempted, as so many monks and nuns, especially in the north, wished to remain in religious life that room could not be found for them in larger monasteries.

The 1536 dissolution was presented as a reform of monasticism, not an attack upon the institution itself. It was, however, the thin end of the wedge. From 1537, the greater houses 'voluntarily' surrendered to the Crown, ending with Waltham Abbey in April 1540. Monasticism had helped to shape the society and landscape of England for almost a millennium. Yet monastic churches were now left as ruins, as their estates passed into the hands of the Crown in the greatest shift in landholding since the Norman Conquest.

Events of almost comparable magnitude were taking place at court in the spring of 1536. Henry was tiring of the sharp wit and independent mind of his Queen, Anne Boleyn, qualities that had once attracted him to her. This might not have mattered if Anne had succeeded in delivering a son for Henry, but, in January 1536, the Queen miscarried for a second time, raising the King's suspicions that God had cursed his second marriage also. Crucially, Anne then quarrelled with her former supporter, Thomas Cromwell, over the direction of foreign policy and the best use for the proceeds from the dissolution of the monasteries.

Meanwhile, the King was increasingly attracted to a lady-in-waiting, Jane Seymour, and proved more than willing to listen to the fantasies and confessions that Cromwell extracted (possibly under torture) from a court musician, Mark Smeaton. On 2 May 1536 Anne was arrested and sent to the Tower, charged with adultery with Smeaton and several others, including her own brother, George. On these trumped-up charges, she was beheaded at Tower Green on 19 May. Two days earlier, Archbishop Cranmer had annulled her marriage with Henry, bastardizing the little Princess Elizabeth.

Supporters of Henry's other daughter hoped that Anne Boleyn's fall from grace would lead to renewed recognition of Mary as heir. However, the King was determined that Mary could be shown no favour until she had agreed to recognize both his Royal Supremacy and her own illegitimacy. Several of her key supporters were arrested, and hints were dropped that if Mary did not capitulate her life might be in danger. Under this pressure, she gave in, telling her father in June what he wanted to hear. Henry and his new Queen, Jane Seymour, now graciously visited the previously isolated princess, but a new Succession Act confirmed the bastardy of Mary and Elizabeth, vesting the Crown in any son born to Queen Jane.

While the factions jockeyed for position at court, the mood in the country was becoming restive, and there were, in the autumn of 1536, a series of linked rebellions, known as the 'Pilgrimage of Grace', that engulfed Lincolnshire and the northern counties. This was the great crisis of Henry's reign, perhaps of the 16th century itself. In Yorkshire alone, 40,000 men were up in arms, marching behind banners of the Five Wounds of Christ – a force far larger than any the Crown could field. The people's grievances, expressed in lists of articles and anxious rumours, focused on the dissolution of the monasteries, a recent attack on saints' days, and a fear that the treasures of parish churches would be taken from them. The gentry leadership, guided by the charismatic Robert Aske, demanded the restoration of Mary to the succession, the punishment of Cromwell and recognition of the spiritual authority of the Pope.

The rebels occupied York on 16 October, and debated whether they should march south to press their demands. Henry was filled with fury at the presumption of his subjects, but the wily Duke of Norfolk persuaded him to temporize and negotiate. At Christmas the rebel armies dispersed, placated with a free pardon and a promise that Parliament would address their grievances. A renewed outbreak of disorder in Yorkshire in early 1537 provided the excuse for Norfolk to impose martial law, and Aske, Lord Darcy and other ringleaders were executed. Yet the outcome had been touch and go. Norfolk probably sympathized with some of the rebel demands (especially the antagonism to Cromwell), as did other powerful loyalist nobles like the Earls of Derby and Shrewsbury. If they had thrown in their lot with the rebels, then the Reformation would have gone into reverse, with Cromwell going to the block while Henry struggled to keep hold of his toppling Crown.

THE DISSOLUTION OF THE SMALLER MONASTERIES

The dissolution (suppression) of the smaller monasteries was carried out under the supervision of Thomas Cromwell, who had recently been appointed Vice-Gerent in Spirituals. Cromwell was hostile to monasticism, critical of clerical wealth and a promoter of evangelical reform. It is not at all certain exactly when and why Cromwell and Henry VIII decided to dissolve some of the monasteries, but the compilation of the *Valor Ecclesiasticus* (a survey of ecclesiastical property for taxation purposes) in 1535 may well have been a powerful inducement, as it revealed the extent of monastic wealth in England that could be diverted into the Crown's coffers. In addition, Henry was probably influenced by the initial reports of six visitors who had been appointed by Cromwell to inspect the monasteries as part of an exercise to assert the Royal Supremacy. The visitors generally exaggerated the abuses within the monastic houses, and their reports were used to justify the closure of the smaller houses, where discipline was thought to be more lax. A statute dissolving houses with an annual income of less than £200 a year was introduced and passed through Parliament in the spring of 1536.

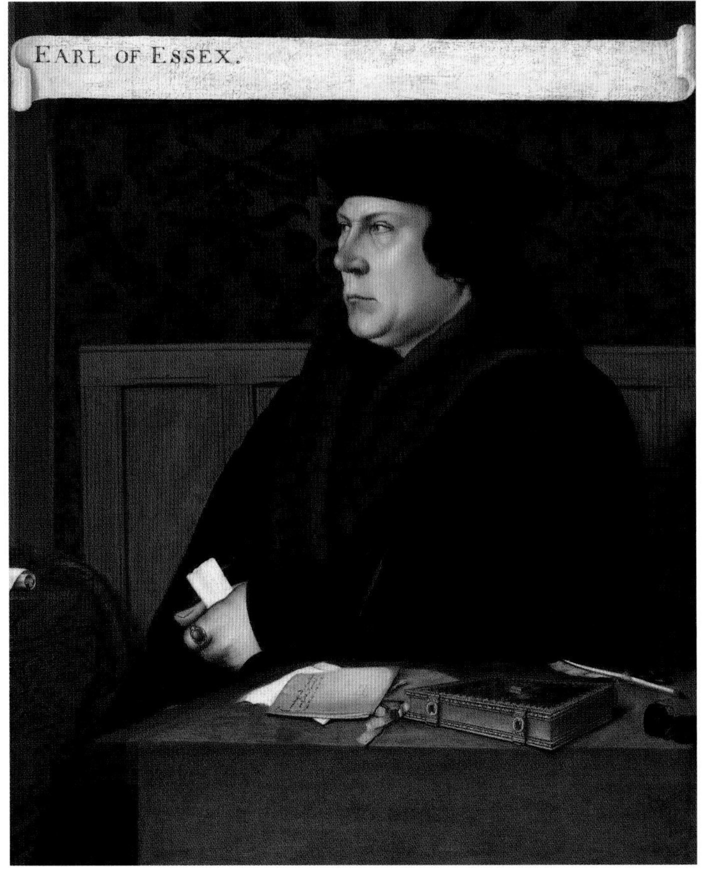

161 Thomas Cromwell

Unknown English workshop, after Hans Holbein the Younger, early 17th century

National Portrait Gallery, London, NPG 1727

Thomas Cromwell (*c*.1485–1540) rose from a modest background to become Henry's chief minister in the 1530s. In the mid-1520s he worked for Wolsey, but, on the Cardinal's fall, he began working for the King and entered the Council at the end of 1530. Cromwell's insight into how to secure the King's annulment and establish Henry VIII as the Supreme Head of the English Church was a key factor in his advancement, while his efficient administration of the dissolution of the monasteries had a fundamental impact on the course of the Reformation in England.

Holbein's original portrait of 1532 showed Cromwell as a consummate statesman, sitting behind a desk, with a letter addressed to him on the table. This portrait is a faithful later version and includes the inscription upon the letter 'To master Thomas Cromwell, trusty and right well-beloved master of our jewel house', one of the first posts which Cromwell held at court. Recent analysis has dated this painting to the early 17th century, indicating a market for key members of Henry's court (and paintings by Hans Holbein) over 60 years later. (TC)

LITERATURE: Elton, *Policy and Police*; Strong, *Tudor and Jacobean Portraits*; Foister, *Holbein and England*

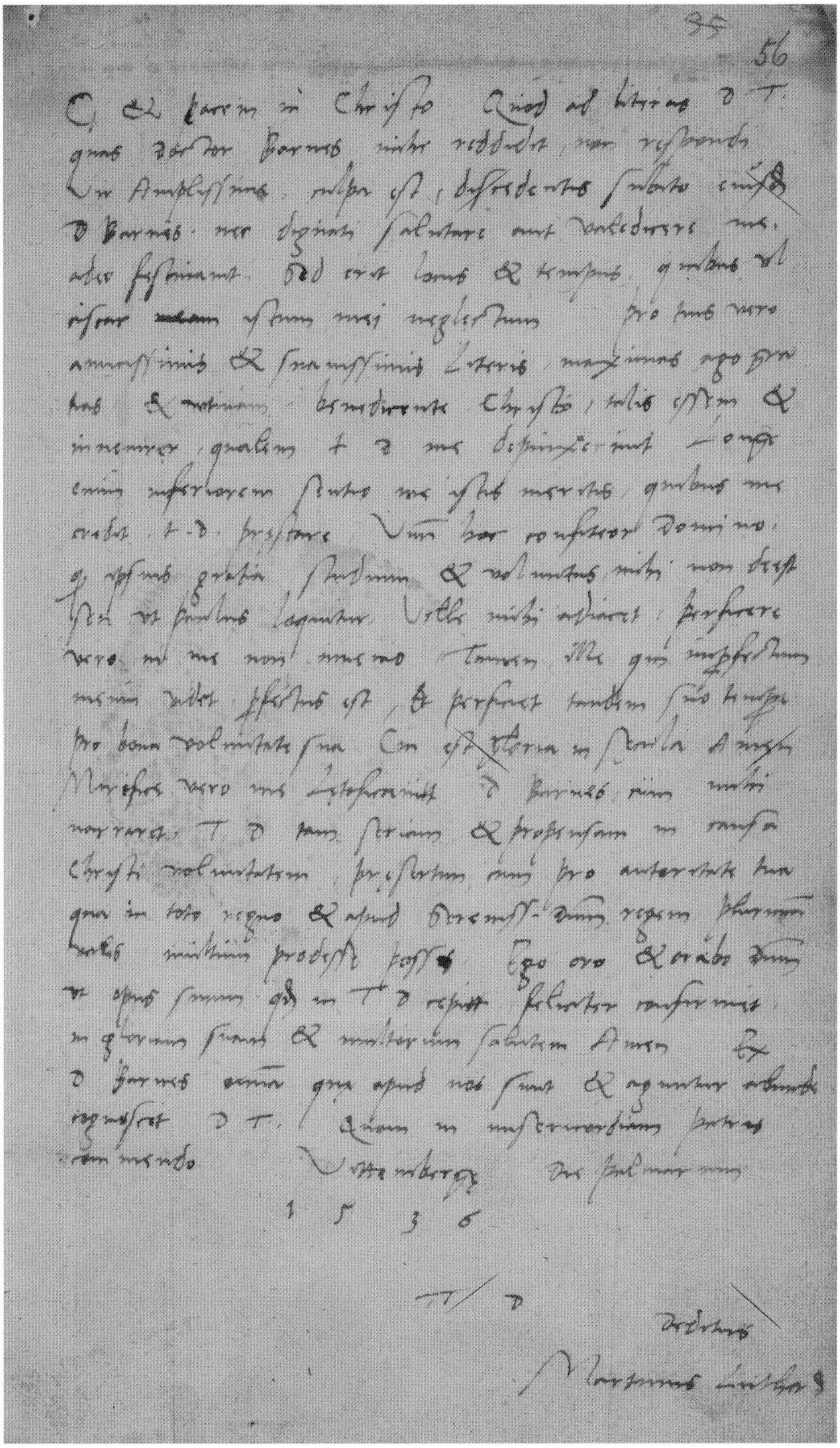

162 Thomas Cromwell's Evangelical Sympathies

Holograph letter from Martin Luther to Thomas Cromwell, from Wittenburg, Germany, 9 April 1536

British Library, Harley MS 6989, fol.56

Cromwell's evangelical sympathies were evident in both his domestic and foreign policies. Abroad, he was a consistent advocate of a close relationship with the Lutheran princes of Germany and was involved in the preparations for two embassies sent to them (from 1533 to 1534 and from 1535 to 1536). On the return to England of the second embassy led by the Bishop of Hereford, Edward Fox, Martin Luther wrote this letter to Cromwell; it was in Latin, the *lingua franca* of the day, and both the text and the signature were in the reformer's own hand. Luther said that he was delighted to hear of 'the earnestness and propensity of your lordship's goodwill in the cause of Christ, and especially of your authority in the realm and about the King, with which you can do much'. This identification of Cromwell as a supporter of the new religious ideas became commonplace in the second half of the decade. (RM)

LITERATURE: McEntergart, *Henry VIII, the League of Schmalkalden and the English Reformation*

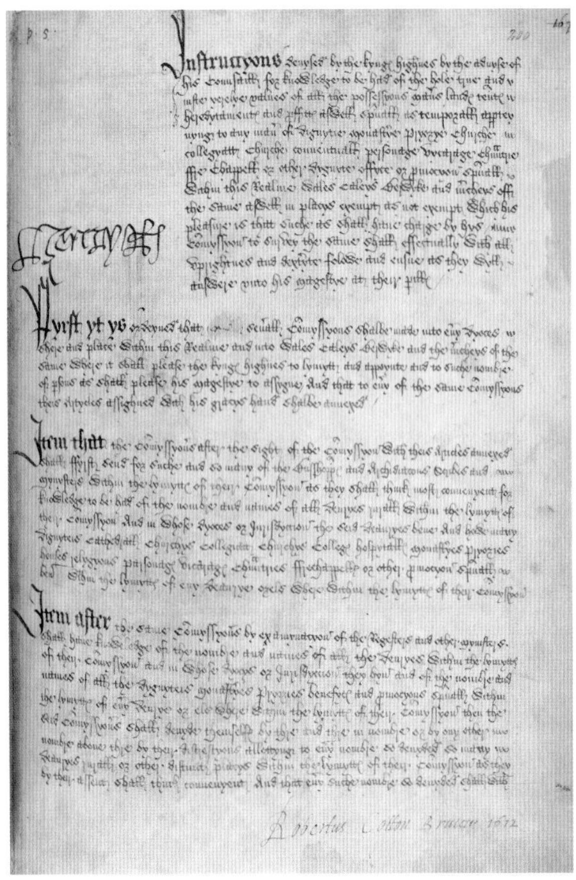

163 Preparations for the *Valor Ecclesiasticus*

Royal instructions to the Commissioners for making a survey and valuation of Church property, 30 January 1535

British Library, Cotton MS Cleopatra E iv, fol.200

The massive survey known as the *Valor Ecclesiasticus*, compiled over the course of 1535, was one of the great administrative achievements of Henry's government, and later one of the most useful sources for social and ecclesiastical historians of the reign. This commission provided for sets of commissioners in every diocese to undertake a systematic investigation and listing of the value of all 'cathedral churches, colleges, churches collegiate, houses conventual, hospitals, monasteries, priories, houses religious, prebends, parsonages, vicarages, chantries, free chapels and other cures, offices and promotions spiritual' in England and Wales. The information was required to enable Henry to extract full value from a statute of 1534 that required the holders of all Church offices or 'benefices' to pay to the Crown the 'first fruits', or first full year's income, along with an annual tenth of the revenue of the benefice thereafter. The commissioners were to 'assemble themselfes and conferre all theyr sev[er]all bokes togey[ther]' before forwarding the information to the Exchequer. (PM)

LITERATURE: Rex, *Henry VIII and the English Reformation*; Savine, *English Monasteries on the Eve of the Dissolution*

164 The *Valor Ecclesiasticus*, 1535

The National Archives, Kew, Richmond, Surrey, E344–22, fol.72

The *Valor Ecclesiasticus* supplied Henry and Cromwell with a comprehensive snapshot of the income of the English Church, allowing them to consider future options for taxation, or confiscation, of the wealth of this newly nationalized corporation. The page displayed here introduces what promises to be a full account of the annual income of all abbeys, monasteries, priories, houses of religion, hospitals, archdeaconries, deaneries, colleges, rectories, vicarages, chantries and free chapels to be found in the county of Nottingham, part of the sprawling archbishopric of York. The first detailed entry describes the income of a middle-ranking Church functionary, Cuthbert Marshall, the Archdeacon of Nottingham, who held the office between 1528 and his death in 1550. This reveals that, after expenses, Marshall received the tidy sum of £59 16*s*. 4*d*. *in sinodalibus et procuracionibus* (synodals and procurations) – fees received from the clergy when he inspected the various rural deaneries in his charge. (PM)

LITERATURE: Horn and Smith (eds), *Fasti Ecclesiae Anglicanae 1541–1857*

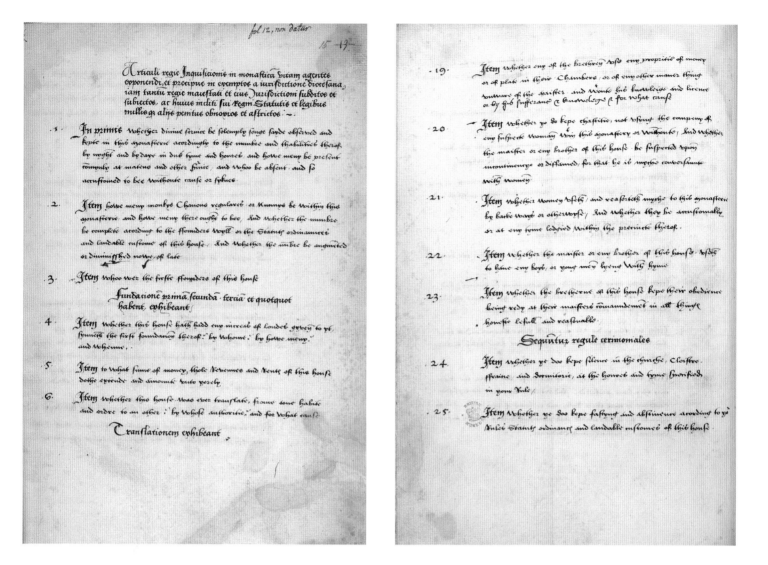

165 Visitation of the Monasteries, 1535

Articles of Enquiry for the General Visitation of the Monasteries in 1535

British Library, Cotton MS Cleopatra E iv, fols 15, 16v

English bishops regularly 'visited' the religious houses in their dioceses to check on standards, but never before 1535 had there been a complete national survey of the state of the monasteries. The visitation was intended as a forceful demonstration of the extent of Henry's new Royal Supremacy; these articles of enquiry were specifically drawn up for those houses which had been exempt from diocesan jurisdiction. Whether the visitation was initially intended to be a prelude to suppression is less clear. The articles are in some ways very traditional, asking, for example, 'whether divine service be solemply songe… in this monasterie'. However, they also exhibit a persistent concern with the property and financial state of the houses, and several of them harp on about sexual misdemeanour, demanding whether any monks 'be suspected upon incontinencye', or whether any 'useth to have any boys, or yong men lyeng with hyme'. It was 'evidence' of this sort, particularly that gathered by Cromwell's visitors for the northern circuit, Richard Layton and Thomas Legh, that was used to justify the suppression of the smaller monasteries in 1536. (PM)

LITERATURE: Hoyle, 'The Origins of the Dissolution of the Monasteries'; Bernard, *The King's Reformation*

166 The Suppression of English Religious Houses, 1536

British Library, Cotton Ch. III. 5

This official listing illuminates both the scale of the first Suppression Act of March 1536, and also the unevenness with which it was implemented. The religious houses to be dissolved comprised all those with an annual income of less than £200 per year, but there were many exemptions. In fact, only 243 of 419 houses falling within the terms of the act were actually closed in 1536. The others survived for a time by making payments to the Crown, or because so many of their inmates wished to transfer to larger monasteries (for which the act made provision) that room could not be found for them all. Others, as this document acerbically notes, 'pretend themselves to be cells' – that is, dependent offshoots rather than freestanding monasteries or priories. The first named of the houses here, Binham Priory in Norfolk, postponed closure by two years by purporting (falsely) to be a cell of St Albans. (PM)

LITERATURE: Woodward, 'The Exemption from Suppression of Certain Yorkshire Priories'; Woodward, *The Dissolution of the Monasteries*

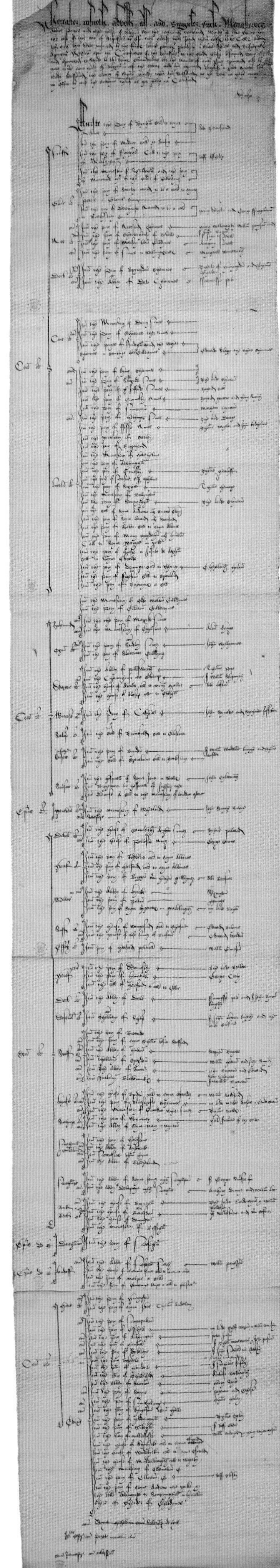

THE DISSOLUTION OF THE LARGER MONASTERIES

In 1536 Henry VIII seems to have planned to reform the monasteries, not to destroy them totally. However, his hostility towards monasteries grew when monks participated in the northern rebellions of 1536 (known as the Pilgrimage of Grace), and religious houses provided succour for the rebels. In March 1537 three Abbots were attainted for treason for their role in the rebellions, and the property of their monasteries was confiscated. Shortly afterwards Henry and Cromwell began to put pressure on the heads of monasteries to surrender their houses and property 'voluntarily' to the Crown. In April 1537 Furness Abbey at Barrow-in-Furness, Cumbria, was the first to be dissolved in this way. Over the next two years the remaining monasteries were individually 'persuaded' or coerced to follow suit. At the same time, the government began an attack on the pilgrimage shrines within the monasteries; clearly Henry had decided that the religious houses were not only centres of opposition but also dens of superstition. The second Act of Dissolution, which Parliament passed in 1539, validated these surrenders and all future dissolutions. By early 1540 monasticism was dead in England.

167 The Surrender of Thetford Priory, 16 February 1540

The National Archives, Kew, Richmond, Surrey, E322/240

This document illustrates the process whereby the larger English monasteries 'voluntarily' surrendered themselves to the Crown. The Cluniac Priory of Thetford in Norfolk was one of the last houses to fall, and this deed, surrendering the house along with its cell at Wangford in Suffolk and properties throughout East Anglia and elsewhere, is signed by the prior, William Ixworth, and thirteen of his brethren. Thetford's closure is noteworthy, for there were powerful forces with a motive to protect it (see cat. no. 168). Henry's insistence on complete closure indicates how relentless he had become in his dissolution policy. (PM)

LITERATURE: Page (ed.), *The Victoria County History of the County of Norfolk*, vol.2; Dymond (ed.), *The Register of Thetford Priory*

168 The Thetford Reliefs

British Museum, London, Prehistory and Europe, 1866,0908.1 & 1866,0908.2

These limestone reliefs from the ruined Priory at Thetford are vivid reminders of religious upheaval and the roller-coaster life during Henry VIII's reign. They once formed part of a projected tomb, in French Renaissance style, for Henry Fitzroy, Duke of Richmond, the King's bastard son who had died in 1536. Fitzroy's father-in-law, Thomas Howard, the religiously conservative 3rd Duke of Norfolk (1473–1554), planned a dynastic mausoleum at Thetford, a project reluctantly abandoned when the priory was dissolved in 1539. Petitioning Henry for permission to adapt the church for collegiate or parish use, Howard claimed to have spent £400 'at the least' on his own and Fitzroy's tombs. Cutting his losses, Norfolk eventually moved his tomb, and parts of Fitzroy's, to the parish church next to his great castle at Framlingham. There he commandeered the chancel and rebuilt it to house them. Norfolk's arrest for treason in 1546, however, and the execution of his son, Henry Earl of Surrey (1516/17–1547), halted work until his rehabilitation under Mary I. (ED)

LITERATURE: Stone and Colvin, 'The Howard Tombs at Framlingham, Suffolk'; Marks, 'The Howard Tombs at Thetford and Framlingham'

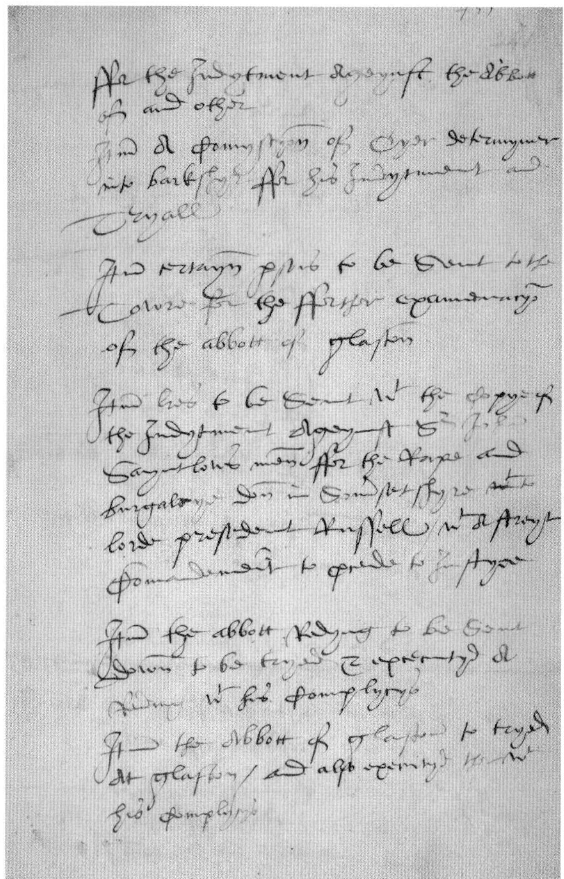

169 The Trials of the Abbots of Reading and Glastonbury, 1539

Cromwell's 'Remembrances': Cromwell's note to himself

British Library, Cotton MS Titus B i, fol.441

Cromwell's working note (in his haste, he omits the word 'Reading' from action to be taken 'ageynst the abbott of') reveals the government's determination to brook no opposition in its campaign to suppress the larger monasteries. Hugh Cook and Richard Whiting – the Abbots respectively of the important Benedictine monasteries of Reading and Glastonbury – were accused of traitorous adherence to the papacy, but their real offence was an obstructionist attitude to the closure of their houses. There was no escape. Even before the trial, Cromwell notes that Cook is 'to be sent down to be tryed & executyd at Reding w[ith] his complycys', as he also comments for Whiting at Glastonbury. Cook was duly condemned by a commission appointed on 27 October 1539, and Whiting was hanged, drawn and quartered at Glastonbury Tor on 15 November of the same year. (PM)

LITERATURE: Elton, *Policy and Police*; Knowles, *The Religious Orders in England*, vol.3

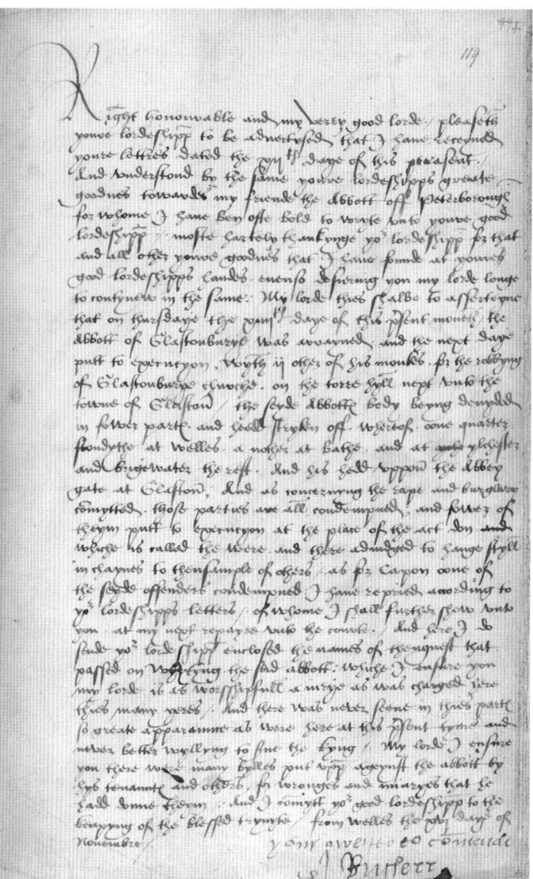

170 The Execution of the Abbot of Glastonbury

Letter from Lord John Russell to Thomas Cromwell, 16 November 1539

British Library, Cotton MS Cleopatra E iv, fol.119

John, Lord Russell's description of the public execution of Abbot Richard Whiting and two of his fellow monks provides graphic evidence of the exemplary use of punishment in the enforcement of government policy. Whiting underwent the usual gruesome punishment for treason, 'the seyde abbotes body being devyded in fower partes, and hedd stryken off'. The quarters were then displayed in four adjacent towns and the head impaled on the abbey gates. Russell (*c*.1485–1555) had been promoted to the King's Privy Chamber by Cromwell's old master Wolsey, and had never put a foot wrong thereafter. He was raised to the peerage after the execution of Henry's cousin, Henry Courtenay, Marquess of Exeter, in 1538, and he was eager to consolidate his position as the now dominant landowner in the south-west. This is perhaps the reason why he supplied Cromwell with a list of the names of those serving on the 'worsshipfull' jury which had convicted Whiting. (PM)

LITERATURE: Bettey, *The Suppression of the Monasteries in the West Country*; Wright (ed.), *Three Chapters of Letters Relating to the Suppression of Monasteries*

171 Fragments of Glastonbury Abbey

Sculpture, 13th century

Glastonbury Abbey Trustees

These fragments of a 13th-century sculpture come from a major stone altarpiece located in Glastonbury Abbey, one of the largest and richest of the English Benedictine monasteries and a famous pilgrimage centre. The Abbey fell into ruins after the dissolution of the monasteries, when the roofs were stripped of their lead, and dressed stones were hauled away and used in the construction of houses, cottages, roads and a market hall. The denuding of the site continued through the 17th and 18th century when former monastic buildings continued to be demolished. In the early 18th century, an antiquary referred to its 'vast Ruins, discovering its former Grandeur'. Eventually, at the turn of the 19th century, a mayor of Glastonbury and a local brickmaker used gunpowder to dislodge stones and turn the site into a quarry. Nonetheless, the framework of the structures still remains today. (SD)

LITERATURE: Carley, *Glastonbury Abbey*

BENEFICIARIES OF THE DISSOLUTIONS

The 1536 Act of Suppression of the smaller monasteries was accompanied by another statute that set up a Court of Augmentations to carry out the suppressions and administer the former monastic lands. Initially, the plan was to increase the flow of money to the King, while granting long leases or selling off some lands to reward loyal royal servants. As time went by, however, Henry sold land to finance his building projects, defences and the wars of the 1540s. The sale of land brought the Crown nearly £30,000 between 1537 and 1538, just over £80,500 between 1538 and 1539, and about £66,000 annually between 1539 and 1543. There was no lack of demand for the former monastic land and even religious conservatives petitioned for grants. Usually, the beneficiaries were already land-owners, many of them local gentlemen who wished to augment their already sizeable land holdings.

172 Sir Richard Southwell

Unknown English workshop c.1589–1610, after Hans Holbein the Younger

National Portrait Gallery, London, NPG 4912

Richard Southwell (1502/3–64) came from a family of Suffolk gentry that was well established in government service. A religious conservative but also a sharp political operator, he was instrumental in the downfall of both Sir Thomas More and his former patron Thomas Cromwell. In 1536, Southwell became a receiver of the Court of Augmentations, a lucrative position dealing with the distribution of land belonging to dissolved monastic orders. In this office he dealt with old monastic estates in East Anglia, obtaining for himself the lands formerly held by several religious houses in Norfolk and the Priory of St John of Jerusalem.

His portrait by Hans Holbein, now in the Uffizi Gallery, Florence, shows him at the age of thirty-three. Holbein has taken considerable care to capture the details of his features, including the scars upon his neck, and a slightly pompous, yet uneasy expression. These details have been copied extremely carefully in this later version dating from the very end of the 16th century (recent dendrochronology dates this picture to after 1588). The copy was probably made in emulation of Holbein's remarkable skill as an artist. (TC)

LITERATURE: Van Suchtelen, Buvelot and van der Ploeg (eds), *Hans Holbein the Younger 1497/98–1543*; Foister, *Holbein in England*; Southwell, Sir Richard, *Oxford DNB*

173 The Spoils of the Dissolved Monastic Houses

Grants of lands and property of dissolved religious houses in Gloucester, Oxfordshire and Sussex

British Library, Additional Ch. 17354

This elaborate Latin patent of June 1540, with its portrait of Henry enthroned with orb and sceptre within the historiated 'H', illustrates the process by which the spoils of the monastic dissolution filtered into the hands of the landed gentry. Sir Thomas Pope is granted the manors of Euston and Preston Crowmarsh in Oxfordshire, lately the possessions of Winchcombe Abbey, Gloucestershire, and Battle Abbey, Sussex. Pope was a trusted royal civil servant, who had served as Treasurer of the Court of Augmentations, the government department responsible for administering the dissolution of the monasteries. He was also, like many of the beneficiaries of the process, a religious conservative. The document additionally illustrates how the dispersal of monastic lands was no reckless give-away by the Crown: an appended receipt in English from his successor as Treasurer of Augmentations, Edward North, records that Pope has paid the substantial sum of £1,204 3*s*. 4*d*. for his manors. (PM)

LITERATURE: Habakkuk, 'The Market for Monastic Property, 1539–1603'; Pope, Sir Thomas, *Oxford DNB*

174 The Lands of Colchester Abbey

British Library, Egerton MS 2164

This survey 'or brefe declaracion of all and singuler lordshippis, manners, landes' belonging to the former Benedictine monastery of Colchester was drawn up by the royal commissioners Richard Pollard and Thomas Moyle after the Abbey's confiscation in 1539. What distinguishes it from other financial records is its deployment of visual propaganda for the royal cause. Depicted in the background is the execution of the Abbot of Colchester, Thomas Marshall *alias* Beche, on 1 December 1539 at Colchester. He was one of three Benedictine abbots executed in that year for treasonous words against the Royal Supremacy. Marshall had also allegedly sworn 'that he shuld never surrender upp hys howse and landes'. The portrayal of the judge riding out of the town after the conclusion of the trial is in fact a copy of a biblical engraving, *The Triumph of Mordecai* (1515) by the Dutch artist Lucas van Leyden (1494–1533). (PM)

LITERATURE: Croft-Murray and Hulton, *Catalogue of British Drawings*; Knowles, *The Religious Orders in England*, vol.3

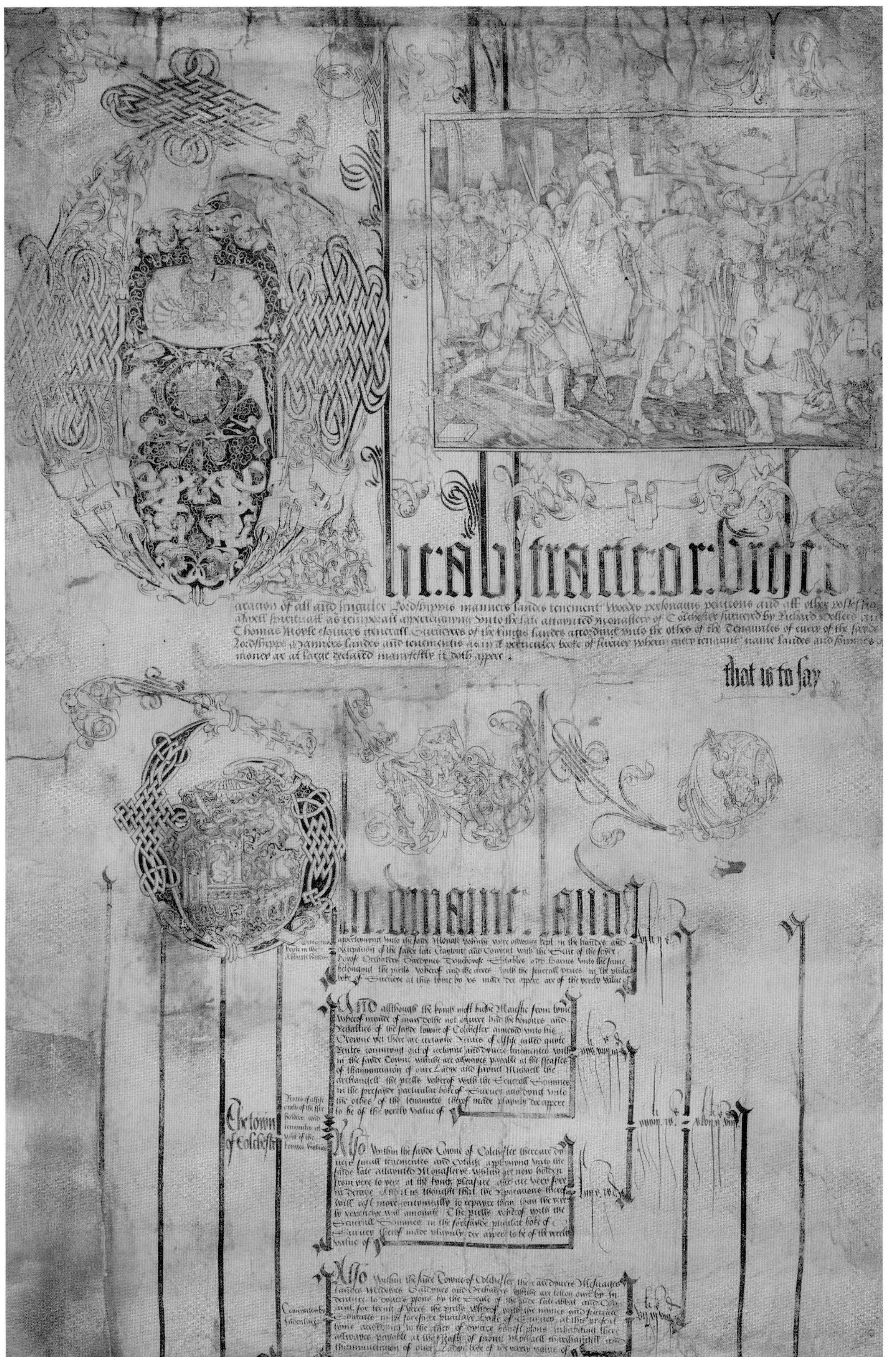

THE DOWNFALL OF ANNE BOLEYN AND THE REHABILITATION OF MARY

After the annulment of her marriage, the Dowager Princess of Wales (as Queen Katherine was now officially known) lived at a house in Kimbolton in Huntingdonshire, where she was not allowed visitors and refused contact with her daughter. On 7 January 1536 Katherine died, and her death was greeted at court with unseemly joy, but disaster struck shortly afterwards. At the end of the month Anne miscarried a male foetus. Dismayed, Henry complained, 'I see that God will not give me male children'. In this mood, and already infatuated with Jane Seymour, Henry was ready to listen to accusations that Anne had betrayed him with several men. Arrested on 2 May 1536, Anne was executed on 19 May and her marriage to Henry declared invalid; their daughter Elizabeth was now a bastard alongside Mary. At the end of the month Henry married Jane Seymour who encouraged Henry to bring Mary to Court. However, Henry would only agree to his daughter's rehabilitation if she signed articles of submission, acknowledging her parents' marriage as invalid and Henry's position as Supreme Head of the Church. After initial resistance, Mary gave way and signed.

175 The Trial of Queen Anne

Commission to Thomas Howard, Duke of Norfolk, as Lord Steward of England to assemble a jury of peers to try Anne Boleyn and George Boleyn, Lord Rochford

The National Archives, Kew, Richmond, Surrey, KB 8/9, membrane 17

On Tuesday, 9 May, Anne, her brother George and four courtiers were accused of conspiring to procure the King's death. This commission provides for the trial of Anne and George by a jury of peers, to which, as nobility, they were entitled. The accusation was that, in the course of courtly repartee, reference had been made to Anne's future if the King died, that this amounted to imagining his death and that, when Henry knew of this, his life actually was endangered. To help divert attention from this nonsense – the King was after all busily pursuing Jane Seymour – Anne was accused of incest with her brother and adultery with the four courtiers. This was not a crime but a moral offence, punishable by the Church courts, but was set out at length to blacken the defendants. Despite an impressive defence, Anne and George were condemned by the peers on Monday, 12 May. The verdict was a foregone conclusion, as the four courtiers had been tried and convicted the previous Friday. (EI)

LITERATURE: Ives, *The Life and Death of Anne Boleyn*

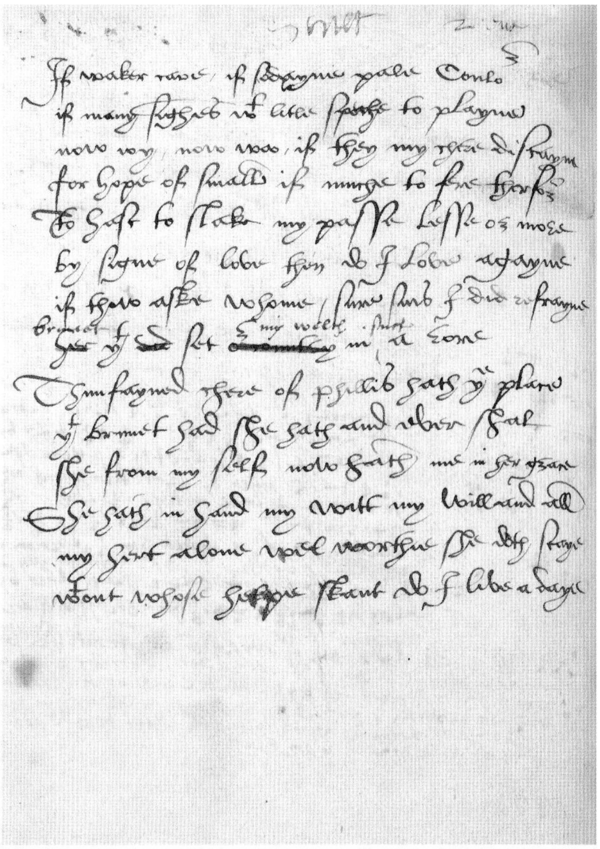

176 Sir Thomas Wyatt

Unknown Anglo-Netherlandish artist, after Hans Holbein the Younger, *c.*1540

National Portrait Gallery, London, NPG 1035

Thomas Wyatt (1503–42) was an influential poet, ambassador and courtier. His inventive poetry based upon classical models was widely celebrated at court and he is credited with introducing the Italian sonnet form into England. At the downfall of Anne Boleyn in 1536, he was associated with those accused of adultery with the Queen and imprisoned. Several sources reported that he had been her lover before her marriage to Henry. Protected by Cromwell, he was released after a few months and went abroad as an ambassador to Charles V.

This bareheaded portrait in profile is probably based on a portrait by Hans Holbein that is now lost. Holbein produced a woodcut of Wyatt using the same composition, also in a roundel, which became the title page to a posthumous edition of Wyatt's poetry dedicated to the Earl of Surrey. Recent analysis using dendrochronology has indicated that the picture was almost certainly painted in the mid-16th century, possibly in Wyatt's lifetime. (TC)

LITERATURE: Strong, *Tudor and Jacobean Portraits*; Foister, *Holbein in England*

177 Thomas Wyatt and Anne

If waker care, if sudden pale colour

British Library, Egerton MS 2711, fol.66v

Speculation about Wyatt's relationship with Anne Boleyn has gone on since Elizabeth's reign, with numerous autobiographical references proposed in his writing. In fact, Wyatt refers to Anne in only four genuine poems. The clearest is *If waker care, if sudden pale colour*, written after he had fallen for Elizabeth Darell, whom he calls Phillis:

> If thow aske whome, sure sins I did refrayn
> Brunet that set my welth in such a rore
> The unfayned chere of Phillis hath the place
> That Brunet had: she hath and ever shal.

That Anne was Brunet is clear because the correction shows that Wyatt originally wrote 'Her that did set our country in a roar'. This does indicate that he had at least been one of Anne's suitors. The other genuine poems suggest that on Wyatt's side his feelings went beyond the flirtatious game of courtly love but were not reciprocated by Anne. Already married but separated from his wife, Wyatt had nothing to offer. (EI)

LITERATURE: Ives, *The Life and Death of Anne Boleyn*

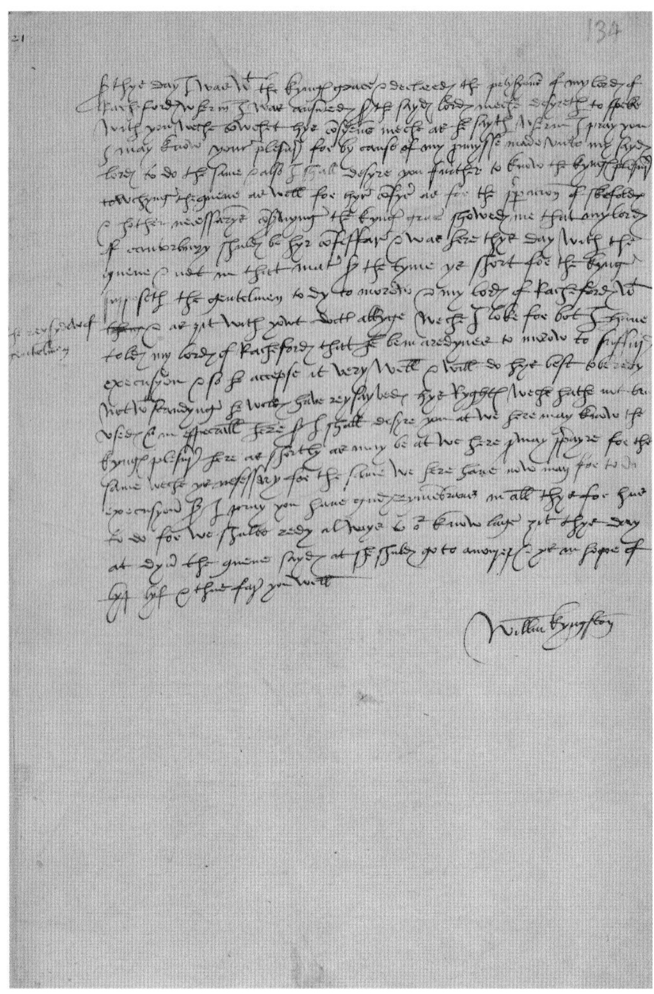

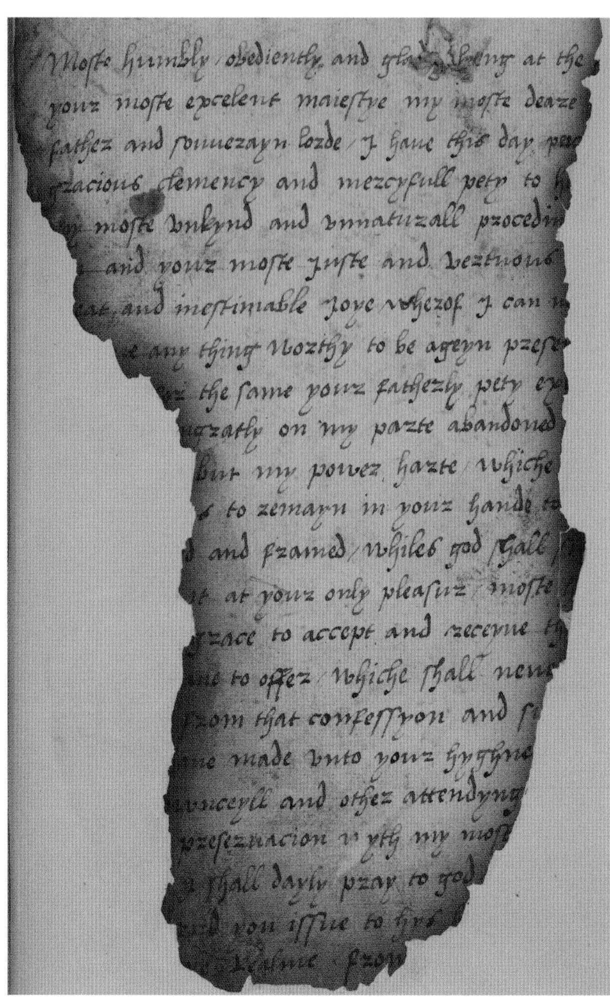

Moste humbly, obediently and [illegible] at the
your moste excelent maiestye my moste deare
father and soueraygn lorde I haue this day per
gracious clemency and mercyfull pety to
my moste unkynd and unnaturall procedin
and your moste juste and vertuous
and inestimable joye wherof I can
any thing worthy to be ageyn prese
the same your fatherly pety
ratly on my parte abandoned
but my power harte whiche
to remayn in your hande
and framed whiles god shall
at your only pleasure moste
grace to accept and receive
to offer whiche shall nev
from that confessyon and
made unto your hyghne
counceyll and other attendyng
preservacion [illegible] my most
shall dayly pray to god
you issue to hys
realme from

178 Preparations for the Death of Anne

British Library, Harley MS 283, fol.134

Between Anne's arrest on Tuesday, 2 May 1536 and her execution on Friday, 19 May, various letters passed between Sir William Kingston, the Lieutenant of the Tower (c.1476–1540), and Thomas Cromwell. Here Kingston refers to his audience with the King to get specific instructions on treating and executing the prisoners. His main concern was to make sure that Rochford was allowed to make his confession and be given absolution. Rochford had also asked for the exceptional privilege of taking Communion – 'he wold have reysayved hys ryghts'. The letter shows the extent of Henry's involvement in the executions. Kingston reports that, on the King's instruction, Thomas Cranmer had that day visited Anne. Although Cranmer might have been attempting to trick her into revealing grounds to annul her marriage, it is more likely that the meeting was pastoral. The reference to Anne still hoping for life is an example of the mood swings that characterized her last days. (EI)

LITERATURE: Ives, *The Life and Death of Anne Boleyn*

179 Mary Tudor's Submission to her Father

Letter from Mary Tudor to Henry VIII, Hunsdon, Hertfordshire, 26 June 1536

British Library, Cotton MS Otho C x, fol.273

Like her mother, Mary persistently resisted Henry's repudiation of his first marriage. But, with Anne Boleyn executed and the sympathetic Jane Seymour as queen, Mary thought that the way was open to reconciliation with her father. Cromwell quickly undeceived her: she must submit herself unreservedly to her 'sovereign Lord and King', acknowledge his ecclesiastical supremacy, repudiate the 'Bishop of Rome' and recognize the nullity of his marriage to her mother 'the Late Princess Dowager'. Mary resisted frantically, until the threat to the life of her friends and supporters forced her to accept her father's terms. Her will broken, she wrote this prostrate letter to her father. 'I have', she wrote, 'this day perc[eived your] gracious clemency and mercyfull pety to [have overcome] my moste unkind and unnaturall procedin[gs towards you] and your moste juste and virtuous [laws]'. (DS)

LITERATURE: Loades, *Mary Tudor*; Richards, *Mary Tudor*; Starkey, *Six Wives*

THE PILGRIMAGE OF GRACE

In 1536, Henry had to face the most serious and largest rising that ever took place in England during Tudor rule. Disturbances first broke out at Louth in Lincolnshire on Monday, 2 October 1536, after false rumours were heard that the government intended to confiscate liturgical plate in the parish churches. Then, under the leadership of a charismatic Yorkshire lawyer, Robert Aske, protests spread into the seven counties of the north. A rebel army of some 40,000 men marched under the religious banner of the Five Wounds of Christ and called their movement the 'Pilgrimage of Grace'. After taking Pontefract Castle, the rebel leaders met Henry's representative, the Duke of Norfolk, who had been sent to quell the rising, and agreed to a truce while Henry considered their grievances. Henry's first reaction was to refuse concessions. But, in view of the rebels' overwhelming strength, he finally allowed Norfolk to negotiate – though in bad faith. The Pilgrim leaders met Norfolk again and agreed to disband their army in return for a pardon and the promise that the King would call a parliament in the north to redress their grievances. However, the parliament was never held, and the following year Aske, Lord Thomas Darcy and other rebel leaders were executed.

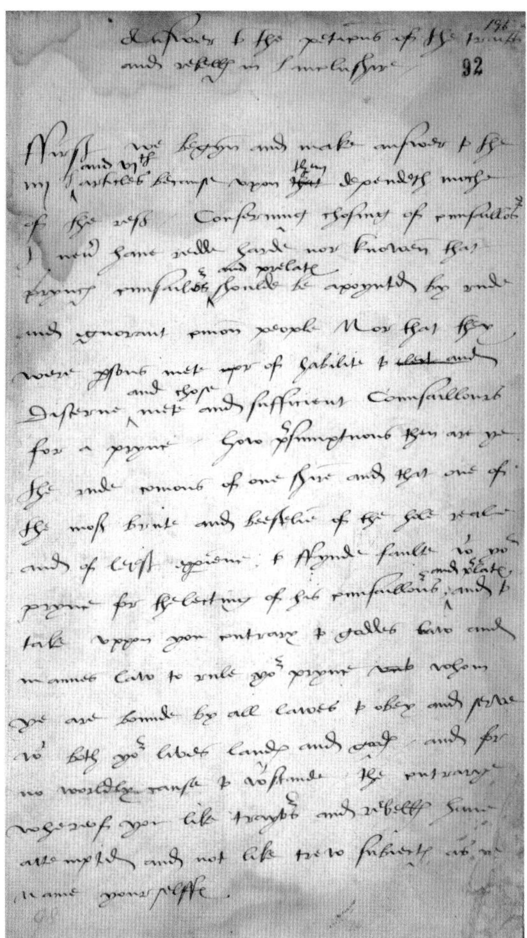

180 The Grievances of the Lincolnshire Rebels

Answer to the Petitions of the Traitors and Rebels in Lincolnshire, 10 October 1536

The National Archives, Kew, Richmond, Surrey, E.36, vol.118, fol.98

The petitions of the Lincolnshire rebels have not survived, but we can see from Henry VIII's reply here what some of their grievances were, namely corrupt and low-born councillors, the suppression of the monasteries and the levying of the fifteenth tax and the Act of First Fruits. In his reply, Henry refuses to accept the justice of the rebels' complaints or offer any concessions. On the contrary, he justifies his policies trenchantly, arguing that these measures had all been passed by Parliament for good reason. For example, the suppressed religious houses were not those 'where God was well served, but where most vice, mischief, and abhomynations of lyving was used'. Henry's tone is far from conciliatory. He berates the rebels for their presumptuousness 'to take upon you, contrary to Goddes law, and mannes law, to rule your Prynce'. The rebels are ordered to disband, and to hand over 100 of 'the provokers of you to this myschief' to the King's lieutenant in the north, with the threat that they would otherwise be destroyed by the royal army. (SD)

LITERATURE: Hoyle, *Pilgrimage of Grace and the Politics of the 1530s*

181 Military Emergency

Letter from Henry VIII to the Mayor and Bailiffs of an English port, Windsor, 29 October 1536

British Library, Additional MS 19398, fol.43

This letter, one of a number sent by Henry VIII to the mayors and bailiffs of strategic ports, provides evidence of the dire military situation in which the Crown found itself at the end of October 1536. It had lost control of virtually all the north from the River Don in Yorkshire to the Scottish borders, and its hastily assembled army was outnumbered and in danger of being routed by the rebels at Doncaster. The letter reveals that Henry VIII 'resolved with an Army Roiall to advannce ourself in personne into the north parts of this our Realme for the Repression of certaine Rebellious traitours assembled in the same', and commanded that in his absence 'a convenyent watche maye be kepte bothe night and daye withyn that townne so as no persone be permittid to enter or departe frome the same' and that 'no strawngers be permittid to land at that porte or nyghe the same with anye meane of weapon or harneyse'.

As was usual with routine documents, this circular is signed, not with the King's own hand but with a stamp of his signature. (AC)

LITERATURE: Hoyle, *The Pilgrimage of Grace and the Politics of the 1530s*

182 A Peaceful Resolution of the Rebellion?

Letter from Lord Thomas Darcy to Robert Aske, 18 November 1536

British Library, Cotton MS Vespasian F xiii, fol.233

After surrendering Pontefract Castle on 20 October 1536 to Robert Aske and his army, Lord Thomas Darcy joined the rebels and became one of the Pilgrim captains. A week later, a truce between the rebels and the King's representative, the Duke of Norfolk, was agreed and two gentlemen – Sir Ralph Ellerker and Robert Bowes (both mentioned here) – were dispatched to London to deliver the rebels' grievances to the King. However, Henry was implacable in his determination not to grant concessions under duress, and told Norfolk only to offer a limited pardon and to demand the disbandment of the rebel army. In the meantime Ellerker and Bowes returned with a message that the Pilgrim leaders should meet with Norfolk in ten days time. When Ellerker and Bowes arrived on Saturday, 18 November, Darcy wrote this letter to Aske, inviting him to come to a council meeting at his house at Temple Hurst. There the leaders decided to convene a meeting of the Pilgrims at York on 21 November and meet with Norfolk later. At this stage it was by no means certain whether the rebellion would end or escalate. But, at a meeting in December with Norfolk, the rebels agreed to disband when the Duke went beyond his instructions and offered them some concessions. (SD)

LITERATURE: Hoyle, *The Pilgrimage of Grace and the Politics of the 1530s*

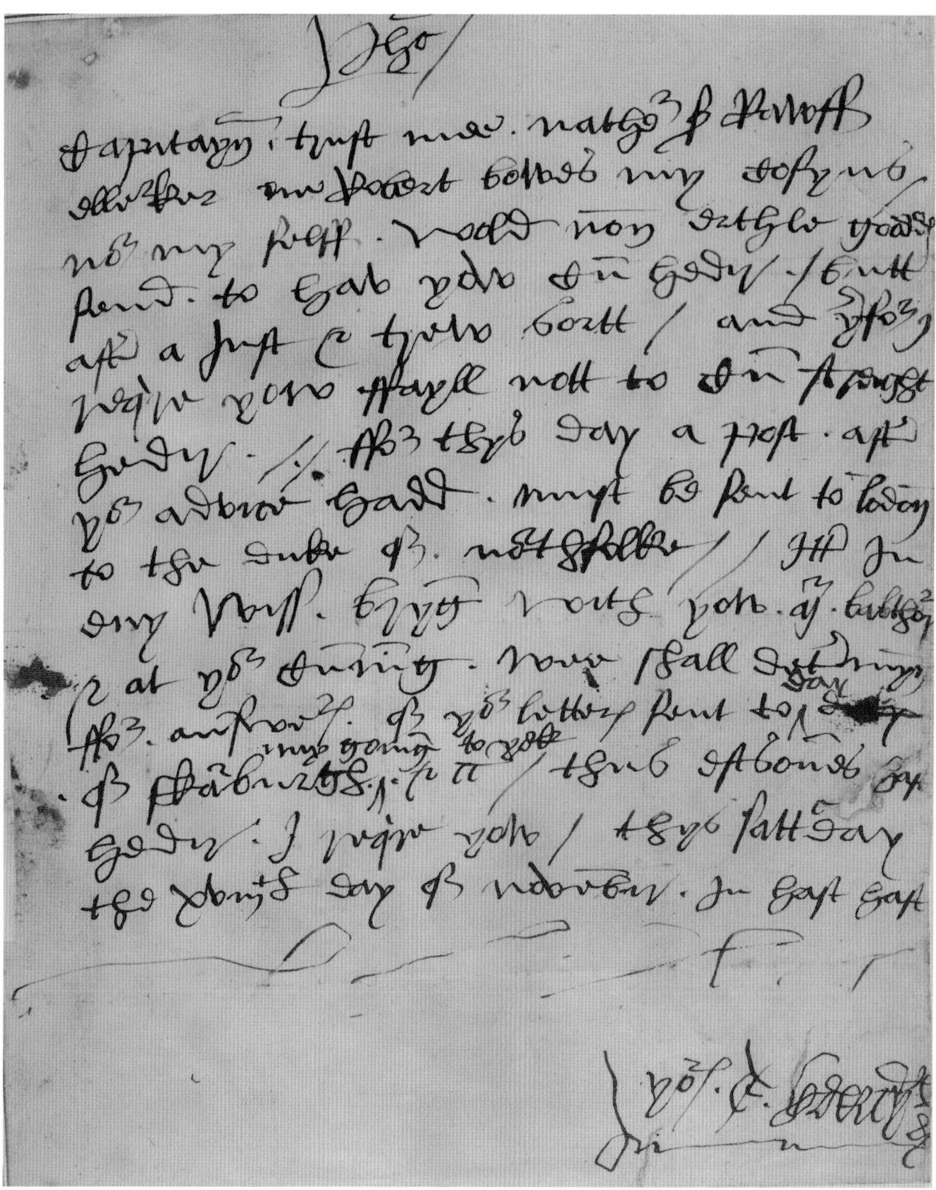

BEATVS vir qui non abiit in consilio impiorum, & in via peccatorum non stetit, & in cathedra pe=stilentiæ non sedit.

nota quis sit bea

THE MAKING OF A NEW CHURCH (1536–40)

Diarmaid MacCulloch

Thomas Cranmer and Thomas Cromwell had very different personalities. Cranmer was the quiet son of a country gentleman, over forty when he entered Henry VIII's service in 1530, after a blameless and undistinguished career at Cambridge University. The most surprising thing about him was that, by 1533, he had become Archbishop of Canterbury; but the years in which Anne Boleyn was Queen were full of surprises.

Cromwell was a shearman's son whose early life was full of adventures which he later glossed over, but which led him through mainland Europe, leaving him mysteriously well educated, and with a curious readiness in an unsentimental career to listen to religious idealists, far more than would be expected in a realistic and not overscrupulous politician.

What came to unite Cranmer and Cromwell was their deep interest in religious changes happening elsewhere in Europe, and a determination to apply them as far as politically possible to the English Church, now that King Henry had detached it from Rome. Cromwell was probably more religiously radical than the Archbishop; from 1536 he pressed for discreet but purposefully close links between England and the Protestant regime in Zurich, at a time when Cranmer still disapproved of the way in which the Zurich leadership and other Swiss Protestant leaders explained the nature of the Eucharist.

Anne Boleyn's 'reign' had seen both men leading religious reform. Cromwell was given a title which made him the day-to-day substitute for the King in running the English Church – 'Vice-Gerent in Spirituals' – an office with no predecessors or successors that, interestingly, reflected the powers over the Church that Cromwell's old master, Cardinal Wolsey, had exercised for the Pope before the break with Rome. Cromwell outranked the Archbishop of Canterbury, yet Cranmer clearly did not mind. He let Cromwell make the big changes. So Cranmer hardly seemed concerned about the speed of the dissolution of the monasteries after the Pilgrimage of Grace, nor about the politicking and business arrangements that led to an official English Bible in 1537. Cromwell did

◀ Detail from cat. no. 194

all this, and issued reforming injunctions in 1538 to destroy shrines and images. Cranmer just applauded from the sidelines and did what he could to help: Cromwell was the politician, not him.

Cranmer was a cautious man by nature – appropriately, in the circumstances. Neither he nor Cromwell was leading a Protestant Reformation as inspired individuals. Unlike other great reformers – Luther, Zwingli, Calvin, Knox, Loyola – they owed their role to a king seeking to build his own peculiar royal Church. In England it was not a question of Cranmer's or Cromwell's Reformation like Knox's Reformation in Scotland or Luther's in Saxony. It was, first of all, Henry's Reformation; moreover, there was good cause to fear the King's selfishness and bad temper. Cranmer found himself in danger, after Cromwell's terrifyingly swift fall in 1540 – and Cromwell died chiefly because Henry had been convinced, rightly in his own terms, that his minister was a heretic. Only a few days later, Henry showed his ecumenical savagery by simultaneously ordering the judicial murder of three papalist Catholics for being papalist Catholics and three Protestants for being Protestants.

Yet, among all Henry's bewildering changes of direction and inconsistencies, he showed real affection for Cranmer, and protected the Archbishop in situations apparently more dangerous than those that destroyed other great men and women. In 1543, conservative churchmen and gentry built up a formidable case against Cranmer for introducing religious change in his diocese without the King knowing or approving: precisely the sort of charges that had ended Thomas Cromwell's life in 1540. Henry let the chorus of hatred build up, and, when it seemed about to overwhelm the Archbishop, he crushed it all, and put Thomas Cranmer in charge of the whole investigation into Thomas Cranmer. Conservatives were humiliated at a time when, in many other ways, they seemed to be triumphant.

Why did Henry spare Cranmer? He had no illusions about Cranmer's religious beliefs. In 1543 he even made it clear that he knew that Cranmer was married, which offended against one of his most savagely expressed prohibitions for the English clergy. The reason was that Henry found in Cranmer a combination of qualities that he needed: honesty, loyalty and weakness. There were many dishonest and strong men around Henry, a few honest and strong – opinions differ as to which combination of characteristics Cromwell exhibited.

Cranmer would say what he thought, then meekly accept what the King wanted. He was bold enough both to argue with him and correct him: when, in 1538, Henry was putting in his pennyworth when preparing a new statement of doctrine for the Church, Cranmer crossed out theological alterations from the King himself, and made schoolmasterly remarks about Henry's grammar.

He gave Henry a lecture on the importance of the Lutheran doctrine of justification by faith. However, the King did not agree, and Cranmer gave way. In spring 1539 he prepared the first version of an English liturgy that would be the basis of the Book of Common Prayer, but he put it aside when Henry moved in a different direction. That year, when Henry forced through Parliament the Six Articles, a savagely conservative set of religious propositions, Cranmer was devastated, but he accepted them, and he sent Mrs Cranmer scurrying back to Germany.

Cranmer would go against his own interests if he felt that those of the King were more important. In 1539, Thomas Cromwell had busily prepared the ground for a diplomatic marriage for the King; his candidate was a German princess – Anne of Cleves – who would represent an asset for his own policy of religious reform, the policy that Cranmer favoured. Yet Cranmer opposed the idea, much to Cromwell's annoyance; Cranmer said that the King should marry someone that he loved, and preferably someone to whom he could talk in English. Given what a disaster the marriage to Anne of Cleves proved, it is a pity that Cromwell then ignored Cranmer's view and pressed ahead. Only when Henry was dead and buried, did Cranmer start emerging from the royal shadow, and a new revolutionary phase of his life began, though it ended in him being burnt at the stake. Yet, in his forties, he had met a man who had changed his life. The two men, Archbishop and King, enjoyed one of the longest-lasting relationships that King Henry ever knew.

QUEEN JANE AND THE BIRTH OF PRINCE EDWARD

Henry VIII's third marriage was his most successful as it produced his only male heir. Jane Seymour's pregnancy was made known in February 1537, and in September she officially withdrew to her chamber at Hampton Court to await the birth of her child. After a long labour of two days and three nights, she gave birth to a healthy son at about 2 am on 12 October. Great rejoicing followed, but it was brought to an abrupt end when Jane fell ill barely a week later and died at about 8 pm on 24 October. She was buried in St George's Chapel at Windsor on 13 November. The court went into mourning; Henry ordered that hundreds of masses be recited for Jane's soul and wore black until 2 February 1538.

183 Jane Seymour

After Hans Holbein the Younger, 1536

Collection of His Grace the Duke of Buccleuch

The imperial ambassador Eustace Chapuys described Jane Seymour (1508/9–37) as 'of middle stature and no great beauty, so fair that one would call her rather pale than otherwise', and he added that she was inclined to be proud and haughty. She first appeared at court about 1529 and served as a lady-in-waiting first to Queen Katherine and then to Anne. Henry probably showed interest in Jane as early as October 1534, but it was only in February 1536 that he seems to have made sexual advances towards her. Like Anne before her, Jane refused his attentions, thereby igniting his ardour. On the day of Anne's execution, 19 May 1536, Cranmer issued a dispensation to allow Jane to marry Henry (as they were fifth cousins, their marriage contravened the laws of consanguinity). The following day the couple were betrothed, and a private marriage took place on 30 May 1536 in the Queen's Closet or Oratory at Whitehall. (SD)

LITERATURE: Jane, née Seymour, *Oxford DNB*; Starkey, *Six Wives*

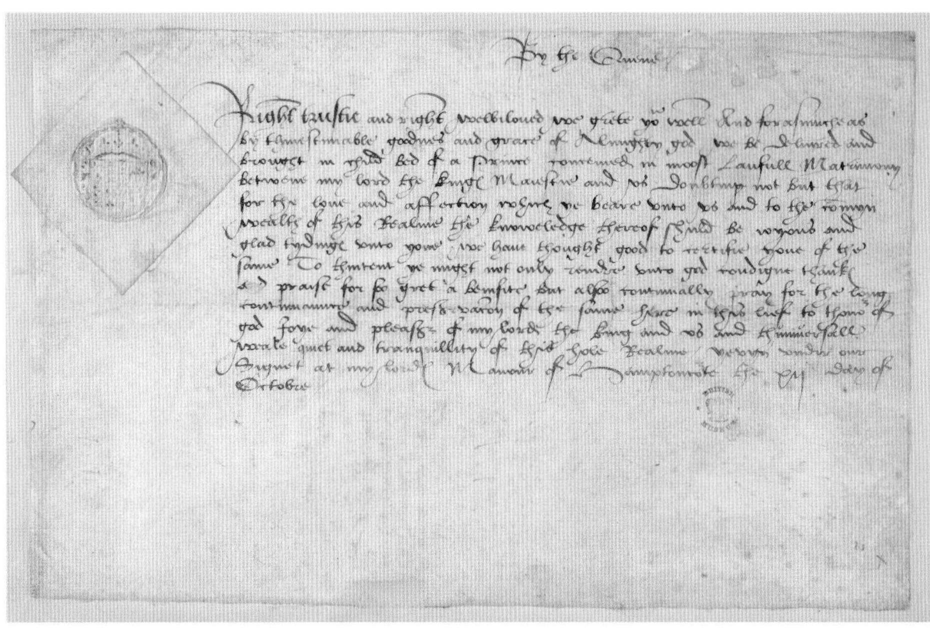

184 'Bound to obey and serve'

Hans Holbein the Younger

Preliminary design for a cup for Jane Seymour, 1536–7

British Museum, London, Department of Prints and Drawings, 1848,1125.9

Inscribed: 'BOVND TO OBEY AND [SERVE] and BOUND TO OBEY'

As a wedding gift to his new bride, Henry VIII commissioned Holbein to design an ornate gold cup enriched with pearls and gems. This drawing shows the preliminary design, which was modified in the final version. The initials 'H' and 'J' are repeated at intervals and tied by a lover's knot. Jane's motto 'bound to obey and serve' is repeated on the lid and foot. Its submissive tone was fairly typical for queen consorts, but it also reflects Jane's personality and helps explain why she was so attractive to Henry. Sir John Russell commended Jane for her gentleness, which had brought the King 'out of hell into heaven'. As in the designs for this cup, Henry ordered the intertwined initials and the Queen's motto to be incorporated in the decorations, just completed in the banqueting hall and at the entrance to the chapel at Hampton Court. In 1629 the cup was melted down and the gold sold. (SD)

LITERATURE: Rowlands, *Drawings by German Artists*; Starkey, *Six Wives*; Wooding, *Henry VIII*

185 Son and Heir

Jane Seymour to Lord Privy Seal (Cromwell) announcing the birth of Edward VI

British Library, Cotton MS Nero C x, fol.2

On 12 October 1537, after a long and difficult labour, Jane succeeded where Katherine of Aragon and Anne Boleyn had failed and presented Henry with his long-desired baby boy. Born on the eve of the feast of St Edward the Confessor, England's royal saint, the infant was named Edward. This is the pre-prepared letter, sent to Thomas Cromwell, Lord Privy Seal, in which Queen Jane proudly announced that 'by the inestimable goodness and grace of Almighty God we be delivered and brought in child bed of a Prince conceived in moost lawfull matrimony betwene my lord the Kinges Maiestie and us'. Henry was overjoyed. After nearly 30 years of waiting he at last had a son and heir and the Tudor dynasty was assured, proof for Henry that God was looking on him favourably and approved of all his policies. (AC)

LITERATURE: Starkey, *Six Wives*; Wooding, *Henry VIII*; Scarisbrick, *Henry VIII*

186 Bitterness of Death

Letter from Thomas Rutland and five other medical men to Cromwell about the Queen's extreme illness, Hampton Court, 17 October 1537

British Library, Cotton MS Nero C x, fol.3

Jane appeared to make a good recovery following the birth of Edward and was well enough to receive guests at Edward's christening on 15 October. The following day, however, her condition suddenly worsened. In this letter to Cromwell, her physicians, including the King's favourite, William Butt (*c*.1485–1545), report that 'all this night she hath bene very syck and doth rather appare (worsen) then amend'. The Queen's confessor, the Bishop of Carlisle, the letter continued, had been with her since dawn and 'even now is preparing to minister to her grace the sacrament of [extreme] unction'. On 24 October, twelve days after the birth of her son, Jane died, probably from puerperal fever caused by unhygienic obstetric practices. That same day, responding to Francis I's message of congratulations on the birth of Edward, Henry told him 'Divine Providence has mingled my joy with the bitterness of the death of her who brought me this happiness'. (AC)

LITERATURE: Starkey, *Six Wives*; Scarisbrick, *Henry VIII*

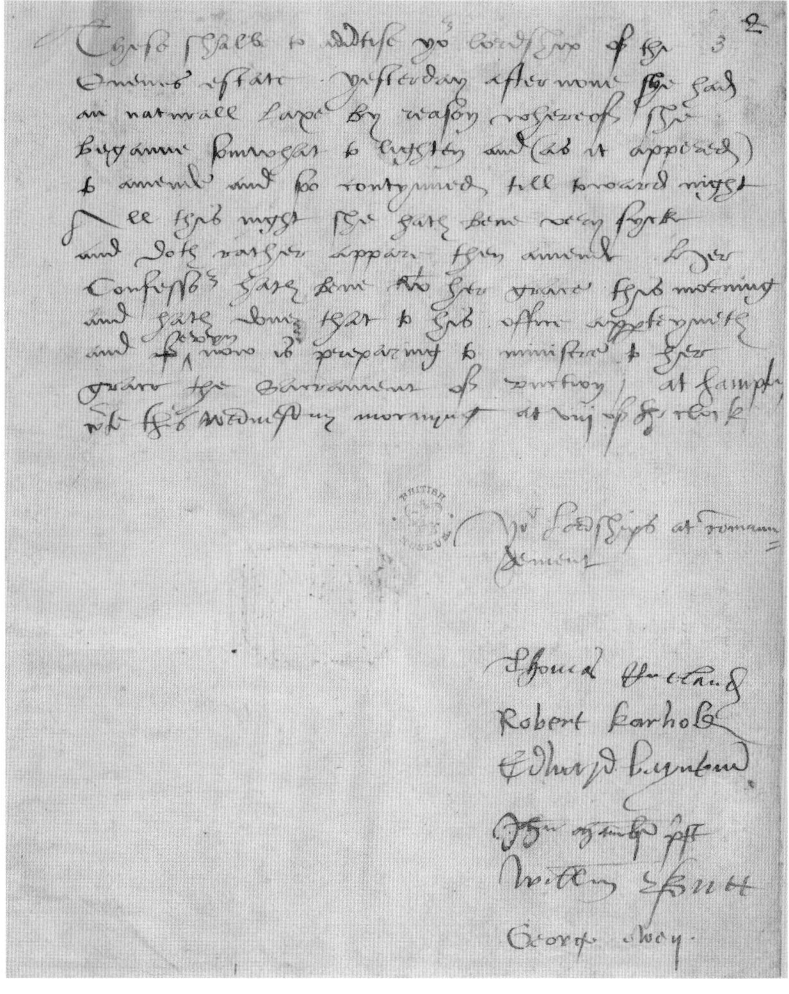

These shalbe to advertise your lordship of the Quenes estate. Yesterday afternoon she had an naturall laxe by reason wherof she began somewhat to lyghten and (as it appered) to amende and soo contynued till towards night. All this night she hath bene very sycke and doth rather appare then amende. Her confessor hath bene with her grace this morning and hath done that to his office apperteyneth and even now is preparing to minister to her grace the sacrament of unction. At Hampton Court this Wednesday morning at viij of the clock.

Your lordships at commandment

[illegible]
Robert Karhole
[illegible]
[illegible]
William Butt
George Owen

187 Edward, Prince of Wales

Hans Holbein the Younger (or copy)

Berger Collection at the Denver Art Museum, 1937.1.64

Inscribed from Latin: 'Little one, emulate your father and be the heir of his virtue; the world contains nothing greater. Heaven and earth could scarcely produce a son whose glory would surpass that of such a father. Only equal the deeds of your parent and men can wish for no more. Surpass him and you have surpassed all the kings the world ever revered and none will surpass you'

In this portrait of Henry's long-awaited male heir, Prince Edward (1537–53) is about fourteen months old and shown as a miniature version of his father in a hat and costume similar to those worn by the King. Even the toy rattle is a composite of an orb and sceptre that is raised in a gesture of authority. The image illustrates the inscription. Written by the humanist Richard Morison (*c*.1510–56), whom Thomas Cromwell had promoted from his own service to that of the King, it exhorts the son to emulate his father and was designed to flatter Henry by maintaining that his achievements could never be surpassed. Almost certainly, the original painting was a New Year's gift to Henry in 1539 from the painter Hans Holbein the Younger, who had just returned to England after a short stay in Basel. Holbein received a silver cup in return.

The juxtaposition of words and image is one of the most striking features of 'official art' under the Tudors. Other striking instances are to be found in the title page of the Great Bible (cat. no. 201), and in the Whitehall mural, with its contrast between Henry VII, who was great because he had ended the War of the Roses, and Henry VIII, who was great because he had reformed the Church. Indeed, these words – and pictures – offer some of the best evidence about Henry's judgement of his own importance and his relationship to the Church (cat. nos 198, 199). (SD and DS)

LITERATURE: Foister, *Holbein in England*; String, *Art and Communication in the Reign of Henry VIII*; Bätschmann and Griener, *Hans Holbein*

PARVVLE PATRISSA, PATRIÆ VIRTVTIS ET HÆRES
ESTO, NIHIL MAIVS MAXIMVS ORBIS HABET.
GNATVM VIX POSSVNT COELVM ET NATVRA DEDISSE,
HVIVS QVEM PATRIS, VICTVS HONORET HONOS.
ÆQVATO TANTVM, TANTI TV FACTA PARENTIS,
VOTA HOMINVM, VIX QVO PROGREDIANTVR, HABENT
VINCITO, VICISTI, QVOT REGES PRISCVS ADORAT
ORBIS, NEC TE QVI VINCERE POSSIT, ERIT.

THE DOCTRINES OF HENRY VIII'S CHURCH

As 'Supreme Head of the Church', Henry VIII had a duty to define 'true doctrine' for his subjects. While some of his bishops recommended little or no substantial change, Cromwell, Archbishop Cranmer and other Evangelicals were keen to rethink and reformulate Roman Catholic doctrines on the Sacraments, purgatory and justification, seeking a move in a Lutheran or even Swiss Reformed direction.

They had an uphill task in convincing their King. Henry disliked Martin Luther (who had not supported his annulment) and refused to accept his central doctrine of justification by faith alone. Henry disliked even more the theologians from South Germany and Switzerland who denied the presence of the body and blood of Christ in the bread and wine at Mass. The King did not see himself as a Protestant but as a reforming and anti-clerical Catholic, very much in the mould of Erasmus.

Nonetheless, the break with Rome, not least on the grounds of the supremacy of Scripture, necessitated some rethinking of traditional doctrines and practices within the Church of England. Furthermore, Lutheran doctrines were given an airing during the 1530s, when Henry sought a political alliance with the Lutheran princes of Germany in order to break his international isolation. Because the princes demanded Henry's subscription to their confession of faith, English and German theologians discussed doctrine together. Ultimately, Henry found himself unable to accept the Lutheran approval of clerical marriage and rejection of private masses, let alone the doctrine of justification by faith alone. However, Henry did gradually become more sceptical about the existence of purgatory and the efficacy of prayers for the dead.

During the mid- and late 1530s Henry called upon his senior clergy to produce a statement of faith for his new Church, but it was not easy to reach agreement. After an acrimonious debate between traditionalists and Evangelicals in Convocation, the Ten Articles – a theological compromise – were cobbled together and endorsed by Henry. Then, in the summer of 1537, a committee of evangelical bishops and theologians produced a more radical statement of religion. Initially, Henry did not have time to read this work properly and the *Bishops' Book* was published without his express approval. However, when the King did have time to read the book, he strongly criticized its contents because it came too close to enunciating Luther's doctrine of justification by faith.

By 1539, Henry's new Church was still without an official doctrine, and a variety of views were being preached in England. Alarmed at the radicalism of some preachers, Henry decided that his Church needed to have a clearly defined set of beliefs to be upheld by law. The Act of Six Articles (1539) began the process, by clarifying Henry's position on some of the key issues dividing conservatives and radicals that had emerged during his negotiations with the German Lutheran princes. On almost all of them the King took a conservative position; the one exception concerned auricular confession. In 1543 the *King's Book* became the authoritative doctrinal formulary of the Henrician Church. Although the King tempered his approach to the efficacy of prayers for the dead in it, the Evangelicals were dismayed by its unambiguous condemnation of justification by faith alone and the need for clerical absolution of sins.

Throughout all the theological debates, Henry tried to find a path between the extremes of Roman Catholicism and Protestantism by following what he saw as a policy of balance. He expressed his standpoint in Parliament in December 1545, when he denounced those who 'be too stiff in their old mumpsimus' (the traditionalists) and those 'too busy and curious in their new sumpsimus' (the Evangelicals).

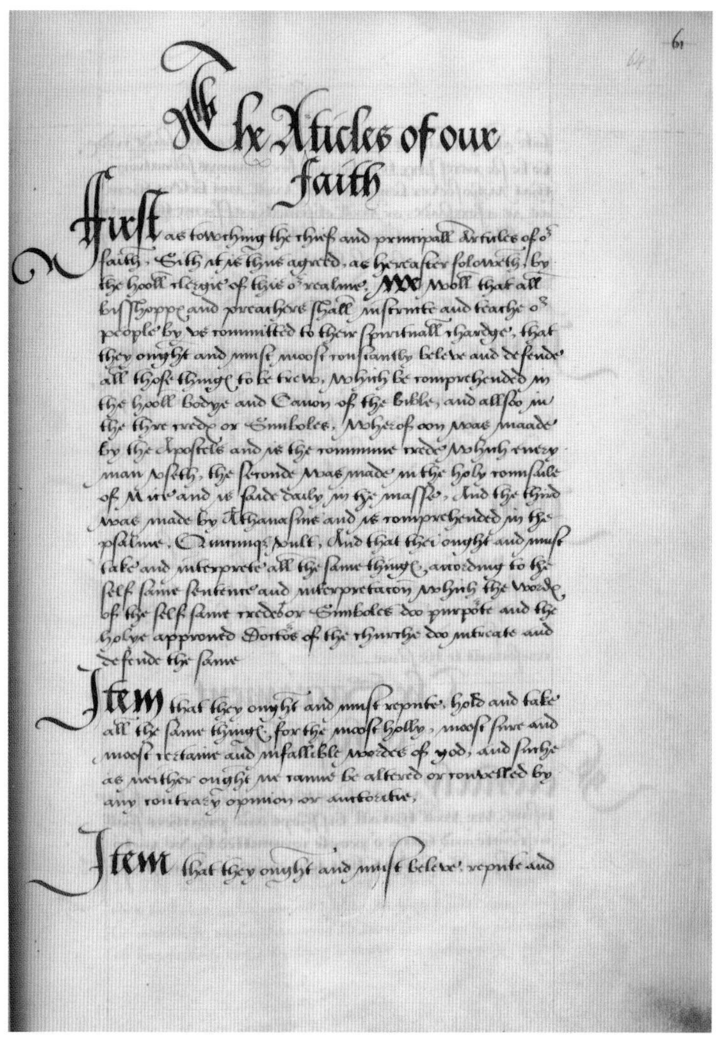

188 The Ten Articles, 1536

British Library, Cotton MS Cleopatra E v, fols 64, 72

In 1536, following negotiations between England and the alliance of German Lutheran princes known as the Schmalkaldic League, these Ten Articles were issued as guidelines for the newly independent English Church's doctrine. They were a puzzle to contemporaries and have remained so since, being neither comprehensive, nor consistent, nor authoritative. Their scepticism towards prayer for the dead and the use of images, and their apparent emulation of Luther in ignoring four of the traditional seven Sacraments, alarmed English religious conservatives. Yet they were conservative enough – especially in their coolness towards Lutheran ideas of justification – to disappoint Evangelicals: one reformer believed that they 'were such that it had bene wickednes not to haue spoken openly against them'. As the product of a particular diplomatic moment, they turned out to be ephemeral, but as the first substantial signal of the ambiguity of Henry VIII's religious policies, they have a lasting significance. (AR)

LITERATURE: McEntegart, *Henry VIII, the League of Schmalkalden and the English Reformation*; Rex, *Henry VIII and the English Reformation*

The sacrament of penaunce.

ficient satisfaction for his synnes. Whiche done, than after-
warde with this feare, shame, and sorowe muste nedes suc-
cede and be conioyned the seconde parte, that is to wytte, a
certayn faithe, trust, and confidence of the mercy and goodnes of god, wherby the penitente muste conceyue certayne
hope and faithe, that god wyll forgyue hym his synnes, and
repute hym iustifyed, and of the nombre of his electe chyldren, not for the worthynes of any merite or worke done by
the penitent, but for the onely merites of the blode and passion of our sauyour Jesu Christe.

Item that this certayne faythe and hope is gotten, and also confyrmed, and made more stronge, by the applyenge of
Christis wordes and promyses of his grace and fauoure
conteyned in his gospell, and the sacramentes instituted by
hym in the newe testament. And therfore to attayne this certayne faythe, the seconde parte of penaunce is necessarye,
That is to say, Confession to a prieste, if it may be hadde.
For the absolution gyuen by the prieste was instituted of
Christe, to applye the promyses of goddis grace and fauour to the penytente.

Wherfore as touchyng CONFESSION we thinke it con-
ueniente, that all bysshoppes and preachers shall instructe
and teache the people, cōmytted unto their spirituall charge,
that they oughte and muste certaynely beleue, that the wordes of absolution, pronounced by the prieste, be spoken by
the auctoritie gyuen to hym by Christe in the gospelle. And
that they ought and muste gyue no lesse faithe and credence
to the same wordes of absolution, so pronounced by the ministers of the churche, than they wolde gyue unto the veray
wordes and voyce of god hym selfe, if he shulde speake unto us out of heuen, accordynge to the sayenge of Christe,
Ioan.20. Whose synnes soo euer you doo forgyue, shall be forgyuen:
Luc.10. Whose synnes so euer you doo reteyne, shall be reteyned.
And ageyne in an nother place Christe saythe, who so euer
Luc.10. hereth you, hereth me.

Item

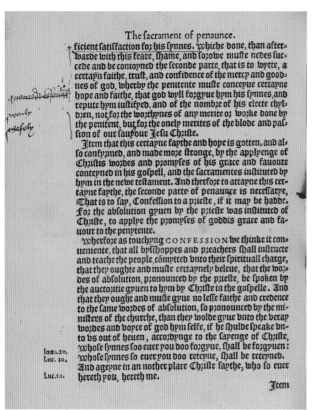

189 The *Bishops' Book*, 1537

'The Institution of a Christen man', otherwise known as the *Bishops' Book*

Printed by Thomas Berthelet (d.1555)

Bodleian Library, Oxford, Bodley 4° Rawlinson 245, fol.37v

This copy of the 1537 *Bishops' Book,* which was kept in Henry's Privy Chamber and corrected in his own hand, shows the King's close involvement in its revisions. Many of the corrections are pedantic, but some are substantial. Henry stripped out the 1537 text's cautious affirmation of the Protestant doctrine of justification by faith. He altered two of the Ten Commandments to fit his own preferences, although Archbishop Cranmer told him tartly that even a Supreme Head could not do that. He also softened attacks on astrology and superstition, and replaced talk of charity for the poor with exhortations to hard work. In the passage displayed, relating to the Sacrament of Penance (confession), Henry altered the meaning of the text with the addition of just two words: 'the penitent must conceive certayne hope and faythe that God wyll forgyve hym his synnes and repute hym iustified, and of the nombre of his electe children, not *wonly* for the worthynes of any merite or worke done by the penitent but *chefely* for the onely merites of the blode and passion of our savyour Jesu Christe'. (AR and AC)

LITERATURE: MacCulloch, *Thomas Cranmer*; Ryrie, 'Divine Kingship and Royal Theology in Henry VIII's Reformation'; Scarisbrick, *Henry VIII*

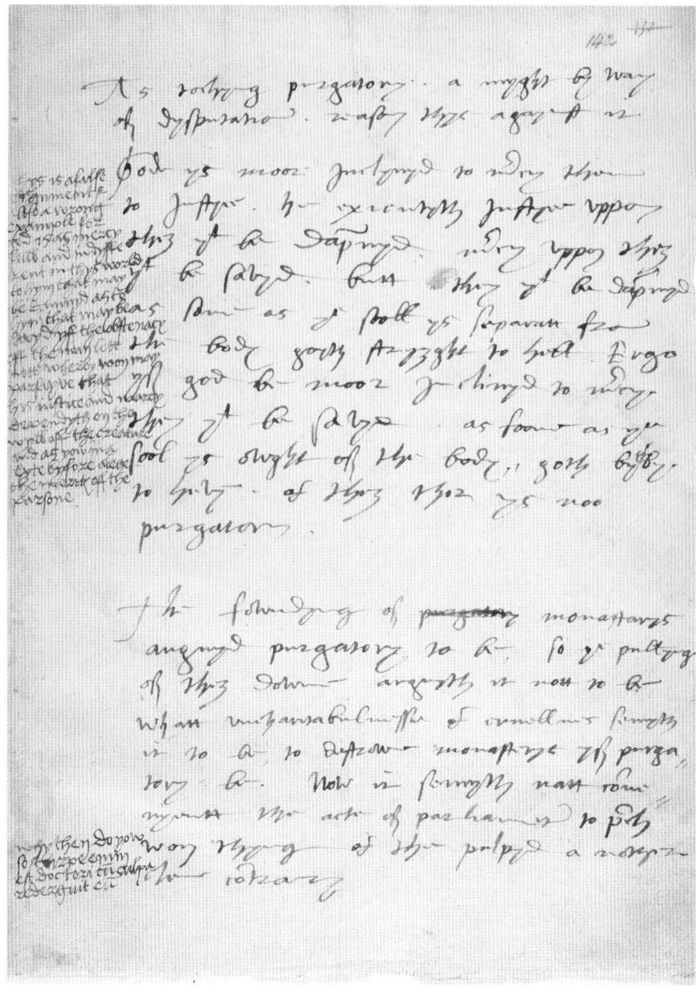

190 Purgatory and Prayers for the Dead

British Library, Cotton MS Cleopatra E v, fol.142

In the 1530s, debate raged about the efficacy of prayers for the dead and the very existence of purgatory. Around 1537 the reformist Bishop of Worcester, Hugh Latimer (*c*.1485–1555), prepared for the King a paper in opposition to what he ironically described elsewhere as 'our old ancient purgatory pick-purse' and Henry's sharp disagreement is apparent in his marginalia in the paper. He alluded to Latimer's false arguments, wrong examples and reprimanded his bishop for 'his carnal wit, which in preaching you dispraise so much'. When Latimer maintained that the dissolution of the monasteries could be justified only if purgatory was negated, Henry responded with a particularly apt quotation from his schoolboy textbook, the *Distichs of Cato*. Ultimately, Henry decided, 'purgatory may yet stond for all this'. Later on he modifed his position. (JC)

LITERATURE: Corrie (ed.), *Sermons and Remains of Hugh Latimer*; Marshall, 'Fear, Purgatory and Polemic'

191 Auricular Confession

Letter from Henry VIII to Cuthbert Tunstall, Bishop of Durham (1474–1559), in reply to arguments in favour of auricular confession, June 1539

British Library, Cotton MS Cleopatra E v, fol.131

In June 1539, when the draft Act of Six Articles was debated in the House of Lords, only one substantive change was made: auricular confession was demoted from being 'necessary by the law of God' to being merely 'expedient'. This letter describes that debate – a lively affair in which evangelical and traditionalist bishops fired biblical and patristic texts at one another until the King overruled the traditionalists. Bishop Tunstall of Durham evidently jibbed at this outcome: the result was this letter, one of the longest surviving in Henry's own hand. It fizzes with indignation, and with the King's pleasure in (as he thought) running theological rings around a bishop. He contrasted his own plain Biblicism with the beliefs of Tunstall, who was 'too muche blyndyd in your awne fansy and jugme[n]t'. He also included a startling analogy between God's laws and his own, making it clear how little difference he saw between the two. (AR)

LITERATURE: Ryrie, 'Divine Kingship and Royal Theology in Henry VIII's Reformation'; Ryrie, *The Gospel and Henry VIII*; Redworth, 'A Study in the Formulation of Policy'

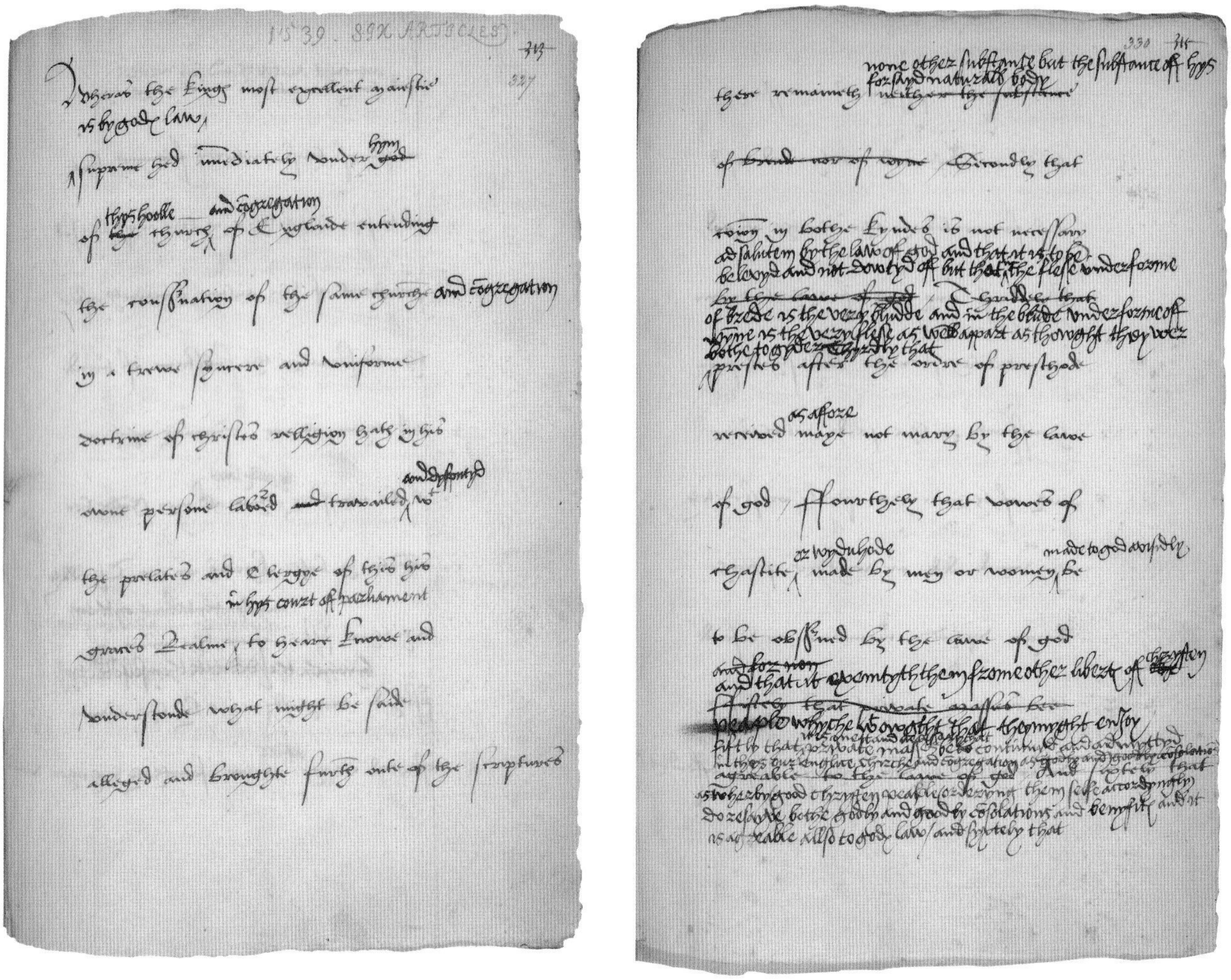

192 The Act of Six Articles, 1539

British Library, Cotton MS Cleopatra E v, fols 327, 330

This is one of the final drafts of the Act of Six Articles, amended in the King's own hand. Some of his changes were minor, indeed pedantic, as in his rephrasing of the first article, which affirms the doctrine of transubstantiation. Others are more substantive. Notably, he entirely rewrote the fifth article of the bill, leaving the text of the statute both awkward and ambiguous. It affirmed that 'private masses' (that is, those celebrated by a priest alone) bring 'godly ... consolations and benyfits' to Christians, without specifying what they might be. Traditionally, such masses were celebrated primarily on behalf of the dead, which Evangelicals found offensive. This phrasing, which implied – but did not assert – prayer for the dead, helped to ease evangelical scruples about the Act. However, Henry would later reprimand Evangelicals who tried to use this as a loophole to criticize masses for the dead. (AR)

LITERATURE: Ryrie, *The Gospel and Henry VIII*; Redworth, 'A Study in the Formulation of Policy'; Lehmberg, *The Later Parliaments of Henry VIII, 1536–1537*

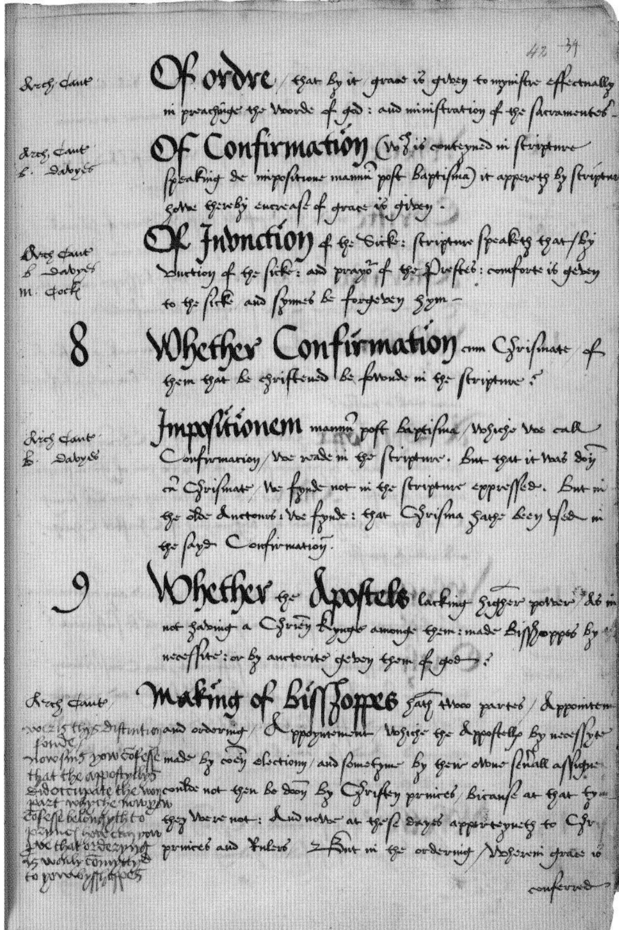

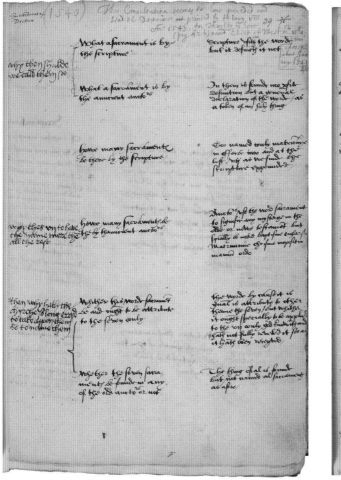

193 Revisions to the *Bishops' Book*

British Library, Cotton MS Cleopatra E v, fols 39, 42

In 1540, a committee of prominent clerics was established as part of the process of revising the 1537 *Bishops' Book*. This document details the committee's replies, in the summer of 1540, to seventeen questions on the Sacraments. These summaries of the committee's views are annotated in the King's own hand. Henry VIII was here in a rumbustiously anticlerical mood, backing the committee's evangelical minority against the traditionalist consensus on several points. He disputed the traditional number of seven Sacraments, the use of chrism in Confirmation, and the necessity of confession to a priest, bluntly demanding scriptural justification for those practices, and accusing the Church of having 'long erryd'. Six of the questions asked pointedly about kings' powers to appoint or ordain clergy, and here Henry was particularly assertive, mocking the distinctions that the traditionalists tried to maintain. His comment on folio 42 is an implicit claim of sacramental power for himself. (AR)

LITERATURE: Cobb (ed.), *The Rationale of Ceremonial, 1540–1543*; Ryrie, 'Divine Kingship and Royal Theology in Henry VIII's Reformation'; MacCulloch, *Thomas Cranmer*

194 Jean Mallard, King Henry VIII's Psalter, 1540

British Library, Royal MS 2 A. xvi

A. Fols 2v–3; B. Fols 29v–30; C. Fols 63v–64; D. Fols 78v–79

Written and illuminated in 1540 by an *émigré* from the court of Francis I, King Henry VIII's Psalter is Mallard's most lavish production. It contains numerous decorated initials, as well as eight larger illuminations that allude to the text of the Psalter which they illustrate, and several link Henry visually to King David and, by analogy, perhaps even to Christ himself. Small and easy to handle, the Psalter was used by Henry in his private devotions, as the miniature accompanying Psalm 1 shows dramatically: the King sits in his Privy Chamber (A) contemplating the Word of God 'day and night', just as the Psalmist admonishes. Henry made many notes in the Psalter and these uniformly witness to his theological concerns and his identification of himself with his Old Testament counterpart. Overweight and increasingly immobile, he regretted the passing of years and considered it a *dolens dictum* when he read in Psalm 36: 25 that 'I have been young and now am old'. Nor did he take much consolation in the second part of the verse, which stated that 'I have not seen the just forsaken, nor his seed seeking bread'. (JC)

LITERATURE: Carley, 'Marginalia by Henry VIII in His Copy of The Bokes of Salomon'; Carley, *King Henry VIII's Prayer Book*

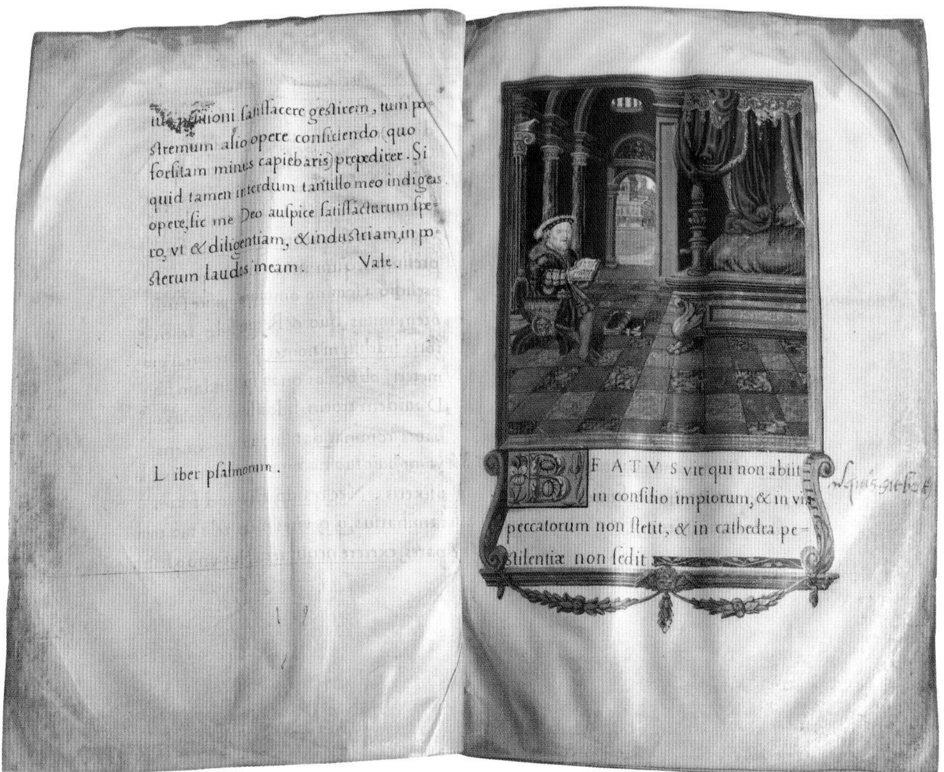

A

B

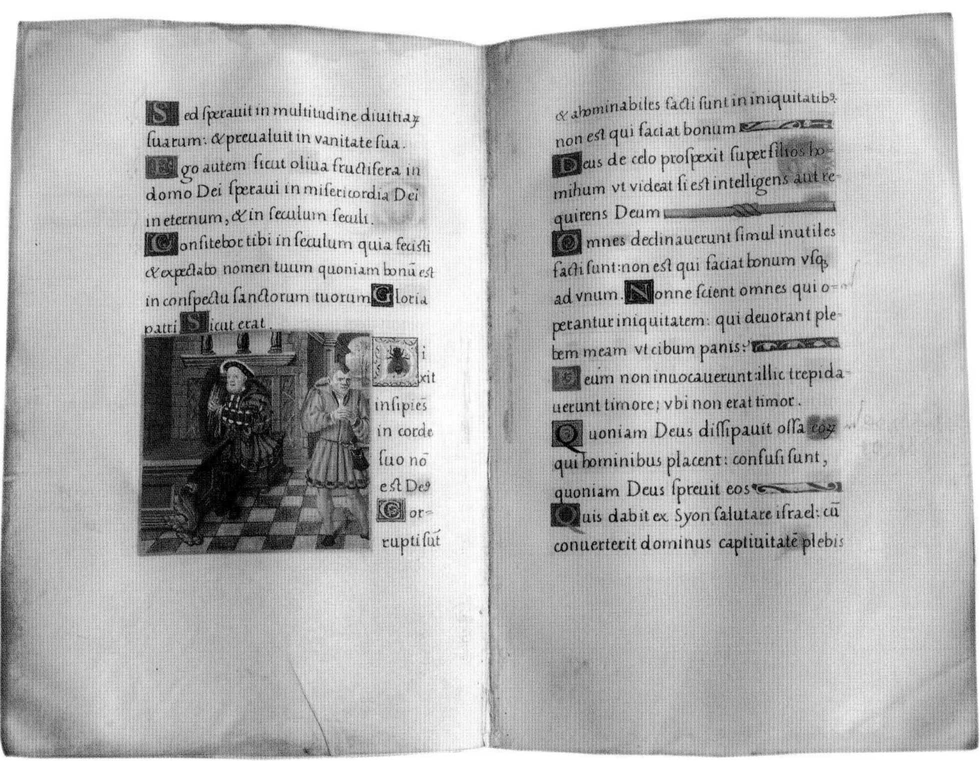
Sed sperauit in multitudine diuitiaꝝ
suarum: & preualuit in vanitate sua.
Ego autem sicut oliua fructifera in
domo Dei speraui in misericordia Dei
in eternum, & in seculum seculi.
Confitebor tibi in seculum quia fecisti
& expectabo nomen tuum quoniam bonū est
in conspectu sanctorum tuorum. Gloria
patri. Sicut erat.
Dixit
insipiēs
in corde
suo nō
est Deus
Cor-
rupti sūt

& abominabiles facti sunt in iniquitatibus
non est qui faciat bonum
Deus de celo prospexit super filios hominum vt videat si est intelligens aut re-
quirens Deum
Omnes declinauerunt simul inutiles
facti sunt: non est qui faciat bonum vsq;
ad vnum. Nonne scient omnes qui o-
perantur iniquitatem: qui deuorant ple-
bem meam vt cibum panis:
Deum non inuocauerunt: illic trepida-
uerunt timore; vbi non erat timor.
Quoniam Deus dissipauit ossa eoꝝ
qui hominibus placent: confusi sunt,
quoniam Deus spreuit eos
Quis dabit ex Syon salutare israel: cū
conuerterit dominus captiuitatē plebis

C

quod operatus es ī nobis. A templo tuo ī hie-
rusalē tibi offerent reges munera.
Increpa feras arundinis congregatio
taurorum in vaccis populoꝝ: vt excludāt
eos qui probati sunt argento
Dissipa gentes que bella volunt. venient
legati ex egipto: ethiopia preueniet manus eius Deo.
Regna terræ cātate Deo psallite dnō.
Psallite Deo qui ascendit super celū
celi ad orientem. Ecce dabit voci
sue vocem virtutis date gloriā deo super
israel magnificentia eius & virtus eius in nu-
bibus. Mirabilis Deus in sanctis suis
deus israel ipse dabit virtutem & fortitudi-
nem plebi sue benedictus Deus. Gloria
Sicut erat.

Saluum me fac Deus quoniam
intrauerunt aque vsq; ad animā
meam.

D

195 Jean Mallard, *Le Chemin de Paradis*, 1540

Bodleian Library, Oxford, MS 883, fol.10v

Written and illustrated around 1540, soon after the French émigré Jean Mallard had become 'poete et orateur en la langue francoyse' to Henry VIII, *Le Chemin de paradis* (The Path to Paradise) contains an elucidation in French verse of the theological issues explicated in The Act of Six Articles of 1539. No theologian, Mallard nevertheless challenged both papalists and Protestants: 'L'ung va preschant le pape et ses bulles / L'aultre Luther, les aultres de leurs mulles' ('One goes preaching the pope and his bulls, / Another Luther and others their (cardinals') slippers'). The miniature shows the poet, wearing royal livery, with the HR monogram (Henricus Rex) stitched on his tunic, and sitting on a path after having fallen by the way. His pilgrim's hat lies in front of him to the side where it landed after his fall. On the right of the path is a church with three tombs in the churchyard. The path carries on to the right past a large rock formation behind which it disappears. What we have, then, is a visual representation of the moment when, as Mallard relates, he was inspired to write a poem to help the faithful avoid death by following the path to paradise, as set out by Henry's Church. (JC)

LITERATURE: Cooper, 'Jean Mallard, Poète et peintre rouennais'; Carley, *King Henry VIII's Prayer Book*

EPISTRE &preface
Apres le temps
que mainte folle erreur
Eut couru sus,
la terre en grand fureur

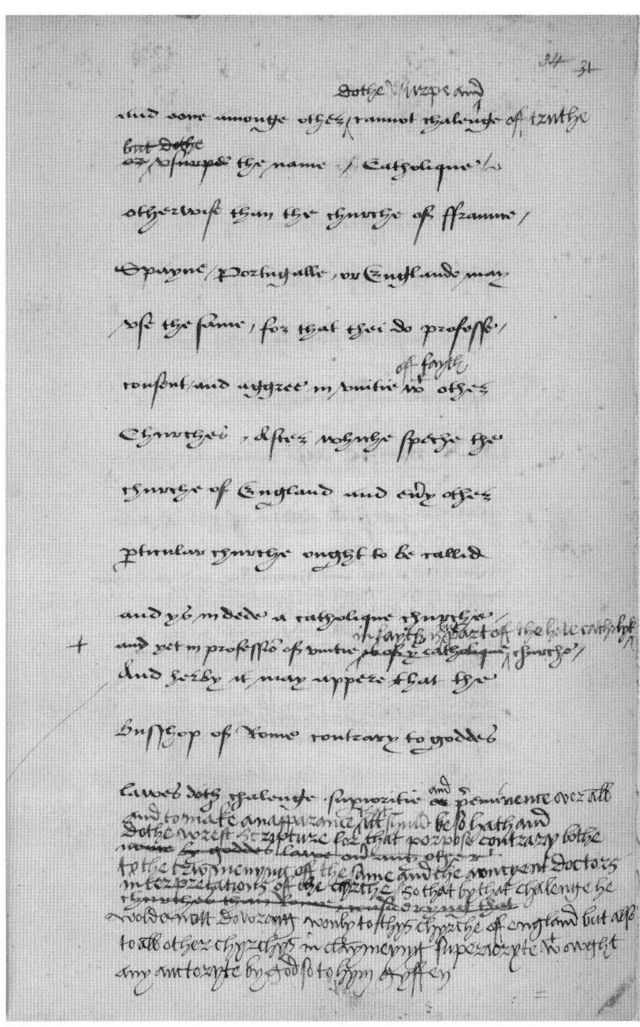

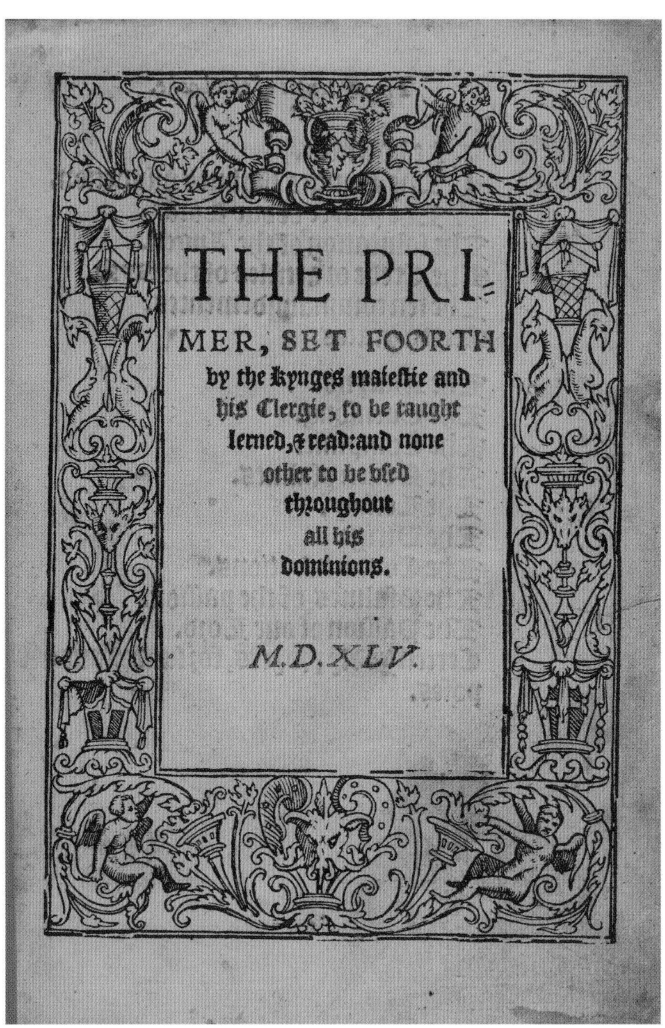

THE PRI=
MER, SET FOORTH
by the kynges maiestie and
his Clergie, to be taught
lerned, & read: and none
other to be vsed
throughout
all his
dominions.

M.D.XLV.

196 The *King's Book*, 1543

'A necessary doctrine and erudition for any Christian man, sette furth by the kynges majestie'

British Library, Cotton MS Cleopatra E v, fol.34

In 1543 an authoritative doctrinal formulary for Henry's Church was published that was universally known as the *King's Book*. Henry was indeed closely involved in its production, as this late draft annotated in his hand shows. Here he rewrites the book's attack on the papacy, inserting a claim that the Pope, to maintain his authority, 'dothe wrest scripture … contrary bothe to the trew memyry off the same and the auncyent doctors interpretations', and so wrongs not only the English Church but all Christendom. The 1543 Act for the Advancement of True Religion enforced the book's doctrine as authoritative, and it remained so until Henry's death. The book's doctrine was in general more robustly conservative than the 1537 *Bishops' Book*, and it rejected justification by faith unequivocally, but it was far more sceptical towards prayer for the dead than earlier Henrician documents. (AR)

LITERATURE: Ryrie, *The Gospel and Henry VIII*; MacCulloch, *Thomas Cranmer*; Rex, *Henry VIII and the English Reformation*

197 The *King's Primer*, 1545

British Library, C.132.i.11, title page

Latin primers were staple devotional texts of the Middle Ages, providing a version of the Church's public liturgy for individual use. From 1529 onwards, Evangelicals set out to subvert, or hijack, the genre, producing English-language primers shorn of many of the traditional devotions centring on the saints and on purgatory. Henry approved of this kind of reform, and in 1539 Cromwell sponsored an English primer produced by Bishop John Hilsey of Rochester (d.1539). In 1545 the Hilsey primer was superseded by this *King's Primer*, whose title declares its exclusive claims over the English people. Although superficially traditional, lengthy chunks of Scripture replaced traditional pieties throughout. An accompanying proclamation claimed that the variety of primers was causing 'contentions and vain disputations', and so required that there now be only 'one uniform order of all such books throughout all our dominion', outlawing centuries of traditional Latin pieties at a stroke. (AR)

LITERATURE: Butterworth, *The English Primers (1529–45)*; Duffy, *Marking the Hours*; Duffy, *The Stripping of the Altars*

THE LAST YEARS (1539–47)

Susan Doran

Had Henry VIII died in 1540 he might be considered one of the greatest monarchs in English history. Until the last years of his life, he fulfilled admirably the role expected of a Renaissance king and in his confident pursuit of glory he successfully displayed power, splendour and energy to fellow European monarchs and his own subjects. Despite England's relatively small size and limited economic resources, Henry acquired by his own efforts a seat at the small top table of the pre-eminent rulers of Europe. To justify and maintain this position, he augmented the size and fighting capacity of the small navy he had inherited from his father, and improved his army by developing its firepower. As a result, even after he withdrew from European warfare during the late 1520s, his international prestige remained substantially intact and an alliance with him was thought worth having. Henry's achievements at home, before 1540, were still more impressive. To project an image of power, he constructed new palaces or enlarged and restyled existing ones, so that they now rivalled the finest Renaissance chateaux built by Francis I. Whitehall Palace in Westminster, started in the 1530s, eventually extended over 23 acres to become the largest royal residence in Europe. Though smaller, Nonsuch Palace in Surrey – begun in 1538 – was more ornately decorated than the grandest palaces on the Continent. Henry also successfully competed with France and the Habsburg Empire in his patronage of artists, musicians, scholars and scientific instrument-makers. His court became a centre of scholarship and the arts.

Furthermore, not all Henry's achievements before 1540 were simply for show. He and his ministers introduced practical measures of reform in government that went beyond the superficial. Most obviously and dramatically Henry enhanced royal power by placing himself at the head of the English Church and expropriating huge amounts of ecclesiastical property. Less well-known reforms – but those that had a long-lasting impact on Tudor government – included the introduction of the peacetime 'subsidy', a tax that became an essential revenue-raising tool for English monarchs throughout the 16th century. In Wales, the

◀ Detail from cat. no. 257

administrative system was entirely and permanently overhauled when JPs and county government were introduced into the Principality and Marcher Lordships (border areas) by a statute of 1536. In Ireland Henry began the process of imposing direct rule through a lord deputy rather than relying on local magnates with delegated authority.

At a cultural level, Henry's reign stimulated England's sense of national identity. Thanks to the break with Rome, England ceased to be a part of international Christendom but instead had its own national Church, and started to develop its own distinctive confession of faith and forms of worship. Governmental propaganda justifying the schism used the language of imperial sovereignty and referred to a realm bound together by law, custom and history – all of which reinforced many English people's belief in their own nationhood.

Henry's Reformation, moreover, gave a great boost to the use of the English language. A newly translated English Bible was printed, authorized by the King and ordered to be placed in every parish. At the same time, writers and poets associated with Henry's court wrote their works in the vernacular for an English readership. Meanwhile, the assimilation of Wales into England extended the dominance of the English language throughout Henry's realm, for the statute of 1536 ordered its sole use in the law courts and administration of the newly created Welsh counties.

Henry VIII's record after 1540 was, however, more mixed. On the positive side, his previous domestic policies and achievements continued. There were more building projects, though perhaps with a greater emphasis on castles and fortifications to meet the perceived defence needs of the time. Henry also continued to extend the vernacular into religious life when he sanctioned an English litany in 1544 and endorsed Hilsey's English Primer in 1545. The 1543 Act of Union completed the integration of Wales into England, while in 1541 Ireland was transformed from a lordship into a kingdom ruled by the English monarch. For the most part, though, the 1540s were years scarred by a foreign policy that drained royal finances and brought economic hardship to England while achieving few of Henry's objectives. Furthermore, the streak of tyranny in Henry's character evident during the 1530s became even more obvious in the 1540s with the high-profile executions of Thomas Cromwell, Margaret Pole, Countess of Salisbury, and Henry Howard, Earl of Surrey, none of whom posed any threat to the King or realm.

Henry's aggressive policy towards the Scots began propitiously with the total defeat of James V's army at the Battle of Solway Moss in November 1542 and the Scottish King's subsequent death. This unexpected success, however, turned into a political disaster. Instead of using patient diplomacy or persistent military force to secure dominance in Scotland, Henry resorted to bullying tactics that encouraged opposition to his plan for a dynastic union of the two realms through a marriage between James V's heir, the infant Queen Mary, and Henry's son Prince Edward. In a show of independence, the Scottish regency government annulled all treaties with England in December 1543 and renewed the Auld Alliance with France. Unwilling to divert his army from France to a war against Scotland, Henry reacted by mounting a series of punitive raids across the border that scorched and plundered the Lowland areas, including Edinburgh. Yet the Scots still refused to submit to his terms and much money was wasted on this so-called 'Rough Wooing'.

War in France was more to Henry's taste. Taking advantage of the renewal of hostilities between Francis I and Charles V, Henry allied with the Emperor in 1543 in a new bid to win military glory and some French territory. Initially Henry won both; in the 1544 campaign his army besieged and took Boulogne. However, this proved to be a Pyrrhic victory, for the town was colossally expensive to maintain and its capture provoked Francis into attacking England's southern coast, burning Brighton and landing troops briefly on the Isle of Wight and at Seaford, Sussex. Henry should have tried to negotiate a favourable treaty by bartering Boulogne, but the town represented an important trophy that he had no intention of letting go. In 1546 both countries were worn down by the expense of the struggle, and their two kings signed an inconclusive peace treaty that seemed unlikely to last in the face of French determination to win back its territory.

The costs of the ongoing war against France, the maintenance and defence of Boulogne, together with the raids into Scotland were crippling: well over £2 million was spent between 1542 and 1547. Such a sum could not be financed out of high taxation or heavy loans, though both were imposed. So Henry had to sell off some 20 per cent of Crown lands, thereby weakening the monarch's future flow of income and losing important sources of royal patronage. Furthermore, between 1542 and 1544, Henry decided to raise money by debasing the coinage (mixing the silver in his coins with base metal). These actions decreased foreign confidence in the currency and helped fuel the steep rise in inflation that created hardship and economic difficulties for well over a decade. Consequently, Henry's legacy to Edward VI was deeply problematic. He left his young heir serious financial and economic problems as well as an unsettled, even dangerous, relationship with Scotland and France.

AN INVASION CRISIS

From 1538 until 1540 the threat of a foreign invasion created alarm in England. In December 1538 Pope Paul III reissued the bull of excommunication against Henry VIII, and sent Cardinal Reginald Pole on an embassy to rally the Catholic powers of France and the Empire in a crusade against Henry's realm. As Francis I and Charles V had recently signed a truce, Henry had good reason to fear that they would join together to execute the papal bull. England was therefore put on invasion alert in 1539: national musters took place; defence fortifications were built; and surveys were commissioned to identify vulnerable points on the coastline.

LIBER

Sed quid opus eſt tam multa me de Roffenſis uirtutibus dice-
re, apud te pręſertim, quam ſcio in uno illo Roffenſis nomine, o-
mnia ea quę ab optimo epiſcopo deſiderari poſſint, prolixa & co
pioſa agnoſcere; ex ſacerdotū autem numero omni habere nemi
nem, cuius fidei plura, aut maiora credere ac committere uelis?
Age uero, collegam ei adiungamus, ipſius quo ad fieri poſſit, ſi-
milem. At illum quo ex ordine? Laicorum cēſeo, ſed eum talem,
qui non facile delabi ad ſuperſtitionē poſſe uideatur. Hoc enim
pene ſolum uerendum eſt in iis qui perpetua ſanctitatis opinione fuerint, ne in illa ſanctitate ſuperſtitionis aliquid inſit, ne ue
ii pro Chriſti oraculo, ſuperſtitioſam aliquam ſententiam nobis
per errorem referant. Quare de tali quopiam cogitemus, qui cū
probitate ac doctrina Roffenſi reſpondeat, tum a ſuperſtitionis
ſuſpicione longiſſime abſit. Eiuſmodi porro hominem ſi reperi-
re uolumus, ad eos accedere neceſſe eſt, qui maxime prudentia,
& rerum humanarum uſu ualent. De iis enim minime dubitan-
dum eſt, ne qua ſuperſtitione capiantur. Quod ſi hæc quæ dixi,
omnia ſpectanda ſunt in eo, quem tanta de re legatum cum Rof
fenſi mittamus: ut ipſa tuos omnes excutias, quem Moro aptio-
rem ad hoc munus inuenies? At ne quęſituram quidem te alium,
edito tibi huius uiri nomine, certo ſcio. Ingeniū enim noſti, tantum, quantum in nullo aliquo tuorum noſti; & quidem ex longa
rerum tuarum adminiſtratione noſti. De hoc igit' qui potes du-
bitare, ne qua eum ſuperſtitioſa reſponſio eludat, cui ſcias a prima ſtatim adoleſcētia ſemper cum hominibus callidiſſimis rem
fuiſſe, & tamen certo teſtari poſſis, ſicut neminem ab ipſo, ſic nun
quam ipſum a quoquam deceptum eſſe, hactenus dumtaxat, ut
culpa in eo ingenii aliqua, aut prudentiæ minus fuiſſe uideret'?
Reliqua porro omnia ſic apta & appoſita ad hoc munus recte
fungendum habet, ut pene ſolus ſit ex laicis, qui hæc omnia con
iuncta habeat, probitatem, literas, prudentiam, ſtudium ſalutis
tuæ. Quibus certe omnibus ita excellit, ut nemo uel lōgo inter-
uallo ſit cum illo comparādus. Quid ergo moramur, cum hic ſe
nobis offerat? quin hoſce duumuiros cōtinuo ad Chriſtū extru
dimus, qui in hac dogmatum confuſione, quæ nos non ſine maxi
mo animarum periculo, circunſtat, certam nobis Dei ſententiam
referant? At illi (aperte nunc loquor) iam pridem, cum tu nihil
minus cogitares, hoc ipſum munus ſponte ſuſceperunt; legatio-
ne functi ſunt, renunciarunt, certiſſimam Chriſti ſententiam at-
tulerunt. Sed tu nimirum adhuc dubitabas, quia nō ſatis crede-
res ex

Roffenſi collega lai-cus non alius potius quàm Morus adiungendus.

Roffenſis & Morus libris ſuis Angliam de Chriſti voluntate certiorem fecerunt.

207 Cardinal Reginald Pole

Pro ecclesiasticae unitatis defensione, 1536

British Library, G.11945, sig R ii v

Reginald Pole (1500–58), grandnephew of Edward IV, was educated in Italy at the expense of his cousin Henry VIII. Briefly employed to secure the support of the University of Paris for the annulment, Pole broke with Henry after the executions of More and Fisher. In September 1535, he began a defence of the unity of the Church under the papacy in a scathing open letter to the King, accusing him of being led by lust and avarice. Pole's royal blood and high reputation made his book dangerous: his arguments coloured all subsequent Catholic accounts of Henry's reign. The book earned Pole a cardinal's hat, and appointment as Legate in 1538 to persuade Charles V to recover England for the Church by force. In preparation for this mission, the Pope printed Pole's treatise, apparently without his consent. Its publication helped ensure Henry's execution of Pole's brother, Henry Pole, Lord Montagu, and their mother, Margaret, Countess of Salisbury. (ED)

LITERATURE: Dwyer (trans.), *Pole's Defence of the Unity of the Church*; Egretier (trans.), *Reginald Pole, Défense de l'Unité de l'Eglise*; Mayer, *Reginald Pole*; Mayer, *A Reluctant Author*

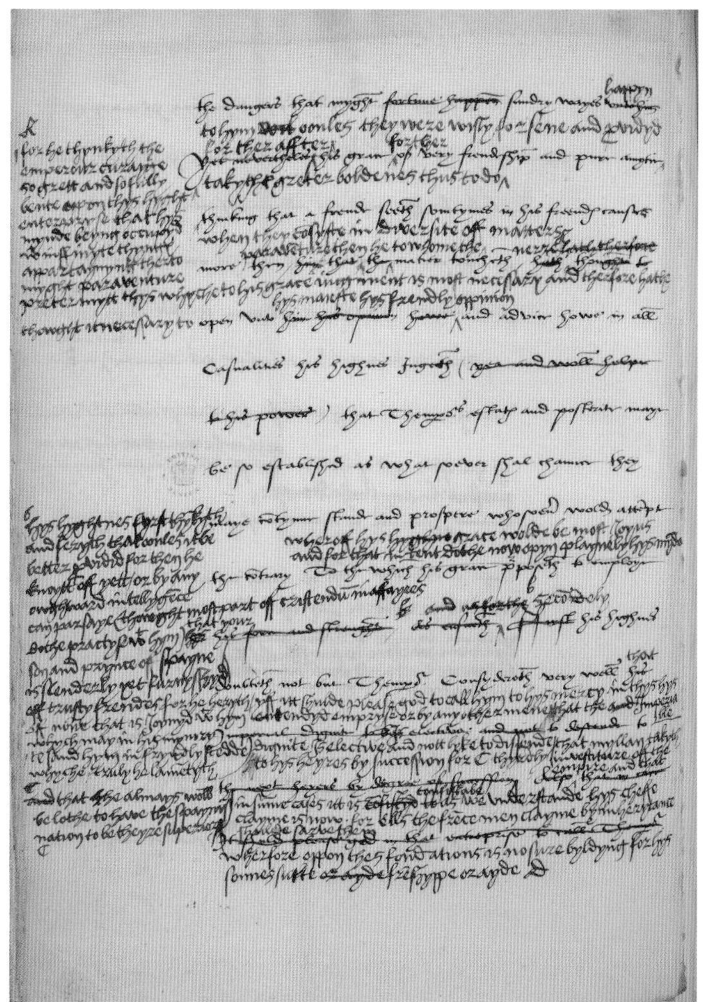

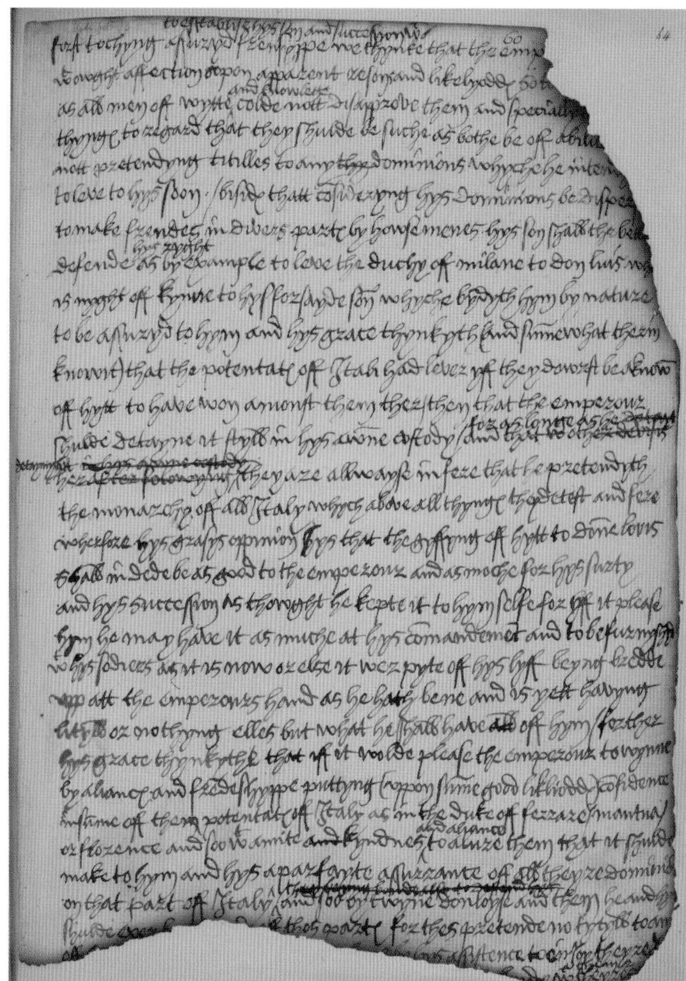

208 Matrimonial Diplomacy

Original draft of instructions from Henry VIII to Sir Thomas Wyatt for his negotiations in Madrid with Emperor Charles V, 16 October 1538

British Library, Cotton MS Vespasian C vii, fol.78v, Cotton MS Vitellius B xxi, fol.64

This is one of numerous letters written by Henry VIII between 1537 and 1539 to Sir Thomas Wyatt, ambassador to Emperor Charles V. With its copious alterations, deletions and additions, it is an excellent example of the interest Henry took in foreign policy and the composition of his diplomatic correspondence. The Franco-imperial rapprochement had prompted Henry's return to the diplomatic arena, his aim being to create rivalry and discord between Charles V and Francis I. As soon as the truce was announced, Henry initiated multiple marriage negotiations with Spain and France for himself and his three children, and in January 1538 a marriage was proposed between Henry and the Duchess of Milan, the Emperor's niece and young widow of the Duke of Milan. In addition, the hand of Mary was offered to the Habsburg Don Louis Infant of Portugal. Here, Henry attempts to exploit the potential rights of the Duchess, artfully suggesting that the Emperor should confer Milan – of great importance to both Charles and Francis – on the Habsburg candidate for Mary. (AC)

LITERATURE: St Clare Byrne (ed.), *The Letters of King Henry VIII*; Scarisbrick, *Henry VIII*

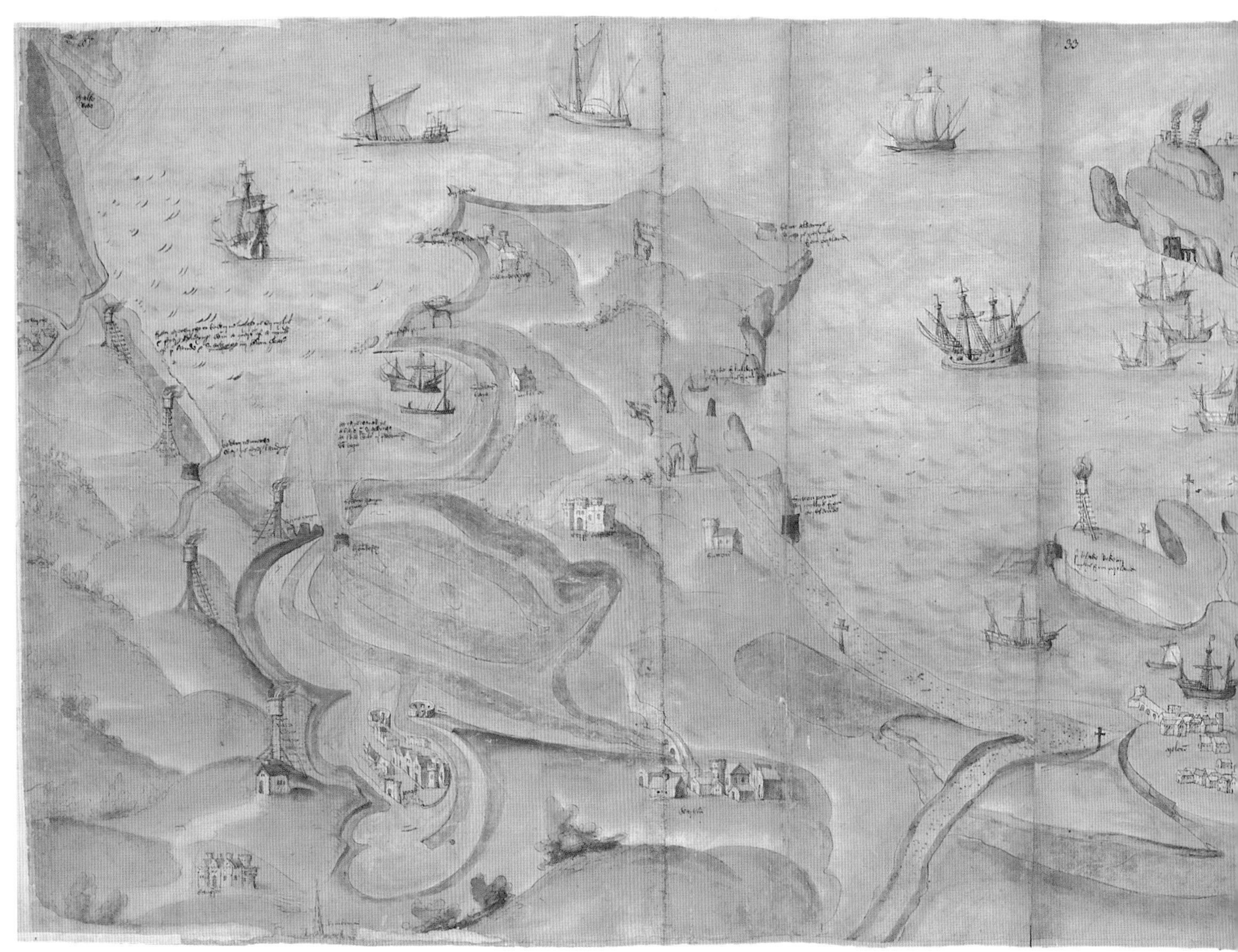

209 'peverels poynte wher ys fayr landyng'

Map of the Dorset coast from Poole to Portland and Lyme Regis, 1539–40

Anon. [Flemish artist in Greenwich?]

British Library, Cotton MS Augustus I.i. 31, 33

In February 1539 Thomas Cromwell ordered certain 'sadde and expert men of every shire in Ingland beyng nere the see … to viewe all the places alongest the secost wher any daunger of invasions ys like to be and to certifie the sayd daungers and also best advises for the fortificacion thereof'. The information was sent to court in the form of sketch plans as well as text. In Greenwich it was compiled into attractive maps that would have appealed to Henry. In order to emphasize the areas at risk of enemy landings, the mapmaker exaggerates the size of the beaches and reduces the size of the cliffs. Defensive measures include real and proposed forts with church towers and beacons for conveying the news of an invasion to court. The map was probably explained to Henry personally and annotated to reflect decisions, such as the positions for additional blockhouses. (PB)

LITERATURE: Robinson, *Marine Cartography in Britain*; Colvin, Ransome and Summerson, *The History of the King's Works*; Beaton, *Dorset Maps*

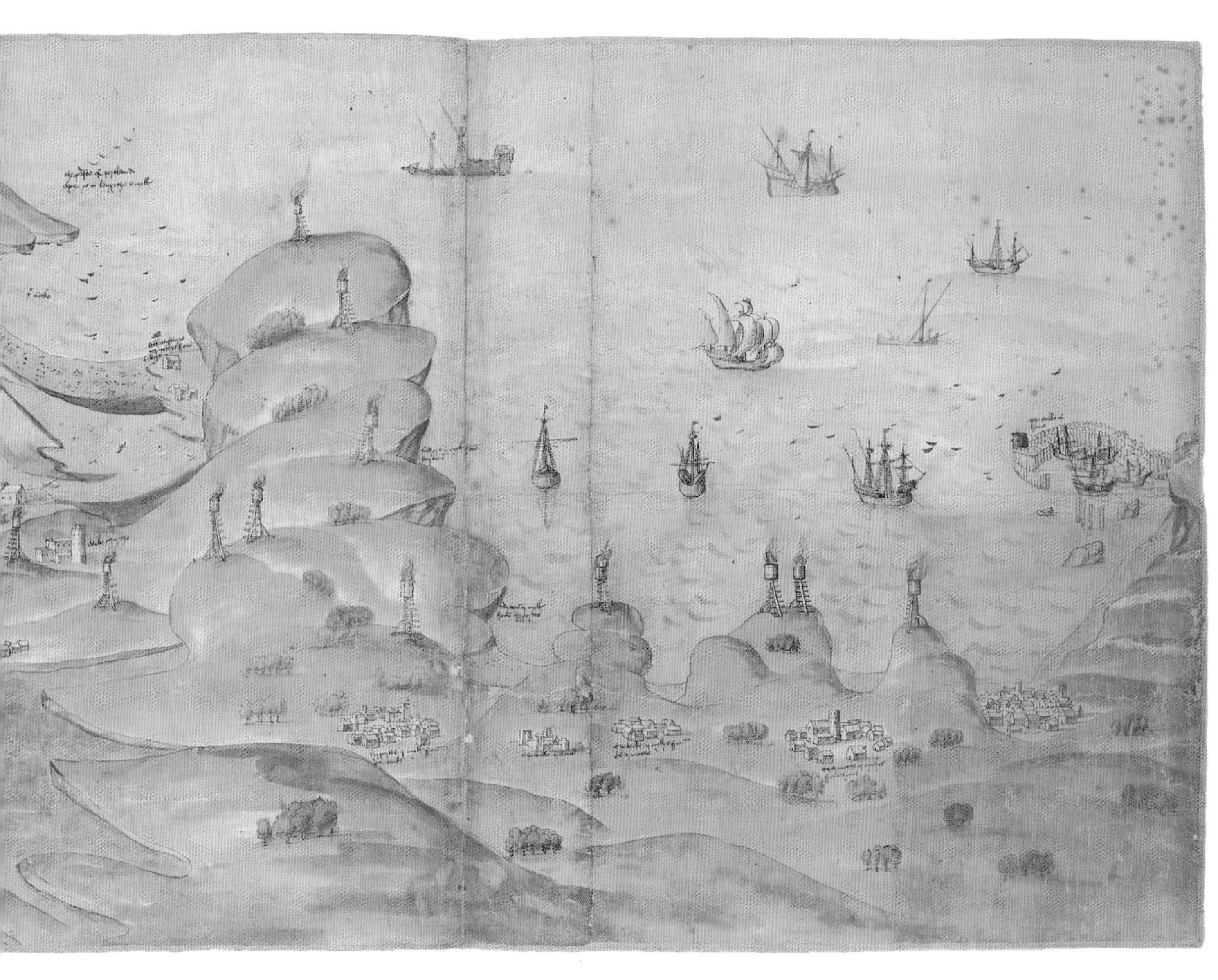

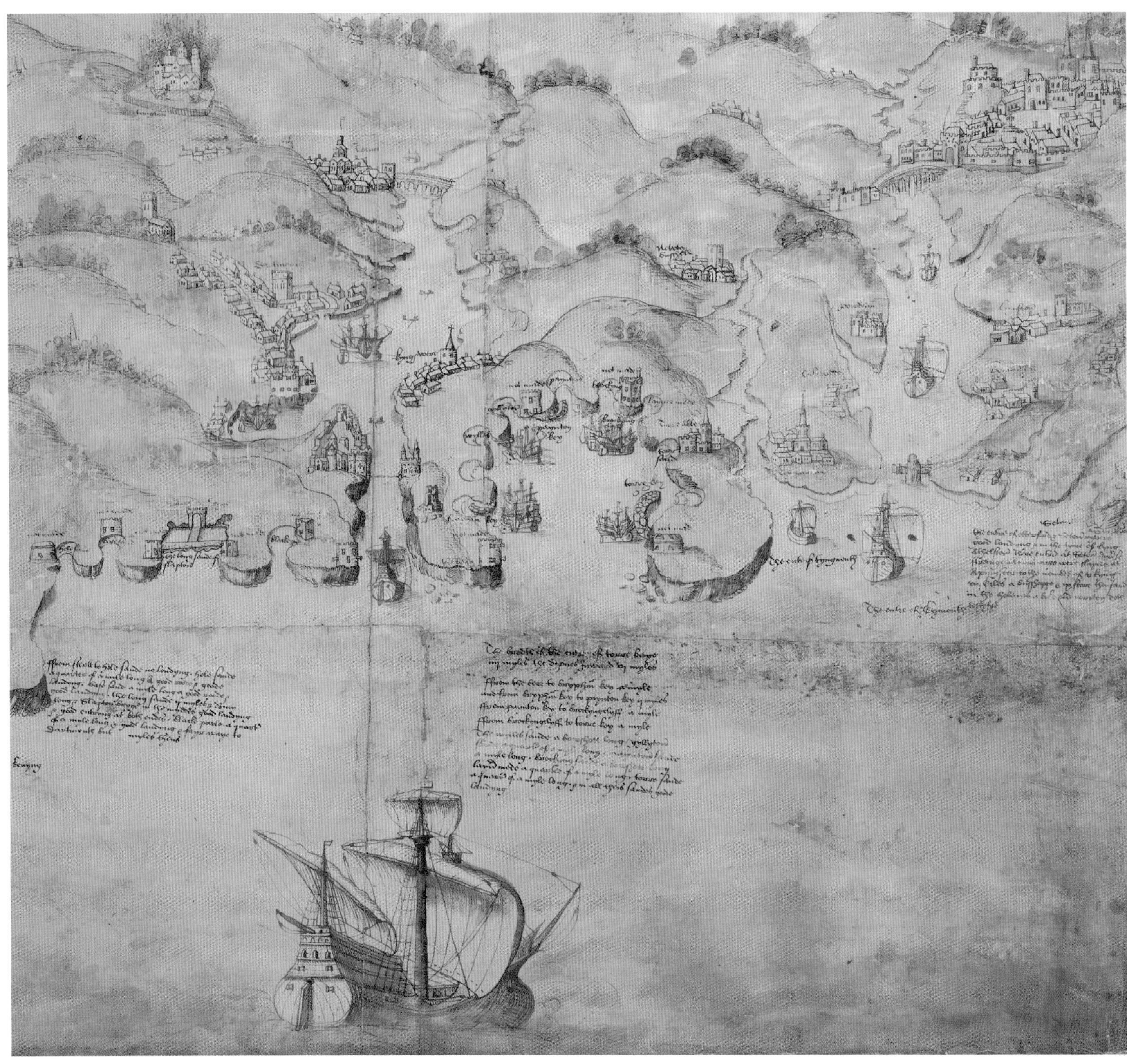

210 'Whitesond bay where parkyn Londed' (see opposite)

Map of coast from Exeter to Land's End, 1539–40

Anon. [Flemish artist in Greenwich?]

British Library, Cotton MS Augustus I, i , 35, 36, 38, 39

This giant bird's-eye view is an outstanding example of the mapping sparked by the fear of invasion from 1538 to 1540. Financed by money from the dissolved monasteries, the coastal survey was the largest single British governmental mapping initiative before the 19th century. The whole of the south-west is shown on the basis of plans sent from the provinces, with towns like Plymouth being portrayed realistically for the first time. There are notes on earlier successful landings by Perkin Warbeck (a pretender to the throne during the reign of Henry VII) and the French; bays are emphasized and cliffs contracted. Beacons feature prominently. The fences enclose parks where musters could be accommodated and fed and horses watered. Forts are shown and recommendations for new fortified sites are added. Annotations inserted a little later indicated whether they had been 'made', 'not made' or left 'halfmade' – as at St Mawes. The map's faded condition suggests the map was displayed and consulted over an extended period. (PB)

LITERATURE: Colvin, Ransome and Summerson, *The History of the King's Works*; Stuart, *Lost Landscapes of Plymouth*; Harvey, *Maps in Tudor England*

211 The Defence of London

Map of the mouths of the Thames and the Medway from Ipswich to Sandwich and Maldon and Rochester to the sea, *c.*1540

British Library, Cotton MS Augustus I.i.53

Inscribed: 'Rychard Candishe made this carde'

It tends to be forgotten that London itself was at risk of attack during the crisis of 1538–40. Knowledge of the sandbanks at the mouth of the Thames was essential for defence and this map, which has no orientation, sets them out in outsized detail. Thomas Elyot considered mapmaking a suitable accomplishment for the governing elite. This example was created by a Suffolk squire, Sir Richard Gernon or Cavendish (d.1554) of Trimley St Martin. The map also contains vignette bird's-eye views of the larger towns, such as Canterbury, Rochester, Colchester and Ipswich. Almost all are the earliest such depictions and were presumably copied from larger plans made in response to royal commands in 1539. Cavendish was experimenting when creating this 'carde', inserting a pencilled circular fretwork of so-called rhumb lines, familiar from contemporary Mediterranean sea charts. Necessity – and royal pressure – bred innovation. (PB)

LITERATURE: Robinson, *Marine Cartography in Britain*; Barber, 'A Revolution in Mapmaking'

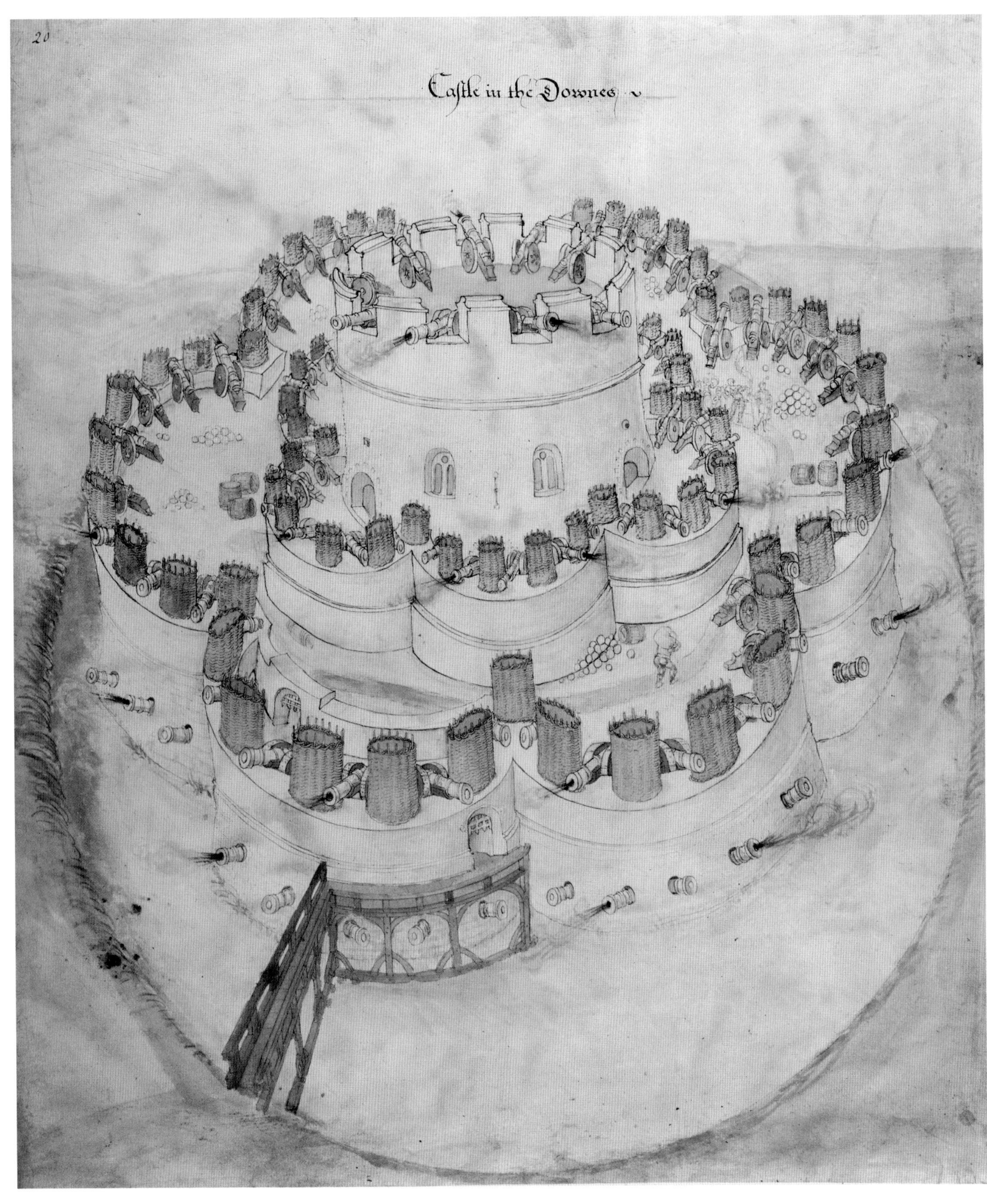
20
Castle in the Downes

212 'Castle in the Downs', 1539

Drawing office of Richard Benese, Christopher Dickenson and William Clement

British Library, Cotton MS Augustus I.i.20

Inscribed: 'Castle in the Downes'

This fortification plan or 'plat' is a survivor of the many that by the 1540s were stuffed into drawers in Henry's office in Holbein Gate in Whitehall Palace. In February 1539 Henry ordered three new castles to be built in the Downs of Kent, at Deal, Sandown and Walmer. This, an early drawing for Deal, originally the largest of the three, must date from a few weeks later. Its relatively high artistic quality suggests that it was presented to the King for his approval. Although possibly adequate for its intended purpose, it is uninfluenced by the latest Italian ideas. The designers of the plan – respectively the surveyor, master mason and master carpenter of the King's Works – had previously only designed palaces. Sandown has been demolished and only Deal Castle is relatively unchanged. Walmer has been expanded and transformed into the official residence of the Lord Warden of the Cinque Ports. (PB)

LITERATURE: Colvin, Ransome and Summerson, *The History of the King's Works*; Starkey (ed.), *The Inventory of King Henry VIII*

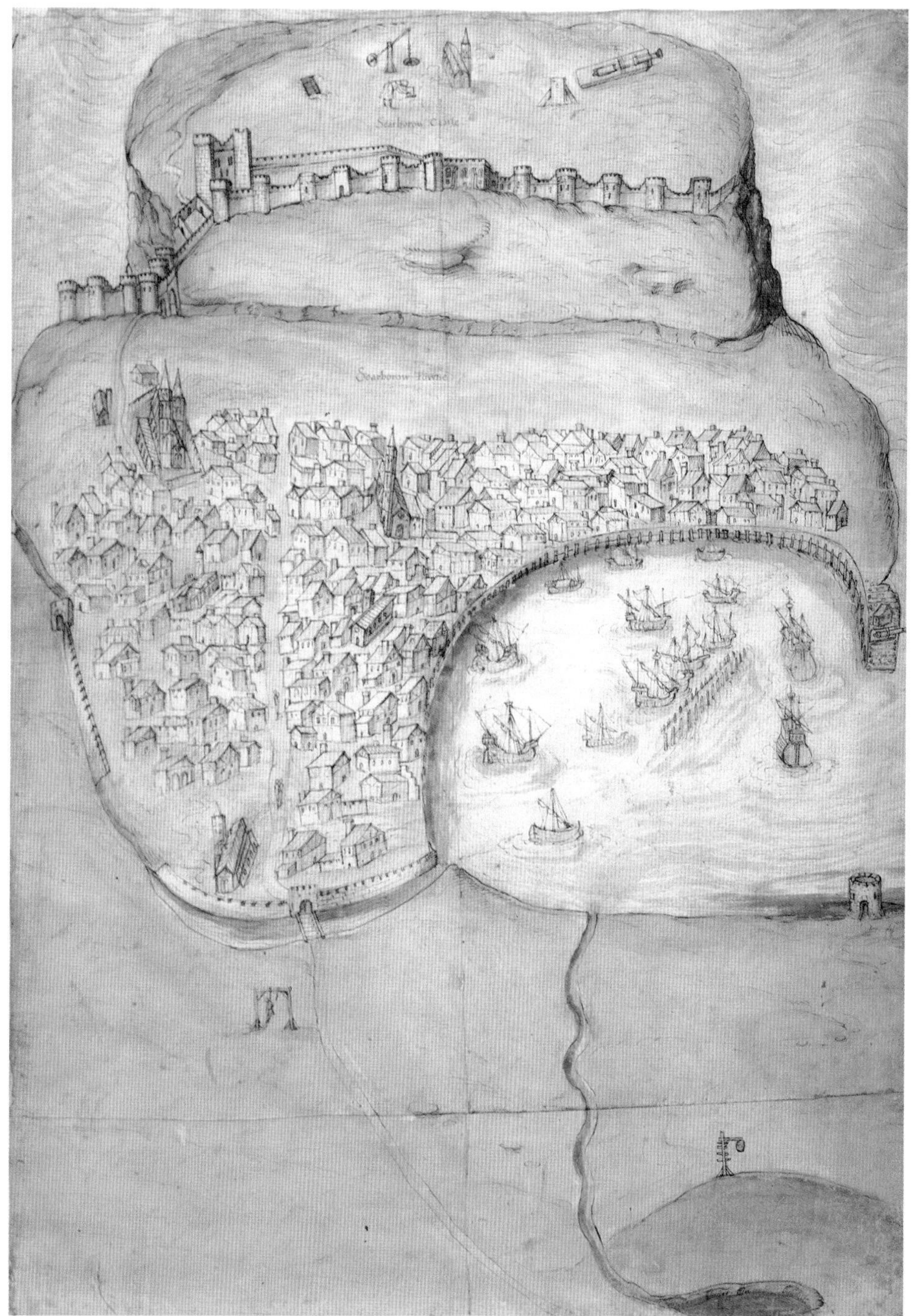

213 An Early Town View

Bird's-eye view of Scarborough with its castle and harbour, *c.*March 1539 (?)

British Library, Cotton MS Augustus I.ii.1

This view of Scarborough, with its castle and harbour, was probably another response to Cromwell's order of February 1539 to the Crown's local representatives for a detailed survey of England's coasts. It is in the same hand as a similar view of Hull and may have been executed locally. The texts are later additions and the plan was probably explained to Henry VIII in person: at that time there was talk of him ordering the refortification of Scarborough Castle. It is one of the earliest relatively accurate English town plans based on observation, though one cannot rely on the details. Henry possessed a number of large and sophisticated printed plan-views of Italian and German towns and grasped their potential. Cromwell and he, while not expecting such expertise, did compel English and Welsh local surveyors to experiment with the hitherto unfamiliar. (PB)

LITERATURE: *Catalogue of Manuscript Maps . . . in the British Museum*; Colvin, Ransome and Summerson, *The History of the King's Works*; Harvey, *Maps in Tudor England*

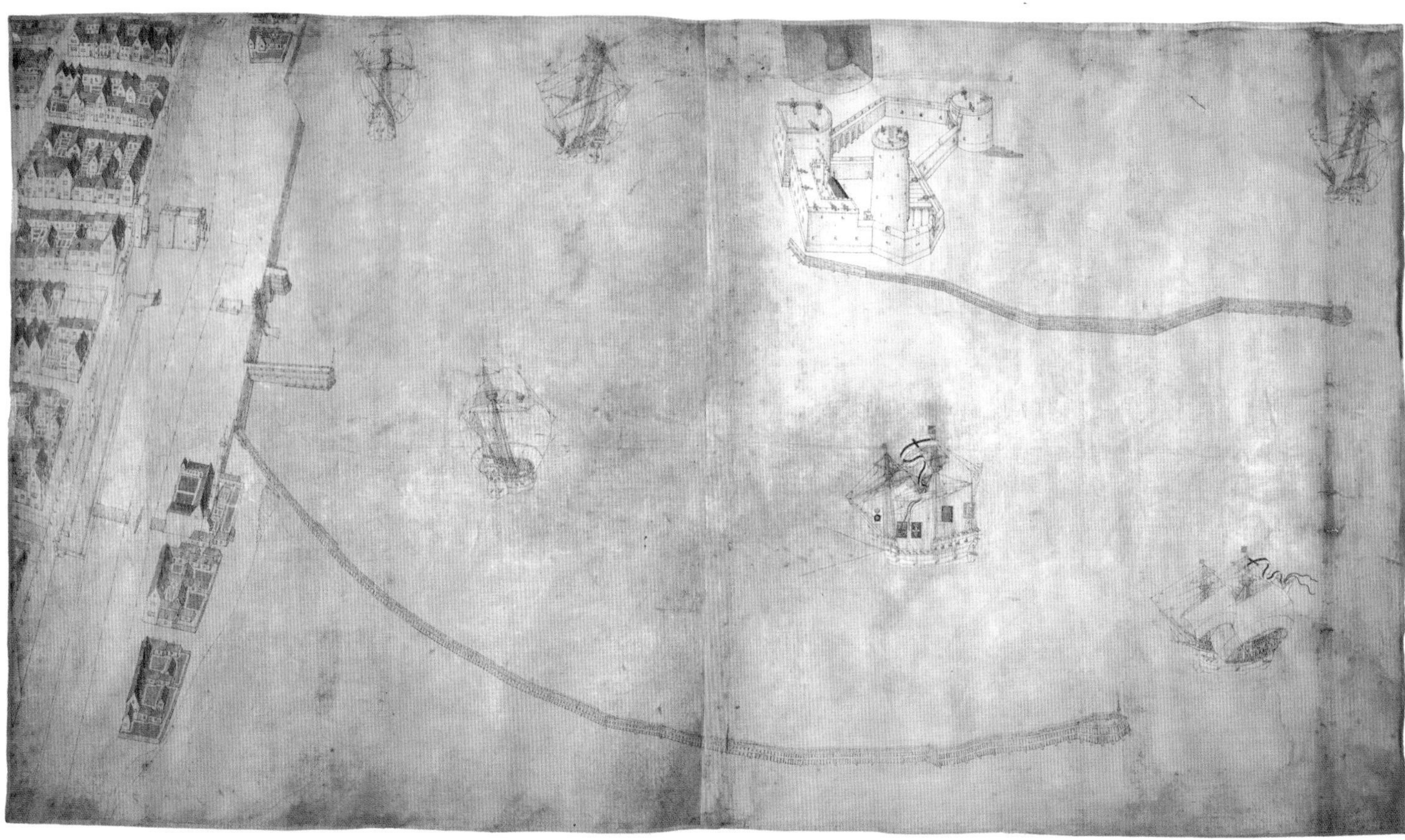

214 New Fortifications for Calais

Richard Lee (1501/2–75)

Calais Harbour with Rysbank Fort, *c.*1543?

British Library, Cotton MS Augustus I.ii.57 A

At the time of the invasion scare of winter 1538/9, commissioners were appointed to inspect the fortifications of Calais. Their report particularly recommended the strengthening of the fortifications of Rysbank Fort, which protected the harbour entrance, through the erection of a D-shaped fort facing seawards and a low circular gun tower facing towards the town. Henry VIII played an active part in the detailed planning. The new fortifications, with the adjoining new quarters for the captain and garrison, are shown on this accomplished view which was perhaps intended for presentation to Henry to mark their completion at the end of 1542: note the attention bestowed on the multi-bannered royal ship.

On stylistic grounds the view is attributable to Richard Lee, the Surveyor of Calais. The angle and the skilful – though not entirely successful – effort to capture the bird's-eye effect are typical of the technical innovations in mapmaking generated under pressure from Henry. (PB)

LITERATURE: Colvin, Ransome and Summerson, *The History of the King's Works*

ANNE OF CLEVES AND THE FALL OF CROMWELL

Responding to the threat of invasion, Henry VIII and Cromwell opened up negotiations for a defensive alliance with the Protestant Schmalkaldic League. During discussions, Cromwell proposed a marriage between Henry and the daughter of one of the German Lutheran princes. As no suitable bride was available, Henry agreed to marry the daughter of Duke John III of Cleves, who, though no Lutheran himself, had repudiated papal authority and was the father-in-law of the Lutheran Duke of Saxony.

Initially enthusiastic about the match, Henry was deeply disappointed on meeting Anne in early January 1540. The marriage went ahead but was a disaster: Henry could not consummate it; he fell in love with Katherine Howard; and by March he realized that an alliance with Cleves was unnecessary, as the Franco-Imperial invasion threat had faded away. Consequently, in June 1540, Henry initiated proceedings for an annulment, while Cromwell, who bore the brunt of Henry's anger at the fiasco, was imprisoned in the Tower on charges of high treason. Cromwell's enemies now poisoned the King's mind against him. He was accused not only of favouring the German Lutherans and the new religious ideas (with justification) but also of unspecified acts of treason that were almost certainly false.

215 Negotiations with the Lutheran Princes

Martin Luther, *Donatio Constantini*

British Library, Royal MS 17 C. xi, fol.14v

Thomas Cranmer, Archbishop of Canterbury, sent this book to Henry VIII in February 1538, when a new set of negotiations were starting with the Lutheran princes in Germany. Cranmer's primary purpose was to remind Henry that Martin Luther shared his dislike of papal pretensions and thereby to allay Henry's habitual suspicions of the German reformer. The book was an anonymous English translation of Luther's attack in German on the discredited Donation of Constantine, an 8th-century forgery that set out to establish the Pope's widespread temporal authority. Through his own annotations Cranmer drew Henry's attention to a passage where Luther mocked the Pope's pretensions to be Lord of England and another where Luther described the unfortunate results of Pope Boniface VIII's attempt to depose the King of England. This is one of the many examples where books were presented to the King with pertinent passages marked for his readings. (JC)

LITERATURE: Carley, *The Libraries of King Henry VIII*; MacCulloch, *Thomas Cranmer*

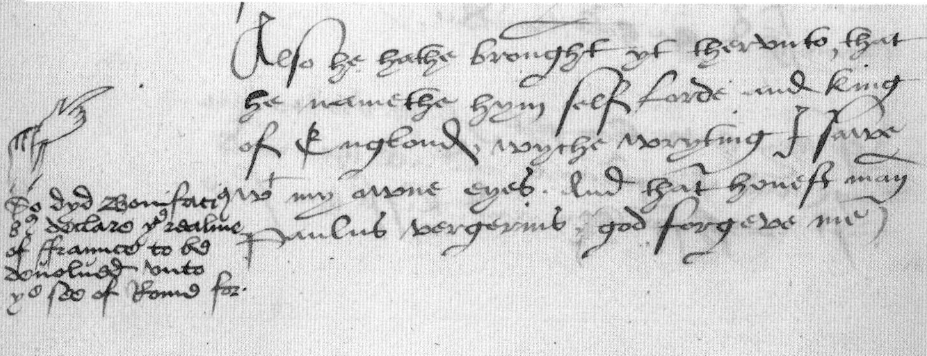

216 The Wrong Impression: A Portrait of Anne of Cleves

Hans Holbein the Younger

Miniature

Victoria and Albert Museum, London, P.153:1, 2-1910

In January 1539 Christopher Mont (1496/7–1572), a German in the King's service, was sent to the Duke of Saxony to propose a marriage between Henry VIII and one of the two unmarried daughters of Duke John of Cleves. However, Henry insisted on seeing a likeness of the two women before choosing between them. Portraits of each were sent to England but thought unsatisfactory as only a part of their faces could be seen 'and that under such a monstruous habyte and apparell'. To create a better likeness, the King's painter, Holbein, was sent out to Cleves at the end of July 1539. By 11 August, the two portraits were completed. The life-size portrait of Anne is now in the Louvre, and it is probable that this miniature was painted at the same time for Henry to view in private. Here Anne's whole face is exposed and the size of her headdress reduced. On the basis of the portrait Henry decided to marry the twenty-four-year-old Anne. (SD)

LITERATURE: Strong, *Artists of the Tudor Court*; Foister, *Holbein in England*; McEntegart, *Henry VIII, the League of Schmalkalden and the English Reformation*

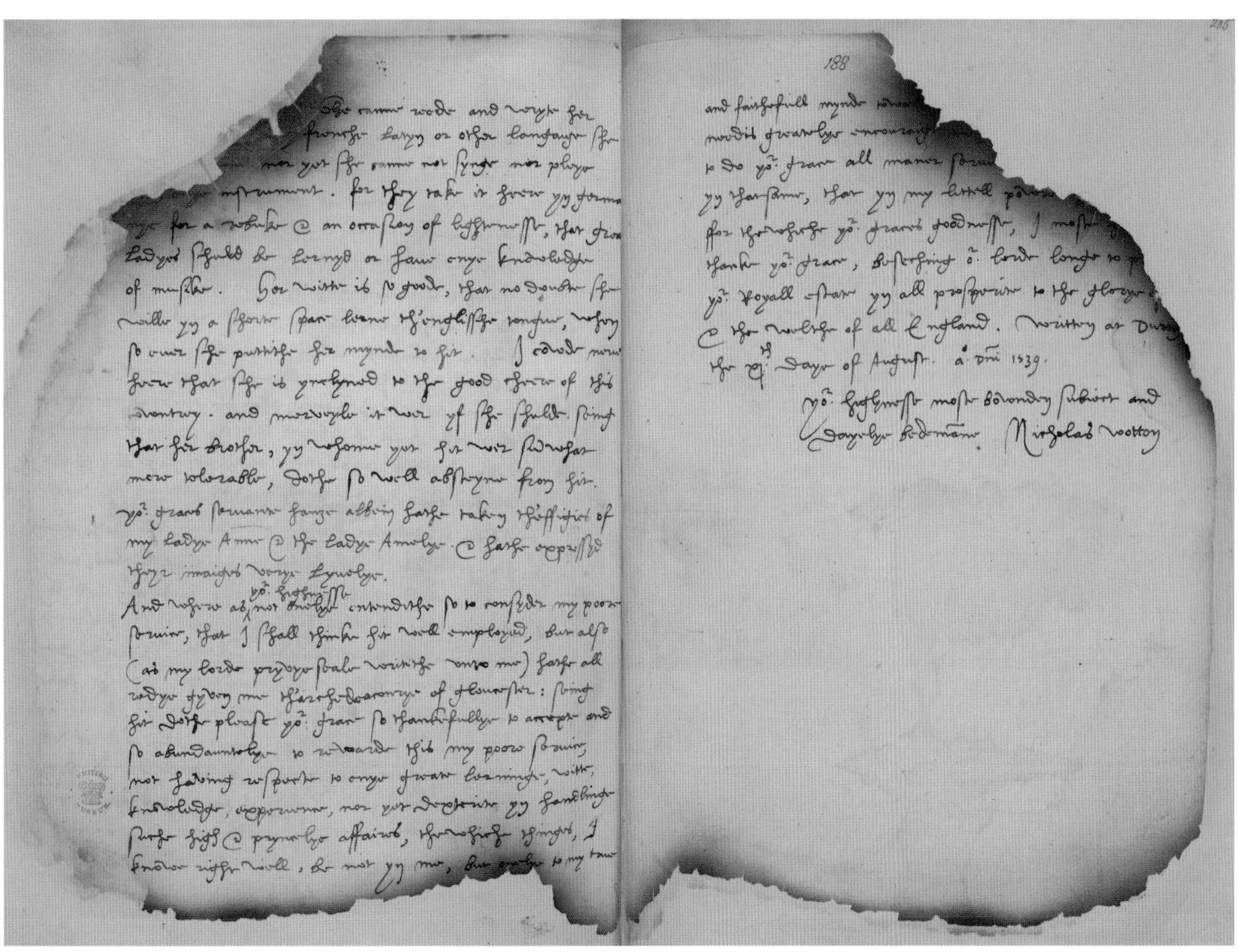

217 The Character and Accomplishments of Anne of Cleves

Letter from Nicholas Wotton to Henry VIII, Düren, 11 August 1539

British Library, Cotton MS Vitellius B xxi, fols 204v–205

Henry VIII received a realistic assessment of Anne from his ambassador Nicholas Wotton (*c.*1497–1567), who was despatched to Cleves to pursue negotiations with the Duke and his council. In this letter, Wotton writes from the Cleves court to the King of his impressions of the Duke's daughters Anne and Amelia, both of whom at this stage were candidates for Henry's hand. Of Anne, Wotton reports that she was of a quiet disposition, occupying 'her time most with the needle'. Although she could 'reede and wryte' her own language, of 'Frenche, Latyn or other langaige she [hath no]ne, nor yet she canne not synge nor playe [upon] enye instrument, for they take it here in Germane for a rebuke and an occasion of lightnesse that great ladyes shuld be lernyd or have anye knowledge of musike'. More promisingly, Wotton observes that Anne was an intelligent woman and would learn English soon when she put her mind to it, and was 'not inclined to the good cheer [excessive drinking] of this country'. A critical matter in the forthcoming marriage was Henry's reaction to Anne's appearance. Wotton closes the letter by mentioning what would be the King's chief evidence for choosing Anne as a physically acceptable wife before he actually met her: 'Your Grace's servant Hanze Albein [Hans Holbein] hathe taken th'effigies of my ladye Anne and the ladye Amelye and hathe expressyd theyr imaiges verye lyvelye [naturalistically]'. (RM)

LITERATURE: McEntegart, *Henry VIII, the League of Schmalkalden and the English Reformation*

218 A Map that 'marvellously inflamed' Henry VIII

Chart showing Anne of Cleves's projected passage to Greenwich, England, October 1539

Anthony Anthony (d.1563) [and another?]

British Library, Cotton MS Augustus I.ii.64

Henry VIII decided to use maps when considering the route that Anne of Cleves should take to England. It was a radically new way of working. This chart illustrates a proposed passage by sea from Harderwijk in Guelderland. It devotes most space to the areas of greatest navigational difficulty with an oversize Zuiderzee at the top and the mouth of the Thames with London at the bottom. A squadron of English ships protects Anne's ship, at the centre, from interference by the French. The map was drafted utilizing sailing instructions and a sketch plan of the Zuiderzee confidentially surveyed in September 1539 by John à Borough and Richard Crouche. These, the earliest English examples of either genre, still survive. Henry was reported as being 'marvellously inflamed' by this map or its prototype, 'supposing many things to be done theron'. Anne's actual route, via Calais, is illustrated on another British Library manuscript map. (PB)

LITERATURE: Ruddock, 'The Earliest Original English Seaman's Rutter and Pilot's Chart'; Buisseret, *Monarchs, Maps and Ministers*; Meurer, 'Op het spoor van de kaart der nederlanden van Jan van Hoirne'

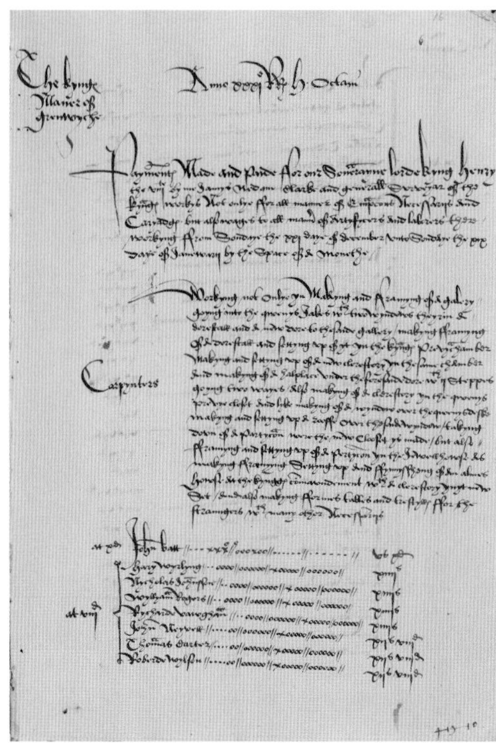

219 Preparing Greenwich Palace for Anne of Cleves

The King's Works: manuscript of James Nedeham, Clerk and Surveyor of the King's Works, 1539–40

Bodleian Library, Oxford, MS Don. c. 206, fol.16

With the conclusion of Henry VIII and Anne's marriage treaty on 4 October 1539, Henry issued a stream of instructions and orders to ensure that everything was ready for Anne's arrival. Two of his finest beds were sent to Rochester and Dartford, where Anne would stay en route to London; plans were drawn up for the formation of the new Queen's household and apartments at Hampton Court; and other palaces were redecorated and repaired. The accounts for works at Greenwich Palace reveal the flurry of building activity that took place there. Alterations were made to the King and Queen's respective privy kitchens, extensive alterations were also made to the Queen's private apartments, including her jakes (latrine) and Privy Closet (private chapel), where Anne and Henry were married. 'Workyng not onlye yn Makyng and ffamyng of a galery goyng into the qwenys Jakes with two wyndows theyrin a dorestall … Also makyng of a clerestory yn the qwenys prevye closet and lyke makyng of a window over the qwenys deske makyng and settyng up a rooffe over the saide wyndow takyng down of a Partycion were the new Clooset ys made'. (AC)

LITERATURE: Colvin, *The History of the King's Works*; Thurley, *The Royal Palaces of Tudor England*

Henricus Octauus Dei gratia Anglie et Francie Rex

220 Anne's Dowry

British Library, Egerton MS 2809

Anne received a very substantial dowry for her marriage to Henry VIII. Several deeds covered the range of grants to be made to the Queen upon her marriage to the King; the deed exhibited here was but one of three that were completed on 5 January 1540, the day before the wedding. Written in Latin by a clerk, the document was signed by the King at Greenwich Palace, and sealed with the seal of the Duchy of Lancaster, appended by green and white plaited silk ribbons. The deed stated that Henry VIII, in view of his marriage to Lady Anne, granted to her, in part satisfaction of dower and jointure, the manors of Waltham Magna, Maysbury, Dunmowe, Lighes Magna, Baddowe Magna and Farneham, Co. Essex, as formerly held by Jane Seymour, late Queen, and worth annually 312 marks 8*s*., 1.25*d*. It was noted that Anne would hold these grants for life, though, if the marriage ended, she would have to continue to live in the realm in order to keep them. In the event, when the marriage failed, Anne remained in England and did retain a goodly share of her marriage endowments until her death in 1557. (RM)

LITERATURE: Anne of Cleves, *Oxford DNB*; Starkey, *Six Wives*

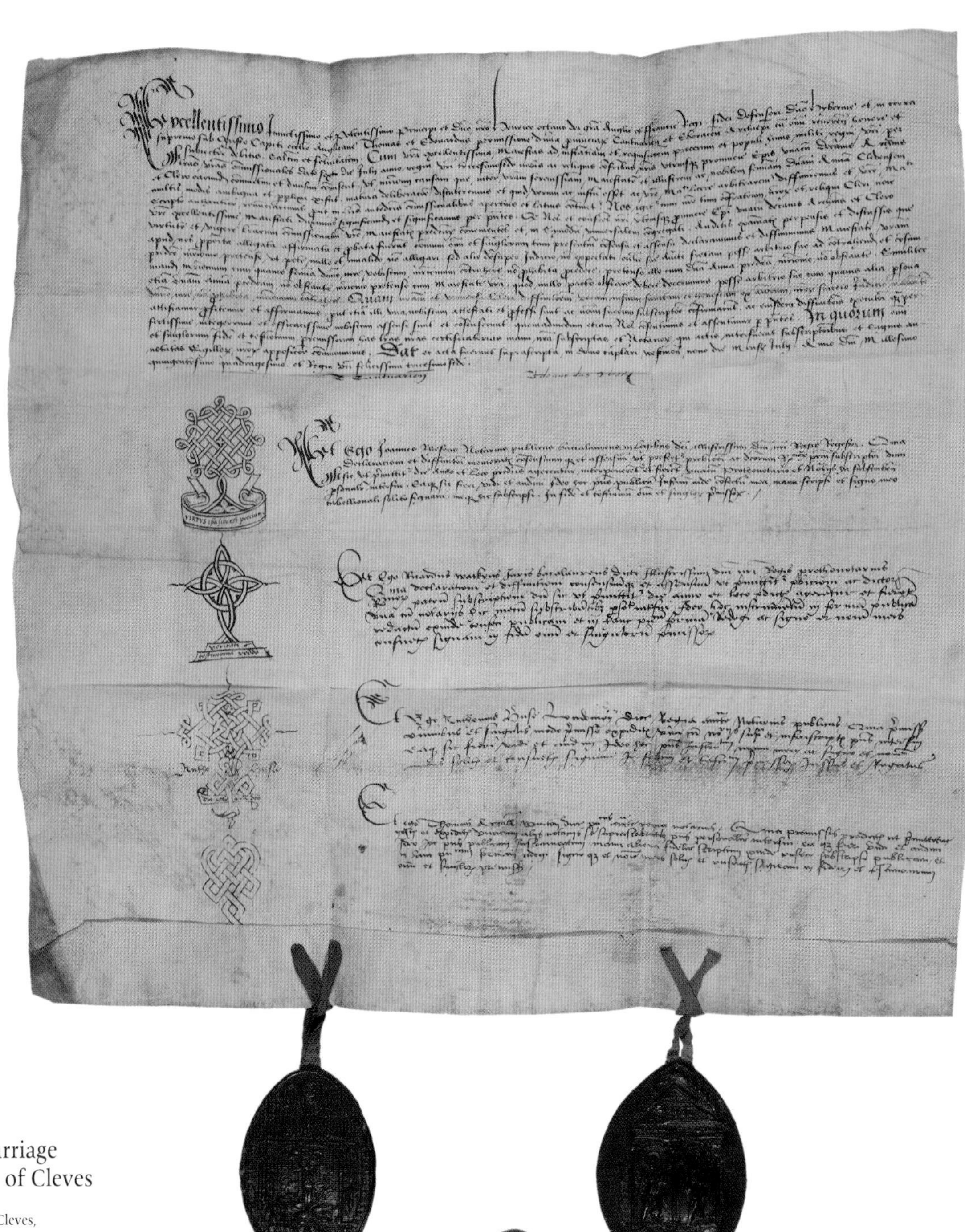

221 The Annulment of the Marriage between Henry VIII and Anne of Cleves

Nullification of Henry VIII's marriage to Anne of Cleves, 9 July 1540

British Library, Cotton Ch. X.13

Anne was devastated when she learned in early July 1540 that Henry VIII was going to leave her. To her ambassador she protested that the King was her 'true lord and husband' and 'cried such tears and bitter moans, it would break a heart of stone'. It was to no avail. On 7 July 1540 the Bishops of the two provinces of Canterbury and York met in convocation, the representative body of the Church of England, and formally examined the depositions of Henry and those involved in the Cleves match. Two days later the double convocation agreed unanimously that Henry and Anne had not been wed and were free to remarry. The document displayed here is the formal record of this decision of nullification, written in Latin, signed by the Archbishops of Canterbury and York and bearing the seals of both provinces. The document nullifying the marriage is dated 9 July; less than three weeks later, on 28 July, the architect of the marriage, Thomas Cromwell, was executed and Henry married his fifth wife, Katherine Howard. (RM)

LITERATURE: Anne of Cleves, *Oxford DNB*; Starkey, *Six Wives*

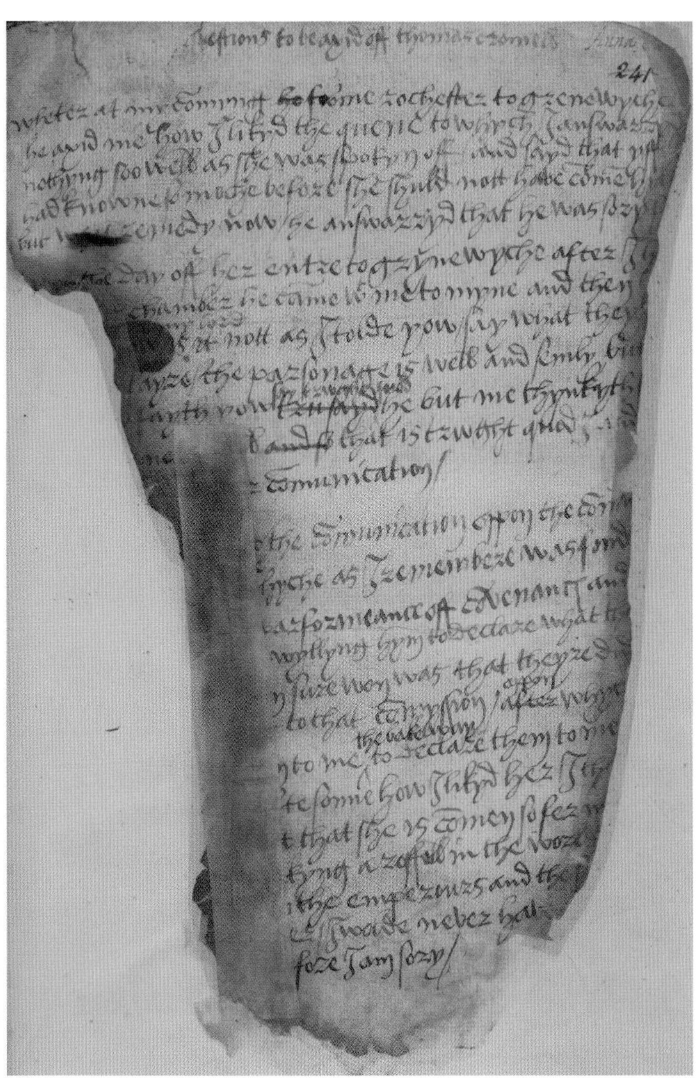

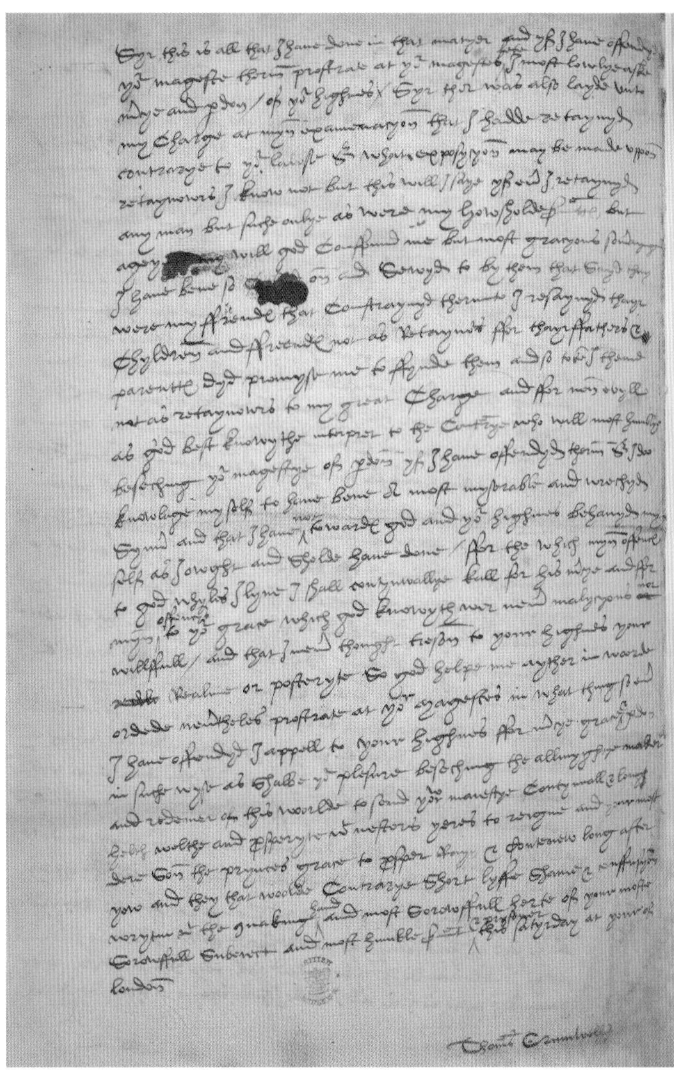

222 Henry VIII's Humiliation

Henry VIII's deposition to Convocation on his marriage with Anne of Cleves and questions to be put to Thomas Cromwell, 1540. In Henry's hand

British Library, Cotton MS Otho C x, fol.246

Once Henry had determined to nullify his marriage to Anne, he drafted in evidence a deposition and a series of questions to be put to Cromwell, who had been imprisoned in the Tower on charges of high treason since 10 June. In his deposition, Henry testified that, from the first encounter with Anne at Rochester, he had found her physically abhorrent and told Cromwell that 'yff [I] had knowne so moche before, she shold nott have come here'. Henry required Cromwell to substantiate his view of events. Henry also wanted Cromwell to acknowledge that it was only because Henry wanted to avoid offending the Duke of Cleves and so drive him into the arms of the Emperor and the French King that Henry consented to put his neck in the yoke and proceed with the marriage. Cromwell would also recall that when he asked Henry the day after the wedding if he liked Anne better, the King replied, not at all for by her breasts and belly he thought her no maid, and when he touched her he had no will to prove otherwise. (RM and SD)

LITERATURE: Starkey, *Six Wives*; Hutchinson, *Thomas Cromwell*

223 Cromwell's Letter from the Tower

Letter from Thomas Cromwell to Henry VIII, 12 June 1540

British Library, Cotton MS Titus B i, fol.274v

Cromwell wrote this letter to Henry VIII two days after his arrest for high treason to protest his innocence of any such charges. Writing with 'the quaking hand and most sorowffull herte of your moste sorowffull subeiect and most humble seruant & prysoner this satyrday at your [Tower] of london', Cromwell implored: 'ffor myne offencys to your grace which god knowyth wer neuer malycyous nor willfful and that I neuer thought treson to your highnes your Realme or posteryte so god helpe me ayther in woorde or dede, neuertheles prostrate at your magestes [feet] in what thing soever I have offendyd I appell to your highnes ffor mercye grace & pardon.' Cromwell's pleas were ignored and, sensing that his chances of survival were slim, he wrote a final letter, now largely damaged by fire, in which he begged the King to be good to his wife, his son and his son's family and made one last plea: 'Most gracyous prynce, I Crye for mercye mercye mercye'. In spite of his appeals to the King, Cromwell was beheaded at the Tower on 28 July 1540. (AC and RM)

LITERATURE: Cromwell, Thomas, *Oxford DNB*; Hutchinson, *Thomas Cromwell*

KATHERINE HOWARD

Katherine Howard (1520/24–1542) was the niece of Thomas, 3rd Duke of Norfolk and a cousin of Anne Boleyn. In 1539 she was appointed a Maid of Honour in Anne of Cleves's household, and by the spring of 1540 she had become the King's mistress. Although only twenty or even younger when she married Henry on 28 July 1540, she was already a woman with considerable sexual experience and (unlike her predecessor) was well able to offer pleasure to the fifty-year-old King.

During their brief marriage he was deeply in love with Katherine, and her betrayal was a severe blow to his feelings and his *amour-propre*. Henry was first told of Katherine's pre-marital sexual relationships in a letter handed over by Archbishop Cranmer at the All Souls' Day Mass in 1541. Disbelieving Cranmer's account, Henry ordered a secret investigation into his wife's reputation and was distraught to discover that the allegations were true. Further investigations revealed that Katherine had also entered a relationship – though it had never been consummated – after her marriage. For this supposed act of treason she went to the block on 13 February 1542.

224 Katherine Howard

Hans Holbein the Younger

Miniature

Collection of His Grace the Duke of Buccleuch

Although the sitter of the portrait is unnamed, she can be identified as the King's fifth wife, Queen Katherine Howard, because of the jewellery she is wearing. Three of the most sumptuous pieces are listed in the inventory of her jewels, shown opposite. On her head her French hood is trimmed with the 'upper habulyment of Goldsmytheswerke ennamuled and garneshed with vii ffery daimondes vii ffeir rubyes and vii ffeyr Perles', which is the first item listed in the inventory. On her bosom, over a translucent chemise, she wears a shaped necklace called a square 'conteyning xxix rubyes and xxix clustres of Peerlles being iiii peerlles in every Clustre' and an 'ooche of golde havyng avery ffeir table diamond and a verey feir ruby with a long peerle hangyng at the same'. According to this likeness, Katherine had auburn hair, pale skin, dark eyes and a come-hither smile. It is easy to see why she was so attractive to the King. (AC and SD)

LITERATURE: Catherine, née Katherine Howard, *Oxford DNB*; Strong, *Artists of the Tudor Court*; Starkey, *Six Wives*

225 Queen Katherine's Jewels

British Library, Stowe MS 559, fol.55

This inventory of Katherine Howard's jewels provides the evidence that the likeness in the miniature, shown left, is indeed the Queen. The inventory lists the jewels – pearls, diamonds and other precious gems – that Henry VIII lavished on Katherine. They are a sign of his deep infatuation for her during their short married life. Many of the jewels were wedding gifts from the King and others were presents he gave her at Christmas and New Year (the traditional time for exchanging gifts). The jewels were worn not only as brooches or chains but also as embellished 'carcanes' (collars or headbands), pomanders, clothes and books. Katherine gave several of the pieces as gifts to her intimates and members of the royal family, including her stepdaughter Elizabeth and Henry's niece, Margaret Douglas. However, when the Queen was disgraced, all were taken away 'by his Grace's commandment, by Nicholas Britowe, His Highness' clerk'. (SD)

LITERATURE: Starkey, *Six Wives*

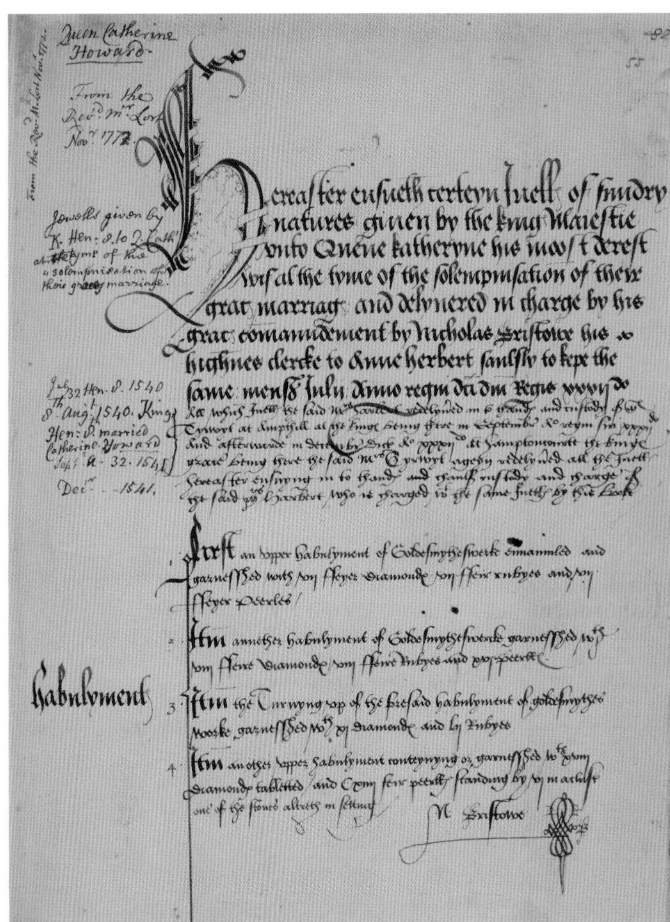

226 Queen Katherine's Infidelity

Letter from members of the Privy Council to Mr William Paget Esquire, Ambassador in France, [12] November 1541

British Library, Cotton MS Otho C x, fol.258

In this damaged letter, the Lords of the Council explain that Archbishop Cranmer had learned of Queen Katherine's infidelities from an informant, John Lascelles. A minor courtier and Evangelical, Lascelles had learned from the Dowager Duchess of Norfolk (who had brought up the Queen as a child) that Katherine had lain with Francis Dereham and had sexual encounters with a servant named Mannock. Cranmer reported the matter to the King in writing, as he had not the heart to tell him in person. At first Henry VIII could not believe it, but when the men were examined and confessed, he broke down in tears. Initially Katherine denied the charge, but later disclosed everything to Cranmer, who took her confession. The writers end: 'That moche we knowe for the beginning' but added that more evidence might well emerge, and, indeed, Henry was soon to learn that his wife had had an adulterous affair with Thomas Culpeper (*c.*1514–41), although some historians now question whether their liaison was sexual. The signatures on the letter that are now visible are: Sir Anthony Wingfield; William Fitzwilliam, Earl of Southampton; and Stephen Gardiner, Bishop of Winchester. (SD)

LITERATURE: Smith, *A Tudor Tragedy*; Starkey, *Six Wives*; Catherine, née Katherine Howard, *Oxford DNB*

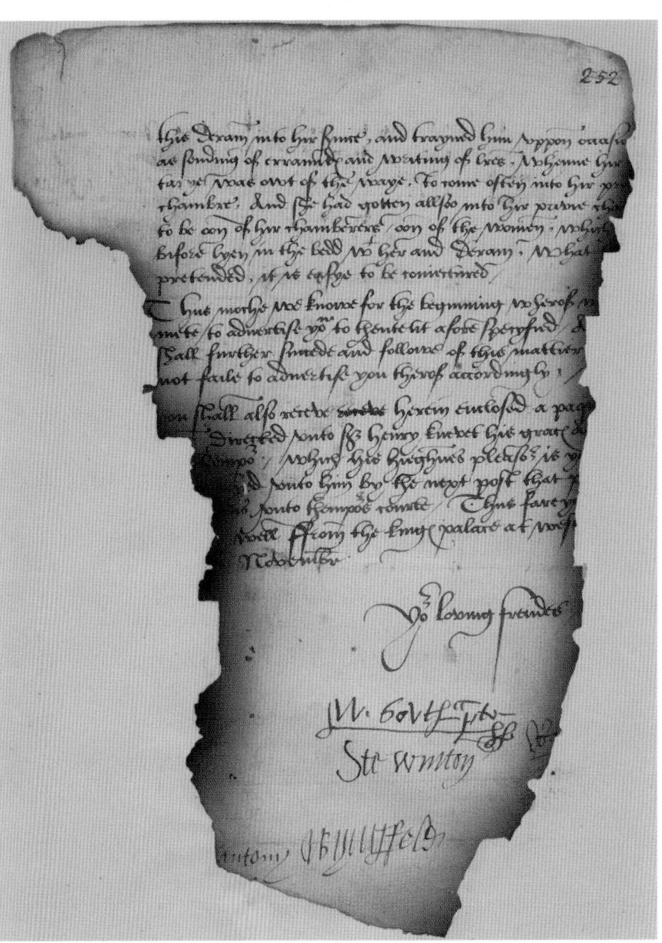

KATHERINE PARR

The thirty-one-year-old Katherine Parr (1512–48) was twice widowed when she married Henry VIII on 12 July 1543. Henry's three children all attended the quiet wedding that took place in the Queen's Closet at Hampton Court, and the following year Katherine used her influence to create a closer royal family by bringing her stepchildren to court whenever possible. For the most part, Katherine fulfilled the role Henry wanted, that of a doting and submissive wife. However, she had an independent mind and sometimes irritated Henry when they discussed theology together. In 1546, Henry – probably encouraged by Bishop Stephen Gardiner – considered charging her with heresy. Warned of the danger she faced, Katherine prostrated herself before the King, promising to defer to his better judgement on all matters spiritual or otherwise. Henry was mollified and Katherine's life was no longer in danger.

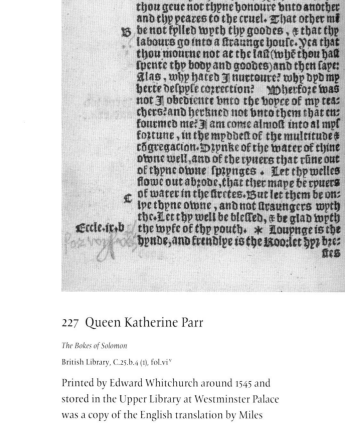

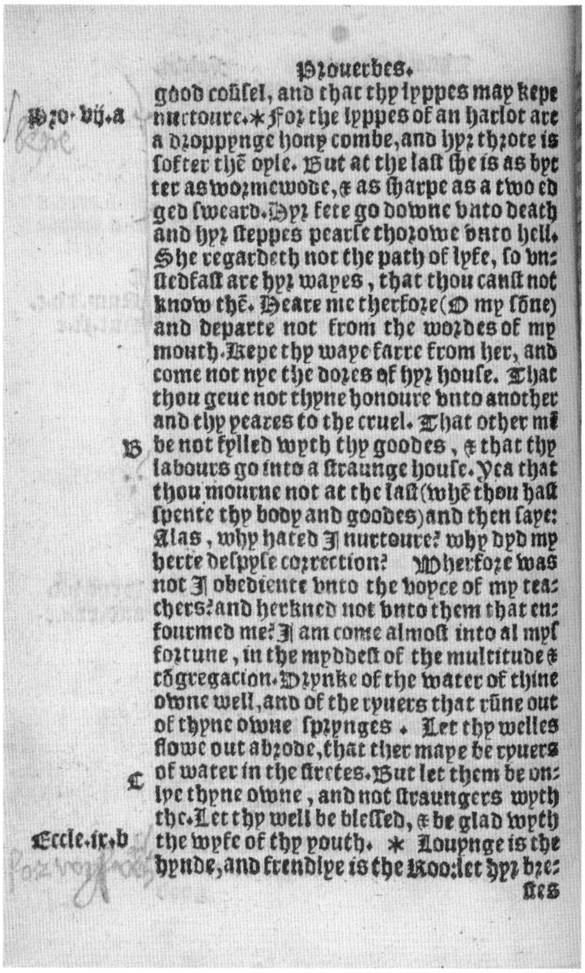

Prouerbes.
good coūsel, and that thy lyppes may kepe
Pro. vii. a nurtoure. * For the lyppes of an harlot are
a droppynge hony combe, and hyr throte is
softer thē oyle. But at the last she is as byt
ter as wormewode, & as sharpe as a two ed
ged sweard. Hyr fete go downe unto death
and hyr steppes pearse thorowe unto hell.
She regardeth not the path of lyfe, so un:
stedfast are hyr wayes, that thou canst not
know thē. Heare me therfore (O my sōne)
and departe not from the wordes of my
mouth. Kepe thy waye farre from her, and
come not nye the dores of hyr house. That
thou geue not thyne honoure unto another
and thy yeares to the cruel. That other mē
B be not fylled wyth thy goodes, & that thy
labours go into a straunge house. Yea that
thou mourne not at the last (whē thou hast
spente thy body and goodes) and then saye:
Alas, why hated I nurtoure? why dyd my
herte despyse correction? Wherfore was
not I obediente unto the voyce of my tea:
chers? and herkned not unto them that en:
fourmed me? I am come almost into al myst
fortune, in the myddest of the multitude &
cōgregacion. Drynke of the water of thine
owne well, and of the ryuers that rūne out
of thyne owne sprynges. Let thy welles
flowe out abrode, that ther maye be ryuers
C of water in the stretes. But let them be on:
lye thyne owne, and not straungers wyth
the. Let thy well be blessed, & be glad wyth
Eccle. ix. b the wyfe of thy youth. * Louynge is the
hynde, and frendlye is the Roo: let hyr bre:
stes

227 Queen Katherine Parr

The Bokes of Solomon

British Library, C.25.b.4 (1), fol.vi^{v}

Printed by Edward Whitchurch around 1545 and stored in the Upper Library at Westminster Palace was a copy of the English translation by Miles Coverdale of the Biblical books ascribed to Solomon. Like David, Solomon was a king with whom Henry VIII associated himself and there are annotations in his hand in the first five chapters of Proverbs. Most consists of wavy lines, nota signs, a tadpole-like mark, or manicules, but Henry does observe that Proverbs 5: 18–19 contains information 'for wyfves'. It is one of several marginalia that indicate his desire to distinguish between good and bad wives. Happily married to Katherine Parr, he clearly rejoices that he had been delivered 'from the straunge woman and from her that is not thyne owne' to end his days with a consort with whose love he could remain 'ever content'. (JC)

LITERATURE: Hattaway, 'Marginalia by Henry VIII in His Copy of *The Bokes of Salomon*'; Carley, *King Henry's Prayer Book*

228 A United Family

Letter from Henry VIII to Katherine Parr, sending news from France, 8 September 1544

British Library, Cotton MS Caligula E iv, fol.56v

Katherine Parr was a loving stepmother to Henry VIII's children and, after her marriage to the King, which was attended by Mary, Elizabeth and Edward, she helped to establish a better relationship between Henry and his children. During Henry's military expedition to France in the summer of 1544, Katherine gathered all the children together at Hampton Court, effectively bringing an end to Elizabeth's exile at Ashridge in Hertfordshire. Katherine is also widely attributed with persuading Henry to restore Mary and Elizabeth to the succession. This personal and loving note, written to Katherine by Henry from France, conveys a sense of the stability and harmony being enjoyed by the King's family for the first time, 'No more to yow att thys tyme swethart bothe for lacke off tyme and grett occupation off bysynes savyng we pray yow to gyff in our name our harte blessynge to all our chyldren and recommendations to our cousin margrett and the rest off the lades and gentyll women and to our consell allsoo, wryttn with the hand off your loving howsbande Henry'. (AC)

LITERATURE: James, *Kateryn Parr*; Starkey, *Six Wives*

229 Katherine Parr's Scholarly Interests

Il Petrarcha con l'espositione d'A. Vellutello; con le figure a i triomphi et con piu cose utili in varii luoghi aggiunte', 1544

British Library, C.27.e.19, binding

Katherine Parr had scholarly interests and enjoyed reading Petrarch and Erasmus. She was fluent in French, Latin and Italian. Shown here is Katherine's personal copy of *Il Petrarcha,* bound in purple velvet and embroidered with gold and silver thread and coloured silks, possibly by Katherine herself, to display her coat of arms surmounted by a royal crown. The supporters are those of the Fitzhugh and Parr families, indicating that the binding was created after the death of Henry VIII and before Katherine's secret marriage to Thomas Seymour in May 1547. Katherine's interest in learning became an important part of her relationship with Mary, Elizabeth and Edward as she inspired and encouraged each of them in their intellectual pursuits, as evidenced by surviving correspondence between Katherine and the children, written in French, Italian, Latin and English. (AC)

LITERATURE: James, *Kateryn Parr*; Starkey, *Six Wives*

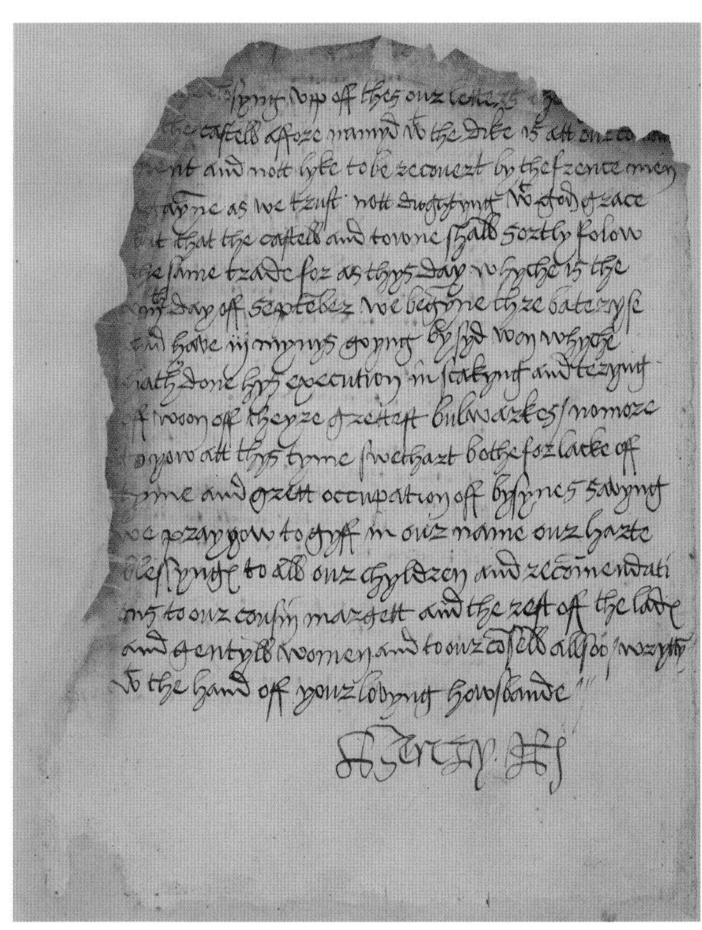

...ynge now off thys our letters ...
the castell afore namyd wt the dike is att our co...
...nt and nott lyke to be recoverd by the frenche men
...tyme as we trust nott doughtyng wt goddes grace
...t that the castell and towne shall shortly folow
the same trade for as thys day whyche is the
...th day off Septeber we begynne thre batteryse
and have iii mynys goyng by syd won whyche
hath done hys execution in shakyng and teryng
off won off theyre grettest bulwarkes / no more
to yow att thys tyme swethart bothe for lacke off
tyme and grett occupation off bysynes savyng
we pray yow to gyff in our name our harte
blessynge to all our chyldren and recommendati
ons to our cousyn margett and the rest off the lade
and gentyll women and to our consell allsoo / wrytt
wt the hand off your lovyng howsbande
Henry R

230 Katherine Parr, *Prayers or Meditations*, 1545

'Precationes ... ex piis scriptoribus per nobiliss. et pientiss. D. Catharinam Anglie, Francie, Hibernieq. reginam collecte, et per D. Elizabetam ex anglico converse.'

British Library, Royal MS 7 D x, binding

Katherine Parr was the first queen to have her own work published. *Prayers or Meditations* appeared in her name on 29 May 1545. The book contained English devotional material collected by Katherine, together with five prayers of her own. This manuscript is a translation of Katherine's work into Latin, French and Italian carried out by Henry VIII's daughter Princess Elizabeth as a New Year's gift for her father. It is dedicated to Henry and dated 20 December 1545. The design and workmanship of the embroidered binding are also credited to Elizabeth. The initials of Henry and Katherine are entwined in the centre of the front cover, and in each corner is stitched a white rose, the emblem of the princess's namesake and paternal royal grandmother, Elizabeth of York. Katherine went on to write *The Lamentation of a Sinner*, which was published after Henry's death in 1547, and describes the Queen's search for religious truth and the soul's salvation initiated by divine grace. (SD)

LITERATURE: James, *Kateryn Parr*; Starkey, *Six Wives*

SCOTLAND

While Henry VIII was on a northern progress with his wife Katherine Howard in 1541, he expected to meet his nephew James V of Scotland (1512–42) at York. Confident in the power of personal diplomacy, Henry hoped that their existing disputes would be resolved at the interview and an alliance be concluded. However, James had not promised to come and did not appear. This 'snub' incensed Henry and convinced him that James was his enemy. Furthermore, Henry feared that the 'Auld Alliance' would be reactivated once he decided to wage war against France again. Henry therefore determined on a pre-emptive strike, both to avenge his honour and safeguard his borders. The result was unexpected: James V raised a huge army that was routed by an English force at the Battle of Solway Moss on 24 November 1542. Three weeks later the Scottish King died, leaving his throne to his six day-old daughter Mary. There now arose an opportunity to marry her to Prince Edward and unite the two realms under England. Over the next four years Henry used a mixture of threats, diplomacy and military force in his endeavours to achieve this end, but to no avail.

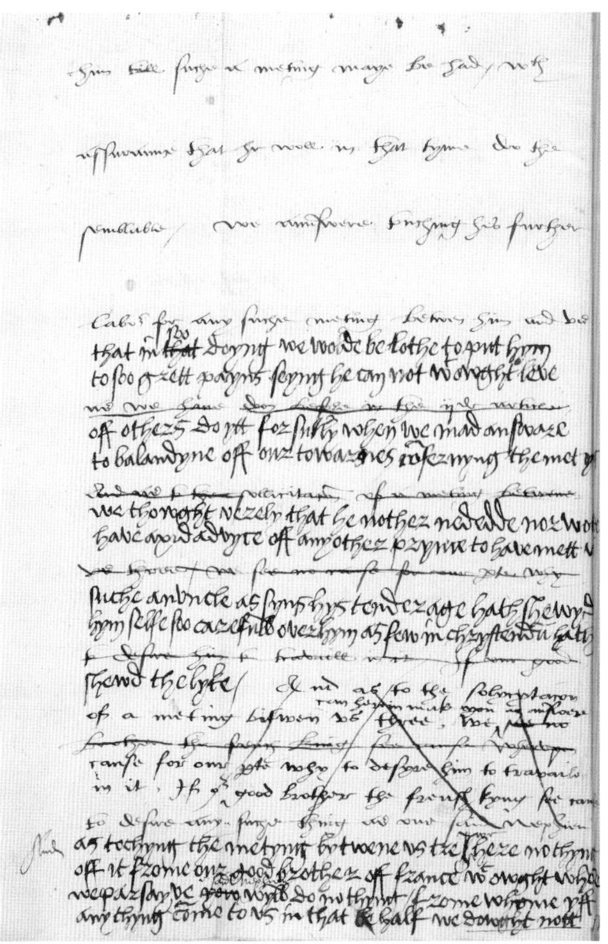

231 Jilted at York

A draft of the King's answer to the articles delivered by the ambassadors of Scotland, 6 February 1542, with many corrections made in Henry VIII's hand

British Library, Additional MS 32647, fol.8v

Henry VIII's anger at waiting in vain to meet James V at York is evident in this exchange with the Scottish ambassadors. Not only had Henry been humiliated by his nephew but he was now equally offended by James's excuses for not turning up, namely that he had not received the consent of his nobles and the French King. Henry consequently added these words to the draft: 'we thowght verely that he nother nededde nor wolde have axid advyce off any other prynce, to have mett with suche an uncle as syns hys tender age hath shewyd hym selfe soo carefull over hym as few in Chrystendum hath shewd the lyke'. Henry took James's nonappearance personally. Furthermore, he recognized that the Scottish King placed a higher premium on an alliance with France than his relationship with his English uncle. Therefore, if England went to war against France, James might well invade England as the ally of Francis I. (SD)

LITERATURE: Hotle, *Thorns and Thistles*; Head, 'Henry VIII's Scottish Policy'; Hoyle and Ramsdale, 'The Royal Progress of 1541, the North of England, and Anglo-Scottish Relations, 1534–1542'

232 Henry VIII and James V

Letter from Henry VIII to the King of the Scots, 23 August 1542

British Library, Additional MS 50825, fol.1

In August 1542, Henry VIII seemed bent on war against Scotland, while James actually showed a willingness to negotiate. In this letter Henry refers to a Scottish raid into Cockdale, Northumberland, that he seems ready to use as a pretext for taking military action. He complains that the Scottish wardens and soldiers had raided the north of England despite James's 'good wordes' and 'desire to the continuaunce of love and amitie between us'. Although Henry purports to believe that James himself is innocent of any 'dissymulacion' and instead holds responsible 'yvel disposed myndes and counsaillours' (a common rhetorical device), the English King demands immediate redress. After receiving this missive, James was conciliatory, and agreed to a meeting on 18 September to discuss Anglo-Scottish disputes. However, the negotiations broke down when the English commissioners put forward Henry's humiliating demands. A punitive invasion was then launched into Scotland. (SD)

LITERATURE: Hotle, *Thorns and Thistles*; Head, 'Henry VIII's Scottish Policy'

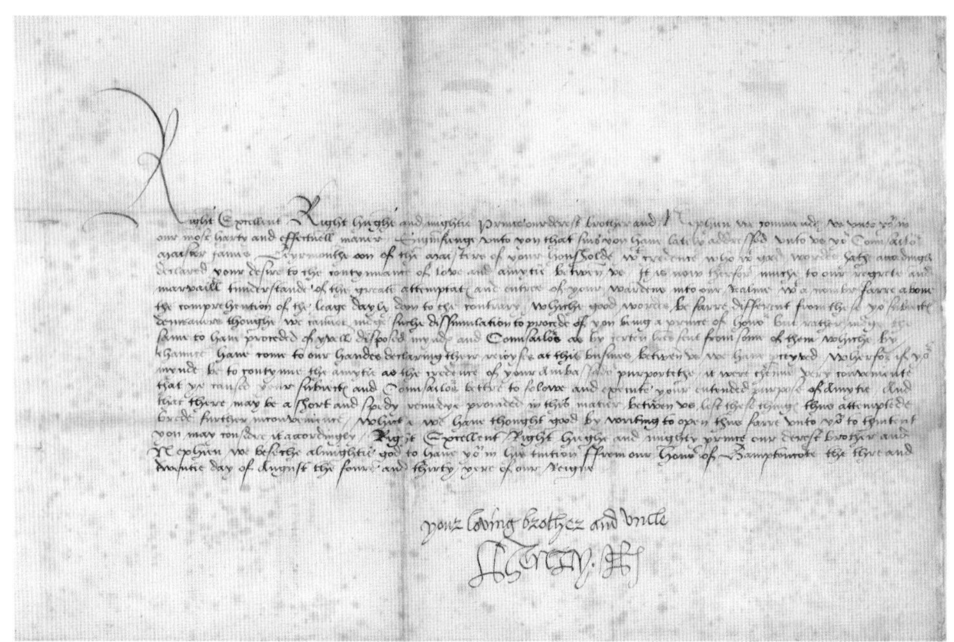

your loving brother and uncle

233 The Rough Wooing

Marriage treaty between Prince Edward and Mary, Queen of Scots, signed by Henry VIII, 1546

British Library, Cotton Vitellius. C xi, fol.225

After the English victory at Solway Moss and the death of James V in 1542, Henry VIII tried to force the Scottish regency government to agree to a marriage between their young Queen Mary and his son Prince Edward. Eventually, it was agreed the marriage would take place as part of the Treaty of Greenwich, signed on 1 July 1543. This is the first page of the articles of the treaty of marriage, signed by Henry at the beginning and end of the document. At some stage the document has been incorrectly dated to 1546, but the text refers to Prince Edward being not yet six years old (*necdem sexennis*) and Mary as not yet one (*necdum primum etatis*), dating the document to 1543. The original marriage treaties were rescinded when the Scots refused to submit to Henry's demand that Mary should live in England until the wedding. Henry's punitive raids on the Lowlands did not make the Scots change their minds. On the contrary, they looked to France for assistance. (AC and SD)

LITERATURE: Hotle, *Thorns and Thistles*; Head, 'Henry VIII's Scottish Policy'

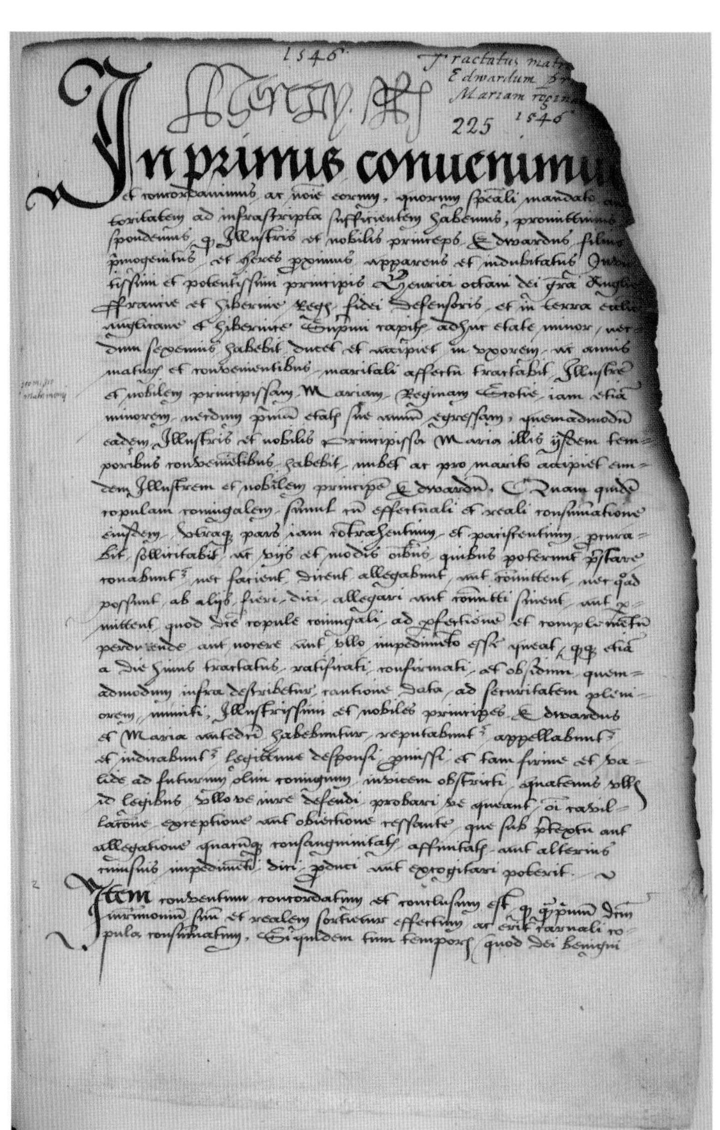

1546 Tractatus inter Edwardum ... Mariam reginam ... 225 1546

In primus conuenimus

234 Italian-style Defences of the Scottish Border

Gian Tommaso Scala, Proposals for the fortification of Tynemouth, February 1545

British Library, Cotton MS Augustus I.ii.7

Early in 1545 the Earl of Hertford (*c.*1500–52) and the military engineers Sir Richard Lee, Gian Tommaso Scala and Antonio da Bergamo were ordered to inspect the defences of Tynemouth, 'a place most … needful to be fortified' near the Scottish border. This bird's-eye view by Scala, with English and Italian annotations, illustrates their proposal that two Italian-style angular bastions and a gun platform be created outside the walls of the dilapidated medieval castle that accommodated the recently dissolved priory. It was the first time that such fortifications had been proposed in an English context. The plan demonstrates how the latest Italian military fashions spread into England. Although these bastions were never built, the *trace italienne* was adopted shortly afterwards for the fortifications of Berwick-upon-Tweed, Yarmouth on the Isle of Wight and Ambleteuse near Boulogne. The plan's pictorial style is traditional: innovation in mapmaking was inspired by German and Netherlandish, not Italian, models. (PB)

LITERATURE: *Catalogue of Manuscript Maps… in the British Museum*, vol.1; Colvin, Ransome and Summerson, *The History of the King's Works*; Merriman, 'Italian Military Engineers in Britain in the 1540s'

235 The Burning of Edinburgh

Richard Lee, fragment of a bird's-eye view of the taking of Edinburgh ('Edenborth') by the English, May 1544

British Library, Cotton Augustus I.ii.56

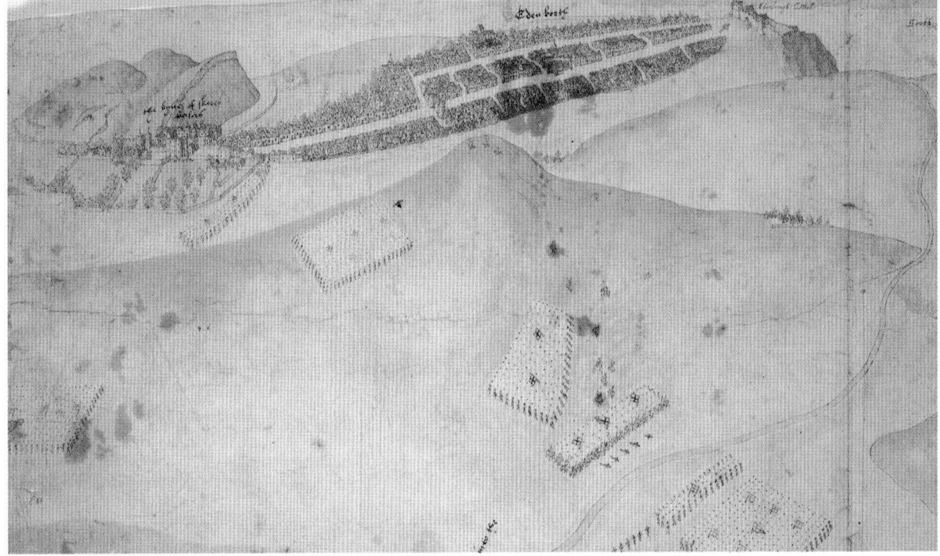

In the spring of 1544 the Earl of Hertford (*c.*1500–52) launched an assault on Edinburgh by sea as part of Henry VIII's 'Rough Wooing' of the young Scottish Queen Mary. Although Hertford would have liked to hold onto and garrison the castle, Henry was unwilling to devote resources to occupying parts of Scotland. Instead, Hertford was ordered to lay waste the city and surrounding countryside before returning to England. This bird's-eye view of Edinburgh shows English forces entering Edinburgh and the English siege works. It is the earliest known realistic view of the city that originally extended to the harbour at Leith and has been convincingly attributed on stylistic grounds to Richard Lee, who was knighted for his achievements during the siege. It is probably the very map that Lee presented to Henry 'so as your majesty will perceive the situation of [Edinburgh] which is undoubtedly set forth as well as possible'. (PB and SD)

LITERATURE: Conway and Boog Watson, *Maps of Edinburgh, 1544–1929*; Robinson, *Marine Cartography in Britain*; Colvin, Ransome and Summerson, *The History of the King's Works*, vol.3

THE WAR AGAINST FRANCE

War against Scotland did not bring Henry VIII the honour he craved; for this he needed to fight on the Continent. The reopening of war between Francis I and Charles V in July 1542 provided the opportunity, while the money from the monasteries gave him the resources. After negotiating with both monarchs, Henry signed an alliance with Charles in February 1543, and, in June 1544, an English army of at least 38,000 men invaded France. Although ailing and overweight, Henry arrived in person to head his army the following month. Wisely limiting his military objectives, Henry decided on a campaign in Picardy rather than a march on Paris, as had been agreed with Charles V. The English armies besieged the towns of Montreuil and Boulogne, taking Boulogne on 14 September. Four days later, Charles and Francis signed a bilateral peace of Crépy. Deserted by his ally and refusing to surrender the trophy of Boulogne, Henry fought on alone in a war of defence against France, as Francis mounted assaults on Boulogne and the south coast of England. Both sides eventually became worn down, and they signed a peace at Camp (also known as the Treaty of Ardres) in June 1546.

236 A Late Triumph

James Basire after Samuel Hieronymous Grimm

A. *The Departure of Henry VIII from Calais*
B. *The Encampment of Henry at Marquison*
C. *The Siege of Boulogne*

Henry VIII considered the siege of Boulogne to be one of his greatest triumphs – on a par with Charles V's conquest of Tunis a decade earlier. It was certainly worthy of commemoration on silver gilt dishes, on swords and particularly in the series of paintings of the great events in his reign that he had been commissioning for Whitehall Palace since about 1540. Foreign prints, tapestries and paintings of other rulers' 'triumphs' would have provided the anonymous artist with plenty of models. The Lord High Admiral, Sir William Fitzwilliam (*c.*1506–1559), had what were almost certainly close copies painted to adorn the dining parlour of his recently completed and magnificent new home at Cowdray in Sussex. They were copied by the Swiss-born artist Samuel Hieronymous Grimm for the Society of Antiquaries of London just a few years before Cowdray House was gutted by fire in 1793 and the paintings destroyed. (PB)

LITERATURE: St John Hope, *Cowdray and Easebourne Priory in the County of Sussex*; Hale, *Artist and Warfare in the Renaissance*; Barber, 'Cartography, Topography and History Painting in *The Inventory of Henry VIII*'

A

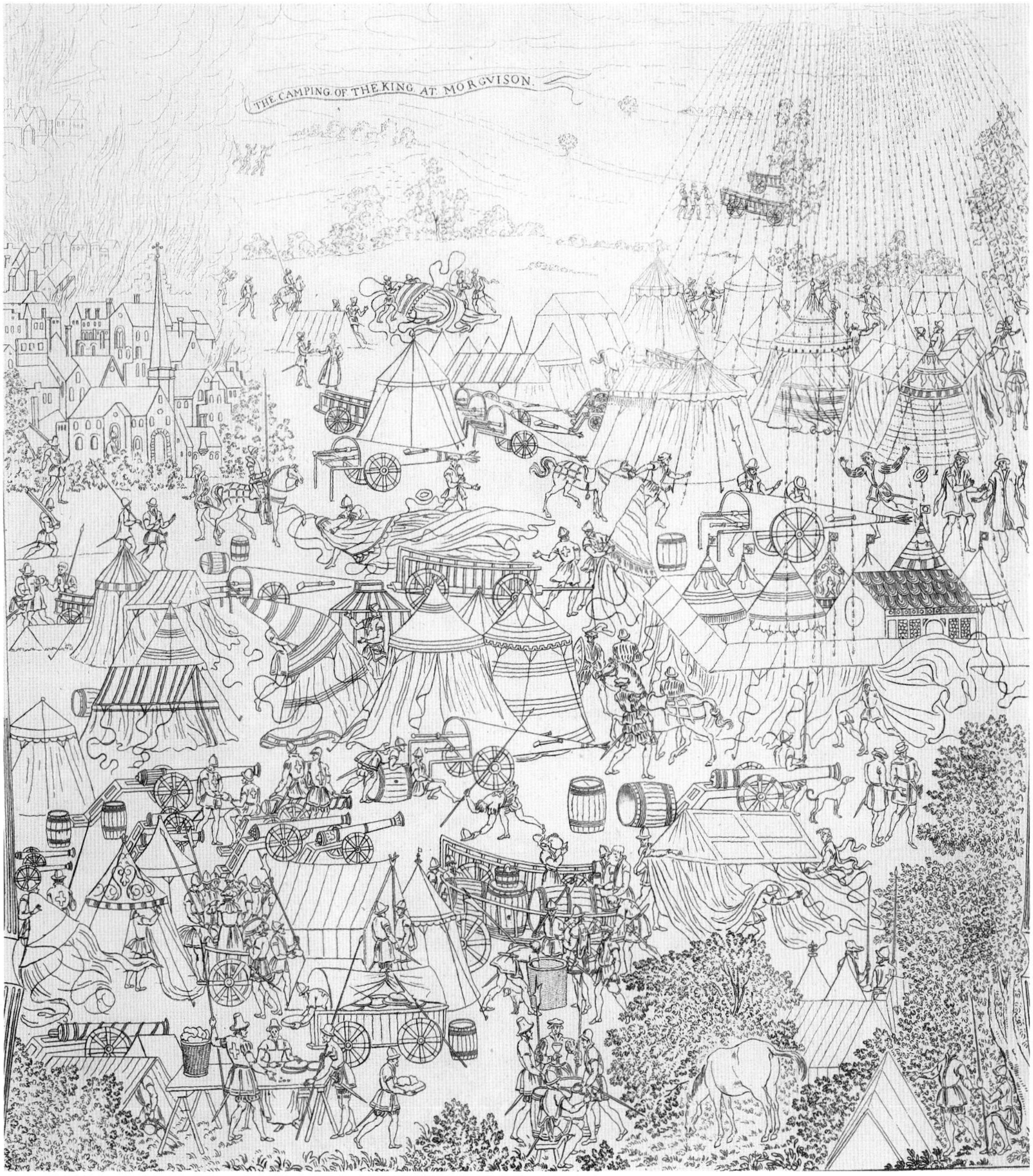

THE CAMPING OF THE KING AT MORGVISON

B

C

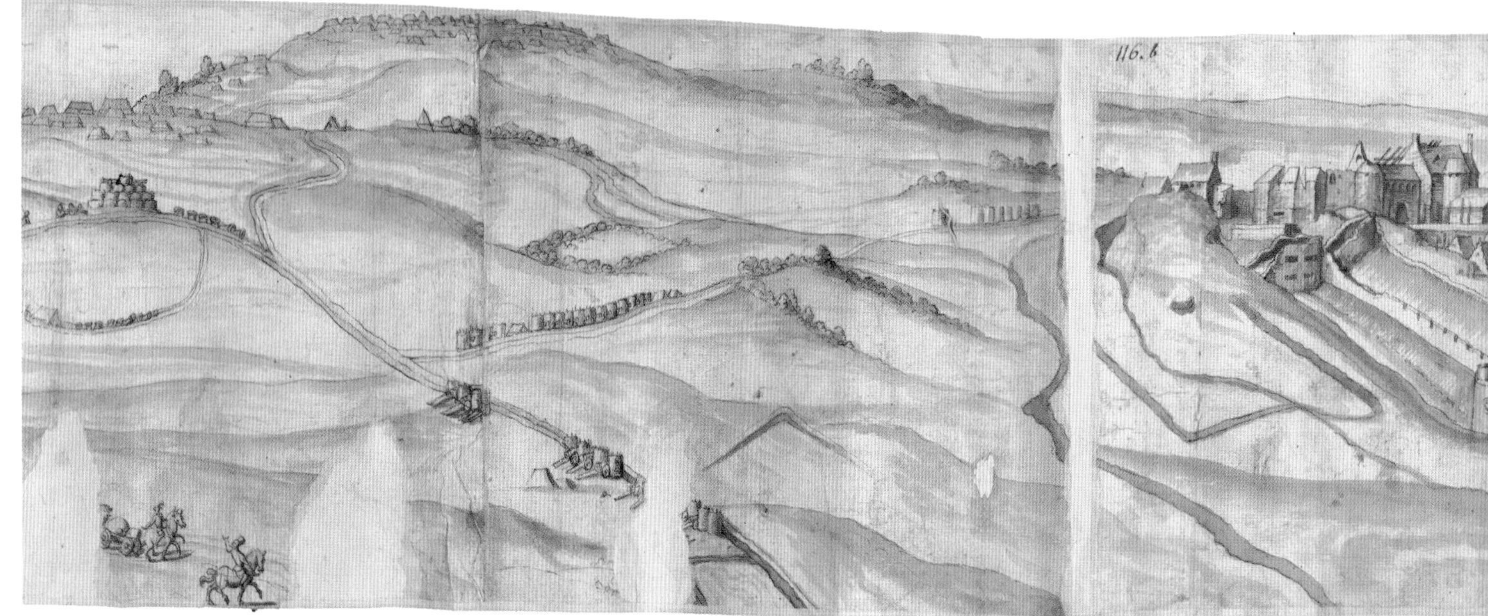

237 The Last Act of the Siege of Boulogne

View of the aftermath of the siege of Boulogne, 1544

British Library, Cotton MS Augustus I.ii.116

This mid-16th-century drawing has recently been recognized as the sole surviving contemporary view of the aftermath of the siege of Boulogne. Inhabitants are seen departing from the battered upper town, while the near-deserted English camp is shown on the left. It cannot be ascertained whether this is a preliminary drawing for a painting or a copy but, like so many of the items in the Cotton Collection, it was probably once in Whitehall Palace. It clearly relates to the series of paintings of the event that was commissioned by Henry VIII for Whitehall Palace. It may not have been copied for Cowdray because there was not enough space for it, with the other paintings on the same wall, in the Dining Chamber. (PB)

LITERATURE: Lloyd and Thurley, *Henry VIII*; Barber, 'Putting Musselburgh on the Map'

238 Henry Draws the Line?

John Rogers

'Boleine with the French Fortresse and the Country towards Hardilo' (late 16th-century annotation)

British Library, Cotton MS Augustus I.ii.77

This surprisingly modern-looking map shows the surroundings of Boulogne (seen at the top left) in about June 1546, when the Treaty of Camp was being negotiated. Precision was needed if it was to serve its purpose and it is one of the earliest predecessors of today's Ordnance Survey maps. It is drawn to a scale of 1,000 feet to the inch (1:12000) and predominantly in plan. Its maker, John Rogers, one of Henry VIII's most capable surveyors, portrays the physical relief both in words and graphically with wavy lines that anticipate the contour lines on modern maps. The dotted red line was probably added later. It shows the preferred English line for the boundary with France and may well have been drawn by Henry himself in consultation with Rogers: Henry had the necessary rulers, compasses and pens in his Whitehall office. The treaty line was much less favourable to England. This map and the very different one showing the taking of Edinburgh demonstrate how pictorial and more mathematical maps coexisted in the 1540s, each being best suited to its particular purpose. (PB)

LITERATURE: Shelby, *John Rogers*

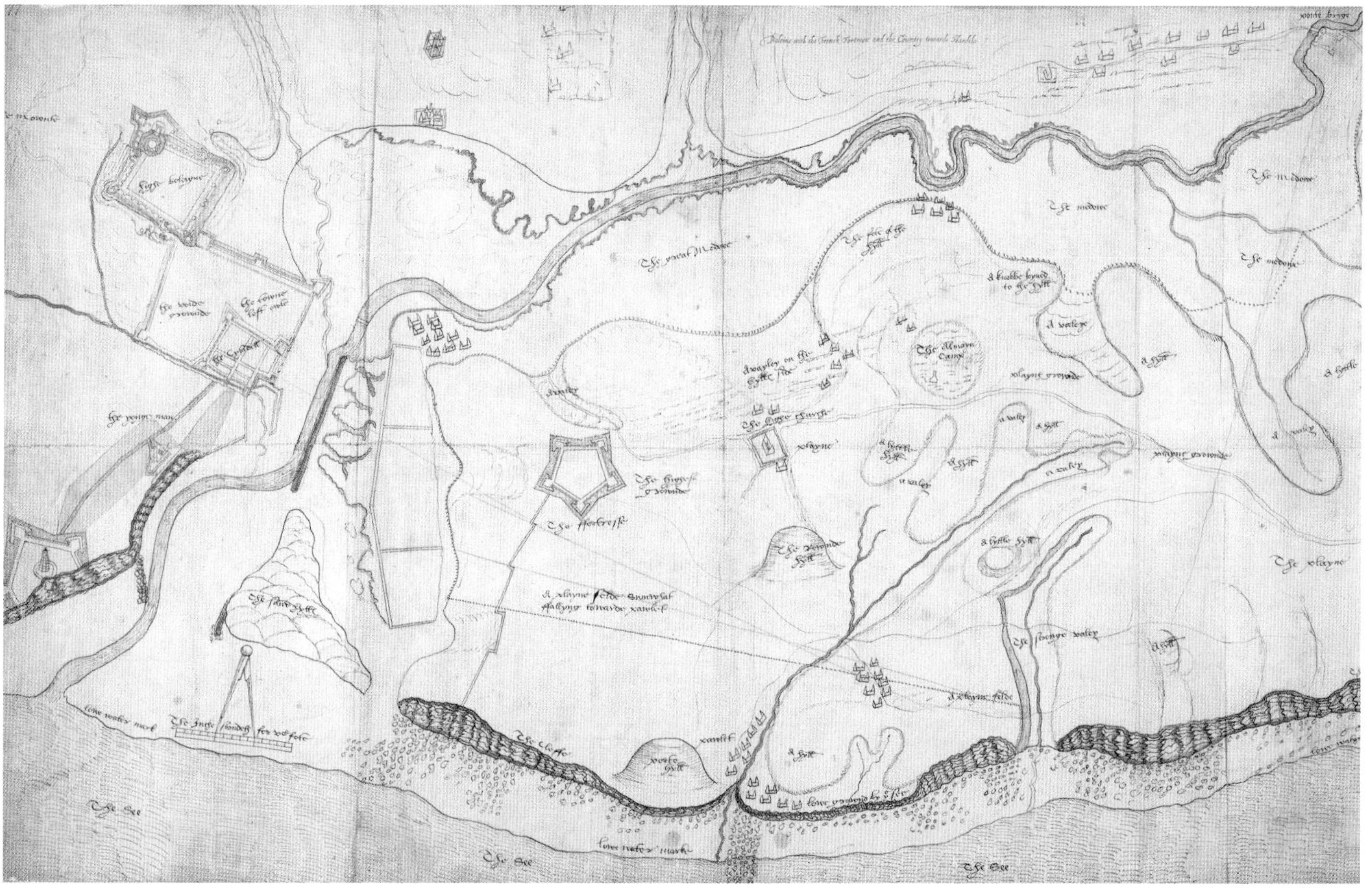

MAPS AND SCIENTIFIC INSTRUMENTS

Henry VIII developed a great enthusiasm for maps and charts during the last decade of his life. As we have already seen, the King valued them as instruments of government during the invasion crisis of 1538–40 and the Scottish and French wars. Among the state papers in Henry's private library in Whitehall, there were drawers full of such 'plats'. But Henry also appreciated maps as cultural artefacts, and on display in his palaces were grander maps and charts that illustrated his military victories, his own territories and those of his neighbours. This enthusiasm for maps was not confined to the King: during his reign there was a new awareness in England of the value of cartography, and maps were drawn up to illustrate a wide variety of texts. At the same time, Henry demonstrated a keen interest in science and mathematics, especially when associated with mapmaking. He offered his patronage to Nicolaus Kratzer (who became his astronomer), Sebastian Le Seney (a clockmaker who entered the King's service in 1537 and produced at least one astrolabe for Henry) and to Jean Rotz, a Dieppe-based sailor and chartmaker of Scottish descent, who was appointed Royal Hydrographer. Henry's inventory of 1542 reveals the extent of the scientific instruments in his possession.

239 Jean Rotz

Jean Rotz (1505–c.1560), *Traicte des differences du compas aymante* (Treatise on the variation of the magnetic compass), 1542

British Library, Royal MS 20 B vii, fols 1v–2

Soon after arriving in England in 1542 to seek service under Henry VIII, Rotz (also known as Ross) presented the King with a navigating instrument that he had invented himself. The '*cadrant differential*' (differential quadrant) was a combined magnetic compass and universal dial and can be seen here, illustrated in the navigational manual that Rotz composed to accompany the gift. The 'Treatise on the variation of the magnetic compass and of certain notable errors of navigation hitherto unknown, very useful and necessary to all pilots and mariners' explains that the instrument was meant to deal with the navigational problem of contemporary charts. In the dedicatory preface to the King, Rotz explains that his work was intended for 'the use and recreation of all those who wish to taste the fruits of Astrology and Marine Science'. The gifts must have indeed delighted Henry as Rotz was appointed Royal Hydrographer in September 1542 and remained in England until the death of Henry VIII in 1547. (AC)

LITERATURE: Taylor, 'Jean Rotz: His Neglected Treatise on Nautical Science'; Rotz, Jean, *Oxford DNB*

240 The World at his Fingertips

Jean Rotz, 'The Boke of Idrography', 1542

British Library, Royal MS 20 E ix, fols 29v–30

High salaries had attracted numerous French mapmakers to Henry VIII's court by the time that Jean Rotz sought to enter royal service by presenting Henry with this magnificent atlas. Although originally intended for Francis I, Rotz covered his tracks by proclaiming his loyalty with Tudor symbols and minute exhortations in Scots English. The atlas was calculated to appeal to Henry's love of maps and the practicalities of navigation. The charts, presenting the fruits of French and Portuguese geographical and ethnographical discoveries in a Portuguese-inspired artistic guise, displayed the latest state of knowledge of the world. The depiction of life in South-East Asia was based on Rotz's personal experience: he seems to have accompanied the French explorer Jean Parmentier on his voyage of 1529–30. Henry was doubtless delighted to be publicly associated with such a prestigious object, but he harboured no known extra-European colonial ambitions. (PB)

LITERATURE: Wallis, *The Maps and Text of the Boke of Idrography presented by Jean Rotz to Henry VIII 1542*

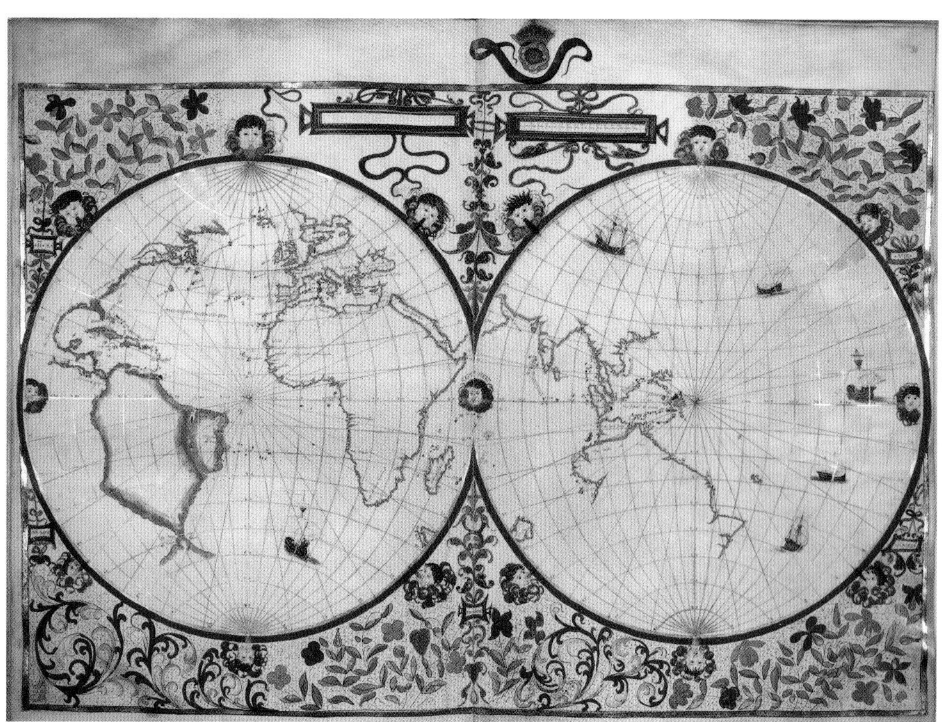

241 A Book of Cosmography

Jean Mallard, *Le Premier Livre de la cosmographie en rhetorique francoyse* (The first book of cosmography in French)

British Library, Royal MS 20 B. xii, fols 4v–5

When in the service of Francis I, Jean Mallard prepared a presentation manuscript for the King of the first volume of an ambitious *Description de tous les portz de mer de l'univers*. The *Description* was basically a poetic rendering of a work by the French navigator Jean Alphonse de Saintonge. Mallard, who described the English as friends of the French, although enemies of the Pope, and noted that Henry VIII was especially welcoming to strangers, soon afterwards emigrated to England where he attempted to find royal patronage through the presentation of a new manuscript of the same work, now entitled *Le Premier Livre de la cosmographie en rhetorique francoyse*. In his preface he promised Henry that, if he were made the royal poet to the English court, he would compose 'histoires et merveilles' that would bring renown to his newly adopted land. This coloured world map, not found in Francis's copy, would have greatly appealed to Henry, who did, in due course, make payments to Mallard as 'poete et orateur en la langue francoyse'. (JC)

LITERATURE: Carley, *King Henry's Prayer Book*; Cooper, 'Jean Mallard, poète et peintre rouennais'

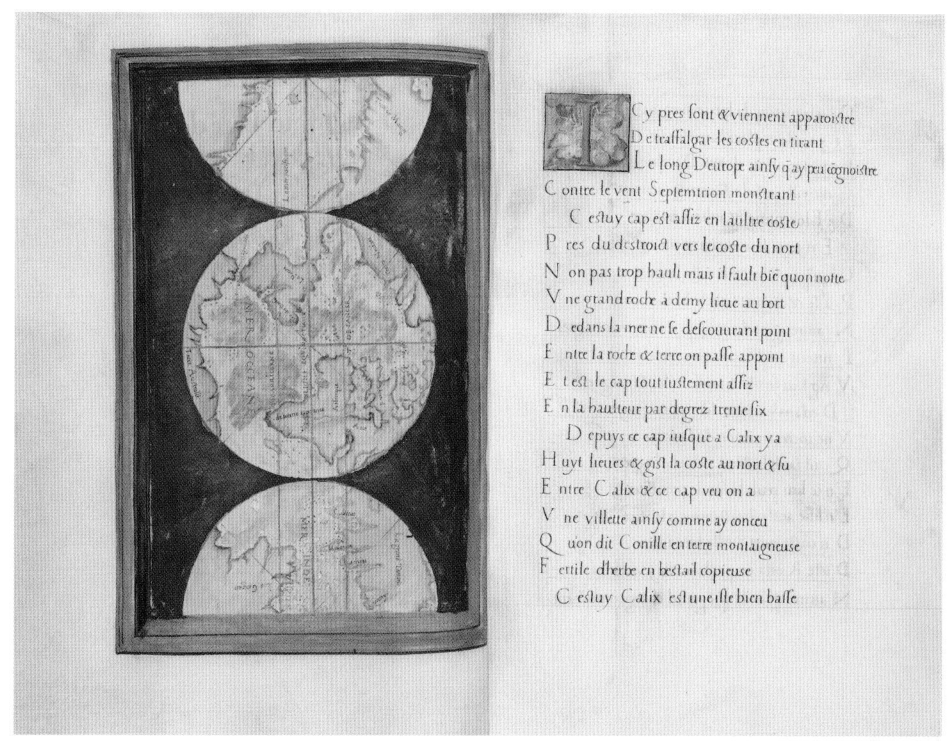

ICy pres sont & viennent apparoistre
De traffalgar les costes en tirant
Le long Deurope ainsy q̃ ay peu cõgnoistre
Contre le vent Septemtrion monstrant
Cestuy cap est assiz en laultre coste
Pres du destroict vers le coste du nort
Non pas trop hault mais il fault biẽ quon notte
Vne grand roche à demy lieue au bort
Dedans la mer ne se descouurant point
Entre la roche & terre on passe appoint
Et est le cap tout iustement assiz
En la haulteur par degrez trente six
Depuys ce cap iusque a Calix y a
Huyt lieues & gist la coste au nort & su
Entre Calix & ce cap veu on a
Vne villette ainsy comme ay conceu
Quon dit Conille en terre montaigneuse
Fertile dherbe en bestail copieuse
Cestuy Calix est une isle bien basse

242 A Modern Map of Britain and Ireland?

Map of the British Isles, also known as 'the Cottonian map of Britain' and 'Angliae Figura'

London workshop *c.*1536–7

British Library, Cotton MS Augustus I. i. 9

This map, the first to name Hampton Court, could be considered the earliest relatively detailed, scientifically constructed map of the British Isles. Drawn on a projection and graduated, relatively accurately, for latitude and longitude, its colouring and decoration subtly reflect English claims to suzerainty over Scotland, France and Ireland. Like so much of the visual culture of Henry VIII's court, however, it is still essentially medieval. The depiction of England owes an enormous debt to a medieval map of about 1290; and that of Wales to Giraldus Cambrensis. Scotland owes much to Hector Boece's description in his history of the Scots published in 1527. Internal evidence suggests that the map was presented to Henry as a New Year's gift in 1537, by Maurice Griffin, alias Griffiths, a Welsh Dominican monk and Archdeacon of Rochester (d.1558), ostensibly to commemorate the union of Wales and England. There is a possible reference to the map hanging in Hampton Court in the 1547 inventory, but precise identification is made difficult because of the ambiguous language employed when describing England and Britain. (PB)

LITERATURE: Crone, *Early Maps of the British Isles AD 1000 – AD 1579*; Marks and Williamson (eds), *Gothic: Art for England 1400–1547*; Barber, *King Henry's Map of Great Britain*

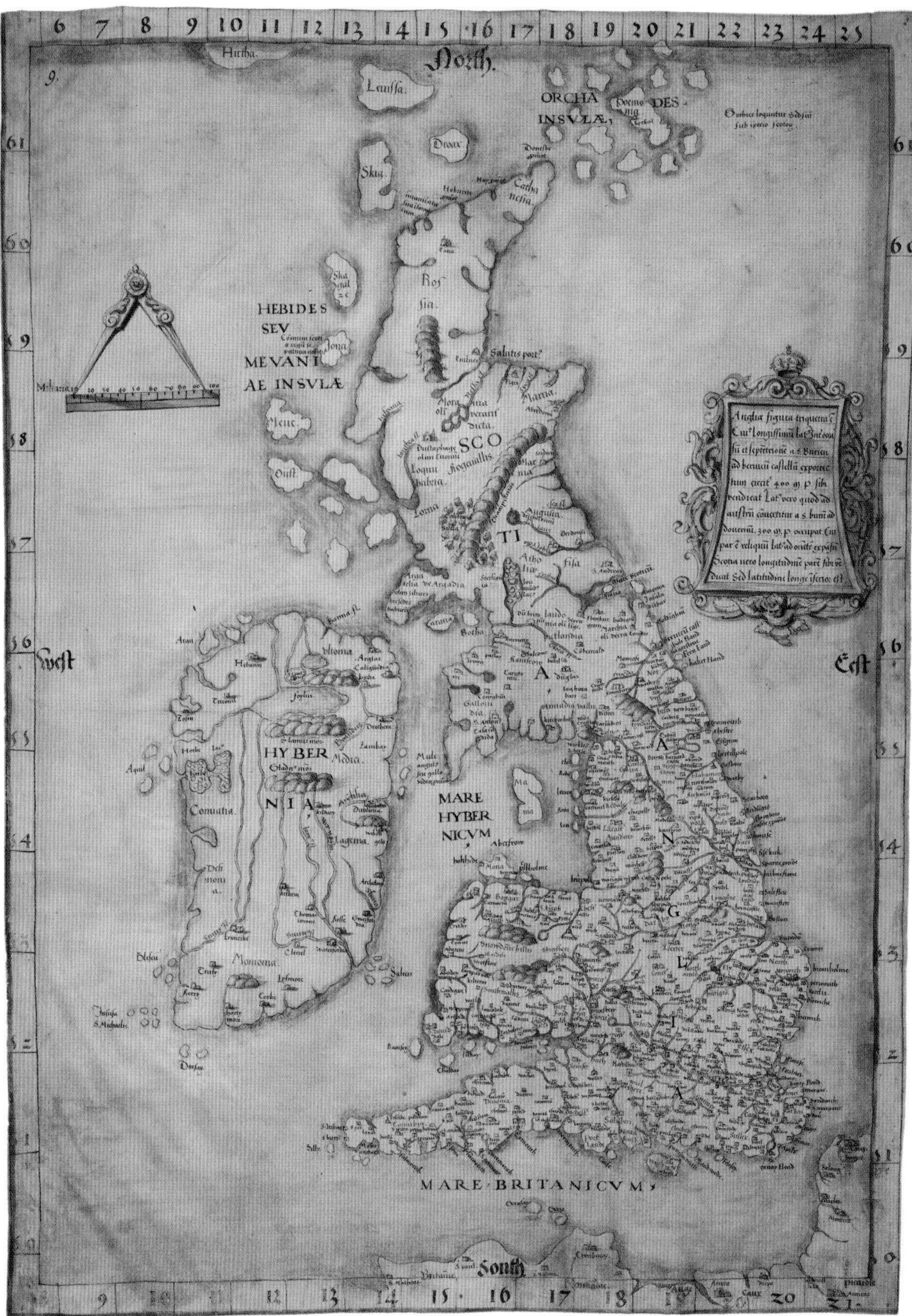

243 The Marvels of Science

Nicolaus Kratzer, *Canones Horoptri*

Copied by Peter Meghen and decorated by Hans Holbein the Younger, 1528–9

Bodleian Library, Oxford, MS Bodley 504, fol.1

Nicolaus Kratzer (1487?–1550) acted as a scientific and cartographic adviser to Henry VIII at a time when the King was becoming increasingly interested in such matters. This treatise, copied by the scribe and scholar Peter Meghen and containing capital letters illuminated by Holbein, was Kratzer's New Year's gift to Henry in 1529. It is a small example of frequent collaboration between Holbein and Kratzer in these years. Kratzer states that he had composed the text in response to repeated requests from a courtier, William Tyler, to explain his invention, the 'horoptrum'. He proceeds to describe how the instrument can be used to find the times of sunrise and sunset, the Golden Number, the position of the sun in the zodiac and more. Though there was nothing radically new in this, such handsomely presented texts served to heighten awareness in court circles of the potential practical benefits of the application of German scientific methods. (PB)

LITERATURE: Pächt, 'Holbein and Kratzer as Collaborators'; Trapp, 'Notes on Manuscripts written by Peter Meghen'; Starkey (ed.), *Henry VIII: A European Court in England*

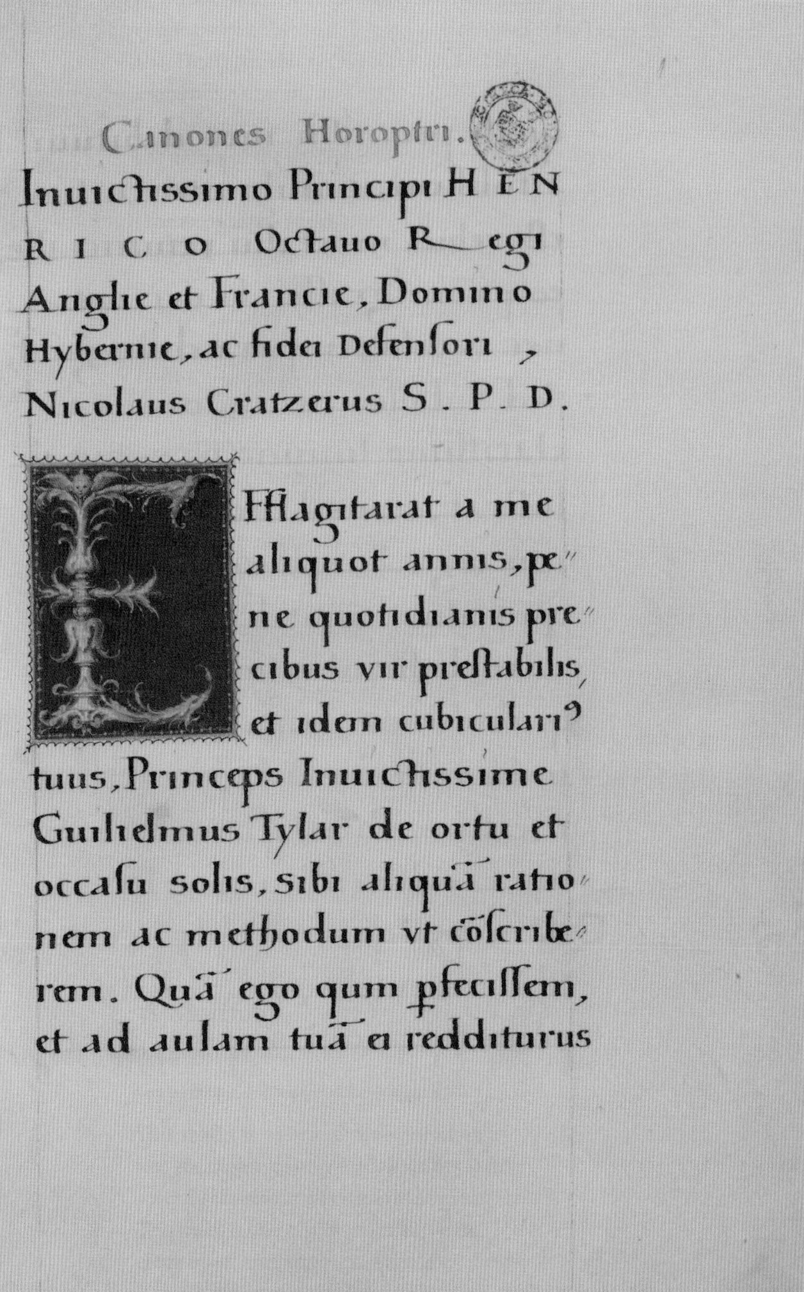

Canones Horoptri.
Inuictissimo Principi HEN
RICO Octauo Regi
Anglie et Francie, Domino
Hybernie, ac fidei Defensori
Nicolaus Cratzerus S. P. D.

Efflagitarat a me
aliquot annis, pe-
ne quotidianis pre-
cibus vir prestabilis,
et idem cubicularius
tuus, Princeps Inuictissime
Guilhelmus Tylar de ortu et
occasu solis, sibi aliquã ratio-
nem ac methodum vt cõscribe-
rem. Quã ego qum pfecissem,
et ad aulam tuã ei redditurus

244 A Terrestrial Table Globe

Gerard Mercator, Louvain, Belgium, 1541

National Maritime Museum, Greenwich, London, GLB0096

Gerard Mercator (1512–94) was most famous as a mapmaker and for devising a new projection named after him, which simplified plotting an accurate course on nautical charts. But he also made globes and mathematical instruments that had a major influence on other makers. This globe indicates the state of geographical knowledge in the later part of Henry VIII's reign. The details on the sphere of the globe include compass bearings, also called rhumb lines or loxodromes, and the presumed position of the magnetic pole. The major European cities are indicated by numbers, with their names given in a table. Several named stars are also plotted on the globe. There is a hypothetical southern continent that was then assumed to exist, in order to balance the land mass in the northern hemisphere. A note on distances is given in a cartouche at the equator, to the left of a pair of dividers. Henry VIII had various similar globes, including a 'great globe of the description of the world' in his new library at Whitehall. (GC)

LITERATURE: Dekker, *Globes at Greenwich*; Crane, *Mercator*; Callendar, *The Caird Collection of Maritime Antiquities*, vol.1; Starkey (ed.), *Inventory no. 11656*

245 Single-handed Dividers

Unknown, 17th century

National Maritime Museum, Greenwich, London, NAV0534

Dividers were an essential tool of the navigator, used with a chart to read off the course from the compass bearings marked on it. Distances could also be worked out by taking them off the chart with the dividers and placing them on a scale rule. Their design changed very little over the centuries. This pair is made of iron and the shape was intended to make them easy to manipulate using only one hand. They are almost identical to those found on the *Mary Rose*. In the 16th century, dividers were often called 'compasses', which can cause confusion for modern readers of early texts on navigation. Henry VIII himself had several 'pairs of compasses', including three that formed part of a drawing box containing ink, counters (for calculation), a foot-rule, pen and pen-knife and pencils, that travelled with him from palace to palace. (GC)

LITERATURE: Waters, *The Art of Navigation in Elizabethan and Early Stuart Times*; Hambly, *Drawing Instruments, 1580–1980*; Callendar, *The Caird Collection of Maritime Antiquities*, vol.1; Starkey (ed.), *Inventory no. 2549*

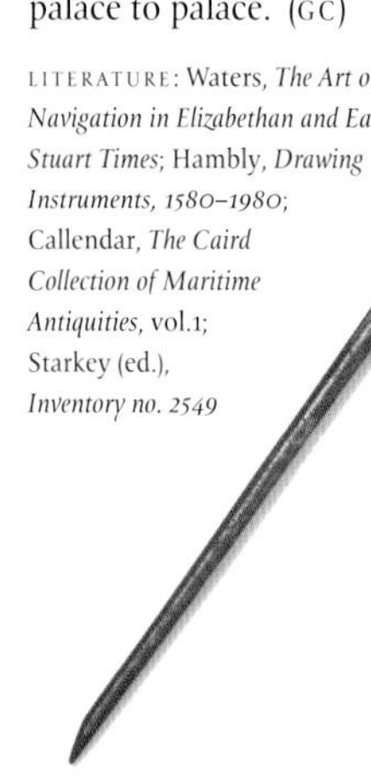

246 Mariner's Compass

Mid-18th century

National Maritime Museum, Greenwich, London, NAV0378

Inscribed around the centre of the compass card: 'Made by Jonathan Eade near King Edward Stairs Wapping'

Compass design changed very little between the early 16th century and the middle of the 18th century. Like the compass found on the *Mary Rose*, this example has a paper card with a soft magnetized iron needle fixed underneath, and the bowl is mounted in brass gimbals in a wooden box, to help it remain level despite the motion of the ship. It is not known for certain when the compass was invented, but it was definitely in use in European waters by the end of the 12th century. It was a very great advance in navigation, enabling mariners to know the direction in which they were sailing even in cloudy weather. (GC)

LITERATURE: Stimson, 'The Navigation Instruments'; Aczel, *The Riddle of the Compass*; Hitchins and May, *From Lodestone to Gyro-compass*

247 Lodestone

17th century

National Maritime Museum, Greenwich, London, NAV0709

The lodestone is a piece of magnetite that is naturally magnetic. This example has been mounted in a silver case. It was used to magnetize compass needles. Until the mid-18th century, when improved compasses were developed, compass needles lost their magnetism quickly and so lodestones were carried on board ship to re-magnetize them. This was done by stroking a lodestone along the needle's length. There is documentary evidence of lodestones being carried on board ships from the early 15th century onwards. (GC)

LITERATURE: Waters, *The Art of Navigation in Elizabethan and Early Stuart Times*; Hitchins and May, *From Lodestone to Gyro-compass*

248 Sounding Lead and Reel

National Maritime Museum, Greenwich, London, NAV1898

The sounding lead is one of the earliest known navigational aids. It was already in use by Roman times and the basic design has changed little since then. It was particularly important in coastal navigation or when entering a port. The lead weight was lowered over the side of the ship on a rope until it touched the seabed, then hauled up and the length of rope measured to determine the depth of water under the keel. It was vital to check the depth repeatedly in shallow water to prevent the ship running aground. To make it easier to measure the rope, by the 16th century fabric or leather markers were attached at one or two fathom intervals, a fathom being six feet or 1.83 metres. Fragments of rope found on the *Mary Rose* show traces of these markers. (GC)

LITERATURE: Waters, *The Art of Navigation in Elizabethan and Early Stuart Times*; Stimson, 'The Navigation Instruments'

249 Mariner's Astrolabe

1964 copy of a late 16th-century original

National Maritime Museum, Greenwich, London, NAV0023

The mariner's astrolabe was an important instrument for long voyages out of sight of land because it enabled the navigator to determine his latitude. In the northern hemisphere he could sight the Pole star directly through the pinholes on the ends of the rule or alidade and measure the altitude of the star above the horizon on the degree scale around the outer edge of the instrument. This corresponded to degrees of latitude. A reading could also be taken of the altitude of the sun, by allowing a beam of sunlight to pass through the upper pinhole on to the lower one. Tables were needed to convert this measurement into latitude. This is an electrotype copy of a 16th-century mariner's astrolabe (NAV0022) in the collections of the National Maritime Museum, Greenwich. (GC)

LITERATURE: Stimson, *The Mariner's Astrolabe*; Waters, *The Art of Navigation in Elizabethan and Early Stuart Times*

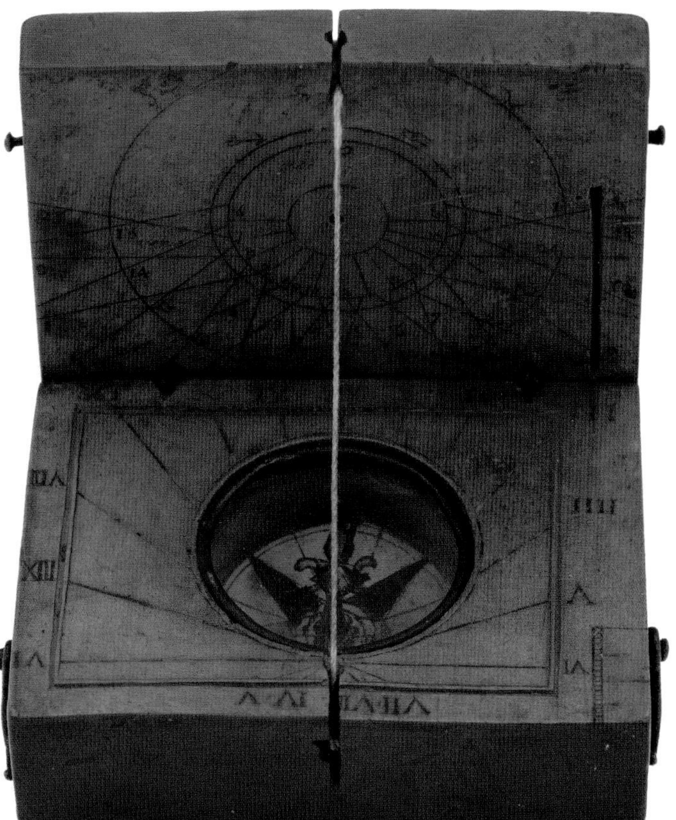

250 Diptych Dial

Maker unknown, but probably Italian, late 16th century

National Maritime Museum, Greenwich, London, AST0478

Travellers often carried small pocket dials for finding local time from the sun. The cheapest versions were made of wood and a number of small wooden sundials were found on the *Mary Rose*. This type, made of two wooden leaves that fold together when not in use, is known as a diptych dial. The small magnetic compass is used to orient the dial north–south and the string joining the two leaves throws a shadow on to the hour scale. This dial was probably made in Italy, because it has additional scales for Italian hours, which were variable hours, the day and night each being divided into twelve equal parts, so that the length of the hour varied throughout the year and daylight hours differed from night-time hours on the same day, except at the equinoxes. (GC)

LITERATURE: Higton, *Sundials at Greenwich*; Higton, *Sundials*; Callendar, *The Caird Collection of Maritime Antiquities*, vol.1

251 Horary Quadrant

Maker unknown, probably French, late 16th century

National Maritime Museum, Greenwich, London, NAV1038

This is a horary quadrant primarily used to tell the time. It is made of brass and the sliding hour-line scale enables the instrument to be set for any day of the year. A sunbeam was lined up through the pinholes on the top edge and the time read from the scale where the weighted string crossed the hour scale. The engraved images are based on a hunting theme and the style suggests it was made in France. The dates on the zodiac scale indicate that the quadrant was made after 1582 and the introduction of the Gregorian calendar, but the design is typical of those made earlier. (GC)

LITERATURE: Higton, *Sundials at Greenwich*; L'E Turner, *Scientific Instruments, 1500–1900*

252 Henry VIII's Astrolabe

Gilt-brass astrolabe, made by Sébastian Le Seney (*c*.1537–47)

British Museum, London, Department of Prehistory and Europe, 1878,1101.113

As a young boy Henry had shown 'remarkable docility' for mathematics and he retained a life-long fascination for the subject as well as science and astronomy, which he enjoyed discussing late into the night with Thomas More. Henry owned a multitude of scientific instruments but few have survived. This astrolabe, which could be used for timekeeping at day and night, navigation at sea, casting horoscopes and surveying, was, without a doubt, made for the King as it carries his initials 'H R' which were engraved on either side of his crowned coat of arms (incorrectly executed in the first quarter). The astrolabe was made for Henry by Sébastian Le Seney, who came from Normandy to England in 1537 and was employed by Henry, principally as a clockmaker. Henry's astrolabe is Le Seney's only known surviving instrument. (AC)

LITERATURE: Gunther, *The Astrolabes of the World*

THE NAVY AND THE MARY ROSE

Henry VIII is often described as the founder of the Royal Navy – and justifiably so, as he expanded the number of its ships and provided an infrastructure for its administration. Warships were for Henry magnificent symbols of royal power, and he commissioned the construction of 46 heavy warships, all built high for dramatic effect and lavishly decorated. When it was launched in 1514, the Henry Grâce à Dieu (called 'Great Harry') was, at over 1,000 tons, the largest warship in the world.

The firepower of English ships was also enhanced during his reign. Warships carried much heavier cannon on board, about 20 heavy and 60 light ones. Gunports (doors that could be opened to run out cannons and closed to allow faster sailing) were placed in the waists of ships (instead of on decks) and allowed the cannons to fire a 'broadside' (all the guns along one side of the ship firing at once). A foundry that experimented with new types and calibres of guns was established at Houndsditch in 1511.

Henry used the navy not only to display his power but also, more practically, to suppress piracy, attack French ports and support his military campaign in France. To build and maintain the ships, new dockyards were built at Deptford, Woolwich and Erith on the Thames, and the harbour at Portsmouth was improved. To meet the navy's needs during the last French war, Henry established a board of professional administrators. This body eventually evolved into the Navy Board that had responsibility for the management of ships, yards and sailors until its abolition in 1832.

253 The Commander of the Mary Rose, Sir George Carew

Hans Holbein the Younger

The Royal Collection © 2009 Her Majesty Queen Elizabeth II, RL 12197

On 19 July 1545, when the French were sailing up the Solent, Henry VIII was at Portsmouth discussing naval strategy with the Lord High Admiral Viscount Lisle John Dudley (1504–53) and Sir George Carew (c.1504–45). After the meeting, the King appointed Carew his Vice-Admiral and personally placed the insignia of his promotion (a gold whistle on a chain) around his neck. Carew took as his flagship the Mary Rose, a royal carrack launched in 1511 that in 1536 had been uprated from 500 to 700 tons and provided with a complete gun-deck. However, as the ship was about to bring her second broadside to bear on the French galleys, her sails caught a sudden breeze and the ship, which was overladen with men and cannon, heeled over. The sea then rushed in through the open gunports. The Mary Rose sank with great speed and Carew drowned, along with nearly all his 500-strong crew. (SD)

LITERATURE: Rodger, *The Safeguard of the Sea*; Starkey (ed.), *Henry VIII: A European Court in England*; Carew, Sir George, *Oxford DNB*

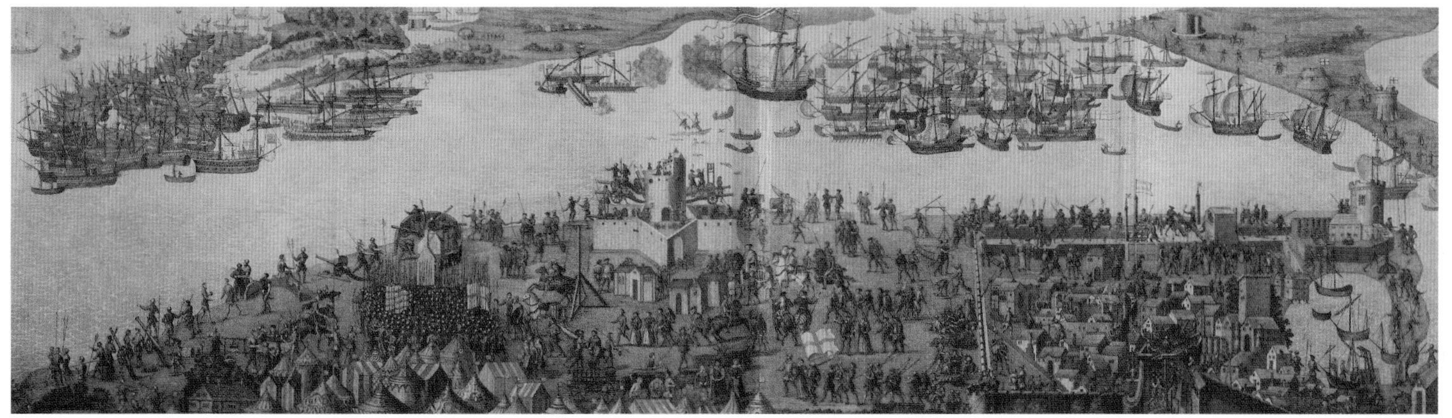

254 Foiling a French Invasion of England

The Encampment of the English Forces near Portsmouth Together With a View of the English and French Fleets at the Commencement of the Action Between Them on the XIX of July MDXLV, 1778

James Basire after Charles Sherwin

British Library, 3 Tab. 24.(2)

In July 1545 the French attempted to invade England from Portsmouth. In an episode that represented as serious a threat as the Spanish Armada of 1588, a fleet of 225 ships carrying about 30,000 men sailed up the Solent, landing troops on the Isle of Wight and elsewhere. Henry VIII was present in Portsmouth when good timing, as well as a sudden change in the weather, enabled the English ships to bar the French from the gates of Portsmouth. Earlier on there had been a squall that had sunk the King's flagship, the Mary Rose, on which Henry had just been dining. This engraving, copied from a contemporary painting in the dining room at Cowdray House, captures the events with a fair degree of topographical accuracy and shows Henry on horseback about to enter Southsea Castle. The mast of the Mary Rose can be seen sinking below the waves in the middle distance. (PB)

LITERATURE: Ayloffe, 'An Account of Some Ancient English Historical Paintings at Cowdray, Sussex'; Rule, *The Mary Rose*; Lloyd and Thurley, *Henry VIII*

255 The Navy

(see between pages 240–41)

Anthony Anthony

The Anthony Roll

British Library, Additional MS 22047

This roll was one of three presented to Henry VIII in 1546 by Anthony Anthony, an official of the ordnance. The illuminated manuscripts provide a visual record of all the ships in Henry's navy at the end of his life, interspersed with a list of their seamen and armaments. This roll shows the galleasses – large, fast, heavily armed three-masted galleys. The other two rolls, which depict the warships, pinnaces and row barges, were bound in one volume after Charles II gave them to Samuel Pepys. The Pepys volume is deposited in the Pepys Library in Magdalene College, Cambridge. (SD)

LITERATURE: Knighton and Loades (eds), *The Anthony Roll of Henry VIII's Navy*

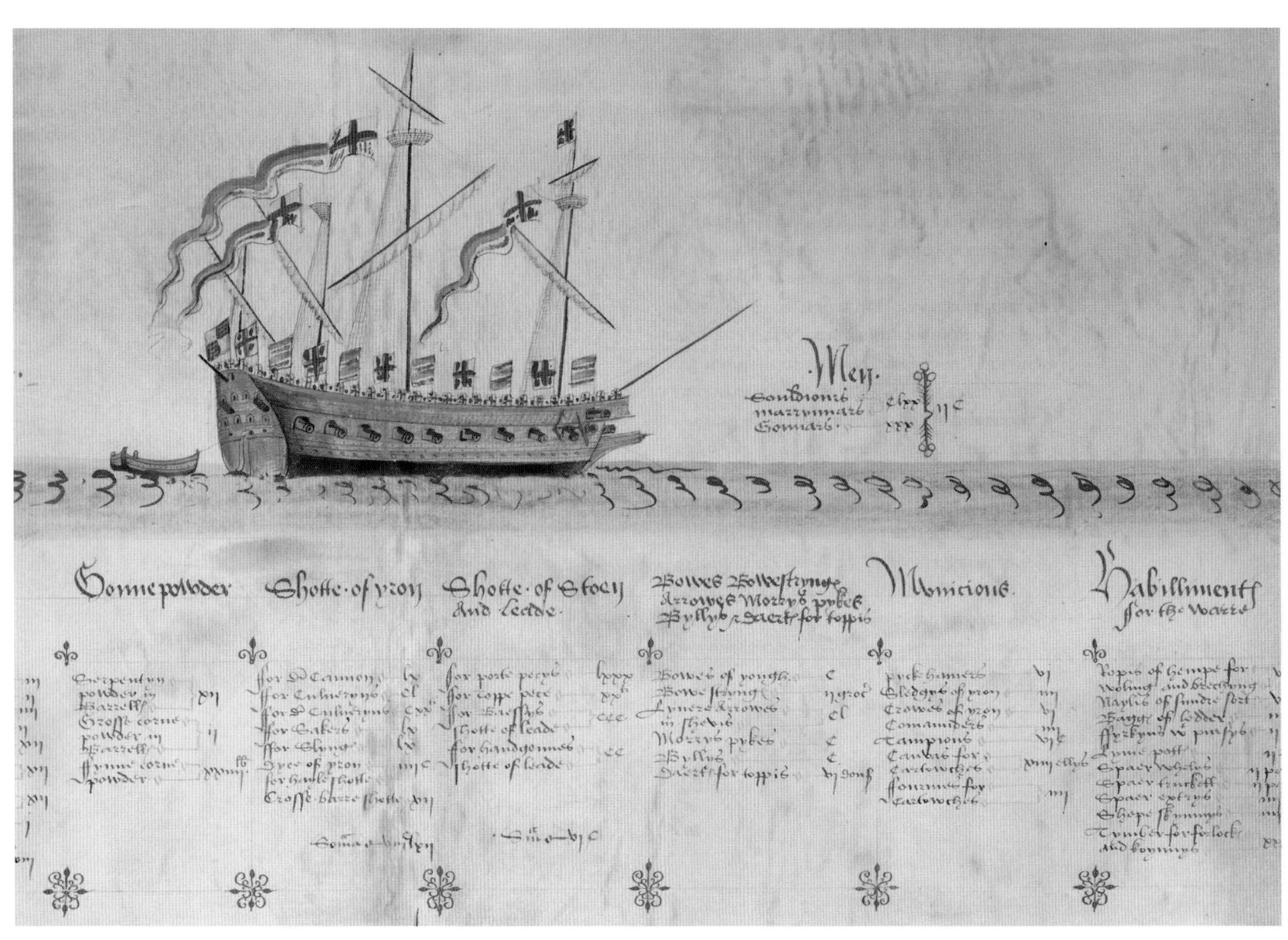

256 Equipping the Mary Rose

Cast iron hailshot piece

Gun-shield

Mary Rose Trust, Portsmouth

These two objects, recovered from the Mary Rose, bear witness to Henry's interest in new innovations and the art of warfare. The hailshot piece is a cast iron muzzle loading small gun, designed to be used by one individual in an anti-personnel role. The Anthony Roll records that the Mary Rose carried twenty such pieces and this is one of four examples to have been recovered from the wreck site. Significantly, they are the earliest securely dated examples of cast iron being used to make guns and therefore provide evidence of the effort made in Henry's reign to find a cheap and convenient alternative to the continental copper used in the production of bronze guns. By the end of the century guns of over three tonnes were being cast in iron. Eight gun-shields have also been found on the wreck of the Mary Rose, including this example with a beautifully decorated copper boss attached. The shielding device would have held a centrally mounted breech-loading matchlock gun and was pierced for sighting. Like the hailshot piece it is illustrative of Henry's interest in new inventions. Thought to be Italian in origin, the earliest reference to gun-shields is found in a letter written to Henry in 1544 by a painter of Ravenna named Giovanbattista, who offered to make for him 'round shields with arm pieces with guns inside them that fire upon the enemy and pierce any armour'. (AC)

LITERATURE: Marsden, *Sealed by Time*; Childs, *The Warship Mary Rose*

NATIONHOOD

The establishment of the Church of England and the emergence of the English Navy under Henry VIII were important contributions to the development of England's nationhood. A sense of an English national identity was also fostered during Henry's reign through an extended use of the vernacular in private devotions, literature and learning. Although Classical (especially Latin) writers dominated the mindset of humanists, many scholars now wrote in English and translated Latin works into the vernacular. Interest in the writings of Geoffrey Chaucer – England's national poet – was stimulated and sustained when the first collected edition of Chaucer's works was printed in 1532.

257 Henry VIII and the Barber-Surgeons

Hans Holbein the Younger and workshop, 1541?

The Worshipful Company of Barbers, London

Inscribed: 'To Henry the eighth the best and greatest King of England ... Defender of the Faith, and next of Christ, supreme Head of the Church of England and Ireland'

Henry VIII embodies power, authority and magnificence in this group painting, while the inscription expresses his place in history as the greatest of English Kings and the Supreme Head of the Church of England and Ireland. Closer to home, the words also compare Henry's reform of the Church to 'the office of a good physician' and hail the King's own learned interest in medicine.

Henry dominates the picture that shows him presenting the Charter of the Incorporation of the Company of Barber-Surgeons to Thomas Vickery, the Master of the Company. The King towers over the other figures in the group: the twenty barbers and surgeons on his left and the royal physicians Dr Butts and Dr Chambers (who were not members of the Company) on his right. Henry's codpiece signified his potency; his crown and sword his majesty. The painting was probably commissioned to mark the occasion of the joining together of the Barbers and the Surgeons Company that was enacted by statute in 1540. (SD)

LITERATURE: Foister, *Holbein in England*

258 Sir Thomas Elyot

Hans Holbein the Younger

Sir Thomas Elyot (*c*.1490–1546) was a humanist scholar, best known as the author of *A Boke Called the Governour*, published in 1531, and his Latin–English *Dictionary*. The former was immensely influential, going into eight editions over the course of the century. Its avowed aim was to incorporate Renaissance learning within the educational programme of Englishmen who were destined to be members of the governing classes. Addressed to 'my natural country' and written 'in our vulgar tongue', Elyot's book prescribes the Classical works that English gentlemen should read in the original Greek and Latin. He also sets out the virtues that governors should display, drawing his illustrations from ancient history. For Elyot, there was no incompatibility between a Classical education and an English identity. This drawing by Holbein was a study for a painted portrait that has not survived. Elyot was probably introduced to Holbein by Sir Thomas More, who, unlike Elyot, and atypically, preferred to write for an international readership in Latin. (SD)

LITERATURE: Elyot, Sir Thomas, *Oxford DNB*; Lehmberg, *Sir Thomas Elyot, Tudor Humanist*; Starkey, 'England'

259 Sir Thomas Elyot's Latin–English *Dictionary*

Printed by Thomas Berthelet, 1538

British Library, C.28.m.2, Ff^{v}–Ff ii

Sir Thomas Elyot's *Dictionary* is the first full-scale Latin-English lexicon to find its way into print. This one was Thomas Cromwell's personal copy and it contains the letter Elyot wrote to accompany its presentation to his patron, reminding him of the duty to protect one's friends in dangerous times. The *Dictionary* itself, which would be expanded and reissued a few years later, was dedicated to the King and in the preface Elyot explained that when he examined the Royal Library, made available to him through Henry's generosity, he found so much new material that he had to stop the presses at the letter M and revise extensively. No doubt Elyot described an actual event – and the Royal Library was an impressive one – but the account also serves to remind readers of the learning and wisdom of their monarch. Like the Great Bible, then, the *Dictionary* can be read as a piece of propaganda for the regime as well as a work of learning. (JC)

LITERATURE: Foley, 'Coming to Terms'

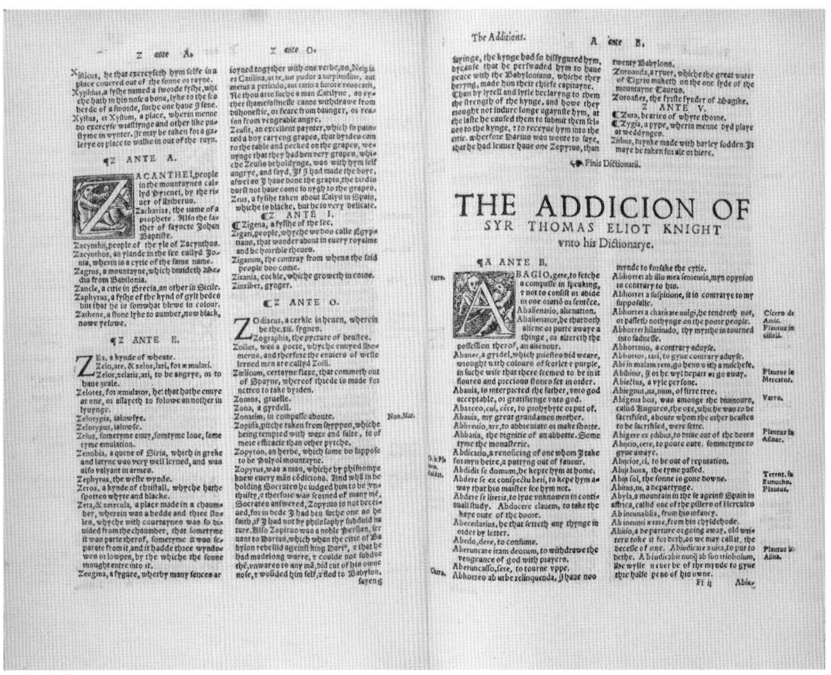
The Addicions.

THE ADDICION OF
SYR THOMAS ELIOT KNIGHT
vnto his Dictionarye.

260 Sir Thomas Elyot and Thomas Cromwell

Letter from Sir Thomas Elyot to Thomas Cromwell, *c.*1538

British Library, Cotton MS Cleopatra E iv, fol.260

This letter to Cromwell is a rare survival from Sir Thomas Elyot's correspondence and was probably written soon after Elyot completed his Latin–English *Dictionary*. He writes, primarily, to thank Cromwell for his favourable report of him to the King and acknowledges that 'the Kinges moste gentill communicacions' with him result from Cromwell's recommendations. Desiring Cromwell to continue 'in augmenting' the King's 'good estimacion of me', Elyot reminds him of his full support for religious reform, declaring 'I wold godd that the king and you mowght see the moste secrete thowghtes of my hart. Surely ye shold than percyve that … I have in as moche detestacion as any man lyving all vayne supersticions, superfluouse ceremonyes, slanderouse iuglynges, counterfaite mirakles, arrogant usurpaciones of men called spirituall and masking religious and all other abusions of Christes holy doctrine and lawes'. Elyot concludes by declaring that he rejoices at the King's 'godly proceding to the due reformacion of the sayde enormyties'. (AC)

LITERATURE: Elyot, Sir Thomas, *Oxford DNB*

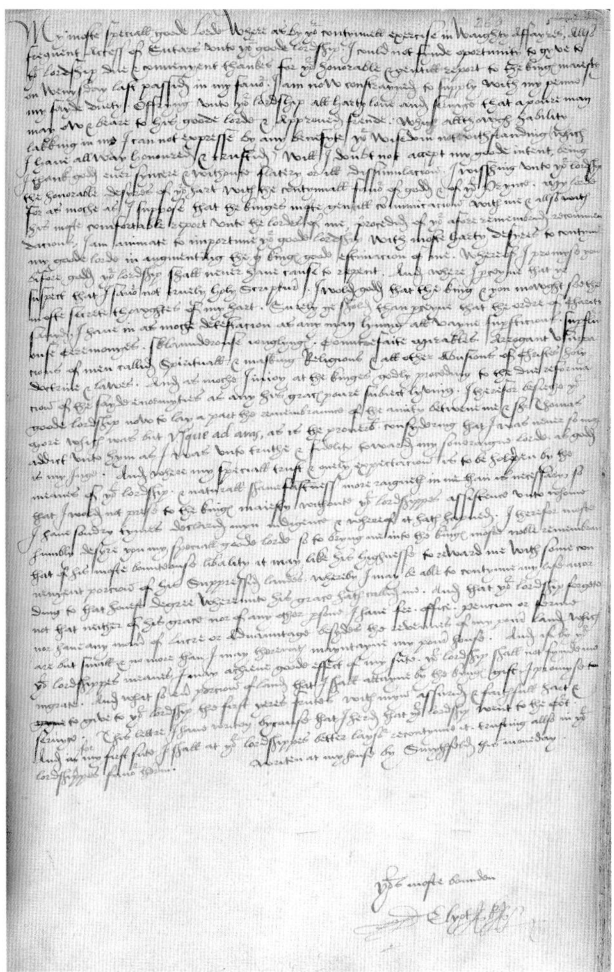

261 Sir Thomas Elyot, *The Image of Governance*, 1541

Printed by Thomas Berthelet

British Library, C.21.b.7, binding

Beautifully bound for the King and stamped with the initials 'HR', this presentation copy of Sir Thomas Elyot's *The Image of Governance* must have held a place of honour in the Royal Library. Ostensibly a translation of a Greek manuscript by Eucolpius (or Encolpius), secretary to the Roman Emperor Alexander Severus, it is in fact an adaptation of the *Lives of the Emperor* attributed to Aurelius Lampridius. Written after the fall of Elyot's quondam patron Thomas Cromwell, *The Image of Governance* is a bitter and grimly comic attack on the consequences of tyranny, one in which cruelty is recommended and abuse of power presented as good kingship. No longer believing that eloquence could reform the King, Elyot recommends, by means of historical examples, a powerful council with coercive force to overrule the monarch. In the preface addressed 'to all the nobilitie of this flouryshynge royalme of Englande', he also points out that the making of books has not brought him profit and, anticipating many a modern author, observes that 'I sette the trees, but the printer eateth the fruites'. (JC)

LITERATURE: Walker, *Writing Under Tyranny*

262 William Thynne, *The Works of Geoffrey Chaucer*, 1532

Clare College, Cambridge, K.1.7

This is the first full (indeed rather too full since it contains some spurious works) printed edition of Chaucer. It was edited by William Thynne, clerk of the Kitchen, but the preface was written by Sir Brian Tuke, as evident from the inscription in this copy: 'This preface I Sir Brian Tuke knight wrote at the request of Mr Clerk of the Kitchen, then being tarrying for the tide at Greenwich.' The preface is Tuke's only known publication. However, it shows his familiarity with humanist theories of language and literature. It is also strongly nationalistic, with its claim for English as a great language, and its praise for Chaucer as its supreme poet. Henry VIII, it also declares, was 'next God and his Apostles', Defender of its Faith. Poetry is thus put at the service of the royal supremacy, first proclaimed that same year.

In the preface to *Confessio Amantis* by Chaucer's contemporary, John Gower, printed the same year, the editor Thomas Berthelet (King's printer), likewise argued for the usage of 'our most allowed old authors' as a model for writing good, clear English. (DS and SD)

LITERATURE: Thynne, William, *Oxford DNB*

The Preface

¶ To the kynges hyghnesse/ my most gratious soueraygne lorde Hēry the eight/ by the grace of god kyng of Englande and of Fraunce/defensor of the fayth/ and lorde of Irlande. &c.

AMonges all other excellencyes/ most gratious soueraygn lord/ wherwt almightye god hath endowed mākynde/ aboue ye resydue of erthly creatures/ as an outwarde declaration of reason or resonablenesse/ wherin consysteth the symylitude of man vnto aungels/ and the differēce betwene the same & brute beestes/ I verayly suppose/ that speche or langage is nat to be reputed amonges the smallest or inferiours. For therby is exprssed the conceite of one to another in open and playne sentence/ whiche in the resydue of lyuely creatures/lacketh and is nat shewed amonges them/but by certayn couert and derke signes/ and that in fewe thyngz hauyng course and operation onely of nature. This speche or langage/ after the confusyon of tonges/ sente by goddes punysshment for pride and arrogance of people/ hath ben by a certayne instyncte & dysposytion naturall diuysed and inuented in sundry partes of the worlde/ as felowshippes or companyenges of folkes one with another chaunced/ moche to the outwarde expressyng of the thyng in worde or soūde/ accordyng to that wherof it had meanyng or sygnification. But in processe of tyme/ by dilygence or polycy of people/ after dyuers fourmes/figures/and impressyons in metall/ barkes of trees/ and other mater vsed for memorie and knowlege of thyngz thay present or passed/sondry letters or carectes were first amōges the Phenices diuysed and founde/ with suche knyttynges and ioynynges of one to another by a marueylous subtylyte and crafte/ as counterueyled was and is equiualent to the same langages. So as the conceite of mānes mynde/ whiche at ye begynnyng was vsed to be declared by mouthe onely/ came to such poynt/ that it was as sensibly and viuely expressed in wrytynge. Hervpon ensewed a great occasion & corage vnto them that shulde write/ to compone and adorne the rudenesse and barbariete of speche/and to forme it to an eloquent and ordynate perfectyon/ wherunto many and many great poetz and oratours haue highly employed their studies and corages/ leauyng therby notable renoume of them selues/and exanple perpetuell to their posterite. Amonges other/ the Grekes in all kyndes of sciēces/ semed so to preuayle and so to ornate their tonge/as yet by other of right noble langages can nat be perfitely ymitated or folowed. The Latyns by example of the grekes/ haue gotten or wonne to thē no small glorie/ in the fourmynge/ order/ and vtterynge of that tonge. Out of the whiche two/ if it be well serched/ that is to saye Greke and Latyn (though by corruptyon of speche it shulde seme moche otherwyse) haue ben deryued the resydue of the langages that be written with the letters or carectes of either of them bothe: But of all speches/ those whiche most approche to the latinite/ be the Italyan and Spaynysshe tonges/ of whom the one by corruption of the Gothes and Longobardes had her begynnynge/ as latyn spoken by straungers of a barbare vnderstādyng/ The other beyng also latyn was by Vandales/Gothes/ Moores/ Sarracenes/and other so many tymes blemysshed/ as marueyle it is to se now vnto what pfection these two formed out of the latyn and barbare speches be reduced. Next vnto them/ in symilytude to the latyn is the Frenche tonge/ whiche by dilygence of people of the same/ is in fewe yeres passed so amended/ as well in pronūciation as in wrytynge/ that an Englysshman by a small tyme exercised in that tōge hath nat lacked groūde to make a grāmer or rule ordinary therof. Though of trouth

A.ii. (whiche

HONY · SOYT · QVI · MAL · Y · PESE
1548

DEATH, WILL AND SUCCESSION (1546–47)

Ralph Houlbrooke

The 1544 engraving by Cornelis Matsys portrays Henry VIII as a grossly overweight king. He had long suffered from chronic ulcers on both his legs, resulting either from varicose veins or osteomyelitis caused by injuries. He had had a severe, temporarily life-threatening seizure in May 1538. During the last decade of his life he suffered several bouts of fever, probably caused by his ulcers. He was ill in September and October 1546. He fell ill again at Oatlands, Surrey, on 10 December, and returned on the 23rd of the same month to Whitehall, where he remained until his death on 28 January 1547. Neither Queen Katherine nor his children were with him.

Early in December 1546, disturbing news had reached the King concerning Henry Howard, Earl of Surrey, and his father Thomas, Duke of Norfolk, the senior nobleman of the realm. After they had been accused of high treason, both were imprisoned in the Tower on 12 December. After his arrival in Whitehall, Henry amended a draft of articles against them on 24 December. The first two concerned the Howards' wrongful inclusion of royal arms in their own heraldic arms. Other articles referred to Surrey's anticipation of Henry's death. He was supposed to have asked, 'If the King die, who should have the rule of the Prince but my father or I?'

The spectre of political instability raised by Surrey's words and actions forced the ailing Henry to confront the likelihood of his own early death and try to secure a smooth succession for his son Edward. Clearly, the Howards would no longer have any place in his plans. Surrey was tried on 13 January 1547 and executed six days later. Norfolk probably escaped execution only because of Henry's own death.

On 26 December 1546 Henry summoned a small group of confidants. They included: Edward Seymour, Earl of Hertford, Prince Edward's uncle; John Dudley, Viscount Lisle; Sir William Paget, Henry's Principal Secretary; and Sir Anthony Denny, chief gentleman of his Privy Chamber. The King told Denny to produce his will, and, after hearing it read, ordered Paget to make certain

◀ Cat. no. 267

changes. Among them was the exclusion of Stephen Gardiner, Bishop of Winchester, one of Henry's ablest servants, from the list of executors of his will. Those present allegedly asked Henry to restore Gardiner, but he steadfastly refused, saying that Gardiner was of such a troublesome nature that his fellow executors would be unable to control him if he were included. On 30 December, the fair copy of Henry's amended will was signed with the dry stamp of the King's signature, which he was presumably now too weak to write himself, sealed with the signet and witnessed. Henry handed it to Seymour.

Henry was seriously ill early in January 1547. He received foreign ambassadors for the last time on 16 January. His condition deteriorated soon afterwards. In the evening of 27 January Sir Anthony Denny warned him to prepare for death. After a short sleep, Henry sent for Thomas Cranmer, Archbishop of Canterbury. By the time Cranmer arrived from Croydon, Henry was speechless. The Archbishop told Henry to give him a token of his trust in God, and Henry gripped Cranmer's hand hard. He died before two o'clock in the morning of 28 January 1547.

The Lord Chancellor announced the news in Parliament three days later. Henry's funeral procession set out from London on 14 February and arrived at Windsor the following day. The funeral Mass, celebrated by Stephen Gardiner, and the King's burial alongside Jane Seymour in St George's Chapel took place on 16 February. The nine-year-old King Edward's record of his father's death in his journal and the conventional letters of condolence he wrote to his two sisters tell us nothing of his personal feelings.

Henry stipulated in his will that his sixteen executors should govern the realm, acting as Privy Councillors. However, on 31 January 1547 Edward Seymour's fellow executors chose him to be Protector of King Edward's realms and Governor of the King's Person. In March, Seymour, by then Duke of Somerset, had his powers further enlarged.

The new government soon began England's Protestant Reformation. Somerset and his colleagues abandoned Henry's provisions for government during Edward's minority and Henry's own religious policy, just as they ignored Henry's own requirement that Mass should be celebrated daily at his tomb. Yet Henry himself had prepared the way for Somerset's assumption of power by striking down his strongest potential opponents, Gardiner and the Howards, by entrusting his will to Somerset and by further strengthening Somerset and his associates after the downfall of the Howards by means of oral bequests that were not included in his will but ostensibly authorized therein by a so-called 'unfulfilled gifts clause'. Did Henry deliberately take all these steps of his own volition? Or did courtiers manipulate him, taking advantage of his weakened state? Had he really intended to abandon the Catholic Mass himself if he had lived? Some Protestants later claimed that he had. Historians have disagreed about all these points.

All acknowledge, however, that Henry VIII hugely enhanced the power, authority and splendour of the English monarchy. His last war with France nevertheless seriously depleted the Crown's resources and left Henry in debt. Boulogne was the war's only gain. A weakened England would have to restore it to France in 1550. The enormous accumulated wealth of precious objects recorded in Henry's inventories after his death was not readily convertible into funds to spend on the military, and without adequate ongoing revenue his successors could not hope to use his huge arsenal or enlarged navy to wage continuing wars against vastly stronger continental monarchies.

The succession of Henry's devoutly Catholic daughter Mary on Edward's early death in 1553 and her restoration of papal supremacy underlined the vulnerability of the Edwardian and Henrician religious changes. After Henry's second daughter Elizabeth came to the throne in November 1558 and broke with Rome once more in 1559, it was clear that the famous successes of her long reign certainly owed much to her father's achievements in government, but set England on a very different course from the one he had followed.

HENRY VIII'S LAST VICTIM

Henry VIII's concerns about the succession and his determination to stamp out dangerous opposition help explain the many executions that took place during the later years of his reign. His last victim was Henry Howard, Earl of Surrey. On 12 December 1546, Surrey was taken on foot through the streets of London to the Tower, where he was soon joined by his father the Duke of Norfolk. Both men were charged with high treason for appropriating royal insignia. In Surrey's case, his use of the coat of arms of King Edward the Confessor was presented in court as evidence of his designs on the throne. Norfolk confessed his guilt on 12 January 1547; Surrey pleaded not guilty at his trial the next day but was convicted and then beheaded on Tower Hill on 19 January. Norfolk likewise received no mercy from the King. On the last day of his life, Henry used his dry stamp to sign a Bill of Attainder against him. Saved from the scaffold by Henry's own death, Norfolk spent the whole of Edward VI's reign in the Tower and was only released when Mary I took the throne.

263 Henry Howard, Earl of Surrey

Unknown Anglo-Netherlandish school, later 16th century, possibly after a lost portrait by William Scrots (fl.1537–53)

National Portrait Gallery, London, NPG 4952

The eldest son of Thomas Howard, third Duke of Norfolk (1473–1554), Henry Howard, Earl of Surrey (1516/17–47) was part of a noble family who boasted descent from Edward I and Edward III. An accomplished scholar and poet, he saw his verse celebrated in his lifetime, along with that of Thomas Wyatt. He commanded forces in France successfully in 1545, but suffered an ignominious defeat in January the following year and feared the loss of royal favour. His attempts to regain power at court alienated his remaining followers, including Richard Southwell, who presented evidence of Surrey's treasonable words to the Council. Surrey sat for Hans Holbein from 1532 to 1535 and for William Scrots in 1546 when a 'great table' or full-length portrait was painted. This striking portrait was previously attributed to William Scrots, but recent analysis using dendrochronology revealed the panel had been felled after 1566, and therefore after this artist's death. As the handling is rather similar to the style of Scrots, this portrait may be after a lost portrait by the artist. (TC)

LITERATURE: Strong, *Tudor and Jacobean Portraits*; Hearn (ed.), *Dynasties*; Childs, *Henry VIII's Last Victim*

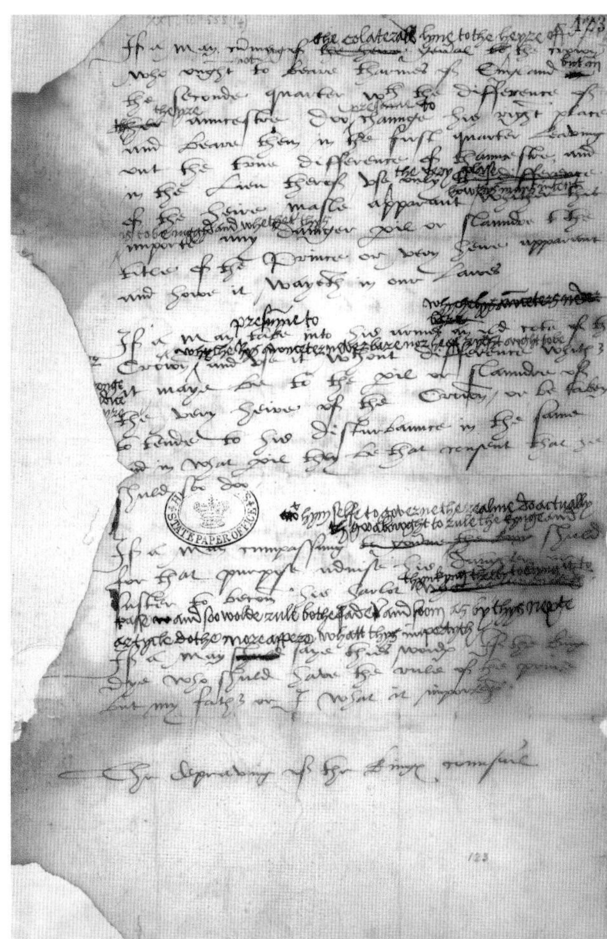

264 Charges against Norfolk and Surrey

Henry's annotations to charges drawn up against Henry Howard, Earl of Surrey, and Thomas Howard, Duke of Norfolk, December 1546

The National Archives, Kew, Richmond, Surrey, SP 1/227, fol.123

In December 1546, the Duke of Norfolk was arrested for high treason, along with his son, the Earl of Surrey. Following the collapse of the initial charges brought against them, both men were accused of incorporating royal heraldry into their own coats of arms. Norfolk was accused of using the three lions of England 'differenced' by a label of three points – the ancient arms of the heir to the throne. Surrey was accused of using the arms attributed to King Edward the Confessor, an act that was interpreted as a direct threat to the heirs of William the Conqueror, including Henry VIII. Although very ill, Henry personally annotated a sheet of charges written by the Lord Chancellor, Thomas Wriothesley (*c.*1505–50), against both men, deleting lines and adding his own amendments. (He did so with a shaky hand, sometimes losing the thread of the heraldic argument.) Henry was fearful that the Howards were seeking to make a bid for the throne or the regency on his death. (AA)

LITERATURE: Moore, 'The Heraldic Charge against the Earl of Surrey, 1546–47'; Childs, *Henry VIII's Last Victim*

265 A Near Escape

Letter from Thomas Howard, Duke of Norfolk, to the Privy Council, from the Tower of London

British Library, Cotton MS Titus B i, fol.101v

This is the last page of a letter written by Norfolk after he was arrested and taken to the Tower on 12 December 1546. Addressing the Council, he reminds them how he had been hated by those traitors, Buckingham, Wolsey and Cromwell, and protests his long service and loyalty to the Crown, 'Who tried out the fulshod of the Lord Darcy, Sir Robert Constable, Sir John Bulmer, Aske and many others … but only I? … I have showed myselff a most trew man to my sovereyne lord and … I have receyved more proffites of his hignes than ever I dyd a fore. Alas who can thynk that I … shuld now be fals? A poor man as I am yet, I am his son, his nere kynsman. For whose sake shall I be an untrew man to them?' Surrey was executed on 19 January and his father's date of execution was set for 28 January, but he was saved by the death of the King himself in the early hours of that morning. (AC)

LITERATURE: Childs, *Henry VIII's Last Victim*; Hutchinson, *The Last Days of Henry VIII*; Starkey, *Rivals in Power*

266 Tyranny

List of executions during the reign of Henry VIII

British Library, Cotton MS Titus B i, fols 136–7

The reign of Henry VIII witnessed more executions of English notables than that of any other monarch before or since. The three pages shown here list the names of some of those struck down by Henry, beginning in 1510 with his father's advisers Sir Richard Empson and Edmund Dudley and ending with Henry VIII's last victim, Henry Howard, Earl of Surrey, in January 1547. Henry's cruel and tyrannical disposition increased notably during the second half of his reign, with far more executions than in the first half. Those who suffered in this second period included: Elizabeth Barton, Nun of Kent, beheaded in 1534; Cardinal John Fisher and Sir Thomas More, both executed in 1535; Lord Darcy, Robert Aske and Sir Robert Constable, put to death in 1537 for their involvement in the Pilgrimage of Grace; Henry Courtenay, Marquis of Exeter (1498/9–1538), Henry Pole, Baron Montagu (1492–1539), and Lady Margaret, Countess of Salisbury (1473–1541), all members of the Pole family; and Richard Whiting, Abbot of Glastonbury, Sir Thomas Cromwell and Thomas Abel, all executed in 1539. (AC)

LITERATURE: Scarisbrick, *Henry VIII*; Ridley, *Henry VIII*

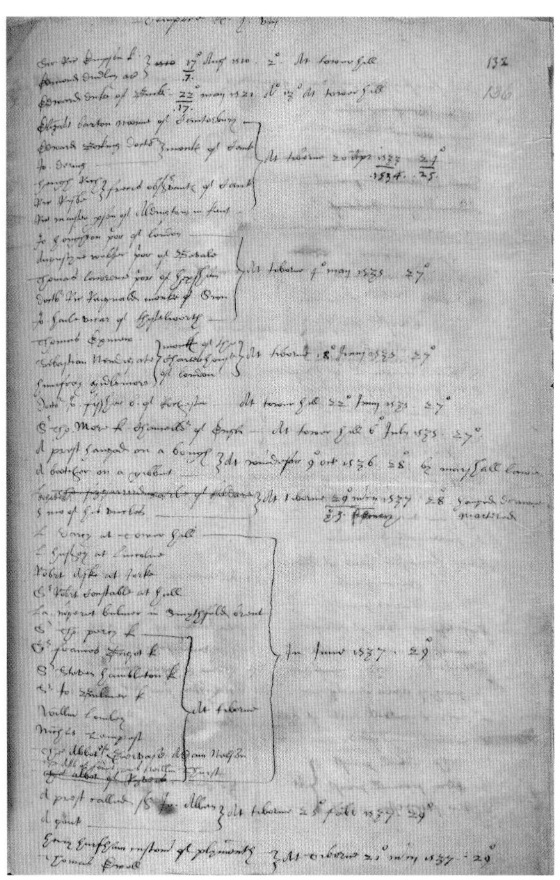

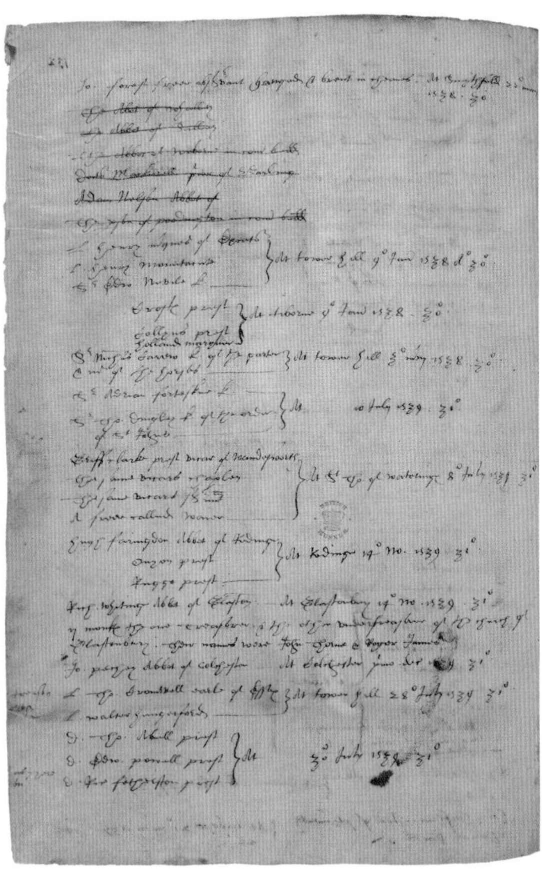

HENRY VIII IN OLD AGE

Henry VIII's health had been periodically poor after a serious fall from his horse during a joust in 1536. Over the next decade he suffered painful ulcers in his legs that brought on bouts of fever. His health was worsened by his obesity: his chest measurement reached 57 inches (144 cm) and his waist 54 (137 cm). During 1546 Henry became seriously incapacitated; not only was he in acute pain for much of the time but he also experienced difficulty in walking and had to be carried around his palaces in a chair. The cause of his ill health was not syphilis (he was never treated for this well-recognized disease) but is thought to have been thrombosis or varicose veins or osteomyelitis. Towards the end of the year it became obvious that the King had not much longer to live and would soon be succeeded by a minor.

267 The King in his Fifties

Cornelis Matsys (1510/11–56/57)

Engraving, 1544

British Museum, London, Department of Prints and Drawings, 0,9.35

Inscribed: *Henricus Dei Gra Rex Anglie* (Henry, by the Grace of God, King of England)

Matsys's highly stylized representation exaggerates the well-known features of Henry VIII: the broad face becomes virtually square; the mouth is disproportionately tiny; his heavy eyes look almost swollen shut here; and his arching, expressive eyebrows are drawn as pencil-thin curves. We are clearly confronting the King in old age – his hairline has receded and there is no indication of his formerly long, thin neck. It is not known whether this engraving was based on a sitting with the King, or if Matsys simply updated the well-known Holbein pose. His monogram and the date 1544 are visible in reverse in the upper right-hand corner of the print. Matsys was exiled from Antwerp in 1543, so it is conceivable that he sought employment from Henry by producing this portrait, or, more likely, that he produced the image hoping to find a market for his print. The only other contemporary printed images of Henry appear in the title pages of the Coverdale Bible and the Great Bible. (TS)

LITERATURE: Van der Stock, *Cornelis Matsys, 1510/11–1556–57*; Lloyd and Thurley, *Henry VIII: Images of a Tudor King*

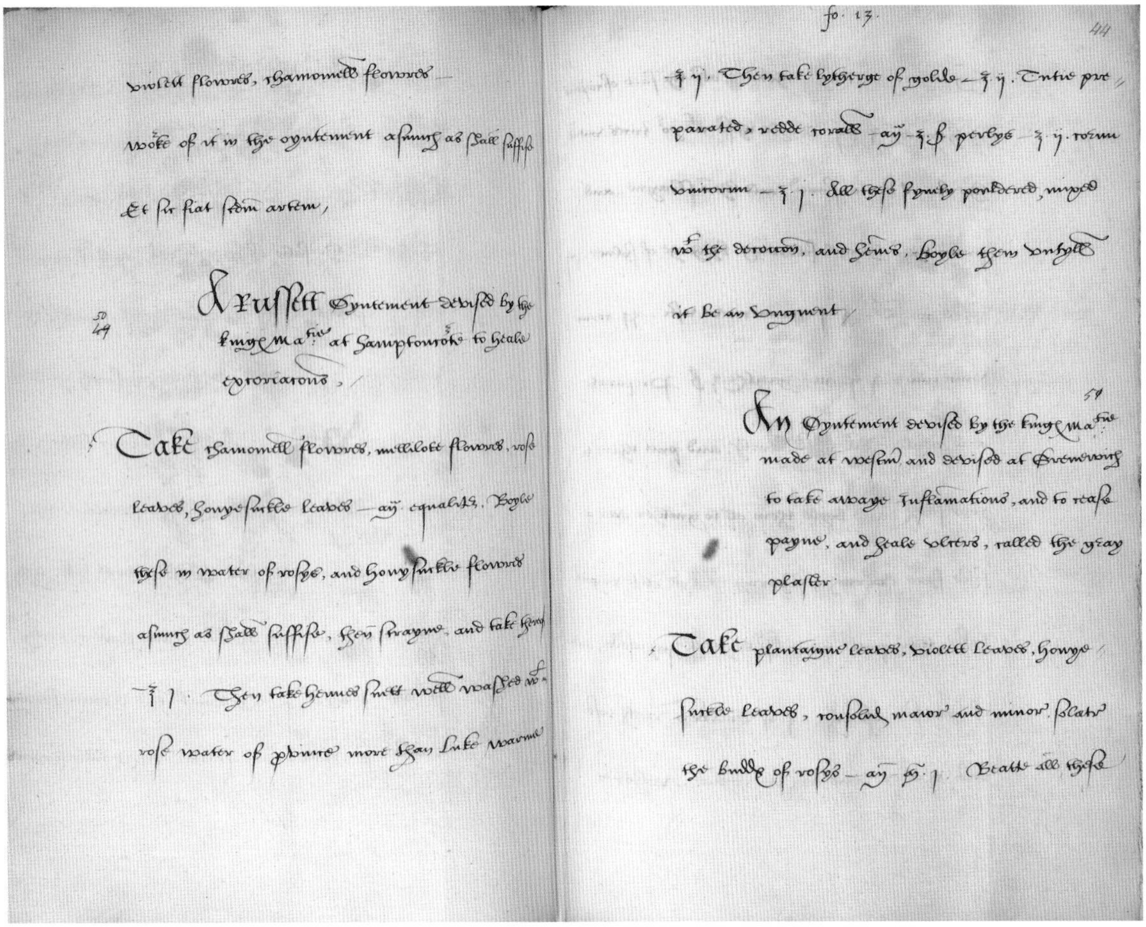

268 Royal Prescriptions ('Receipts')

British Library, Sloane MS 1047, fols 43v–44

Sir Brian Tuke (a secretary employed by the King and Cardinal Wolsey), in a letter to Wolsey, referred to Henry VIII's knowledge of medicine and stated that the King 'shewed me remedyes as any connyng physician in England coude do'. Henry's interest in medical matters increased during the last decade of his life when he was tormented by ill health and painful ulcers on what Chapuys described as the 'worst legs in the world'. This volume records many 'receipts' for plasters, spasmadraps (dipped plasters), ointments, waters, lotions, decoctions and poultices, some devised by Henry himself and others by his physicians.

Displayed here is a recipe for 'An oyntement devised by the kinges Majes]tie made at Westm[inster] and devised at Grenewich to take awaye inflamations and to cease payne, and heale ulcers, called the gray plaster'. The ingredients required for this particular ointment include plantaigne, violet, honeysuckle leaves, rosebuds, the suet of capons or hens, litharge of silver, red coral, margarite, a mucilage of quinseed and linseed, rose water and white wine. (AC)

LITERATURE: Hutchinson, *The Last Days of Henry VIII*; Scarisbrick, *Henry VIII*

HENRY VIII'S WILL AND DEATH

During the final weeks of his life the increasingly immobile King spent most of the time in his Privy Chamber. He even sent Queen Katherine away to Greenwich for Christmas while he remained at Whitehall. After the trial of Norfolk, Henry called for his will to be brought before him and revised. Probably he then excised the Duke's name from the list of executors and councillors who were to rule during his son's minority; he certainly removed the name of Bishop Gardiner of Winchester, as he was 'a wilful man not meet to be about his son'.

Henry died at Whitehall Palace in the early hours of Friday, 28 January 1547. His body was embalmed and lay in state in the presence chamber at Whitehall until 14 February, when it was moved in stages to Windsor. On 16 February, Henry was buried in the vault of St George's Chapel, next to the grave of Jane Seymour, the only one of his six wives to deliver a male heir.

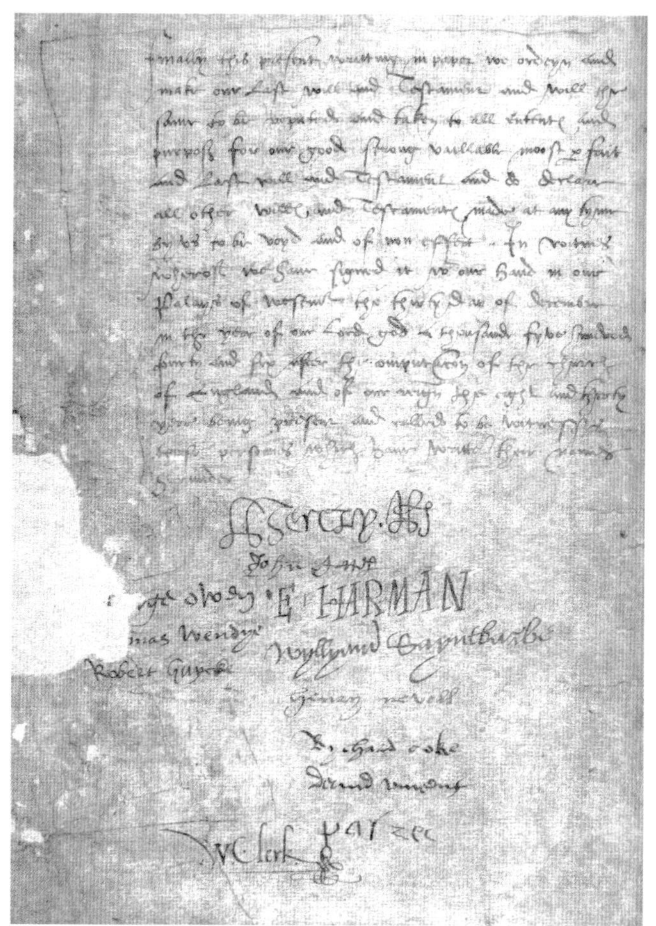

269 Henry VIII's Will

The National Archives, Kew, Richmond, Surrey, E23/4, fol.16v
Dry stamp register, SP 4/1 membrane 19

Henry's will, authenticated on 30 December 1546, entrusted the government of England to his executors, acting as a privy council, until his son Edward's eighteenth birthday, and laid down the succession to the Crown in case he had no further children and in case his existing children – Edward, Mary and Elizabeth – died without legitimate offspring of their own. Henry provided that the Crown should pass to the descendants of his younger sister Mary and did not mention those of his elder sister Margaret, including her granddaughter Mary, Queen of Scots. The will, however, failed to prevent the succession of Mary Stuart's son James VI to the English throne in 1603.

A long statement of personal faith takes up much of the first three pages of the will. In addition, the will provided for both the burial of Henry's body and Masses and charitable benefactions for the good of his soul. The last page, shown here, ends with a facsimile of Henry's signature made with the 'dry stamp'. This used a screw-press to form an impression in the paper which was filled in with ink by a skilled clerk. The application of the dry stamp was carefully recorded in a register. Below is the entry noting the stamping of Henry's will. (RH)

LITERATURE: Levine, *Tudor Dynastic Problems 1460–1571*; Starkey, *The Reign of Henry VIII*; Ives, 'Henry VIII's Will – A Forensic Conundrum'

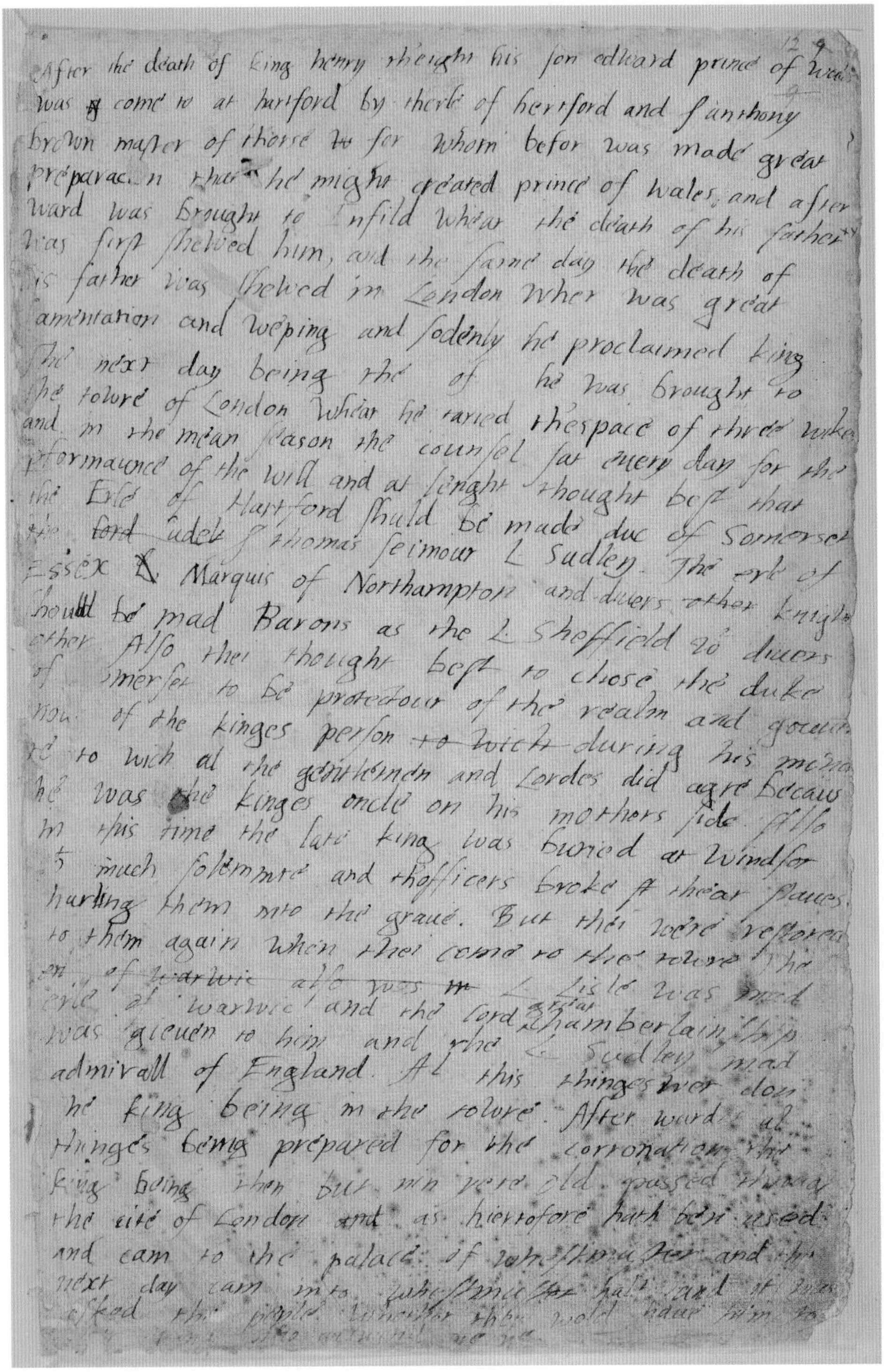

270 Edward VI's Diary

British Library, Cotton MS Nero C x, fol.12

Edward VI reveals here that he and his sister Elizabeth learnt of their father's death from his uncle Edward Seymour, Earl of Hertford, at Elizabeth's Enfield residence on 30 January 1547. Although he writes that it caused great grief in London, he reveals nothing of his personal feelings. He describes the Privy Council's choice of Edward Seymour as Protector and Governor of the King's Person and mentions how his father's officers broke their staffs of office and threw them into Henry's grave at his burial. Edward may have been prompted to write his 'diary' by one of his tutors. It begins with a description of his childhood until 1547. For the years 1547 to 1549 the 'diary' is a chronicle of past events that mostly refers to Edward in the third person. From March 1550 until November 1552, when it ends, it is more like a diary, with entries for individual days. (RH)

LITERATURE: Jordan (ed.), *The Chronicle and Political Papers of King Edward VI*; Jordan, *Edward VI*

271 Inventory of Henry VIII's Goods

British Library, Harley MS 1419 A, fol.206

Commissioners appointed in September 1547 took some eighteen months to compile an inventory of Henry's movable goods. The first part of the surviving inventory includes money, jewels, plate, artillery, munitions, ships, arms, armour, horses, masque garments, tents, liturgical vestments and books. The second covers other items in the principal royal residences and wardrobes or stores. The inventory includes hundreds of thousands of objects. The contents of Henry's palaces, particularly Whitehall, show that he was an insatiable collector of beautiful and costly things. They presented to his subjects and to foreign visitors a cumulative impression of dazzling royal magnificence. He possessed lavishly decorated furniture, numerous pictures, great quantities of jewellery, over 2,000 pieces of tapestry (the largest collection on record) and 2,028 pieces of plate. Henry's military resources included 70 ships, 400 guns and 6,500 handguns in the Tower of London and 2,250 guns in other coastal and border fortresses. (RH)

LITERATURE: Starkey, *The Inventory of King Henry VIII*

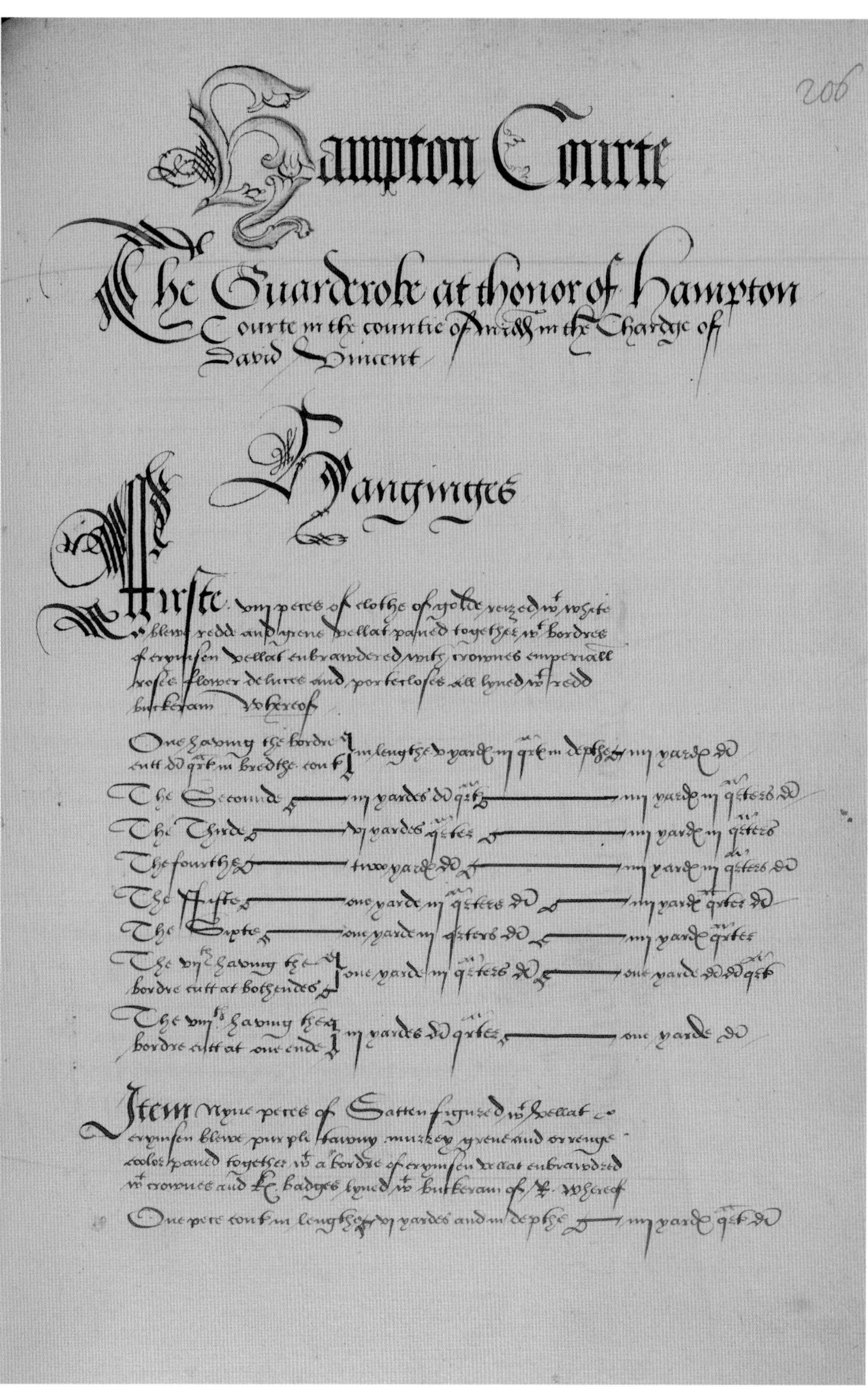
206

Hampton Courte

The Guardrobe at thonor of Hampton Courte in the countie of Midd in the Chardge of David Vincent

Hanginges

HENRY'S SUCCESSION AND LEGACY

By an Act of Parliament in 1544 and in his last will and testament of December 1546, Henry VIII restored both his daughters Mary and Elizabeth to the succession, although he never removed from them the taint of bastardy. On Edward VI's death in July 1553 an attempt was made to overturn this arrangement and place Lady Jane Grey (the granddaughter of Henry's younger sister), rather than Mary or Elizabeth, on the throne. However, both his daughters did indeed succeed, as Henry had intended, and Elizabeth I followed closely in the footsteps of her father. Unlike Mary, who returned England to Rome, Elizabeth retained Henry's policy of breaking with Rome, establishing a national Church, and trying to resist religious extremism. Furthermore, like Henry, Elizabeth understood the importance of the royal image and was painted in equally memorable portraits.

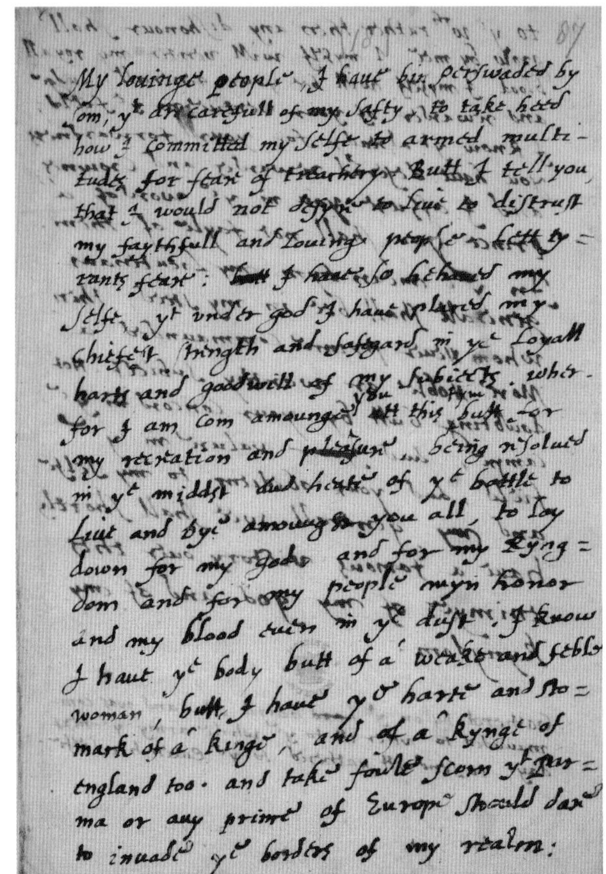

My louinge people, I haue bin persuaded by
som, yt ar carefull of my saffty, to take heed
how I committed my selfe to armed multitudes for fear of treachery. Butt I tell you
that I would not desyre to liue to distrust
my faythfull and louinge people. lett ty=
rants fear: I haue so behaued my
selfe, yt under god I haue placed my
chiefest strength and saffgard in ye loyall
harts and goodwill of my subiects. wherfor I am com amounge you at this tyme
my recreation and plesure, being resolued
in ye middst and heate of ye battle to
liue and dye amoung you all, to lay
down for my god and for my kyng=
dom and for my people myn honor
and my blood euen in ye dust. I know
I haue ye body butt of a weake and feble
woman, butt I haue ye harte and sto=
mack of a kinge, and of a kynge of
england too. and take foule scorn yt par=
ma or any prince of Europe should dare
to inuade ye borders of my realm:

272 The Heart and Stomach of a King

The Tilbury Speech

British Library, Harley MS 6798, fol.87

This speech was undoubtedly the most famous of Elizabeth's many speeches. Delivered in July 1588 to her troops assembled at Tilbury Camp to defend the realm against the Spanish Armada, Elizabeth projected a heroic persona that was intended to remind listeners of the courage and power of her father. In referring to her royal blood and by claiming that, although she has 'the body butt of a weake and feble woman' she has 'the harte and stomack of a kinge, and of a kynge of England too', Elizabeth draws attention to her descent from the warrior king, Henry VIII. The heart was believed to be the seat of courage and the stomach the home of violent deeds. Surprisingly, the speech was not printed at the time. This manuscript copy was probably made by the Reverend Dr Lionel Sharp, chaplain to the Queen's Lieutenant General, the Earl of Leicester. A version of it was eventually printed in the mid-17th century. (SD)

LITERATURE: Green, '"I My Self": Queen Elizabeth's Oration at Tilbury Camp'

273 The Armada Portrait

The Armada Portrait, after George Gower, *c.*1600

Collection of Mark Pigott OBE

Like her father, Elizabeth I used royal portraiture to project an image of legitimacy, magnificence and power. In this portrait, she is shown as an embodiment of the English nation that has just repulsed the Spanish Armada. Like Henry VIII's broad-shouldered stance in Holbein's later portraits, the posture of the Queen and the enormous sleeves of her dress dominate the pictorial space. However, Elizabeth's power is shown to reside in her feminine virginity, whereas Henry's came from his masculine virility; the pearls and bows on Elizabeth's dress (symbols of virginity) converge to meet in the place where Henry usually displayed his prominent codpiece. (SD)

LITERATURE: Montrose, *The Subject of Elizabeth*

274 The Family of Henry VIII

William Rogers (fl.1584–1604)

Engraving after Lucas de Heere's *An Allegory of the Tudor Succession*

British Museum, London, Department of Prints and Drawings, 1842,0806.373

Elizabeth I, the dominant figure in this engraving, is represented as the true heir of Henry VIII and the culmination of the Tudor dynasty. Henry turns his gaze towards Elizabeth and to a lesser extent her half-brother Edward VI (on his knees by Henry's side), who continue their father's work of promoting true religion (namely Protestantism) and not allowing England to fall under the sway of a foreign power. Away from Henry's eye and in a recessed plane is the smaller figure of Mary, Elizabeth's polar opposite; for, whereas the independent Elizabeth brings peace and prosperity to England (signs of divine favour), Mary is shackled to Spain (represented by her husband Philip), ushers in a disastrous war (the figure of Mars) and incurs divine displeasure by returning England to Rome and burning Protestants. This engraving, produced in the late 1590s, was based on an earlier painting attributed to Lucas de Heere, a Flemish painter who settled in England to escape religious persecution. Rogers added the verses in the cartouches and updated Elizabeth's clothes to reflect the fashions of the later period. Both allegories were typical of Elizabethan propaganda. (SD)

LITERATURE: Montrose, *The Subject of Elizabeth*

275 'The Pope Suppressed by King Henry the Eighth'

John Foxe (1516/17–87)

Actes and Monuments of These Latter and Perillous Dayes, Touching Matters of the Church …, 2 vols, 1570, vol.2, 1201

British Library, 4824.k.3, p.799

This illustration first appeared in the second edition of John Foxe's *Actes and Monuments,* one of the most widely read books in Elizabethan England and popularly known as the 'Book of Martyrs'. In truth the Protestant martyrologist Foxe found it difficult to reconcile the King's praiseworthy act in breaking from Rome with his violent persecution of Evangelicals, and for this reason his depiction of the King changed over each of the four editions printed during his lifetime. Nonetheless, the picture of Henry VIII trampling on Pope Clement VII has become the iconic representation of the Henrician Reformation. Also depicted and named in the illustration are: 'B. fisher' leaning over the body of the Pope; 'Cromwel' standing behind; and 'Cranmer', who receives a book from King Henry. The picture is an inversion of the story told in Foxe of Pope Alexander treading on the neck of the Emperor Frederick Barbarossa. (SD)

LITERATURE: Mark Rankin, 'Rereading Henry VIII in Foxe's Acts and Monuments', *Reformation,* 12 (2007)

799.

Here folovveth the ſecond Volume AND THE VII. BOOKE, BEGINNING WITH THE REIGNE OF KING HENRY E THE EIGHT.

Anno. 1509.

As touching the ciuil ſtate and adminiſtration of the Common wealth, and likewiſe of the ſtate of the Churche, vnder the raign of king Henry 7. how he entred firſt in poſſeſſion of ẏ crowne: how the two houſes of Yorke and Lancaſter were in hym conioyned through marriage with Elizabeth the eldeſt daughter to King Edwarde 4. by the prudent counſail of John Morton then Biſhop of Ely, after Archbiſhop of Canterbury, and Cardinall: howe long the ſayd King reigned, and what perſecution was in his time for lacke of ſearche and knowledge of Gods word, both in the dioceſſe of Lincolne vnder biſhop Smith (who was erector of the houſe of Brasen noſe in Oxforde) as alſo in the dioceſſe of Couentrie, and other places moe; and further, what puniſhment and alteration God commonly ſendeth vpon cities and realmes publique for neglecting the ſafety of his flocke, ſufficiently in the former booke hath bene already ſpecified: wherin many things more amply might haue ben added, incidēt in the raigne of this Prince, which we haue for breuitie pretermitted. For hee that ſtudieth to comprehend in ſtory all things, which the common courſe & vſe of life may offer to the wryter, may ſooner finde matter to occupye himſelfe, then to profite other. Otherwiſe I myght haue inferred mention of the ſeditious tumult of Perkin werbecke, wyth his retinue, Anno 1494. alſo of Blackheath field by the Blacke ſmith, An. 1496. I myght alſo haue recited the glorious commendation of Georgius Lilius in his Latine Chronicle teſtifying of King Henrie 7. howe hee ſent three ſolemne Oratours to Pope Iulius 2. to yeelde his obedience to the ſea of Rome. An. 1506. and likewiſe howe Pope Alexander 9. Pius 3. and Iulius 2. ſent to the ſayde king Henry 7. three ſundrie famous Am-

Notes ſummarely collected and repeated of things done in the tyme of K. Henry the ſeuēth.

AAa. ii. baſſa-

Tabula librorum de historiis antiquitatibus ac diuinitate tractantium in librariis et domibus religiosis subscriptis repertorum nulla mentione habita de libris communibus impressis seu de materiis predictis minime tractantium

Libraria ecclesie cathedralis beate Marie Lincoln

+ Iuo Carnotensis episcopus ante collectionem ecclesiasticarum regularum

Historia de vita et gestis sancti Hugonis Lincoln episcopi

+ Petrus de aureolis

+ Culton abbreuiat super librum sententiarum

+ Pronosticon futuri seculi

Liber canonum romanorum pontificum

+ Liber statutorum romanorum pontificum

Vegesius de re militari

Cassiodorus super psalterium

Breuiarium Bernardi Papien. extra

+ Cronica Cestrensis

HENRY VIII AS BIBLIOPHILE:

HIS BOOK COLLECTIONS, THEIR STORAGE AND THEIR USE

James Carley

Like all collectors, medieval and modern, Henry VIII owned books that were meant primarily for show and others that had been acquired for study or reference (fig.1). All of Henry's palaces would have been provided with devotional books for the chapel, as well as other religious texts in Latin. Favourite books would have been transported in the coffers that accompanied the royal party on its travels. At the grand houses, if not elsewhere, there were specific rooms set aside for books. In some of these rooms display books predominated, often arranged by binding; in others scholarly books were organized alphabetically for easy retrieval. There were inherited books, many of these beautiful manuscripts dating from the 15th century; books sequestered from the estates of fallen favourites, including former wives; and books purchased by Henry or his agents, some relatively humble printed books in quarto, cheaply bound in parchment.

The King's tastes in reading changed over the decades and one of the last books he commissioned was a beautiful Psalter, small enough to be conveniently held in his hands or placed on his lap, written and illuminated by the French scribe Jean Mallard. His annotations in this manuscript are those of a man looking back over his life and preparing for death: *monitio ne in rebus mundi fidem habeamus* (a warning not to have faith in the things of the world). They contrast forcefully with the shallow and platitudinous notes scribbled in his schoolboy copy of Cicero: 'He that cannot suffer shall not joye'.

BOOKS FOR SHOW

Nonsuch

Among the more than 25 books elaborately bound by an individual known as the King's Binder are a group of sixteen with the royal arms stamped on the covers, flanked by the greyhound and dragon as supporters, as well as the motto 'Rex Henricus VIII: Dieu et Mon Droit'. Of these, fifteen have a 'K' to the left of the central panel (or of the crowned Tudor rose), and an 'H' to the right. The Katherine denoted by the initial cannot be Katherine of Aragon, as one of the books was not printed until 1534, a year after Henry's marriage to Anne Boleyn, and it is unlikely that it was Katherine Parr, as this binder was no longer working by the time she and Henry were married (fig.2). The group can, therefore, almost certainly be associated with the brief period of Henry's marriage (28 July 1540 – 13 February 1542) to Katherine Howard, by far the least bookish of his wives.

The majority of the books consist of works by the Latin Fathers, several edited by Erasmus, and deriving from the Froben press in Basel. They were precisely the sorts of elegantly printed books in folio that were filling the libraries of those with pretensions to humanist tastes in the second quarter of the 16th century and Henry's long-standing association with Erasmus, dating to his boyhood, made him especially partial to this type of work. Dates of printing range from 1523 to 1530, but the identical bindings must all have been applied at the same time, and no doubt for a reason. What might this be?

On 22 November 1538 construction was begun on Nonsuch, some six miles away from Hampton Court, and the palace was substantially completed by January 1541. It was beautifully designed and the rooms elaborately fitted, every detail reflecting Henry's mature taste. No doubt, then, this gorgeously bound and perfectly matching set of books was put together for the new residence, the binding mirroring the decorative scheme throughout. The books, most of which are in mint condition and not soiled by marginalia, were not chosen for close perusal – this was after all a hunting lodge – but for their aesthetic value.

Richmond

John Leland, royal chaplain and antiquary, was part of the royal entourage when Henry VIII made his northern progress to York in 1541. Above all a bibliophile, Leland was especially impressed by the library at the Earl of Northumberland's castle at Wressle:

FIG. 1
Conventionally pious throughout his life, Henry VIII is shown here at prayer, his Book of Hours open before him.
Black Book of the Garter. St Georges's Archives, Windsor. The Dean and Canons of Windsor

FIG. 2
Edward Foxe's highly provocative *De uera differentia regiae potestatis et ecclesiasticae* was printed by the King's Printer, Thomas Berthelet, in 1534. The date of publication establishes that the 'K' on the cover cannot be identified as Katherine of Aragon.
British Library, C.24.a.25

> One thing I likid excedingly yn one of the towers, that was a study caullid *Paradise*, wher was a closet [cabinet] in the midle, of 8. squares latisid aboute: and at the toppe of every square was a desk ledgid to set bookes on cofers [chests] withyn them, and these semid as yoinid hard to the toppe of the closet: and yet by pulling, one or al wold cum downe, briste highe in rabettes [grooves], and serve for deskes to lay bokes on.

This ingenious device was constructed to make it possible to place several large manuscripts – too heavy to rest on one's knees – on secure surfaces where they could be examined by a standing reader. Although Richmond Palace had nothing similar – this invention was almost Heath Robinsonesque in its complexity – it would have been well equipped with lecterns, as it was at Richmond that the grand manuscripts inherited by Henry from his predecessors, especially his father-in-law Edward IV, were stored. Weighty tomes, they could by no means have been consulted without appropriate stands.

Henry VII was proud of the library at Richmond and was willing to spend substantial sums of money on keeping it up to date. The French ambassador Claude de Seyssel described it as 'tres belle et tres bien acoustree' and it was the first English Royal Library where printed books competed with manuscripts for pride of place. In particular, Henry VII collected books issued by the fashionable French publisher and bookseller Antoine Vérard, patronized by the French royal family. On occasion, moreover, he bought two copies of the same book at the same time, one on paper and one on vellum.

An example is the *Le Jardin de santé*, one of the earliest printed herbals in Europe, issued by Vérard around 1501 (figs 3, 4). The vellum copy, now owned by Transylvania University in Lexington, Kentucky, has been printed on vellum and personalized for its royal purchaser – the woodcut miniature facing the

FIG 3 (ABOVE) FIG 4 (RIGHT)
In 1502 Henry VII acquired two copies of *Le Jardin de santé* that had been recently published by the fashionable French bookseller and printer Antoine Vérard. The woodcut presentation miniature has been left untouched in the workaday paper copy. In the embellished copy on vellum, it has been hand-painted, with Henry's arms and supporters inserted in the lower border.
Above: British Library, C.22.f.9.
Right: Clara S. Peck Collection, Transylvania University (Photographed by Kurt Gohde)

dedication page has been painted over as a portrait of Henry VII and the royal arms along with other Tudor devices inserted. This superior – and highly expensive – tome was kept at Richmond as an object for viewing by visiting dignitaries, whereas the more humble paper copy, meant for consultation, was housed at Westminster, where it appears in the 1542 inventory. This pair thus provides a powerful piece of evidence of the different functions of the various libraries.

HENRY VIII'S WORKING LIBRARY

A description by the Secretary to Cardinal d'Aragona of Francis I's library at the Château de Blois survives from early in Henry VIII's reign: 'in the chateau, or rather palace, we saw a sizeable library not only furnished with shelves from end to end but also lined with bookcases from floor to ceiling, and literally packed with books – to say nothing of those put away in chests in an inner room'. By the 1540s Francis's collection – vastly superior to that of his English rival – had been consolidated at Fontainebleau: it was on the top floor of a wing and was lit from either side by windows and had, so it has been conjectured, wall-shelves, and double-sided desks placed at right angles to the windows. This represented a very efficient use of space and shows parallels with the arrangements in the upper, working library of Henry VIII's palace at Westminster. It was here that the ever-increasing numbers of books, printed books as well as medieval manuscripts seized from the monasteries, were stored in alphabetical order. Here too a numbering system was instituted that made the books easy to track by consulting a list. Henry and his advisers knew the library well and made canny use of the materials it contained.

Although always an avid reader, Henry VIII was particularly engaged in sustained research at three different junctures: when he was gathering up evidence for the *Assertio septem sacramentorum contra Martinum Lutherum* around 1520; when, in the late 1520s and early 1530s, he was examining his conscience about his first marriage, as well as showing himself concerned about the limits of papal power; and when, in the late 1530s/early 1540s, cut off from the papacy and exercising his role as Defender of the Faith of his people, he considered ways in which the *Bishops' Book* should be revised as the *King's Book*, to be a definitive statement of the position of the Church of England.

Especially after 1527, the Royal Collection expanded quickly as royal agents scoured the monastic libraries looking for ancient documents that might justify Henry VIII's doubts about his first marriage and, soon afterwards, those that might be used in the dispute with Rome. Henry was closely involved in the process and, in at least one case (Lincolnshire), he himself examined the lists of medieval manuscripts available and decided what should be brought to London. The majority of what was chosen was fairly obvious – commentaries on the book of Leviticus with its convenient prohibition on marriage to one's brother's widow, English historians such as Geoffrey of Monmouth, who celebrated the imperial pretensions of King Arthur, or William of Malmesbury, who recorded the acts of the English bishops, including their disputes with the Pope. Much of this material was quoted in the *Epistola cardinalibus missa* put together in the King's name for the legatine trial concerning the validity of the royal marriage in 1529, or in the *Collectanea satis copiosa* documenting England's struggles against the duplicitous papacy.

There were, however, more recondite texts that could be used to help the cause, such as John Baconsthorpe's commentary on the *Sentences* of Peter Lombard. In his commentary Baconsthorpe maintained that 'the pope cannot dispense on degrees of consanguinity prohibited by divine law'– precisely Henry's position concerning the papal annulment permitting his first marriage – and it is not surprising that Baconsthorpe was one of medieval authorities on canon law cited, under the determination of the University of Toulouse, in the government-sponsored *Grauissimae atque exactissimae illustrissimarum totius Italiae et Galliae academiarum censurae* published anonymously in 1531.

One of Henry VIII's most remarkable agents was Leland, who, armed with a laissez-passer from the King himself, spent some three years, from 1533 to 1536, trawling through even the most inaccessible monastic libraries and returning to London with treasures for the King to peruse. As every scholar knows, research depends on what is available for examination and

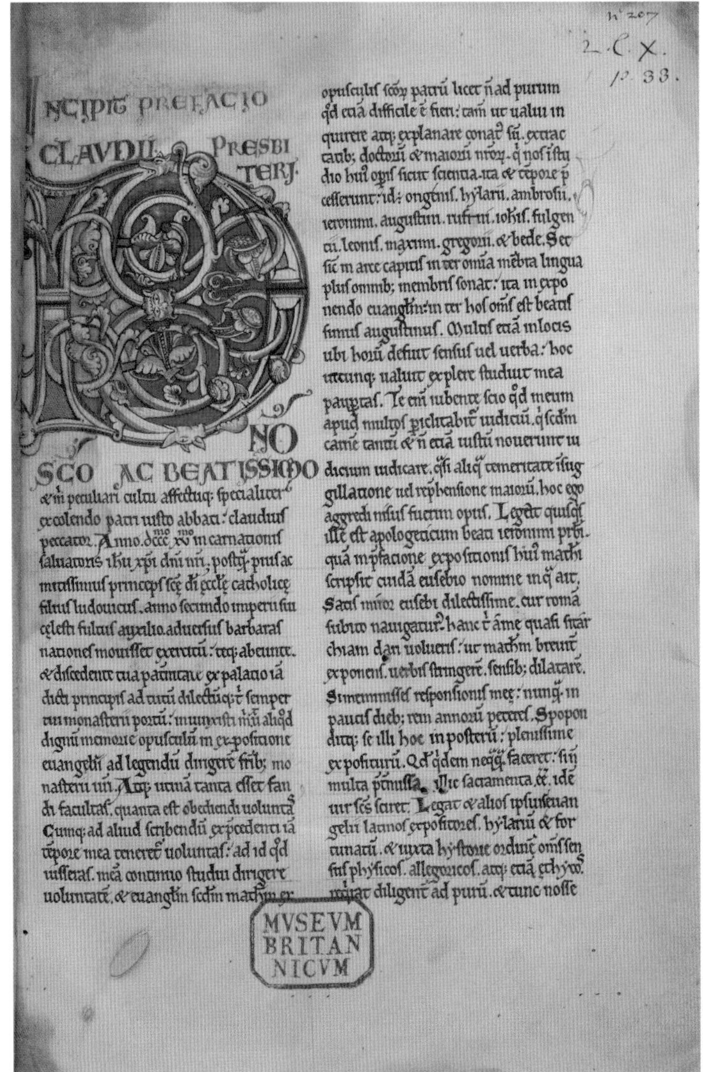

FIG. 5
The characteristic Westminster inventory number was entered on the first folio of this 12th-century copy of Claudius of Turin's Commentary on the Gospel of Matthew after it came into the Royal Library in 1533.
British Library, Royal MS 2 C.X

Henry was lucky in Leland, who had a fine training at Oxford and Cambridge and in Paris, as well as an unusually sharp mind. Leland knew, almost instinctively, what would benefit the royal cause (fig.5).

In 1533, for example, he came across a copy of a commentary on the Gospel of Matthew by the 9th-century scholar Claudius of Turin at the Augustinian priory at Lanthony in Gloucestershire and he sent it back to London for future use. Entered in the Westminster inventory as No. 207, it still survives as British Library, MS Royal 2 C.x. Leland would probably not have seen this text before he began his trip and he would have had only the briefest time to examine it among the other items in the library at Lanthony. Yet he immediately realized its pertinence to the reforms that were being contemplated by his patron Thomas Cromwell: Claudius attacked the cult of images and relics and rejected pilgrimages, as well as the intercession of the saints. Claudius was thus a man whose writings were well worth preserving in Henry's arsenal of anti-papal documents. It was this sort of work that justified Leland's prolonged 'research leave' from his so-called clerical duties.

Henry did not annotate his copy of Claudius on Matthew, but he did mark up many of the other books in his collections and his responses to what he read find echoes in the policies of his regime. He knew, above all, how to manipulate his sources to serve his own ends. Possessing a retentive memory, he was able to deploy material he had read years earlier in debates with opponents. When, in 1537 or so, he read a paper prepared for him by Hugh Latimer, Bishop of Worcester, attacking 'our old ancient purgatory pick-purse', Henry not only pointed out Latimer's 'false arguments' and 'wrong examples', he also quoted the *Distichs of Cato*, a book he had studied in his childhood, as a means of drawing attention to the Bishop's hypocrisy: *Turpe enim est doctori, cum culpa redarguit [ipsum]* (Those things you are accustomed to blame do not do yourself; it is bad for a wise man when his own guilt comes back to haunt him). Although, by the time the *King's Book* appeared in 1543, he had revised his opinion of this doctrine, it was not because of Latimer and, after having read the paper, he affirmed that purgatory 'may yet stand for all this'.

No mean theologian, Henry found the writings of his biblical prototypes David and Solomon particularly struck a chord with him and, as his annotations show, he measured himself against these two Old Testament rulers. One of his last sets of marginalia appear in his copy of the *c.*1545 edition of *The Bokes of Solomon*, a translation by Miles Coverdale of Proverbs (fig.6). As his markings show, Henry rejoices in having escaped the clutches of 'the straunge woman', Katherine Howard, that fifth wife who 'forsaketh the husbande of hyr youth', and congratulates himself for having found in his sixth, Katherine Parr, a woman with whom to be glad. Unlike his fourth, Anne of Cleves, whose 'breasts so slack' appalled and unmanned him, he could at last say with Solomon 'let hyr brestes alwaye satisfye the, and holde the ever content wyth hyr loue'. No wonder he complacently inscribed in the margin 'for wyfves'.

The.ii.Chapter. Fol.iiij.
That thou mayest be delyuered also C
*from the straunge woman, and from her Pro.v.a
ŷ is not thyne owne, whych gyueth swete and.vij.a
wordes, forsaketh ŷ husbande of hyr youth
and forgetteth the couenaunt of hir God.
For hyr house is enclyned vnto death, and
hyr pathes vnto hell. Al they that go in vn
to her, come not agayne, nother take they
holde of the waye of lyfe.
That thou mayest walke in the good
waye, and kepe the pathes of the ryghte-
ous. For the iuste shall dwell in the lande,
and the innocentes shall remayne in it: but
the vngodly shalbe rooted out of the lande
and the wycked doers shalbe takē out of it
The.iij.Chapter.
¶ He exhorteth vs to the feare of God &
to pacience, he commendeth wysedome and
requyreth vs to cleue vnto the same.
My sonne, *Forget not my law, but A
se that thyne herte kepe my cōmaū- Deute.xi.c.
dementes. For they shall prolonge
the dayes and yeares of thy lyfe, &
brynge the peace. Let mercye and faythful-
nesse neuer go from the, bynde thē aboute
thy necke, and wryte them in the tables of
thyne herte. So shalt thou fynde fauoure,
and good vnderstandynge in the syghte of
God and men. Put thy trust in the Lorde
wyth al thyne herte, and leane not to thyn
owne vnderstandynge. In all thy wayes
haue respecte vnto hym, and he shall ordre
thy goynges. *Be not wyse in thyne owne Esa.v.c.
concepte, but feare the Lorde and departe Rom.xij.c
A iiij from

FIG. 6
Henry VIII noted with approval the admonition that one should 'Put thy trust in the Lorde with al thyne herte, and leane not to thyn owne understandynge'.
British Library, C.25.b.4.(1).f.iiiir

SELECT BIBLIOGRAPHY

BOOKS

Amir D. Aczel, *The Riddle of the Compass* (San Diego, California, 2001)

Sydney Anglo (ed.), *The Great Tournament Roll of Westminster: A Collotype Reproduction of the Manuscript* (Oxford, 1968)

Sydney Anglo, *Images of Tudor Kingship* (London, 1992)

Ian Arthurson, *The Perkin Warbeck Conspiracy, 1491–1499* (Stroud, 1994)

C. Augustijn, *Erasmus: His Life, Works and Influence*, trans. J.C. Grayson (Toronto, 1991)

Roland H. Bainton, *Here I Stand: A Life of Martin Luther* (London, 2002)

Peter Barber, *King Henry's Map of Great Britain* (London, 2009)

C.R. Baskervill (ed.), *Pierre Gringore's Pageants for the Entry of Mary Tudor into Paris* (Chicago, 1934)

Oskar Bätschmann and Pascal Griener, *Hans Holbein* (London, 1997)

Frederic J. Baumgartner, *Louis XII* (Basingstoke, 1996)

David Beaton, *Dorset Maps* (Wimborne, 2001)

Guy Bedouelle and Patrick Le Gal, *Le 'Divorce' du roi Henri VIII: etudes et documents* (Geneva, 1987)

G.W. Bernard, *War, Taxation and Rebellion in Early Tudor England: Henry VIII, Cardinal Wolsey and the Amicable Grant of 1525* (Brighton, 1985)

G.W. Bernard, *The King's Reformation: Henry VIII and the Remaking of the English Church* (New Haven and London, 2005)

J.H. Bettey, *The Suppression of the Monasteries in the West Country* (Gloucester, 1989)

T.A. Birrell, *English Monarchs and Their Books from Henry VII to Charles II* (London, 1987)

Wim Blockmans, *Emperor Charles V, 1500–1558* (London, 2002)

Julia Boffey and A.S.G. Edwards, *A New Index of Middle English Verse* (London, 2005)

Gerald Bray, *Tudor Church Reform: The Henrician Canons of 1535 and the Reformatio legum ecclesiasticarum*, vol. 8, Church of England Record Society (Woodbridge, 2000)

John Butler, *The Quest for Becket's Bones* (New Haven and London, 1995)

Charles C. Butterworth, *The English Primers (1529–45): Their Publication and Connection with the English Bible and the Reformation in England* (Philadelphia, 1953)

Geoffrey Callendar, *The Caird Collection of Maritime Antiquities*, vol.1 supplement, 5 vols (Greenwich, 1933–37)

Lorne Campbell, *The Early Flemish Pictures in the Collection of Her Majesty the Queen* (Cambridge, 1985)

Thomas P. Campbell, *Henry VIII and the Art of Majesty: Tapestries at the Tudor Court* (New Haven and London, 2007)

James P. Carley, *Glastonbury Abbey: The Holy House at the Head of the Moors Adventurous* (Woodbridge, 1988)

James P. Carley, *The Libraries of King Henry VIII* (London, 2000)

James P. Carley, *The Books of King Henry VIII and his Wives* (London, 2004)

James P. Carley, *King Henry's Prayer Book: Commentary* (London, 2009)

David R. Carlson, *The Latin Writings of John Skelton* (Chapel Hill, North Carolina, 1991)

David R. Carlson, *English Humanist Books* (Toronto, 1993)

Catalogue of the Heralds' Commemorative Exhibition 1484–1934 held at the College Of Arms (London, 1936)

Catalogue of the Manuscript Maps, Charts and Plans, and of the Topographical Drawings in the British Museum (London, 1844)

Albert Châtelet, *Early Dutch Painting: Painting in the Northern Netherlands in the Fifteenth century* (New York, 1981)

David Childs, *The Warship Mary Rose: The Life and Times of King Henry VIII's Flagship* (London, 2007)

Jessie Childs, *Henry VIII's Last Victim: The Life and Times of Henry Howard, Earl of Surrey* (London, 2008)

C.S. Cobb (ed.), *The Rationale of Ceremonial 1540–1543: with Notes and Appendices* (London, 1910)

H.M. Colvin, D.R. Ransome and J. Summerson, *The History of the King's Works: Vol. IV 1485–1660* (London, 1982)

H.M. Colvin and Susan Foister (eds), *The Panorama of London circa 1544 by Anthonis van den Wyngaerde* (London, 1996)

William Conway and Charles B. Boog Watson, *Maps of Edinburgh 1544–1929* (Edinburgh, 1932)

George Elwes Corrie (ed.), *Sermons and Remains of Hugh Latimer*, Parker Society, 2 vols (Cambridge, 1845)

Janet Cox-Rearick, *The Collection of Francis I: Royal Treasures* (New York, 1995)

Nicholas Crane, *Mercator: The Man who Mapped the Planet* (London, 2002)

P.J. Croft, *Autograph Poetry in the English Language*, vol.1 (London, 1973)

Edward Croft-Murray and Paul Hulton, *Catalogue of British Drawings: Vol.1. Sixteenth and Seventeenth Centuries* (London, 1960)

G.R. Crone, *Early Maps of the British Isles A.D. 1000–A.D. 1579*, Royal Geographical Society Reproductions of Early Maps 7 (London, 1961)

C.G. Cruickshank, *Army Royal: Henry VIII's Invasion of France, 1513* (Oxford, 1969)

C.G. Cruickshank, *Henry VIII and the Invasion of France* (Stroud, 1990)

Sean Cunningham, *Henry VII* (London, 2007)

Robert de Balsat [*sic*], *La Nef des princes et des batailles de noblesse…* (Lyons, 1502)

Elly Dekker, *Globes at Greenwich: A Catalogue of the Globes and Armillary Spheres in the National Maritime Museum, Greenwich* (Oxford, 1999)

Lord Howard de Walden, *Banners Standards and Badges from a Tudor Manuscript* (London, 1904)

Anne Dillon, *The Construction of Martyrdom in the English Catholic Community, 1535–1603* (Aldershot, 2002)

Susan Doran and Glenn Richardson (eds), *Tudor England and its Neighbours* (Basingstoke, 2005)

Susan Doran, *The Tudor Chronicles* (London, 2008)

Maria Dowling, *Fisher of Men: A Life of John Fisher* (Basingstoke, 1999)

Eamon Duffy, *The Stripping of the Altars* (New Haven and London, 1992)

Eamon Duffy, *Marking the Hours: English People and their Prayers, 1240–1570* (New Haven and London, 2006)

Theodor Dumitrescu, *The Early Tudor Court and International Musical Relations* (Aldershot, 2007)

Joseph G. Dwyer (trans.), *Pole's Defence of the Unity of the Church* (Westminster, Maryland, 1965)

David Dymond (ed.), *The Register of Thetford Priory*, Norfolk Record Society, vols 59–60 (Oxford, 1994–6)

John Edwards, *Ferdinand and Isabella* (Harlow, 2004)

Mark U. Edwards, *Printing, Propaganda and Martin Luther* (Berkeley, California, 1994)

Noelle-Marie Egretier (trans.), *Reginald Pole, Defence de l'Unite de l'Eglise* (Paris, 1967)

G.R. Elton, *Policy and Police: The Enforcement of the Reformation in the Age of Thomas Cromwell* (Cambridge, 1972)

G.R. Elton, *The Tudor Constitution* (Cambridge, 1982)

Mark Evans, *The Sforza Hours* (London, 1992)

Susan Foister, *Holbein in England* (London, 2006)

Alistair Fox and John Guy (eds), *Reassessing the Henrician Age: Humanism, Politics and Reform 1500–1550* (Oxford, 1986)

S.J. Gunn, *Charles Brandon, Duke of Suffolk* (Oxford, 1988)

Robert T. Gunther, *The Astrolabes of the World*, 2 vols (Oxford, 1932)

John Guy, *A Daughter's Love: Thomas and Margaret More* (London, 2008)

Peter Gwyn, *The King's Cardinal: The Rise and Fall of Thomas Wolsey* (London, 1990)

John Hale, *Artist and Warfare in the Renaissance* (London and New Haven, 1990)

Maya Hambly, *Drawing Instruments 1580–1980* (London, 1988)

Barbara J. Harris, *Edward Stafford, Third Duke of Buckingham, 1478–1521* (Stanford, California, 1986)

P.D.A. Harvey, *Maps in Tudor England* (London, 1993)

Edward Hawkin, Augustus W. Franks and Herbert A. Gruber, *Medallic Illustrations of the History of Great Britain and Ireland* (London, 1885)

Maria Hayward, *The 1542 Inventory of Whitehall: The Palace and its Keeper*, vols 1 and 2 (London, 2004)

Karen Hearn (ed.), *Dynasties: Painting in Tudor and Jacobean England 1530–1630* (London, 1995)

Anne D. Hedeman, *The Royal Image: Illustrations of the 'Grandes Chroniques de France' 1274–1422* (Berkeley, Los Angeles and Oxford, 1991)

Henry VIII, *Assertio septem sacramentorum adversus Martinum Lutherum*, ed. Pierre Fraenkel, Corpus Catholicorum 43 (Münster, 1992),

Heralds' Commemorative Exhibition, 1484–1934: Enlarged and Illustrated Catalogue (London, 1970)

Hester Higton, *Sundials: An Illustrated History of Portable Dials* (London, 2001)

Hester Higton, *Sundials at Greenwich: A Catalogue of the Sundials, Nocturnals and Horary Quadrants in the National Maritime Museum, Greenwich* (Oxford and London, 2002)

Sir George Hill and J. Graham Pollard, *Medals of the Renaissance* (London, 1978)

H.L. Hitchins and W.E. May, *From Lodestone to Gyro-compass* (London, 1955)

Dale Hoak (ed.), *Tudor Political Culture* (Cambridge, 1995)

Pearl Hogrefe, *The Life and Times of Sir Thomas Elyot* (Ames, Iowa, 1967)

Holbein and the Court of Henry VIII: Drawings from the Royal Library at Windsor Castle (London, 1978)

Joyce M. Horn and David M. Smith (eds), *Fasti Ecclesiae Anglicanae 1541–1857: vol 4: York Diocese* (London, 1975)

C. Patrick Hotle, *Thorns and Thistles, Diplomacy between Henry VIII and James V 1528–1542* (Lanham, Maryland and London, 1996)

Richard W. Hoyle, *The Pilgrimage of Grace and the Politics of the 1530s* (Oxford, 2001)

Philip Hughes, *The Reformation in England*, 3 vols (London, 1950–4)

P.L. Hughes and J.F. Larkin, *Tudor Royal Proclamations*, vol.1: *1485–1553* (New Haven and London, 1964)

Robert Hutchinson, *The Last Days of Henry VIII: Conspiracy, Treason and Heresy at the Court of the Dying Tyrant* (London, 2005)

Robert Hutchinson, *Thomas Cromwell, The Rise And Fall of Henry VIII's Most Notorious Minister* (London, 2007)

E.W. Ives, *The Life and Death of Anne Boleyn: 'The Most Happy'* (Oxford, 2004)

Susan James, *Kateryn Parr: The Making of a Queen* (Stroud, 1999)

M.K. Jones and M.G. Underwood, *The King's Mother: Lady Margaret Beaufort, Countess of Richmond and Derby* (Cambridge, 1992)

W.K. Jordan (ed.), *The Chronicle and Political Papers of King Edward VI* (London, 1966)

W.K. Jordan, *Edward VI: The Young King. The Protectorship of the Duke of Somerset* (London, 1968)

Herbert Kellman, *Renaissance Music in Facsimile*, vol.9 (New York, 1987)

Herbert Kellman (ed.), *The Treasury of Petrus Alamire: Music and Art in Flemish Court Manuscripts, 1500–1535* (Ghent, 1999)

Henry Ansgar Kelly, *The Matrimonial Trials of Henry VIII* (Stanford, 1976)

John N. King, *Tudor Royal Iconography: Literature and Art in an Age of Religious Crisis* (Princeton, 1989)

R.J. Knecht, *Francis the First* (Cambridge, 1984)

R.J. Knecht, *Renaissance Warrior and Patron: The Reign of Francis I* (Cambridge, 1994)

C.S. Knighton and D.M. Loades (eds), *The Anthony Roll of Henry VIII's Navy: Pepys MS 2991 and British Library Add MS 22047 with Related Material* (Aldershot, 2000)

David Knowles, *The Religious Orders in England*, vol. 3: *The Tudor Age* (Cambridge, 1959)

Angus Konstam, *Pavia 1525, The Climax of the Italian Wars* (Oxford, 1996)

Thomas Kren (ed.), *Renaissance Painting in Manuscripts: Treasures from the British Library* (New York, 1983)

Thomas Kren and Scot McKendrick, *Illuminating the Renaissance: The Triumph of Flemish Manuscript Painting in Europe* (Los Angeles, California, 2003)

Gerard L'E Turner, *Scientific Instruments 1500–1900: An Introduction* (London and Berkeley, California, 1998)

Damian Riehl Leader, *A History of the University of Cambridge*, vol.1: *The University to 1546* (Cambridge, 1988)

Stanford E. Lehmberg, *Sir Thomas Elyot, Tudor Humanist* (Austin, Texas, 1960)

Stanford E. Lehmberg, *The Later Parliaments of Henry VIII, 1536–1547* (Cambridge, 1977)

Mortimer Levine, *Tudor Dynastic Problems, 1460–1571* (London and New York, 1973)

Christopher Lloyd and Simon Thurley, *Henry VIII. Images of a Tudor King* (London, 1990)

David Loades, *Henry VIII: Church, Court and Conflict* (Kew, Richmond, Surrey, 2007)

David Loades, *Mary Tudor: The Tragical History of the First Queen of England* (Kew, Richmond, Surrey, 2007)

Diarmaid MacCulloch, *Thomas Cranmer* (New Haven and London, 1996)

R.L. Mackie, *King James IV of Scotland: A Brief Survey of His Life and Times* (Edinburgh, 1958)

Making History: Antiquaries in Britain, 1707–2007 (London, 2007)

Richard Marks and Ann Payne (eds), *British Heraldry from its Origins to c.1800* (London, 1978)

Richard Marks and Paul Williamson, *Gothic: Art for England 1400–1547* (London, 2003)

Peter Marsden, *Sealed by Time: The Loss and Recovery of the Mary Rose* (Portsmouth, 2003)

Garrett Mattingly, *Catherine of Aragon* (London, 1950)

Thomas F. Mayer, *A Reluctant Author: Cardinal Pole and his Manuscripts*, Transactions of the American Philosophical Society, 89:4 (Philadelphia, 1999)

Thomas F. Mayer, *Reginald Pole, Prince and Prophet* (Cambridge, 2000)

Rory McEntegart, *Henry VIII, the League of Schmalkalden and the English Reformation* (Woodbridge, 2002)

P. Mellen, *Jean Clouet* (London, 1971)

Konrad Meuschel, *Antiquariat Achtzigster Katalog: Handschriften, Bücher und Einblattdrucke aus dem Späten Mittelalter bis 1600* (Bad Honnef, 1997)

Robert F. Michaelis, *Antique Pewter of the British Isles* (London, 1955)

Robert F. Michaelis, *British Pewter* (London, 1969)

Oliver Millar, *The Tudor, Stuart and Early Georgian Pictures in the Collection of Her Majesty The Queen* (London, 1963)

Eduard Mira and An Delva (eds), *A La Búsqueda del Toisón de Oro. La Europa de los Príncipes. La Europa de las Ciudades*, vol.1 (Valencia, 2007)

Louis Montrose, *The Subject of Elizabeth: Authority, Gender and Representation* (Chicago, 2007)

J.A. Muller, *Stephen Gardiner and the Tudor Reaction* (London, 1926)

Frank Mumby, *The Youth of Henry VIII: A Narrative in Contemporary Letters* (London, 1913)

Beverley A. Murphy, *Bastard Prince: Henry VIII's Lost Son* (Stroud, 2001)

Music for King Henry: BL Royal MS 11 E XI, with commentary by Nicolas Bell, performing edition by David Skinner (London, 2009)

Clifford Musgrave, *Life in Brighton from the Earliest Times to the Present* (Rochester, 1981)

H.M. Nixon and Mirjam M. Foot, *The History of Decorated Bookbinding in England* (Oxford, 1982)

Oxford Dictionary of National Biography (Oxford, 2004)

William Page (ed.), *The Victoria County History of the County of Norfolk*, vol.2 (London, 1906)

K.T. Parker and Susan Foister, *The Drawings of Hans Holbein the Younger in the Collection of Her Majesty the Queen at Windsor Castle* (London and New York, 1983)

Maria Perry, *The Sisters of Henry VIII: The Tumultuous Lives of Margaret of Scotland and Mary of France* (London, 1998)

Nicolas Pocock, *Records of the Reformation: The Divorce 1527–1533*, 2 vols (London, 1870)

A.W. Pollard, *Records of the English Bible* (London, 1911)

H.C. Porter, *Reformation and Reaction in Tudor Cambridge* (Cambridge, 1958)

Glyn Redworth, *In Defence of the Church Catholic: The Life of Stephen Gardiner* (Oxford, 1990)

Richard Rex, *The Theology of John Fisher* (Cambridge, 1991)

Richard Rex, *Henry VIII and the English Reformation* (Basingstoke, 2006)

E.E. Reynolds, *Saint John Fisher* (London, 1972)

Judith Richards, *Mary Tudor* (London, 2008)

Glenn Richardson, *Renaissance Monarchy: The Reigns of Henry VIII, Francis I and Charles V* (London, 2002)

W.C. Richardson, *Mary Tudor, the White Queen* (London, 1970)

Jasper Ridley, *Henry VIII* (London, 2002)

J. Roberts, *George III and Queen Charlotte: Patronage, Collecting and Court Taste* (London, 2004)

A.H.W. Robinson, *Marine Cartography in Britain: A History of the Sea Chart of 1855* (Leicester, 1962)

N.A.M. Rodger, *The Safeguard of the Sea: A Naval History of Britain*, vol.1: *660–1649* (London, 1997)

E.F. Rogers (ed.), *The Correspondence of Sir Thomas More* (Princeton, 1947)

John Rowlands, *Drawings by German Artists: The Fifteenth Century and Sixteenth Century by Artists born before 1530*, 2 vols (London, 1993)

Margaret Rule, *The Mary Rose: The Excavation and Raising of Henry VIII's Flagship* (London, 1983)

Joycelyne G. Russell, *The Field of Cloth of Gold: Men and Manners in 1520* (London, 1969)

Alec Ryrie, *The Gospel and Henry VIII: Evangelicals in the Early English Reformation* (Cambridge, 2003)

M. St Clare Byrne (ed.), *The Letters of King Henry VIII: A Selection, with a few Other Documents* (London, 1936)

William H. St John Hope, *Cowdray and Easebourne Priory in the County of Sussex* (London, 1919)

L.F. Salzman, *The Victoria History of the County of Sussex*, vol.7 (Oxford, 1937)

Lucy Freeman Sandler, *Gothic Manuscripts, 1285–1385* (London, 1986)

Alexander Savine, *English Monasteries on the Eve of the Dissolution* (Oxford, 1909)

J.J. Scarisbrick, *Henry VIII* (London, 1968)

Thomas Schauerte, *Die Ehrenpforte für Kaiser Maximilian* (Munich, 2001)

Kathleen L. Scott, *Later Gothic Manuscripts, 1390–1490*, 2 vols (London, 1996)

Lon R. Shelby, *John Rogers: Tudor Military Engineer* (Oxford, 1967)

Lacey Baldwin Smith, *A Tudor Tragedy: The Life and Times of Catherine Howard* (London, 1961)

Hugo Soly (ed.), *Charles V 1500–1558 and his Time* (Antwerp, 1999)

David Starkey, *Rivals in Power: The Lives and Letters of the Great Tudor Dynasties* (London, 1990)

David Starkey (ed.), *Henry VIII: A European Court in England* (London, 1991)

David Starkey, *The Reign of Henry VIII: Personalities and Politics* (London, 1991)

David Starkey (ed.), *The Inventory of Henry VIII. Society of Antiquaries MS 129 and British Library MS Harley 1419* (London, 1998)

David Starkey, *Six Wives: The Queens of Henry VIII* (London, 2003)

David Starkey, *Henry: Virtuous Prince* (London, 2008)

John Stevens, *Music and Poetry in the Early Tudor Court* (Cambridge, 1961)

John Stevens, *Music at the Court of Henry VIII*, vol.18 (London, 1962)

Alan Stimson, *The Mariner's Astrolabe: A Survey of Known, Surviving Sea Astrolabes* (Utrecht, 1988)

Tatiana C. String, *Art and Communication in the Reign of Henry VIII* (Aldershot and Burlington, Vermont, 2008)

Roy Strong, *Tudor and Jacobean Portraits*, 2 vols (London, 1969)

Roy Strong, *Artists of the Tudor Court: The Portrait Miniature Rediscovered 1520–1620* (London, 1983)

Elisabeth Stuart, *Lost Landscapes of Plymouth* (Stroud, 1993)

Edward Surtz and Virginia Murphy (eds), *The Divorce Tracts of Henry VIII* (Angers, 1988)

Tim Tatton-Brown and Richard Mortimer, *Westminster Abbey; The Lady Chapel of Henry VII* (Woodbridge, 2003)

Simon Thurley, *The Royal Palaces of Tudor England: Architecture and Court Life, 1460–1547* (New Haven and London, 1993)

James D. Tracy, *Emperor Charles V, Impresario of War: Campaign Strategy, International Finance and Domestic Politics* (Cambridge, 2002)

J.B. Trapp, *Erasmus, Colet, and More: The Early Tudor Humanists and their Books* (London, 1991)

J.B. Trapp and H. Schulte Herbrüggen (eds), *'The King's Good Servant': Sir Thomas More, 1477/8–1535* (London, 1977)

Jane Turner (ed.), *The Dictionary of Art*, 34 vols (London, 1996)

Jan van der Stock, *Cornelis Matsys 1510/11–1556–57: Oeuvre Graphique* (Brussels, 1985)

Ariane van Suchtelen, Quentin Buvelot, Peter van der Ploeg (eds), *Hans Holbein the Younger 1497/98–1543: Portraitist of the Renaissance* (The Hague, 2003)

Greg Walker, *Writing Under Tyranny: English Literature and the Henrician Reformation* (Oxford, 2005)

Helen M. Wallis, *The Maps and Text of the Boke of Idrography presented by Jean Rotz to Henry VIII 1542* (Oxford, 1981)

H.L.D. Ward, *Catalogue of Romances in the Department of Manuscripts of the British Museum*, vol.1 (1883)

J.C. Warner, *Henry VIII's Divorce: Literature and the Politics of the Printing Press* (Woodbridge, 1998)

David W. Waters, *The Art of Navigation in Elizabethan and Early Stuart Times* (London, 1978)

Alison Weir, *The Six Wives of Henry VIII* (London, 2000)

Leopold G. Wickham Legg (ed.), *English Coronation Records* (London, 1901)

Franklin B. Williams, Jr (ed.), *The Gardyners Passetaunce* (London, 1985)

H.R. Willoughby, *The First Authorized English Bible and the Cranmer Preface* (Chicago, 1942)

Lucy Wooding, *Henry VIII* (Abingdon and New York, 2008)

G.W.O. Woodward, *The Dissolution of the Monasteries* (London, 1966)

C.E. Wright, *English Heraldic Manuscripts in the British Museum* (London, 1973)

Thomas Wright (ed.), *Three Chapters of Letters Relating to the Suppression of Monasteries*, Camden Society, old series, 26 (1843)

ARTICLES AND ESSAYS

Sydney Anglo, 'Archives of the English Tournament', *Journal of the Society of Antiquaries*, 2 (1962), pp.103–62

Joseph Ayloffe, 'An Account of some Ancient English Historical Paintings at Cowdray Sussex', *Archaeologia*, 3 (1776), pp.239–72

Peter Barber, 'England I: Pageantry, Defense and Governent: Maps at Court to 1550' in David Buisseret (ed.) *Monarchs, Maps and Ministers: The Emergence of Cartography as a Tool of Government in Early Modern Europe* (Chicago, 1992), pp.26–40

Peter Barber, 'The Maps, Town-Views and Historical Prints in the Columbus Inventory' in Mark R. McDonald (ed.), *The Print Collection of Ferdinand Columbus 1488–1539: A Renaissance Collector in Seville*, 3 vols (London, 2004), vol.1, pp.246–62

Peter Barber, 'A Revolution in Mapmaking' in Peter Barber (ed.), *The Map Book* (London, 2005)

Peter Barber, 'Putting Musselburgh on the Map: Two Recently Discovered Cartographic Documents from the "Rough Wooing" ' in Paula van Gest-van het Schip and Peter van der Krogt (eds), *Mappae Antiquae Liber Amicorum Günter Schilder* (Amsterdam, 2007), pp.327–32

Peter Barber, 'Cartography, Topography and History Painting' in *The Inventory of Henry VIII*, vol.3 (forthcoming)

George W. Bernard, 'The Fall of Wolsey Reconsidered', *Journal of British Studies*, 35 (1996), pp.277–310

George W. Bernard, 'The Tyranny of Henry VIII' in George W. Bernard and Steven J. Gunn (eds), *Authority and Consent in Tudor England: Essays Presented to C.S.L. Davies* (Aldershot, 2002), pp.113–29

James P. Carley, 'Marginalia by Henry VIII in His Copy of The Bokes of Salomon', *Transactions of the Cambridge Bibliographical Society*, 4 (1965), pp.166–70

James P. Carley, 'John Leland and the Contents of English Pre-dissolution Libraries: the Cambridge Friars', *Transactions of the Cambridge Bibliographical Society*, 9 (1986), pp.90–100

James P. Carley, 'John Leland and the Contents of English Pre-dissolution Libraries: Lincolnshire', *Transactions of the Cambridge Bibliographical Society*, 9 (1989), pp.330–57

James P. Carley, 'Marks in Books and the Libraries of Henry VIII', *Papers of the Bibliographical Society of America*, 91 (1997), pp.583–606

James P. Carley, 'Sir Thomas Bodley's Library and its Acquisitions: An Edition of the Nottingham Benefaction of 1604' in James P. Carley and Colin G. C. Tite (eds), *Books and Collectors 1200–1700* (London, 1997), pp.357–86

James P. Carley, 'The Royal Library as a Source for Sir Robert Cotton's Collection: A Preliminary List of Acquisitions', in C. J. Wright (ed.), *Sir Robert Cotton as Collector: Essays on an Early Stuart Courtier and his Legacy* (London, 1997), pp.209–11

James P. Carley, 'The Royal Library under Henry VIII', in the *Cambridge History of the Book in Britain*, (1999), vol.3, pp.274–81

James P. Carley, '"A Great Gatherer Together of Books": Archbishop Bancroft's Library at Lambeth (1610) and its Sources', *Lambeth Palace Library Annual Review* (2001), pp.55–7

James P. Carley, 'Misattributions and Ghost Entries in John Bale's *Index Britanniae Scriptorum*', in S. Echard and G. R. Wieland (eds), *Anglo-Latin and Its Heritage* (Turnhout, 2001), pp.229–42

James P. Carley, 'Religious Controversy and Marginalia: Pierfrancesco di Piero Bardi, Thomas Wakefield, and their Books', *Transactions of the Cambridge Bibliographical Society* 12 (2002), pp.206–45

James P. Carley, 'Henry VIII's Library and Humanist Donors: Gian Matteo Giberti as Case Study', in Jonathan Woolfson (ed.), *Reassessing Tudor Humanism* (New York, 2002), pp.99–128

James P. Carley, 'French Evangelical Books at the Court of Henry VIII', in Jean-François Gilmont and William Kemp (eds), *Le Livre évangelique en français avant Calvin* (Turnhout, 2004), pp.131–45

James P. Carley and Ann M. Hutchison, 'Chapter 10. 1534–1550s: The Fall of the Monasteries and Its Consequences' in S. Fanous and V. Gillespie (eds), *The Cambridge Companion to Medieval English Mysticism* (Cambridge, forthcoming)

David R. Carlson, 'Royal Tutors in the Reign of Henry VII', *Sixteenth-century Journal*, 22 (1991), pp.253–79

David R. Carlson, 'The Writings of Bernard André (*c*.1450–*c*.1522)', *Renaissance Studies* 12 (1998), pp.229–50

Andrew A. Chibi, *'Turpitudinem uxoris fratris tui non revelavit*: John Stokesley and the Divorce Question', *The Sixteenth-century Journal*, 25 (1994), pp.387–97

C.H. Clough, 'A Presentation Volume for Henry VIII: the Charlecote Park Copy of Erasmus's *Institutio Principis Christiani*', *Journal of the Warburg and Courtauld Institutes*, 44 (1981), pp.199–202

Philippe Contamine, 'The War Literature of the Late Middle Ages', in his *La France au XIVe et XVe siècles: hommes, mentalités, guerre et paix* (Aldershot, 1981)

Richard Cooper, 'Jean Mallard, poète et peintre rouennais', in Jean-Claude Arnould and Thierry Mantovani (eds), *Première poésie française de la renaissance: autour des Puys poétiques normands* (Paris, 2003), pp.193–213

D.M. Derrett, 'The Trial of Sir Thomas More', *The English Historical* Review, 79 (1964), pp.449–77

Maria Dowling, 'Anne Boleyn and Reform', *Journal of Ecclesiastical History*, 35 (1984), pp.30–46

David Dunlop, 'The Politics of Peace-Keeping: Anglo-Scottish Relations from 1503 to 1511', *Renaissance Studies*, 8 (1994), pp.138–61

F.S. Eden, 'Heraldic Parliament Rolls', *The Connoisseur*, 94 (1934), pp.363–6

Timothy Elston, 'Transformation or Continuity? Sixteenth-century Education and the Legacy of Catherine of Aragon, Mary I and Juan Vives' in Carole Levin, Debra Barrett-Graves and Jo Eldridge Carney (eds), *'High and Mighty Queens' of Early Modern England: Realities and Representations* (New York, 2003), pp.11–26

G.R. Elton, 'The Evolution of a Reformation Statute', *The English Historical Review*, 64 (1949), pp.174–97

David Fallows, 'Henry VIII as a Composer', in Chris Banks, Arthur Searle and Malcolm Turner (eds), *Sundry Sorts of Music Books: Essays on the British Library Collections Presented to O.W. Neighbour on his 70th Birthday* (London, 1993), pp.27–39

J.M. Fletcher, 'A Group of English Royal Portraits Painted Soon after 1513: A Dendrochronological Study', *Studies in Conservation*, 21 (1976), pp.171–8

Stephen Merriam Foley, 'Coming to Terms: Thomas Elyot's Definitions and the Particularity of Human Letters', *ELH*, 61 (1994), pp.211–30

Thomas S. Freeman, 'Research, Rumour and Propaganda: Anne Boleyn in Foxe's Book of Martyrs', *The Historical Journal*, 38 (1995), pp.797–819

H.W. Garrod, 'Erasmus and his English Patrons', *The Library*, 5th series, 4 (1949), pp.1–13

Charles Giry-Deloison, 'Mary Tudor's Marriage to Louis XII' in David Grummitt (ed.), *The English Experience in France c.1450–1558* (Basingstoke, 2002), pp.132–59

Janet M. Green, '"I My Self": Queen Elizabeth I's Oration at Tilbury Camp', *Sixteenth-century Journal*, 28 (1997), pp.421–45

Steven Gunn, 'The Accession of Henry VIII', *Bulletin of the Institute of Historical Research*, lxiv (1991), pp.278–88

John Guy, 'Thomas Cromwell and the Intellectual Origins of the Henrician Revolution', in A. Fox and J. Guy (eds), *Reassessing the Henrician Age* (Oxford, 1986), pp.151–78

John Guy, 'The Henrician Age' in J.G.A. Pocock and Gordon J. Schochet (eds), *The Varieties of British Political Thought 1400–1800* (Cambridge, 1996), pp.13–46

John Guy, 'Wolsey and the Tudor Polity' in Steven J. Gunn and Philip G. Lindley (eds) *Cardinal Wolsey: Church, State and Art* (Cambridge and New York, 1991), pp.54–75

H. J. Habakkuk, 'The Market for Monastic Property, 1539–1603', *The Economic History Review*, 2nd series, 10 (1958), pp.362–80

Michael Hattaway, 'Marginalia by Henry VIII in His Copy of The Bokes of Salomon', *Transactions of the Cambridge Bibliographical Society*, 4 (1965), pp.166–70

David M. Head, 'Henry VIII's Scottish Policy: A Reassessment', *The Scottish Historical Review* 61 (1982), pp.1–24

Daniel Hobbins, 'Arsenal MS 360 as a Witness to the Career and Writings of Bernard André', *Humanistica Lovaniensia*, 50 (2001), pp.161–98

R.W. Hoyle, 'The Origins of the Dissolution of the Monasteries', *Historical Journal*, 38 (1995), pp.275–305

R.W. Hoyle and J.B. Ramsdale, 'The Royal Progress of 1541, the North of England, and Anglo-Scottish Relations, 1534–42', *Northern History*, 41 (2004), pp.239–65

E.W. Ives, 'The Fall of Wolsey' in Steven J. Gunn and Philip G. Lindley (eds), *Cardinal Wolsey: Church, State and Art* (Cambridge and New York, 1991), pp.286–315

E.W. Ives, 'Henry VIII's Will – A Forensic Conundrum', in *The Historical Journal*, 35 (1992), pp.779–804

E.W. Ives, 'Ann Boleyn and the Early Reformation in England: The Contemporary Evidence', *Historical Journal* 37 (1994), pp.389–400

J.R. Liddell, '"Leland's" List of Manuscripts in Lincolnshire Monasteries', *The English Historical Review*, 54 (1939), pp.88–95

Jennifer Loach, 'The Function of Ceremonial in the Reign of Henry VIII', *Past and Present*, 143 (1994), pp.43–68

F. Donald Logan, 'The First Royal Visitation of the English Universities, 1535', *The English Historical Review*, 106 (1991), pp.861–88

Richard Marks, 'The Howard Tombs at Thetford and Framlingham: New Discoveries', *The Archaeological Journal*, 141 (1984), pp.252–68

Thomas H. Mayer, 'Becket's Bones Burnt! Cardinal Pole and the Invention and Dissemination of an Atrocity' in T.S. Freeman and T.F. Mayer (eds), *Martyrs and Martyrdom in England c. 1400–1700* (Woodbridge, 2007), pp.126–43

Peter H. Meurer, 'Op het spoor van de kaart der nederlanden van Jan van Hoirne', *Caert-Thresor* 21 (2002), pp.33–40

Barbara Hochstetler Meyer, 'Marguerite de Navarre and the Androgynous Portrait of François Ier', *Renaissance Quarterly*, 48 (1995), pp.287–325

Marcus Merriman, 'Italian Military Engineers in Britain in the 1540s', in Sarah Tyacke (ed.), *English Map-Making 1500–1650: Historical Essays* (London, 1983), pp.57–67

Peter R. Moore, 'The Heraldic Charge against the Earl of Surrey, 1546–47', *The English Historical Review*, 116 (2001), pp.557–83

Virginia Murphy, 'The Literature and Propaganda of Henry VIII's First Divorce', in Diarmaid MacCulloch (ed.), *The Reign of Henry VIII* (Basingstoke, 1995), pp.135–58

G.D. Nicholson, 'The Act of Appeals and the English Reformation', in C. Cross, D. Loades and J.J. Scarisbrick (eds), *Law and Government under the Tudors* (Cambridge, 1988), pp.19–30

J.D. North, 'Nicolaus Kratzer, the King's Astronomer', in *Science and History: Studies in Honor of Edward Rosen* (Ossolineum, 1978), pp.205–34

M. Orth, 'A French Illuminated Treaty of 1527', *Burlington Magazine* 122 (1980), pp.125–6

Otto Pächt, 'Holbein and Kratzer as Collaborators', *Burlington Magazine*, 84, pp.134–9

Ann Payne, 'An Artistic Survey' in C.S. Knighton and D.M. Loades (eds), *The Anthony Roll of Henry VIII's Navy: Pepys MS 2991 and British Library Add MS 22047 with Related Material*, Navy Records Society, occasional publications, 2 (Aldershot, 2000), pp.20–7

Mark Rankin, 'Rereading Henry VIII in Foxe's *Acts and Monuments*', *Reformation*, 12 (2007), pp.69–102

Glyn Redworth, 'A Study in the Formulation of Policy: The Genesis and Evolution of the Act of Six Articles' in *Journal of Ecclesiastical History*, vol.37 (1986), pp.42–67

R. Rex, 'The English Campaign against Luther in the 1520s', *Transactions of the Royal Historical Society*, 5th series, 39 (1989), pp.85–106

R. Rex, 'Redating Henry VIII's A Glasse of the Truthe', *The Library*, 7th series, 4 (2003), pp.16–27

Glenn Richardson, 'Eternal Peace, Occasional War: Anglo-French Relations under Henry VIII' in Susan Doran and Glenn Richardson (eds), *Tudor England and its Neighbours* (London, 2005), pp.44–73

Glenn Richardson, 'The French Connection: Francis I and England's Break with Rome' in Glenn Richardson (ed.), *Contending Kingdoms: England and France 1420–1700* (Aldershot, 2008), pp.95–115

Nicholas Rogers, 'Patrons and Purchasers: Evidence for the Original Owners of Books Produced in the Low Countries for the English Market' in Bert Cardon, Jan Van der Stock, Dominique Vanwijnsberghe et al. (eds), *Als ich Can: Liber Amicorum in Memory of Professor Dr Maurits Smeyers, Corpus of Illuminated manuscripts* (Louvain 2002), pp. 1165–81

A. Ruddock, 'The Earliest Original English Seaman's Rutter and Pilot's Chart', *Journal of the Institute of Navigation*, 14 (1961), pp.409–31

David Rundle, 'A New Golden Age? More, Skelton and the Accession Verses of 1509', *Renaissance Studies*, 9 (1995), pp.58–76

Alec Ryrie, 'Divine Kingship and Royal Theology in Henry VIII's Reformation' in *Reformation*, 7 (2002), pp.49–77

John Scattergood, 'A Defining Moment: The Battle of Flodden and English Poetry' in Jennifer Britnell and Richard Britnell (eds), *Vernacular Literature and Current Affairs in the Early Sixteenth Century* (Aldershot, 2000), pp.62–77

Cesare Sinistri and Luigi Casali, 'Il Ritrovamento della più antica pianta di Pavia', *Bolletino della Società Pavese di Storia Patria*, Nuova Serie, 48 (1996), pp.481–5

J.K. Sowards, 'Erasmus and the Education of Women', *The Sixteenth-century Journal*, 13 (1982), pp.77–89

David Starkey, 'England' in Roy Porter and Mikulás Teich (eds), *The Renaissance in National Context* (Cambridge, 1992), pp.146–163

David Starkey, 'King Henry and King Arthur' in James P. Carley and Felicity Riddy (eds), *Arthurian Literature*, XVI (Woodbridge, 1998), pp.171–96

Alan Stimson, 'The Navigation Instruments', in Julie Gardiner with Michael J. Allen (eds), *Before the Mast: Life and Death aboard the Mary Rose. The Archaeology of the Mary Rose*, vol.4 (Portsmouth, 2005), pp.267–81

W.R. Streitberger, 'John Skelton: The Entertainments, Plays, and Revels at Court' in David R. Carlson (ed.), *John Skelton and Early Modern Culture: Papers Honoring Robert S. Kinsman* (Tempe, Arizona, 2008)

T.C. String, 'Henry VIII's Illuminated *Great Bible*', *Journal of the Warburg and Courtauld Institutes*, 59 (1996), pp.315–24

Lawrence Stone and Howard Colvin, 'The Howard Tombs at Framlinghham, Suffolk', *The Archaeological Journal*, 122 (1965), pp.159–71

E.G.R. Taylor, 'Jean Rotz: His Neglected Treatise on Nautical Science', *The Geographical Journal*, 73 (1929), pp.455–9

J. Topham, 'A Description of an antient Picture in Windsor Castle, representing the Embarkation of King Henry VIII at Dover May 31, 1520; Preparatory to his Interview with the French king Francis I', *Archaeologia*, 6 (1782), pp.179–220

J.B. Trapp, 'Notes on Manuscripts Written by Peter Meghen', *The Book Collector*, 24 (1975), pp.80–96

W. Ullmann, 'This Realm of England is an Empire', *Journal of Ecclesiastical History*, 300 (1979), pp.175–203

N. Vian, 'La presentazione e gli esemplari Vaticani della *Assertio Septem Sacramentorum* di Enrico VIII', *Studi e testi*, 220 (1962), pp.355–75

Anthony Wagner and J.C. Sainty, 'The Origin of the Introduction of Peers in the House of Lords', *Archaeologia*, 101 (1967), pp.119–50

Daniel Williman, 'Guillaume de Nangis' in *Encyclopedia of the Medieval Chronicle* (Leiden, forthcoming 2009)

G.W.O. Woodward, 'The Exemption from Suppression of Certain Yorkshire Priories', *The English Historical Review*, 76 (1961), pp.385–401

THESES

Pamela Ayers Neville, 'Richard Pynson, King's Printer (1506–1529): Printing and Propaganda in Early Tudor England', University of London, Ph.D. thesis, 1990

M.J. Kelly, 'Canterbury Jurisdiction and Influence during the Episcopate of William Warham, 1503–1532', University of Cambridge, Ph.D. thesis, 1965

INDEX

Page numbers in *italics* refer to illustrations

LIST OF MANUSCRIPTS

INDEX OF PAINTINGS

INDEX OF ARTEFACTS AND OTHER OBJECTS